New Homes In a New Land

German Immigration to Texas

1847 - 1861

New Homes In a New Land

German Immigration to Texas

1847 - 1861

BY ETHEL HANDER GEUE

CLEARFIELD

Reprinted for
Clearfield Company, Inc. by
Genealogical Publishing Co., Inc.
Baltimore, Maryland
1994, 1999, 2002

First printing, 1970
Reprinted, by arrangement,
Genealogical Publishing Co., Inc.
Baltimore, 1982
Library of Congress Catalogue Card Number 81-86306
International Standard Book Number 0-8063-0980-6
Made in the United States of America

DEDICATION

To my grandfathers

Christian Wolfer and Christian William Hander
who, amid the rumblings of war, left Europe in the 1850's to
build new lives in Texas and through an unpredictable fate,
found themselves involved in a war in the United States between
the North and the South. The former served in the Confederate
Navy at the Battle of Galveston, and the latter in the Confederate Army at the Siege of Vicksburg.

PREFACE

The widespread interest shown in *A NEW LAND BECK-ONED, German Immigration to Texas, 1844-1847,* inspired the compilers, Chester W. and Ethel H. Geue, to continue research on German immigration to Texas.

The *Verein zum Schutze deutscher Einwanderer nach Texas,* Society for the Protection of German Immigrants to Texas, had brought 7,200 immigrants to Texas between 1844 and 1847 without fulfilling its promise to care for these settlers in a new land. What happened to these colonists who had survived hunger, disease, death? What did the future hold for them? What effect did reports of their plight have on further immigration to Texas?

Much remained to be told about this story. Newspapers in Germany were very critical of the Verein and its management of this large colonization project. German immigration to Texas did continue, however, abetted by conditions in Europe that caused many thousands to leave.

The research covered in the present study was limited to the years 1847, the demise of the Verein, through 1861, the beginning of the War between the North and the South in the United States. From German newspapers in Texas, microfilm records of passenger lists of ships that arrived at the port of Galveston, Texas, and from emigration lists in the Hamburg Archives, information was gathered about German immigrants to Texas from 1847 to 1861.

Since this is only a part of the history of the German settlers in Texas, it seemed pertinent to tell the story of those who had preceded them. Hence, a short history of German immigration is included from the time the first one set foot on Texas soil.

Research was done mostly in the Texas State Archives; and to Director John M. Kinney and his staff, together with Mrs. Fischer Osburn, retired Assistant Archivist, sincere appreciation is expressed by the compiler.

The Verein and Wied Collections in the University of Texas Archives contained much valuable information. Dr. Chester

v

Kielman and his research assistant, Mr. William Richter, provided access to this important material. For their help I am very grateful.

Microfilm records in the Fort Worth Public Library, the Microfilm Newspaper Collection of the Amon Carter Museum of Art in Fort Worth, at Rice University, and the Texas State Archives provided numerous passenger lists of ships arriving at the ports of Galveston and Indianola; for the use of these and the help of the personnel in each place, I am greatly indebted.

Two men in Europe sent excellent material not available in the United States, as well as assistance in correcting the spelling of names of immigrants and the towns in Europe from which they came. Karl Friedrich von Frank, internationally-known genealogist in Austria, gave advice on this spelling; and Karl Werner Klüber, Kulturhistoriker und Genealoge in Hamburg, forwarded passenger lists collected from material in the Hamburg Archives. Their assistance is greatly appreciated.

For valuable help in the immense task of locating and securing the correct spelling of towns in Europe as written on passenger lists, on microfilm, or printed in German newspapers, I am very grateful to Miss Heide Ochs of Fort Worth. The proofreading of Mrs. Ray Chandler of Fort Worth and her suggestions for improvement of the historical portion of the manuscript were of great value.

Last, but by no means least, my sincere gratitude is given to my husband for his patience, his assistance in all phases of the research, and especially his knowledge of German which was needed so greatly in reading German newspaper lists of passenger ships and translating material in German magazines and books. I can truly say that without his help, this work would not have been accomplished.

Ethel Hander Geue

CONTENTS

ILLUSTRATIONS

following page 36

Fachwerk houses: In Bicken, Nassau, houses on immigrant road from Leipzig to Bremen.

Fachwerk house of Lieutenant von Claren in New Braunfels, showing two stages used in such houses: 1) original wooden beam and limestone construction; 2) plaster covering.

Limestone house of Peter Tatsch in Fredericksburg.

Restored home in New Braunfels of George Ullrich, wagon master of the Verein.

The frigate *Guttenberg*, picture taken from model in the Deutsches Museum in Munich, Germany.

Immigrant ship similar to the *Johann Dethardt*, from picture sent by Kurt Klotzbach, city editor of *Ruhr Nachrichten*, Dortmund, West Germany.

Between decks on immigrant ship, 1847.
from *Allegemeine Auswanderungs-Zeitung 1847*, p. 291, by permission of CommerzBibliothek, Hamburg.
Picture sent by Karl Werner Klüber, Hamburg, Ger.

Passenger list of *Neptune*

Passenger list of *Friedrich Grosse*

Passenger list of *Bassermann*

Passenger list of *Texas*

ix

History of German
Immigration to Texas

The Germans in Texas
before the Texas Revolution
against Mexico in 1836

The first German to set foot on Texas soil was probably a man named Heins or Heims. He was a member of the colony that La Salle established in Texas in 1685.[1] It is perhaps a curious coincidence that this group landed on the same beach at Matagorda Bay where one hundred and sixty years later several thousand Germans arrived. This area on the coast was nameless in 1685, inhabited at that time by Karankawa Indians. Called Powderhorn at first, then Indian Point, this place was selected by Prince Carl of Solms-Braunfels in 1844 as the harbor for the debarkation of German immigrants sent to Texas by an organization of noblemen in Germany. Prince Carl named the site Carlshafen in honor of himself . Many of these colonists remained there, and the name was changed to Indianola. Today this name may still be found on Texas maps, but the town is no longer there. It was severely damaged by hurricanes in 1875 and 1886, and completely destroyed by hurricane Carla in 1962. There remain, however, two reminders of historical events that took place on this beach: a large statue of Robert Cavalier Sieur de la Salle and a historical marker commemorating the arrival of the German colonists who disembarked at this port and later went inland.

The seventeen hundreds were years of Spanish power in the area that now is Texas. At that time it was part of Mexico governed by the crown of Spain, and its prairies were the homes of Indians and buffaloes. By means of their system of establishing presidios the Spanish hoped to win control of the Indians. These presidios were both missions and forts, built to convert the Indians and to protect the priests, soldiers, settlers and their families. Gradually, towns grew up around them. Ten presidios were established in Texas; the best known is San Antonio de Bexar. With the exception of these establishments, Texas was a vast land of forests, prairies, hills, and streams, inhabited by Indians and Spaniards. No other attempt at colonization was made during this century by Europeans or Americans.

A few adventurers came into Texas during the latter part of the eighteenth century, but it is not known if there were any Germans among them. In 1821 Ernst von Rosenberg and fifty-three men came to Texas with James Long who led a filibustering expedition to conquer Texas. Long and his men were captured by the Mexicans at Goliad in 1821. Five other Germans were in this group: Eduard Hanstein, Joseph Dirksen, Gaspar Porton, Wilhelm Mueller, and August Blaccher.[2] A few Germans from Oldenburg settled in Bastrop County in the early 1820's. At this time there were only Indians in that area, and men carried guns on their shoulders while plowing the fields.

The most accurate source for further information on names of Germans in Texas is the list of land grants in the General Land Office in Austin. Here, however, there is chance for error since names that were German were often written in English with phonetic spelling. For instance, in 1821 Gabriel Strohschneider settled in Austin's colony; but since he could not write, his land title is in the name of Gabriel Strawsnider. At the same time five others secured land grants in Austin's colony: John and Francis Keller, Peter Bertrand, Peter Conrad, and F. W. Grassmeyer. In the same year, a German by the name of Henry Rueg settled in Nacogdoches. In the 1820's at least two others had located in Texas, J. Becker of Bevil's Settlement and F. Swetenburg of St. Augustine.[3]

The first German family to come to Texas and establish a permanent settlement was the family of Friedrich Ernst. With Charles Fordtran, they came to Mill Creek in Austin County in 1832. Fordtran surveyed the land, and Ernst founded the town of Industry. With the Ernst family there lived a Mr. Tiedemann and also a man named B. Scherer who taught Mr. Ernst the skill of cigar making. Other settlers soon arrived, and the town grew.

Caroline, daughter of Mr. and Mrs. Ernst, gave this description of their first home. It was a small hut with a thatch roof, and there were six sides made of logs and moss. The cows often ate the moss; consequently it was neither waterproof nor warm. Her father tried to build a chimney and fireplace, but they were afraid to build a fire since there was danger of destroying the whole house. By 1838, Friedrich Ernst had built a large house which, under Mrs. Ernst's supervision, served as a hotel that was looked upon as an oasis by immigrants from other states and travelers in Texas.

Mr. Ernst came from Varel, Oldenburg. A letter written to a friend in that city was published in an Oldenburg newspaper; and its description of the beautiful rolling land, the fertile soil, and the pleasant climate of Austin County brought many more German settlers to Texas. Among these were William Bartels, J. Juergens, Jacob Wolters, Joseph Biegel, William Frels who established Frelsburg in Colorado County, and D. F. F. Yordt.

The town of Cat Spring was founded in 1835 by Robert Kleberg. He was soon joined by the von Roeder family, Marcus and Karl Amsler, John Heinike, John Reinermann, Hans Hollien and Levermann, and Dr. John D. Varrelmann. One of the young von Roeder boys killed a wildcat near a spring on the San Bernard River, thus giving Cat Spring its name.

Not all early German immigrants came to Austin County, however. In 1834, there were in Power and Hewitson's colony Franz Dietrich, John A. Baumann, William Langenheim, and Cornelius P. Hermans. In 1835 George B. Erath, Friedrich Niebling and Sarah Wilhelm settled in Robertson's colony. In Burnet, Vehlein, Zavala, and Taylor's colonies we find the names of John Falk, Friedrich Kistler, Jacob Roth, Edmund Altiz, Joseph Hartz, Christian Hillebrandt, Georg Kuhn, and Alexander Thornburg (Dornburg?).[4]

There are several others who are deserving of special mention. In 1826 Adolphus Sterne arrived from New Orleans and played an important part in the Texas Revolution. Before 1836, he was the Alcalde of Nacogdoches. Eduard Harcourt, Hermann Ehrenberg, and Friedrich von Wrede arrived shortly before hostilities began. Charles Gieseke settled in Washington County in 1836; and Henry Fisher, partner with Burchard Miller in the Fisher-Miller grant, was also in Texas at that time.[5]

There were about one hundred and fifteen German settlers who were in Texas before March 2, 1836, according to a list compiled from patents in the General Land Office in Austin. L. F. Lafrentz in the *Deutsche-Texanische Monats-Hefte* for September, 1906, page 92, records the names.[4] It is indeed possible, even probable, that this is not a complete list of Germans in Texas at that time since no registration system was kept of persons entering this area.

Early German settlers in Texas as given in
DEUTSCH-TEXANISCHE MONATS-HEFTE
September 1906, pages 88-92
Gewidmet den Deutsch-Texanertum Der Kunst und Wissenschaft.
(GERMAN-TEXAN MONTHLY MAGAZINE)
Devoted to the Arts and Knowledge of German Texans
by L. F. Lafrentz of San Antonio, Texas
Issue of September, 1906:
Page 92—A list compiled from the patents in the General
Land Office of the following [Germans who were in Texas
before March 2, 1836:][1]
Ibid., p. 90.

Johann Appelmann
Heinrich Aschabrannar
  (Aschebrenner?)
Jacob Bicker
Jacob Borkmann
Alfred Benze
Heinrich Bergner
Henry Beymer
Wm Brockner
Heinrich Buckner
H. Bürge (Buerge)
Richard Bushel (?)
E. S. Cabler
F. G. Cabler
Jacob Cassner
A. Constante
David Cornelius
Philipp Cornelius
David Crüger (Crueger)
Georg Dedrick
Andreas Dorsheimer
Conrad Eigenauer
Bernhard Eilers
Chas. Eisterwald
Jacob Eyler
F. B. Earnest (Ernst?)
Jacob Eberly
Joseph Ealender
Friedrich Elm
E. C. Findelmann
Peter Fleming
Robert Fleming
John Frederick*
Wm Friedlander

Friedrich Giebenrath
Johann Grunder
Casper Habermacher
Georg Habermacher
Eduard Harcourt*
Kasper Heymann
Friedrich Hellmiller
Johann Hennecke
Franz Hennecke
Friedrich Heneker (perhaps
  the same name as the
  foregoing)
F. W. Hüssmann (Huessmann)
L. S. Hagler
Leander Harl
Heinrich Hartzell
Friedrich Heminger
A. Holshausen
C. Holshausen
A. M. R. Hoppe
C. Hermann Jäger (Jaeger)
Johann W. Kirchhoffer
Bernhard Klecamp
Ludwig Kraatz
Johann Kaiser
Wm. Kibbe
Chas. Kneass
Louis Kneip
Georg Knust
Chas Lantz
Anton Lehmkuhl
Rudolf Lehmkuhl
E. Leichtle
Jacob G. Lentz

Heinrich Lentz
Ludwig Lidstrand
Friedrich Lüders (Lueders)
Johann Lüsch (Luesch)
Friedrich Lundt
Peter Mattern
Chas. Messer
Theodor Miller
Adolf Moormann
Heinrich Mordorff
Chas. Murhard
Jacob Mast
Wm R. Mook
Johann Moll
Joseph Müchem (Muechem)
Albert Nautz
Johann Obeländer (Obellaender)
Peter Ornik
Conrad Overland (?)
Peter Pieper
Franz Potthast
Wm. G. Preusch
Georg Peermann
Heinrich Platte
Wm E. Probst
Heinrich Reinermann
Johann Reinermann

Ernst Richter
Wm Rosenberg
Johann Schröder (Schroeder)
Friedrich Siebenmann
Ferdinand Schwinghammer
Chas. Santz
J. H. Schnell
J. N. Schaffner
Martin Setzer
Friedrich Schrack
Robert Spack
Adolf Sterne (Nacogdoches) *
Jacob Stiffler
Meinhard Stiffler
B. Strunk
Christoph Tranz
Joseph Urban
Anton Vanderhoya
Jos. T. Vanderhoya
Joh. Vanderwerth
Friedrich W. Weide [Wrede?]
Louis Willmuth
Wm. Willmuth
Sam. Wolfenberger
Edward Wickmann
S. W. Yeager
Abraham Zuber

The Germans in the Texas War of Independence

One of the first Germans to deserve mention for his aid to Texas in its struggle for freedom from Mexico is Adolphus Sterne. He lived in Nacogdoches, Texas and was appointed by the Provisional Government of Texas to go to New Orleans in the fall of 1835 to secure help for Texas in the coming war with Mexico. Great enthusiasm was aroused in New Orleans for the Texas cause, and a fund of ten thousand dollars was raised for the Texas army. Posters asking for volunteers were placed on street corners, and three companies were organized to go to the aid of Texas: the New Orleans Greys, the Tampico Greys, and the Mobile Greys. Adolphus Sterne equipped the New Orleans Greys; and when they left New Orleans on October 2, 1835, he paid their way by steamboat to Natchitoches, Louisiana. From this place they marched to Nacogdoches where they went to his home. Sterne welcomed them with a hot supper which had been prepared in anticipation of their arrival.[1]

The story of the New Orleans Greys is taken up at this point by Hermann Ehrenberg who, as one of their number, gave valiant service to the Texas cause. In his book, *Texas und Seine Revolution** published in Leipzig in 1843, he tells in detail the story of the battle in December 1835, when San Antonio was captured from the Mexicans, and of the death of brave Ben Milam. Following this, the New Orleans Greys marched with the Texas army to Goliad to join the forces of Colonel Fannin. In March 1836, the commander of the fort at Goliad received orders from General Sam Houston to blow up the fort and either fall back to Victoria or march to the aid of the Alamo in San Antonio. William B. Travis had also sent a letter asking for help in the Alamo, but Fannin delayed until it was too late, preferring to await the enemy in the fort at Goliad. Finally, on March 19, Fannin started. He and his troops with nine cannon were intercepted by General Urrea and, after a bloody fight,

---

*Translated by Charlotte Churchill and published under the title **With Milam and Fannin**, Pemberton Press, Austin, Texas, 1968.

surrendered on March 20. The Mexicans agreed to set Fannin's men free, according to the story as told by Ehrenberg.[2] However, General Urrea made a treaty privately with Fannin by which the Texans were to be prisoners of war "at the disposal of the Mexican government."[3] Fannin's men gave up their arms and were marched back to Goliad.

When General Urrea wrote to Santa Anna about Fannin's surrender, Santa Anna ordered immediate execution. For seven days the Texans, including the New Orleans Greys, were given scanty rations of food and water. On the eighth day the men were marched to the upper ford of the San Antonio River in a line, with Mexican soldiers at their side. Immediately following an order to halt, the Texans heard a command given in Spanish. Shots were fired, clouds of smoke arose, and men began to fall. Seeing his comrades fall, Ehrenberg took advantage of the heavy smoke to make a dash for the river. As he dived into the water, he shouted "The Republic of Texas forever!" He swam to the opposite bank with bullets flying over his head and escaped; but he carried with him the sight of his comrades bleeding and dying. After about a week of wandering helplessly, he came to a deserted farm house whose owners had fled in advance of Santa Anna's army which was pursuing the army of General Sam Houston. Here he feasted on a dozen eggs which renewed his strength. Finally, Thomas Kelly, the owner of the house, walked in bringing the good news of the defeat of Santa Anna by the Texian army under General Sam Houston at San Jacinto, Ehrenberg set out again. He reported to David Burnett, the president of the new Republic of Texas; and on June 2, 1836 he received an honorable discharge from the Secretary of War, Mirabeau B. Lamar. Many of his comrades were not as fortunate as Ehrenberg; some were detained by the Mexican general as helpers in the Mexican army; but most were massacred.

Germans at Goliad[4]

Dietrich, Franz—detained by Mexicans
Dombrinski, M.—killed
Ehrenberg, Herm.—escaped
Eigenauer, Conrad—killed
Finner (Fenner), Robert—killed

Fisher, J. H.—killed
Griebenrath, F.—killed
Heiser, J.—killed
Kemp, Thomas*—escaped
Kolmann (Coleman), Jacob—killed

*Name added by H. Yoakum in his **History of Texas**, Vol. II, pg. 100, note.

Kurtmann (Curtmann, Courtmann), George F.—killed
Langenheim, Wm.—captured
Lantz, Charles—killed
Mattern, Peter—killed
Mayer, William—killed
Miller, J.—killed
Peterswich, F.—killed
Rosenberg, Wm—detained by Mexicans
Preusch, Wm.—escaped (killed?)

Reese, John*—escaped
Schultz, H.—killed
Strunck, B.—killed
Spiess, John—captured
Spohn, Joseph—escaped
Volkmar, J.—killed
Voss, Georg—detained by Mexicans
Winter, A.
Wutherich, Ulrich—detained

There were 342 Americans killed in the massacre at Goliad, 28 escaped, and 20 were spared and kept by the Mexicans for use as doctors, nurses, interpreters, and mechanics.

Much has been written about the battles of the Alamo and San Jacinto; the deeds and sacrifices of the men who gave their lives for the freedom of Texas have been recorded in magazines and books, engraved in stone on monuments, and acknowledged as supreme contributions in the history of Texas.

The best sources list the number of defenders in the Alamo as 180 to 188. Among these were men from many states of the United States, as well as from four foreign countries. Fighting at the side of Americans against Santa Anna's army of more than five thousand were men from Scotland, England, Ireland, Denmark, and Germany. The two Germans in the Alamo were Henry Thomas, age 25, and Henry Courtman (also spelled Curtman or Kurtman), age 28.

Following the fall of the Alamo, General Sam Houston and his army retreated toward the San Jacinto River. On April 21 he and his forces attacked the large Mexican Army under Santa Anna and defeated them in a short battle that began with shouts of "Remember the Alamo! Remember Goliad!" In this one brief encounter Sam Houston and the brave men in his army won for Texas the freedom from Mexico that they had longed for.

In addition to the list of Germans who were with Fannin at Goliad and the two who died in the Alamo, the following Germans fought in the Texas War for Independence:

Germans in the Texas War for Independence[5]
(In addition to those killed in the Alamo and at Goliad)

Ahlert, William
Albrecht, Jacob

Amelung, Louis
Amsler, Carl

Balch, Benjamin and John
Baumbacher, Joh.
Bernbeck, Wilh. Christoph
Bertram, Thomas
Biegel, Joseph
Burch, W. M.
Burgiesky, Joh.
Courtman, Henry*
Eilers, Bernard
Ellinger (Ehlinger), Joseph
Elm, F. G.
Emanuel, Albert
Erath, Georg
Ernst, Fritz
Felder, Carl
Fordtran, Carl
Formann, Abraham
Friedlander, William
Frels, Wilhelm
Fullenweider, Peter
Geiger, Jacob
Giesecke, C.
Grassmeyer, F. W.
Gross, Jacob
Halt, H.
Hammacher, C.
Harkort (Harcourt), Ed
Heinrich, Moritz
Heuser, J. A.
Hellmueller, F.
Herder, G.
Herz, J.
Heunecke, Joh.
Heusemann, F.
Hildebrandt, Christian
Hollien, Joh.
Jurgens, Conrad
Keller, F.
Kessler, L. D.
Kinschel, A.
Kleberg, Louis
Kleberg, Robert J.
Kopf, Joh.
Kranz, L.
(Kraatz, Louis?)

Krup, L.
Lemsky, Frederich
Lantz, Charles
Lehmkuhl, A.
Luck, G.
Luders, F.
Luenenburg, C.
Luckenhoger, G.
Lundt, F.
Messler, C.
Miller, J.
Niebling, F.
Oberlander, J.
Peske, J.
Pieper, P.
Pucholaski, E.
Redlich, A. C.
Reinhardt, J. (Asa?)
Ricks, G. W.
v. Roeder, Joachim
v. Roeder, Louis
v. Roeder, Otto
v. Roeder, Rudolph
v. Roeder, William
Schrack, F.
Schroeder, F.
Schultz, C.
Schulz, L.
Schur, J.
Stern, A.
Stolke, A.
Sullsbach, G.
Tapps, C.
Thuerwachter, H.
Vardemann, Henry W.
Wagner, William
Weppler, Phil.
Wertzner, Chr. G.
Wilhelm, A. and R.
Wilke, Henry
Wolfenberger, Sam
v. Zacharias, L.
Zekainski, J.
Zuber, William
Zumwalt, Andrew

*Died in the Alamo.

German Colonization of Texas, 1836-1844

The struggling Republic of Texas, successful in winning its freedom from Mexico, soon found itself in financial difficulty. Its treasury was empty ; there was no money to run the new government. However, while poor in funds, it was rich in land. Millions of acres lay ready for the plow of the settler. The answer to the need for money lay in taxation. This meant granting land to new settlers. As an inducement to immigrants to come to Texas, whether from the United States or from other countries, the Congress of the Republic passed a law granting 640 acres of land to each married man and 320 acres to a single man who settled in Texas after 1837. Taxes on these grants would help to provide funds needed for the operation of the government.

In addition to grants to individual settlers, large grants were offered to men who could establish a designated number of families in a colony. Contracts made with these men, called *empresarios,* required that the agreed number of families and single men be settled on the land granted by the government of the Republic of Texas within a specified length of time; otherwise the contract would be forfeited.[1]

While Moses Austin's contract for land was not made with the Republic of Texas, mention of it should be made since this was the first of such contracts for land that was made. Early in 1821 the Spanish government granted him the authority to settle three hundred families in his proposed colony. He died, however, before he could fulfill this agreement, and his son, Stephen F. Austin, assumed the contract. In December of 1821, the first settlers arrived near the present town of Washington-on-the-Brazos.

A grant in North Texas was made by the Republic of Texas to empresario W. S. Peters. In addition, many other grants were made. John Power and James Hewitson brought Irish into the lower Rio Grande area while McMullen and McGloin located Europeans near San Patricio. Green DeWitt's colony lay on land east and west of the Colorado River. Adjoining

Austin's colony on the east were the lands of Joseph Vehlein, and north of this was the large grant of Sterling G. Robertson. Hayden Edwards, Lorenzo de Zavalla, and Martin de Leon settled hundreds of families on lands for which they held contracts.[2]

In 1844, a large colony was founded by Henri Castro on the Medina River about fifty miles southwest of San Antonio. This was composed of three hundred French settlers who were of Alsacian descent. The heart of the colony was the town of Castroville, located in the middle of Medina County. Henri Castro went bankrupt on this venture, and the colonists suffered much at first, as did most ethnic groups in early Texas; but they persevered, and today Castroville is one of the most charming towns in West Texas.

Until the organization of the Adelsverein colonization project, no contract was made for the introduction of German settlers in Texas. However, they came before this in small groups and established characteristic German settlements. In the area near Industry in Austin County, the towns of Cat Spring and Frelsburg are two most representative of such towns. In Fayette County, small German groups settled near La Grange, Round Top, and Ross Prairie. Washington County also drew many German settlers to its area. Many immigrants, coming into the port of Galveston, chose to remain there while others went fifty miles farther to the larger town of Houston. Some traveled on to Independence, Washington-on-the-Brazos, Columbus, and even San Antonio.

The greatest impetus to German settlement in Texas came in 1844-47 with the arrival at Indianola of thousands of immigrants brought to Texas under the auspices of the Adelsverein. This led to the founding of the two most characteristic German towns in Texas, New Braunfels and Fredericksburg. Many smaller communities near these towns were started shortly after.

It is difficult to say how many Germans were in Texas at the end of the days of the Republic in February, 1846, since no official census of Texas was taken until 1850. Including those who came as Verein colonists in 1844, 1845, and 1846, perhaps an estimate of twenty thousand is not too high.

The Adelsverein Immigration to Texas, 1844-1847

No very large scale colonization had been planned for Texas until the Adelsverein (Society of Noblemen) was organized in Germany and initiated its project to send thousands of Germans to Texas. This group, consisting of fourteen German princes and noblemen, met at Biebrich on the Rhine on April 20, 1842. Its purpose was to form an organization known as the *Verein zum Schutze deutscher Einwanderer in Texas*, or "Society for the Protection of German Immigrants in Texas." It became known simply as the "Verein" in Texas. This organization decided to secure land in Texas for immigrants who wished to settle there and, as stated in its constitution drawn up on March 25, 1844, "to protect the emigrants on their long journey and in their new home, and to employ every means to secure for them a new home across the seas."[1]

The Society, or *Verein* as it was known in Texas, was incorporated for $80,000, a sum that seemed ample to the directors of the organization in Germany but was entirely insufficient for the needs of the thousands who were sent to Texas under its auspices. It promised[2]

1) free transportation (by ship) and food to the port of disembarkation, as well as free land transportation from the port of disembarkation to the colony itself in wagons and tents of the Verein, and also to provide a dwelling house at about 60 florins.
2) 320 acres of land free to each family and 160 acres to each single male person over 17 years of age.
3) procurement and provision of all utensils and materials for agriculture and livelihood at the lowest price from the storehouse of the Verein.
4) establishment of churches, schools, and hospitals, apothecary, a means of communication, as well as construction of navigable rivers, and especially an overall provision for the welfare of the immigrants who had placed their trust in the Verein.

With such glowing promises as these, it was not hard to secure emigrants. Conditions in Germany added an incentive for the people to find homes in a new country. The industrial revolution, whereby machinery was invented to do work formerly done by hand labor, caused a difficulty in finding the means to support a family. Overcrowding of farm lands made the raising of crops sufficient to feed families another reason for seeking a new home in a foreign land. Added to this were glowing pictures of Texas painted by such writers as Friedrich Wilhelm von Wrede in his *Lebensbilder aus den Vereinigten Staaten von Nord Amerika und Texas* (Sketches of Life in the United States of North America and Texas), published in Cassel in 1844; Ferdinand Roemer in *Texas, with Special Reference to German Immigration*, Bonn, 1849; Gustav Dresel in his *Houston Journal, Adventures in North America and Texas, 1837-1841*, and Victor Bracht in *Texas in 1848*, published by Julius Baedeker in Elberfeld in 1849. Letters written to friends and relatives from emigrants who were living in Texas often brought many from their former residences in Germany, each seeking an opportunity to make a better living than he had in Germany. Revolutions, such as those in 1848, and the threat of war caused hundreds to leave. Evidence of the latter is found in the large number of emigrants from Schleswig, Holstein, and Mecklenburg who left in the 1850's due to apprehension over the approaching Austrian-Prussian War of 1864 with Denmark.

The Verein began its project by securing a contract for land in Texas. The first contract was made with Alexander Bourgeois d'Orvanne for the Bourgeois-Ducos grant. This had been granted on June 3, 1842 and carried the stipulation that four hundred families would be settled on the land within eighteen months. This specification had not been met; and the contract had expired on December 3, 1843, four months before it was signed by the Verein. Bourgeois assured the directors of the Verein that he could obtain a renewal of his grant from the government of the Republic of Texas.

On the basis of this promise, the directors sent two men to Texas to prepare for the arrival of the colonists, Bourgeois d'Orvanne as Colonial Director and Prince Carl of Solms-Braunfels as Commissioner General. They arrived at Galveston, Texas on July 1, 1844. It was not long, however, before Prince Solms learned that the Bourgeois-Ducos contract had expired and could neither be renewed nor extended. The German immigrants were expected to arrive in the fall of 1844; and there was no tract of land on which they could be located.

Prince Carl faced this emergency by going to San Antonio de Bexar to inspect various grants on the Medina, Cibolo, and San Antonio rivers, as he wrote to the directors of the Verein on August 20, 1844 in his second report.[3] In the meantime, the directors had signed, on June 26, 1844, a contract with Henry Fisher for an interest in the Fisher-Miller grant of 3,800,000 acres between the waters of the Colorado and Llano rivers. Henry Fisher returned to Texas to take the place of Bourgeois d'Orvanne as Colonial Director.

The Fisher-Miller contract provided for the introduction of six hundred families and single men into Texas, two hundred families and single men to be located within a year. Each married man was to receive 640 acres of land and a single man 320 acres. Fisher and Miller, upon request, could get title from the Republic of Texas for one-half of the land received by the families and single men, provided they made such an agreement. This was done, and every married immigrant was promised 320 acres and every single immigrant 160 acres.

The grant for which the Verein had contracted was by no means favorable to the settlement of the colonists. In the first place it was situated too far inland. Transportation of the immigrants and their possessions would take many days, or even weeks if rivers had flooded the route to be traversed. Then, too, the land was not fertile, and farming would not be productive. A third disadvantage was the presence of Indians on the lands which the directors had selected. No one could safely establish a home in the area of the Fisher-Miller grant until peace had been made with these Indians. The Verein had made the contract even though no member had inspected the land to be colonized.

Meanwhile, in Germany, agents of the Verein had begun to sign agreements with persons who wished to go to Texas. Then the prospective emigrant made preparations for the long journey, first by water and then by land, to his new home. At the harbor from which he would leave, he signed an immigration contract[4] which entitled him to 320 acres of land in Texas if he was married, or 160 acres if he was single. Then he boarded one of the Verein's ships for the voyage across the ocean. These were sailing vessels which were dependent on the weather. Often they were delayed by storms or calm seas; but the length of the journey from Bremen, Hamburg, or Antwerp was usually two months.

The port of arrival in Texas was Galveston where the immigrants were listed by an agent of the Verein and were "hereby entered by the State Department of Texas as settlers on the Grants ceded to Messrs Hry F. Fisher and Bd. Miller."[5] Then they were transferred, with their baggage, to a smaller ship to make the short trip to Indianola, the port of debarkation.

Prince Carl of Solms-Braunfels, realizing there would be need for way stations on the way to the Fisher-Miller grant, searched for the first such place. The immigrants had encampments or "halting places" at Agua Dulce, McCoy's Creek, Gonzales, and Seguin. However, it also seemed important to secure land for a permanent settlement on the way to the grant. Therefore, acting on the advice of an old settler, Jacob Rahm, he purchased from the Veramendi and Raphael Garza families a beautiful tract of land about thirty miles from San Antonio. This was known as "Las Fontanas" or "the fountains." Clear water from the nearby hills gushed forth from seven springs. The stream flowing from these was called Comal River, which flowed into the Guadalupe River. No more delightful place could have been found for the weary immigrants.

The first three ships sent by the Verein, the *Johann Dethardt,* the *Ferdinand,* and the *Herschel,* arrived in November and December of 1844 with 292 colonists. On March 21, 1845 the colonists crossed the Guadalupe River and founded the town of New Braunfels. Prince Carl had given the first Verein settlement this name in honor of his home town, Braunfels, in Germany. Each immigrant was given a town lot for a home, and ten acres to be used for farming. Immediately, crops were planted; then log houses were built. It is estimated that about 167 immigrants were the first settlers of New Braunfels. Others among the number who came on these first three ships remained at Indianola or Galveston, or stayed in some of the towns through which they passed. The new residents of New Braunfels raised the flag of the Republic of Texas and built a fort for protection from the Indians. In his eleventh report to the directors of the Verein, Prince Solms wrote, "It is a cheerful sight to see this beauty spot of nature developing and the land becoming occupied."[6]

Eleven reports were sent by Prince Carl of Solms-Braunfels to the directors of the Verein in Germany. In these he gave details of the progress of the settlement in Texas. However, he was eager to return to Germany to make an oral report. On

May 15, 1845, he left New Braunfels; and on the 28th of July, 1845, he made this report at Wiesbaden. In this he wrote, "I gave my successor both verbal and written reports of all events and detailed information on things he needed to know, and especially on matters that had to be taken care of in the future."[7] However, the thing which his successor, Baron Meusebach, needed to know most was the financial condition of the new colony.

Baron Ottfried Hans von Meusebach of Dillenburg, Nassau, arrived in Texas late in May 1845. Immediately he discarded his baronial name and became to everyone just plain John O. Meusebach. As the new Commissioner General of the Verein in Texas, he found himself in a difficult position. There was a most unsatisfactory condition in the financial affairs of the new colony of New Braunfels, due to the fact that "the Commissioner General (Solms), the doctor, and the engineer had contracted debts in the name of the Society without making any record of them. They had signed promissory notes and had issued certificates of credit."[8] There was a debt of $20,000 in the books and no money to pay the creditors who besieged Meusebach for the amounts that had been promised them. The situation was serious. The settlers were angry and even made threats on the life of Meusebach.

Immediately he went to work on the records books and soon had them in better order. By judicious business methods he soon restored the confidence of the colonists. However, the treasury was empty, but expenses of the settlement continued. Meusebach sent an itemized report to the directors on August 7, 1845, stating the precarious financial situation at New Braunfels.

Before he could receive a reply, he learned that several thousand immigrants were due to arrive at Indianola in November, 1845. This staggering news would have caused a man of less fortitude to lose hope and return to Europe. Not so with John O. Meusebach!

It was evident that this large number of settlers could not be located in New Braunfels. Therefore, Meusebach left on a journey that would take him northwest toward the area of the Fisher-Miller grant. He was fortunate in finding land on the Pedernales River that would make an excellent place on which to found a new town for these colonists. It had good soil, plenty of water, and ample timber for houses. Meusebach selected a ten thousand acre tract and had it surveyed. Town lots were laid out as well as ten-acre plots for farming. The name Fredericksburg was chosen in honor of Prince Frederick of Prussia, a member of the Verein.

When he returned to New Braunfels, Meusebach learned that a total of $24,000 had been credited to him in a New Orleans bank. This was an amount of money that probably seemed ample to the directors of the Verein in Germany, but it was a very small sum to supply the needs of the colonists who were coming to Texas depending on the promises of the Verein. Four thousand immigrants would have to be transported over one hundred and fifty miles from Indianola to New Braunfels; the promised log cabins must be built for them; food had to be provided to sustain them through the winter until they could raise a crop; utensils for farming were needed. The sum of six dollars per person was assumed sufficient by the directors to supply all of these needs!

Between October 1845 and April 1846, thirty-six ships brought 5,257 immigrants to Texas under the auspices of the Verein. Those who came in the fall and winter fared well enough, but tragedy struck those who came in the spring and summer of 1846.

Meusebach had made a contract with a Houston transportation company to take the immigrants from Indianola to New Braunfels. However, war broke out between the United States and Mexico in April, 1846; and all available wagons, oxen, and horses were needed by the United States army. One hundred wagons had left the coast before the transportation company broke its contract with Meusebach to be at the service of the United States in moving troops.

Over four thousand immigrants were left on the beach at Indianola in whatever shelter they could find or in no shelter at all. Heat and rain, impure food and water, exhaustion from their long journey—all these contributed to the beginning of an epidemic of dysentery, typhoid and malaria fever that took the lives of over one thousand immigrants in the summer of 1846. Four hundred died at Indianola; others started their long trek to New Braunfels, the town which they had hoped would be their new home. Leaving their prized possessions on the beach along Matagorda Bay, walking over rough wagon tracks, stopping at times to help those who had fallen by the wayside or to bury friends or relatives, they made their way with heavy hearts to New Braunfels. The germs of disease were brought there and also to Fredericksburg; and a terrible epidemic broke out in both places. Sometimes all members of a family died; more often a mother or father, or both, were taken away by the disease. So many children were left parentless that Louis C. Ervendberg, pastor of the Protestant Church at New Braunfels, took the orphans about five miles out of the city, built a house or orphanage, and cared for these homeless children. The epidemic took the lives of two or three every day in New Braunfels; and over three hundred deaths are listed in the Register of the First Protestant Church there for the summer months of 1846.

On April 23, 1846, a wagon train left New Braunfels with one hundred men, women, and children. After a trip that lasted sixteen days, they reached their destination—the new Verein settlement of Fredericksburg. The town was founded on May 8, 1846 when the settlers claimed the town lots and ten-acre plots that had previously been surveyed and assigned to them. Cultivation of the fields was started at once in order that a harvest could be reaped before winter. One month after the first settlers arrived a second wagon train brought many others. Life was not pleasant in Fredericksburg during the first few months. The same diseases that claimed so many lives in New Braunfels were brought to Fredericksburg, and an epidemic broke out there.

It was evident that the German immigrants could not go into the area of the Fisher-Miller grant to claim their land until peace was made with the Comanche Indians who lived there. As far as could be ascertained, no white man had dared to venture into this land, the home of the Red Man and the buffalo for so many centuries. In February, 1847, John O. Meusebach, with forty-five men, dared to be the first to do this so that peace could be made and the land opened up for new settlement. Wherever he and the men met a band of Indians, they assured them that they came with friendly feelings. Gifts were also brought for the purpose of inducing the Indians to make a peace treaty. A meeting with twenty Comanche chiefs was arranged for March 1, 1847 on the bank of the lower San Saba River. Meusebach reported in his *Answer to Interrogatories*, page 24, that he with seven men had met the Indians and "made a treaty with the head chiefs Buffalo Hump, Santa Anna, and Mopechucope, and their people for all the western bands of Comanches, promised them $3,000 worth of presents, for which consideration they on their part promised and agreed not to disturb our surveyors in their work, nor to do any harm to our colonists."

Was this peace treaty kept? Yes, and no. There were Indian depredations, theft of cattle, and sometimes kidnapping of children. Settlers were killed in the vicinity of Fredericksburg and other towns that were established in the Fisher-Miller grant. In 1855, Hermann Runge was killed and scalped on the farm of one of the Dresel brothers. Among others who suffered the same fate were Heinrich Arhelger, Heinrich Kensing and his wife, and Conrad and Heinrich Meckel. Two officers of the Verein, Friedrich Wilhelm von Wrede and Lieutenant Oscar von Claren, lost their lives when they were returning to New Braunfels from a business trip to Austin. On their way back to New Braunfels, they stopped at Manchaca Springs to rest and have supper when suddenly a band of Comanches dashed out of the woods, killed, and scalped them.

On the other hand, Victor Bracht, in his *Texas in 1848*, wrote to a friend in Germany on August 30, 1847 that Santa Anna, the war chief of the Comanches, and a number of his followers had spent three days in New Braunfels and had assured the people of the town that friendship for the Germans would continue. This pledge had been given on March 1, 1847 when he and two other Comanche chiefs had made a peace treaty with John O. Meusebach. Colonel Jack Hayes, Texas Ranger and famous Indian fighter, reported to Meusebach, when he stopped at Meusebach's house near Comanche Springs, that he had made a trip to El Paso and was surprised to find that the Indians had kept the treaty so well. He said that he had not been molested nor had he lost any horses as long as he was within the bounds of the German colony, but as soon as he passed the line, he had losses. The Indians had great respect for John O. Meusebach. They called him *El Sol Colorado* (the Red Sun) because of his red beard.

The treaty of peace with the Indians opened the area of the Fisher-Miller grant to colonization by the German immigrants. Within a year five settlements were made in the former lands of the Comanche Indians: Castell, Bettina, Leiningen, Schoenburg, and Meerholz. The only town of these five which remains on a Texas map today, however, is Castell.

Texas, since February 1846, had been a state of the United States. For the protection of its newly-acquired territory, a line of forts was established, some of them in the Fisher-Miller grant. As the German colonists moved westward to claim their lands or settlers from other states arrived to secure land for farming or ranching, they needed the assurance that they would have help in case of attack by Indians or bands of marauders. Fort Martin Scott was constructed in 1848 near Fredericksburg. Fort Croghan, about three miles south of the present town of Burnet, was manned by a company of Rangers under the command of Lieutenant Henry McCulloch of Captain Jack C. Hayes's Texas Rangers. Fort McKavett in Menard County was established in 1852. From Fort Mason, built in 1851, cavalry units were sent wherever help was needed and were used especially to suppress raids by Apache and Kiowa Indians. These were the most important forts within the borders of the Fisher-Miller grant. Not far away, however, and of great importance to settlers going farther west, were other forts such as Fort Stockton, established in 1850, Fort Terrett, Fort Clark, Fort Davis, and Fort Concho. This line of forts was important not only for protection but for their value as markets for the produce of the settlers. Their surplus vegetables, corn, and other grains brought needed income to farmers who lived far from any large town.

Many university students and well-educated men came to Texas in the late 1840's as a result of the revolutions in Europe in 1848. These gathered in colonies where they could enjoy their common interests in music, literature, philosophy, and politics. At least five so-called "Latin Settlements" were made in Texas. Latium, near Brenham in Washington County, was founded in 1848. Among its earliest settlers were Victor and Bernard Witte, Dr. Henry Brandt, Carl F. Gieseke, Carl William Groos, Hermann von Bieberstein, Hermann Otto Cornitius, Professor Krug, and Albert Eversburg.

The Darmstaedter Farm, near New Braunfels, was another "Latin Settlement," its members being some of those among "The Forty" who established the communistic colony at Bettina in Llano County. They were joined by six young men from their native city in Germany, Darmstädt: Ernst Dosch, Ernst and Ludwig von Lichtenberg, Baron von Rotsmann, Hermann Schenck, and a man named Keller. This colony, however, lasted only one year.

In 1849, five members of Bettina, another Latin settlement, organized a Latin group on a communistic farm, named *Tusculum*. This was near the present town of Boerne in Kendall County. Its members were Philip Zoeller, Adam Vogt, Wilhelm

Friedrich, Leopold Schulz, and Christian Flach. They were joined later by Fritz Kramer, a medical student from Darmstadt. The largest and best known of the "Latin Settlements" was Sisterdale, situated in a beautiful valley of the two Sister Creeks which flow into the Guadalupe River about fifty miles north of San Antonio. The first settler, Nicolaus Zink, built a cabin there in 1847. He was followed by a number of well-educated Germans: Ernst Kapp, Eduard Degener, Dr. Adolf Douai who later became editor of the *San Antonio Zeitung*, Emil, Julius, and Rudolph Dresel, Dr. W. I. Runge, Baron Westphal, Louis von Breitenbach, Adolph and Otto Neubert, Fr. Brunckow, and August Siemering, also an editor of the *San Antonio Zeitung*. Practically every house had a library, and the men gathered in the the evenings for songs and discussion. At one time, when one of the men was discussing the doctrine of the socialists, St. Simon and Fourier, several dozen Comanche Indians appeared at the front door and, with perplexed expressions on their faces, watched the speaker who was so engrossed in his subject that he was completely unaware of their presence.

As early as 1845, the German immigrants had made a favorable impression on the inhabitants of Texas. A Houston newspaper, *The Morning Star*,[10] dated October 21, 1845, quoted this item from *The Galveston News*: "It must be gratifying to every Texian to witness the arrival of people so well calculated to add to the wealth of the country. Among this new accession to our population we discover many whose appearance is an evidence of superior character and standing. They will receive a hearty welcome among our citizens who know well how to appreciate the steady and industrious habits of German farmers to whom America is indebted for much of her agricultural wealth."

Aftermath of the Adelsverein

In 1847, the Adelsverein was bankrupt. The $80,000 which the directors had considered ample to fulfill the promises made to the settlers had been far from sufficient. Two years after the establishment of its first colony there were no storehouses to provide the necessities of life, no farm implements or seeds to furnish food, no hospitals for those who had been so desperately ill, no apothecary with medicines, and above all no funds with which these things could have been bought in the larger cities. Furthermore, not one colonist had received or even seen the land which his Immigration Contract had mentioned.

Reports of this situation reached Europe and were published in newspapers, creating great condemnation of the Verein. Much of this was deserved since the directors had made no effort to have the grant inspected before they signed the contract nor were all plans complete before the first group of immigrants departed. Moreover, the fact that they considered $80,000 sufficient to settle thousands in a place which had no provisions for human habitation indicated a lack of knowledge concerning the financial requirement for such a large project.

In his book, *For Those Intending to Emigrate! Letters from an Emigrant under the Protection of the Mainzer Verein to Texas,* published in Leipzig in 1847, Alwin Soergel, who had come to Texas on the *Franziska* in 1845, listed an account of the cost of such an undertaking. The number of immigrants considered in this statement is 2,500. In the final count as recorded by John O. Meusebach on page 16 in his *Answer to Interrogatories,* 7,380 immigrants were brought to Texas in the years 1844, 1845, and 1846. This is almost three times the number on which Soergel based his account. Therefore, if his final estimate for 2,500 persons is more than doubled, it is evident that the Verein colonization was greatly underfinanced. Soergel's account is listed as follows:[1]

For 2,500 persons:	
700 wagons @ $80	$ 56,000
5,600 oxen @ $20	112,000

700 drivers, 3 months @ $30 per month	63,000
3,000 oxen advanced to settlers @ $20	60,000
1,500 horses @ $20	30,000
3,000 cows @ $8	24,000
For 2,500 persons, provisions for 6 months @ $20	50,000
	$395,000

Such figures as these are more realistic than the $80,000 which the Verein had considered sufficient. During the three years in which the Verein had sent immigrants to Texas (1844, 1845, and 1846), it had brought 7,380 persons. How little they must have received of the things they needed so badly in a strange new land! Very few had received transportation to New Braunfels or Fredericksburg; no houses were provided; no tools for farming; and no funds, not even the funds which the immigrants had placed for credit with the Verein.

By 1847, no immigrant had entered the land of the Fisher-Miller grant except John O. Meusebach and his party of forty-seven men. Until the peace treaty[2] was signed with the Comanches on May 9, 1847, it was impossible for them to locate or claim land granted by the Verein. Many sold their 320 acres for ten cents an acre; others waited and benefited thereby. The Verein ceased to exist in 1848. For the purpose of transacting whatever business remained, the German Emigration Company was formed. Meusebach had resigned, and Hermann Spiess was appointed Commissioner General. He, in turn, was succeeded by Louis Bene who, as trustee for the company, tried to get an act approved by the Legislature "to assure to the German Emigration Company and its colonists their lands." On September 13, 1853 the company, after many involved transactions, transferred to creditors its property and all rights accruing to it by colonization contracts.[3] After the creditors had gained the land, the Legislature divested it from the former and granted it to the colonists or their assignees. The act to accomplish this was passed by the Legislature on February 3, 1854.

John Meusebach himself issued 729 certificates for land to colonists. These amounted to 324,160 acres. Altogether, a total of 1,735,200 acres was granted to the colonists brought to Texas by the Verein.[4]

In his "MEMORIAL of the Trustee of the German Emigration Company to the Legislature of the State of Texas,"[5] Louis

Bene, last Commissioner General of the organization, wrote this summary of the accomplishments of a project that had so many adversities, yet in the final analysis added much to the development of a new land:

> In compliance with the conditions and obligations of said contract, they [the directors of the Verein] sent direct from different ports of Europe to the ports of Texas, their own ships and emigrants, as follows: In the year 1844, five ships with 415 emigrants; in 1845, thirty ships with 4,304 emigrants; in 1846 twenty-one ships with 2,376 emigrants—total ending in 1846, fifty-six ships and 7,095 emigrants. They also sent in 1847, nineteen ships with 1,500 emigrants; in 1848, ten ships with 1,100 emigrants; in 1849, five ships with 700 emigrants, and in 1850, three ships with 300 emigrants. Total number of vessels arriving in Texas under the auspices of said company at the end of the year 1850, ninety-three ships and 10,695 emigrants. So that it is apparent that they not only contributed to the population and the development of the internal resources of the State but materially aided in establishing and extending its foreign commerce.

Were these all of the achievements that resulted from such a large project? Others are obvious when viewed in the light of history. An industrious people had added materially to the economy of Texas. As soon as the German colonists realized that they must take care of themselves, they began to shape their lives anew. Necessity made men of those who had been forlorn, gave strength for the tasks ahead, and courage for the hardships that they had to endure.

Since most settlers had lost their possessions, there was need for cabinet makers to replace these, and to make furniture and other essential articles for housekeeping. Shoemakers found themselves supplying footwear; wheelwrights were busy making wagons; and wagoners hauling supplies from Indianola, San Antonio, or Austin. Merchants began to open stores for trade, and mills were constructed for grinding grain. Farmers were busily occupied raising vegetables, corn, and other crops, and hunters in killing deer, turkey, and other animals for food.

As seasons passed and more time was allowed for other things, the colonists began to improve their homes or to build new ones. The log cabins were reinforced, and perhaps other rooms were added. Some immigrants, remembering the manner in which houses were built in Germany, used a *fachwerk* type of construction for their homes. This method employed half-timbering, mostly of logs, filled in with sand brick or a combination of straw and rocks mixed with native soil. The logs for walls were fastened together horizontally, vertically, and diagonally, thus making strong sides for the house. The outside, as well as the rooms inside, was covered with plaster and whitewashed.[4] Later the outside was covered with wood siding. This type of house construction was used mostly in New Braunfels where many houses over one hundred years old are still standing. In Fredericksburg, San Antonio, and the towns established later by settlers, the houses were built of native limestone or adobe brick.

Towns near New Braunfels and Fredericksburg began to be founded as typical German settlements, often started by a few families. Among these were York's Creek, Neighborsville, Smithson's Valley, and Buffalo Springs in Comal County; Grape Creek and Cherry Springs in Gillespie County. Later, in 1854 after the peace treaty was made, Comfort, in Kendall County was established by Ernst Altgelt, also Boerne which grew out of the Tusculum Latin Colony. Mason, Llano, San Saba, Brady, Paint Rock, and Menard were founded in the land that was once the home of the Indian and buffalo. Today many large cattle and sheep ranches are found in the seven counties that were carved out of the 3,800,000 acres of the Fisher-Miller grant: Kimble, Concho, Llano, Mason, Menard, McCulloch, and San Saba.

In 1852, Frederick Law Olmsted, who later was superintendent of Central Park in New York, was commissioned to write a series of articles for the *New York Sun*. He and his brother made a trip by horseback through the South. In his *Journey Through Texas*, published in New York in 1857, he wrote:[6] "On entering Texas we had been so ignorant as not to know that there were larger settlements there than in any Southern state." Of New Braunfels, his description of the main streets stated that they were "very wide—three times as wide as Broadway in New York."[7] He stayed in a small inn with the sign *Guadalupe Hotel, J. Schmitz*. This he described as having[8]

A long room, extending across the whole front of the cottage, the walls pink, with stenciled panels, and scroll ornaments in crimson, and with neatly-framed and glazed pretty lithographic prints hanging on all sides; a long, thick, dark oak table with rounded ends, oak benches at its sides;

chiseled oak chairs; a sofa, covered with cheap pink calico, with a small vine pattern; a stove in the corner; a little mahogany cupboard in another corner, with pitcher and glasses upon it; a smoky atmosphere; and finally, four thick-bearded men, from whom smoke proceeds, . . .

The landlady enters; she does not readily understand us, and one of the smokers rises immediately to assist us. Dinner we shall have immediately, and she spreads the white cloth at the end of the table, before she leaves the room, and in two minutes' time, by which we have got off our coats and warmed our hands at the stove, we are asked to sit down. An excellent soup is set before us, and in succession, there follow two courses of meat, neither of them pork, and neither of them fried, two dishes of vegetables, salad, compote of peaches, coffee with milk, white bread from the loaf, and beautiful and sweet butter.

In New Braunfels, Olmsted learned from Pastor Ervendberg the story of the Verein colonization and the suffering which the immigrants had to endure. "Such was the unhappy beginning," he wrote.[9] "But the wretchedness is already forgotten. . . . Now, after seven years, I do not know a prettier picture of contented prosperity than we witnessed at Neu-Braunfels. A satisfied smile, in fact, beamed on almost every German face we saw in Texas."

Northwest of New Braunfels, lands between the Colorado and Llano rivers were opened for settlement. This added greatly to the development of Texas. New industries were started in the settlements such as saddle-making, cotton ginning, grist milling, and gun making in Fredericksburg and Bastrop. George Ulrich, assessor and collector for Comal County, reported in the 1861 *Texas Almanac*, page 190, that there were in cultivation "200 acres in cotton, 15,000 acres in corn, and 600 acres in wheat." . . . "In the county there were four grist mills, one flour mill, two saw mills, one cotton gin, one sash factory, all propelled by water power." Until lately cattle had been considered the most profitable stock, but sheep were preferred at that time. Farms, large and small, were found along the Cibolo River on the road to Fredericksburg. This is also the pleasing picture of other counties where the German colonists settled. They had overcome adversities that seemed overwhelming when they first arrived in this new land.

Three German newspapers were published in Texas before the War Between the States: the *Neu-Braunfelser Zeitung*, edited and published by Ferdinand Lindheimer; *Der Union*, published by Ferdinand Flake in Galveston; and the *San Antonio Zeitung* with Dr. Adolf Douai as editor. A number of books written by Germans in Texas found their way to the population in Germany and had an effect on future emigration to Texas. Ferdinand Roemer's *Texas* gave much information about the geology of Texas, while Victor Bracht's *Texas in 1848* and Prince Solms's *Texas* gave advice to those preparing to emigrate. John O. Meusebach in his *Answer to Interrogatories* explained the problem of the land which was promised to the immigrants by the Verein. The geography of Texas and the announcement of the organization of the Verein, as well as his travels in the United States, are three of the subjects in Friedrich von Wrede's *Sketches of Life in the United States of North America and Texas.* Alwin Soergel in his *Letters to Those Intending to Emigrate* had a great influence on prospective emigrants.

After the first necessities of life were taken care of in a new settlement, schools and churches were the next consideration. The Protestant Church in New Braunfels held its first services under an elm tree and was incorporated in 1845 with Louis C. Ervendberg as pastor. Other well-known pastors in early German Protestant churches in Texas were: Henry Bauer, Carl Biel, C. Braun, S. W. Basse, B. Dangers, H. Braeschler, G. Geubner, J. G. Ebinger, G. W. Eisenlohr, R. Jaeggli, A. Sager, J. C. Roehm, F. Weisgerber, H. Wendt, and Ph. Fr. Zizelmann. Before the arrival of Father Gottfried Menzel who came from Bohemia on the ship *Canapus* in December, 1849, there was no priest of the Catholic Church in West Texas from the Colorado to the San Antonio rivers and from Victoria to the Llano River. The towns of New Braunfels and Fredericksburg were visited by a priest from Castroville in Medina County. The Catholic Church had as its first bishop in Texas the Rt. Reverend Odin of Galveston. Father Mueller arrived in Fredericksburg in 1852 and remained there until 1855. He was followed by Father Zoeller.

The Verein had felt a moral obligation to provide for the education of the immigrants' children and declared in its constitution that it would cause schools to be built in the colony according to the needs of the settlers. Shortly after the founding of New Braunfels in March 1845, the first school was started with Hermann Seele as teacher. In 1846, when the church was erected, L. C. Ervendberg became the teacher as part of his work as pastor of the Protestant Church. The severe epidemic of the summer 1846 caused many children to be parentless, and he established a *Waisenfarm* or orphanage about five miles from the city. There he and his wife were not only father and mother to these children but he was also minister and teacher. The school was granted a charter in 1848 which gave the director authority to begin an agricultural school and a school of arts and sciences as needed. Private schools were organized in New Braunfels in 1852 by Dr. Adolf Douai and in 1853 by Adolf Schlameus.

The first city school was started in New Braunfels in 1853 with Heinrich Guenther and Adolf Schlameus as teachers. The New Braunfels Academy was incorporated in 1858 and the first teachers were S. H. Franks, C. H. Holtz, and Adolf Schlameus. The first district school was constructed with walls twenty inches thick. At first there was only one room, but others were added as the list of students increased. There were also two private schools in the city, a Catholic school and a school for the study of Greek and Latin.

Nor was education neglected in Fredericksburg, the other town which the Verein founded. Its first school was established in 1846 with Johann Leyendecker as teacher. He was succeeded in 1847 by Jacob Brodbeck. Other schools were organized in nearby areas, and by 1860 there were ten schools in Gillespie County, with an enrollment of 290. At Cherry Springs, the teachers were Theodor Huelsemann and Frances Stein; at Grape Creek, Jacob Brodbeck, Louis Techner, and Edward L. Theumann.

No modern conveniences were found in the first schoolhouse at Comfort in Kendall County. There was no floor in the small log cabin, and only one door and one window. The benches had no backs, and there was no blackboard. This school was organized by a Mr. Glass in 1856, two years after Comfort was founded. At Boerne, between Comfort and San Antonio, H. W. Toepperwein taught school for one year at a salary of $25 a month.

Galveston organized a German school in 1846, and Austin in 1848. In San Antonio a German-English school received a charter in 1860, and Julius Berends was the first teacher.

In Austin County, there were elementary schools as early as 1840. The first of these was founded by Pastor Ervendberg and Dr. Johann Fischer at Industry. Other schools held in connection with Protestant churches were at Cat Spring, Biegel Settlement, La Grange, and Columbus. At Cat Spring Adolphus Fuchs was the teacher in the early 1850's. One of the best elementary schools in Texas before the Civil War was at Millheim; Ernst Gustav Maetze was the excellent teacher at the school. In Fayette County two church schools were organized by ministers of the Evangelical-Lutheran Church. A school at La Grange was taught by Reverend P. F. Zizelmann; one at Berlin, near Brenham, had Reverend Johann G. Ebinger as teacher. Professor Daniel Weber was an instructor at Texas Military Institute in Rutersville.

An attempt was made by Germans to establish a school of higher learning in Texas. Hermann's University was chartered in 1844 and received one league of land from the Republic. A two-story building was erected in Frelsburg, but the school never opened. The property was sold, and the building used as a public school in Frelsburg.

The German immigrants sent to Texas by the Verein were a hardy group and also people who could put their hands to a plow not only for their own families but likewise for those less able to accomplish the tasks required by life on a frontier. The soil in the areas chosen for the first two settlements was relatively fertile but less so in the land of the Fisher-Miller grant. Farmers in Comal and Gillespie counties had small gardens which produced vegetables sufficient for the family and sometimes abundant enough to provide income. The Germans who started homes on the Fisher-Miller grant turned to ranching as a better source of income, and today large ranches in the western part of Texas bear German names.

Social life on the frontier in the 1850's revolved around such organizations as agricultural societies, singing clubs similar to the Germania in New Braunfels and Sängerbunde in Austin, San Antonio, Houston, and other cities with a large German population; Schützenvereins (rifle clubs), and activities in the churches. Since a settler received a town lot and a ten-acre plot on arrival at New Braunfels and Fredericksburg, most of the farmers chose to have their homes on the ten-acre farms. In the latter town, a delightful compromise was made by having so-called Sunday houses on their town lots. These were small homes built to accommodate the farmer and his family overnight. They would drive into town and buy supplies for the week on Saturday, attend church services on Sunday morning, and return to the farm in the afternoon. These houses usually had only two rooms, but a staircase on the outside led to another room in the attic if this was needed. Many of these Sunday houses in Fredericksburg, over one hundred years old, have been restored and are reminders of a time when social life in Texas was more difficult to achieve.

German Immigration to Texas, 1847-1861

Many reasons have been given for emigration of a people to a new country: economic insecurity, overpopulation, political oppression, revolution, and war. The Verein colonization was accomplished mostly because of the first three situations, with the added enticement of promises made by the Verein and attractive publicity in newspapers and books in Germany. The adversities suffered by the German settlers in Texas during the years 1846 and 1847, however, could have been reasons for discouraging further immigration to Texas had it not been for conditions in Germany that caused thousands to leave in the years ahead.

In 1848, revolutionary movements broke out in many countries of Europe. In Italy, a revolution was directed by the middle classes who forced rulers in the various provinces to grant constitutions giving them political privileges. In Prussia and Austria, the people gained promised constitutional governments, but these did not last. Nearly all the German rulers withdrew the constitutions which they had granted. There was also much hatred and discord among the Slavic groups, and the Austrian emperor tried to appease them by granting the Bohemians the right to govern Bohemia as they liked, giving the same privilege to other racial groups in the empire. These rights, however, were later taken away.

Wars also were brewing in several places. Schleswig and Holstein in the southern part of the Danish peninsula were parts of Denmark. Prussia, under the leadership of Bismark, together with Austria, made war on Denmark in 1864 and annexed these two provinces. In the 1850's this impending war caused hundreds to leave Schleswig and Holstein. This was also true in nearby Mecklenburg. The Crimean War of 1854 and 1855 involved several countries of Europe, although it was fought in the area of the Black Sea. In the eastern part of Europe, the people of Poland revolted against Russia, demanding national independence. Poland had been divided between Prussia, Austria, and Russia at the Congress of Vienna in 1815. In an attempt to crush the insurrection, Russia ordered all Polish universities closed, confiscated large areas of Polish land, and deported thousands of Poles to Russia. These harsh measures led hundreds of Polish nationals to seek refuge in other countries, and many came to Texas. This is very evident in passenger lists of vessels arriving at the port of Galveston in the 1850's. The latter part of this decade brought large numbers of emigrants from other eastern European countries who left their homes in an effort to escape impending war. People from Bohemia, Silesia, and Austria sought a more peaceful life overseas, and Texas with its vast undeveloped lands and air of freedom was especially attractive to them.

In order to understand the location of towns and areas named in the immigrant list, one cannot use a present day map. Within the past two or three centuries many changes have been made in the boundaries of the countries of Europe. First and foremost, it should be remembered that neither Italy nor Germany was united until 1870 for the former and 1871 for the latter. Both countries before that time were merely a group of provinces.

During the first decade of the nineteenth century Napoleon had completely disrupted the political system and boundaries of countries in Europe as a result of his conquests. After the first overthrow of Napoleon the leaders of Russia, Prussia, Austria, England, and France met at Vienna to settle territorial differences. The Congress of Vienna in 1815 made several decisions that resulted in a state of discontent in Europe. This was particularly true in the case of Poland. This country was divided into three parts, one part to be annexed to Prussia, one to Russia, and one to Austria. This division and other changes are reflected in a map of Europe after 1815. Germany, not united until 1871, consisted of thirty-nine different states or provinces between 1815 and 1871.

The perplexing situation of boundaries between the principalities, duchies, provinces and electorates at this time is the cause of a situation in which it is sometimes impossible to give the location of a town named by a German immigrant who came to Texas between 1815 and 1871. Therefore, the use of a map covering the time 1815-1871 is recommended to those wishing to locate a certain town named in the 1847-1861 immigration list.

From all available sources an attempt was made to find passenger lists of Germans who came to Texas between 1847 and 1861. However, the ravages of time and war made this difficult. Any records that might have been kept at Galveston, where most of the ships arrived, had been lost in the great hurricane that struck the island of Galveston in September, 1900. The United States National Archives has preserved on microfilm a list of thirty-five ships from Hamburg and Bremen with the names of passengers on these ships.

Letters written to the port authorities in Antwerp and Bremen brought replies that they had no records for this period and added the information that the archives in both cities had been destroyed during World War II. The Hamburg Port Authority forwarded the letter of inquiry about ships leaving Hamburg for Texas, 1847-1861, to the Hamburg Archives who in turn recommended Herr Karl Werner Klüber, Kulturhistoriker and Genealoge. He researched the Hamburg Archives and compiled passenger lists of twenty-four ships that brought German immigrants to Texas during this period.

In the Texas State Archives, a rich source of passenger lists was found in the *Neu-Braunfelser Zeitung* for the years 1852 to 1861 and the *Galveston Zeitung* for June 25, 1851. The latter contained the list of passengers on the *Magnet* and *Reform*, both of which arrived at Galveston in 1851. In *Die Union*, another German newspaper published in Galveston, eleven lists were found, some in the Microfilm Newspaper Collection of the Rice University Library in Houston, and some in bound volumes of this newspaper in the Texas State Archives in Austin.

From these three sources all names were copied from the ship lists, together with whatever information was included about each immigrant. These names were indexed and placed in a master file. This does not represent a full count of Germans coming to Texas from Europe during the years from 1847 to 1861 since many ship lists were lost, and many settlers came through the port of New Orleans. The list as compiled and presented in this book is only a partial number of the Germans who came to Texas during those years.

The total number of single men and men with families from all sources is 5,629 entries. With the addition of wives and children, plus four members added for each family when only the words "with family" were written with the name of an immigrant, the total count is about 11,900. Including the 495 Wends, who arrived at Galveston from Lausitz and Rothenburg in 1854, the number would be about 12,400.

In tabulating the entries, a chart was kept of the place in Europe from which each immigrant came and also the county in Texas where he settled. It was not possible to locate the residences of all immigrants in Texas for several reasons: 1) some may have moved to other states; 2) some died and no record was kept; 3) time did not allow for research of naturalization, tax, or U.S. Census records for all counties in Texas where the German immigrants settled; 4) some lived on isolated farms and left no record.

The location of towns in the following lists is based on a map of Central Europe, 1815-1871, in Hammond's *World Atlas,* 1851, p. H-29. The percentages arrived at do not include the 495 Wends from Lusatia and Rothenburg in Eastern Europe who arrived at Galveston in 1854. Under the listing "Undetermined" are immigrants from towns that the compiler was unable to locate because of incorrect spelling, because they were too small to be listed in a gazetteer, or because there were numerous towns with the same name in different areas. The listing "No record" was used when an immigrant gave no name of his residence in Europe nor was any Texas destination located by the compiler. The designation "Texas" indicated that a town or county in Texas was named by the immigrant.

However, for the purpose of determining the proportion of immigrants coming from different parts of Germany between 1847 and 1861, a modern map was superimposed on a map of 1815-1871. Then, using the line of demarcation (or the so-called Iron Curtain) between the present West Germany and East Germany, each immigrant from these areas was listed as having resided in the western or eastern part of the present Germany. From this study certain percentages were arrived at which reflect a larger number of people having left the eastern part of Europe than the western in the immigration of Germans to Texas from 1847 to 1871. The number of single persons or families leaving countries other than Germany is listed numerically since the percentage is so small.

Under these listings, the following percentages were compiled:

From	East Germany (or DDR)	38.8%
"	West Germany	30. %
"	No record	11.5%
"	Texas record	7.0%
"	Undetermined record	4.6%
"	Austria	3.7%
"	Schleswig and Holstein	2.7%

98.3%

From	Denmark	32	imm.
"	Switzerland	28	"
"	United States	14	"
"	Russia	4	"
"	Norway	3	"
"	England	3	"
"	Belgium	2	"
"	Alsace Lorraine	2	"
"	France	2	"
"	Sweden	1	"
"	Spain	1	"

From these other countries 92 " or 1.7%

100%

The following information was found regarding the residences of the 1847-1861 German immigrants in Texas counties:

Austin County	388
Bexar County	167
Gillespie and Comal	291
Bastrop and Fayette	349
Gonzales and Goliad	39
Galveston	360
Guadaulpe and Victoria	135
Wharton and Harris	192
Colorado and Washington	204
Lee and Travis	111
West Texas (all counties west and north of Gillespie County)	78
Calhoun, DeWitt and Matagorda	138
Total	2,452

In analyzing these figures on a regional basis, we find a new concentration of Germans in Texas as compared to the Verein immigrants who settled mostly in West Texas. The region around Austin, Fayette, Washington, Bastrop and Colorado counties became the focal areas for new German settlers in Texas in the 1850's.

East Central Texas Counties

Austin County	388
Bastrop and Fayette	349
Colorado and Washington	204
	941

Galveston County	360
Harris County	192
	552

West Texas Counties

Gillespie and Comal	291
Bexar County	167
Lee and Travis	111
West Texas	78
	647

Coastal Region Counties

Gonzales and Goliad	39
Guadalupe and Victoria	135
Calhoun, DeWitt and Matagorda	138
	312

FACHWERK HOUSES IN BICKEN, NASSAU

These houses, on the emigrant road from Leipzig to Bremen, are representative of this type of half-timber construction in Germany.

HOUSE OF OSCAR VON CLAREN IN NEW BRAUNFELS
Oscar von Claren together with Friedrich Wilhelm von Wrede
were two officials of the Verein who were murdered by Indians
about twenty miles southwest of Austin in 1845. This house shows
fachwerk construction, a covering of white-washed plaster, and
later addition of wood siding. Picture furnished by Mr. Roger
Nuhn of New Braunfels.

PETER TATSCH HOME, FREDERICKSBURG, TEXAS

Built by Peter Tatsch in 1856, this house shows the native stone used in Fredericksburg. Tatsch, a cabinet maker, did the woodwork himself. Fireplace at the rear was large enough to roast an ox. *San Antonio Express* photo.

Restored fachwerk home (built in 1855) of George Ullrich, wagonmaster of the Verein.

PICTURE OF THE FRIGATE GUTENBERG

The *Gutenberg* which arrived at the port of Indianola, Texas on October 2, 1855 was chosen as an example of an emigrant ship in the Transportation Exhibit in the Deutsches Museum, in Munich Germany

AN EMIGRANT SHIP OF THE 1840's, SIMILAR
TO THE *JOHANN DETHARDT*
Picture furnished by Kurt Klotzbach, editor of the *Ruhr Nach-
richten*, Dortmund, West Germany.

PICTURE OF BETWEEN-DECKS SCENE ON EMIGRANT SHIP ABOUT 1847, SHOWING CONDITIONS UNDER WHICH MANY IMMIGRANTS CAME TO TEXAS. Picture from *Allegeneine Auswanderungs Zeitung* 1847, page 291, by permission of Commerzbibliothek, Hamburg, West Germany, sent by Karl Werner Klüber, Kulturhistoriker und Genealoge, Hamburg.

List of Passengers arrived from ...
during the quarter ending June

Date / Vessels name	Master's name	Where From	Passengers Name
June 13 Bark Neptune	[illegible]	Bremen	Edward Wagner
			Edward Harter
			Victor Witte
			Anna Witte
			Ferdinand Hagendorn
			Marie Witte
			Helene Witte
			Amelie Becker
			Albert Cornelius
			Emilie Cornelius
			Julius Cornelius
			Alfred Müller
			Franz Lange
			Catharina ,
			Ludwig ,
			Lena ,
			Eva ,
			Johann ,
			Carl ,
			Wilhelm Prötzel
			Carl Papermans
			Friedr. Salter
			Johann ,
			Heinrich ,
			Friedr ,
			Carl ,

From Microfilm RG 36, Records of the U. S. Bureau of Customs: Lists of Passengers Arriving at the Port of Galveston, Texas from Foreign Ports, 1846-1871. Copy in Fort Worth, Texas, Public Library: list of passengers on Bark *Neptune* from Bremen which arrived at Galveston, Texas on 13 June, 1850.

...gn Ports in the port of Galveston
30. 1850.

Age	Sex	Occupation	Country to which they belong	Country to which they intend to become inhabitants	Died
35	male	Junst	Auerbach	Texas	
30	,		Cassinkel		
29	,		Hanover		
21	female				
12	male				
2	fem				
3/4	,				
43	,		Burg		
35	male	Merchant	Sannebom		
24	fem				
3/4	male				
50	,	Lace maker	frohnsm		
45	,	Miller	Aakenheim		
35	fem				
11	male				
8	fem				
5	,				
4	male				
3	,				
37	,	farmer	Fallersleben		
35	,				
43	,	Draper	Blankenburg		
32	,				
1	,				
...	,				
44	,	Dues			

Passagierliste

der am 18. Octbr. von Bremen in Galveston angekommenen Barke „Friedrich Grosse", Capt. Sanders:

Doro. Sachtleben 6 Pers., J. S. Thürge 3 Pers., Auguste Michael, Carl Wagner, Carl Aurich, Friedr. Wesser, Joh. Model, Carl Oberländer, Gottl. Reuß, Carl Kenßler aus Sachsen; Andr. Langbein, 7 Pers., Ch. Behrends 4 Pers., Ida Winström 4 P., Carl Hoffmann 4 Pers., W. Brudisch, A. Thiel, C. Urbede, Marie Baumann, Ant. Pechner 2 Pers., C. Bore, B. Colmar, A. Müller, C. Borsch 4 Pers., F. Böhmer, F. Sachtleben 3 Pers., H. Markworth 5 Pers., J. Wegener 6 Pers., J. Korsch 8 Pers., A. Lux, P. Fenig, Joh. Willmann 8 Pers., A. Tannhäuser 5 Pers., J. Steller, A. Stach, W. Wisuer, Alb. Degenhardt, M. Dübeler 5 Pers., A. Seidel, F. Büttner, M. Jaschke, M. Klenger, A. Urner, H. Markworth, J. Wagener, J. Rehberg, R. Bittermann, H. Rußland, K. Schröder, 2 Pers., A. Hofmann, G. Hampel, 6 Pers. A. Büttner, F. Fränkel, S. Eggeling, J. Pier, A. Reinlich, P. Strumann, H. Wennbofer, W. Beckmann, P. Siegmann, C. Hübener, M. Hahn, J. S. Nechels, aus Preußen; A. Richter aus Rudelstadt; Elis. Klein, C. Wuth, C. Vogt, A. Eck, K. u. A. Barum, C. Banger, M. Rust, A. Mateus, C. Friesmann, M. Vogt, G. Rohrbach, H. Altmüller 2 Pers., F. Marschall, W. Waldschmidt, aus Hessen; J. Elsterer 5 Pers., K. Schäfer 2 Pers., W. Bachfe, A. Brückner, J. Hausmann 2 Pers., F. Abelt 6 Pers.; W. Meier, 6 P., Fr. Schäfer, K. Knebel, Fr. Kräßer, Th. Meier 7 Pers., Fr. Hausmann, Fr. Schulz aus Böhmen; Fr. Pupille, Chr. Schütz 3 Pers., Mar. Springmann, F. Brecht, H. Hennig aus Hanover; G. u. F. König aus Oldenburg, M. Güntel aus Baiern; zusammen 194 Personen.

From *Neu-Braunfelser Zeitung* dated 24 October, 1853, copy of passenger list of the ship *Friedrich Grosse* from Bremen which arrived at Galveston, Texas on 18 October, 1853.

Zusammengestellt aus den alphabetischen Hamburger Auswandererprotokollen von 1851 durch **Karl Werner Klüber**
Kulturhistoriker und Genealoge
2000 Hamburg-Altona 1

Passag. Zahl	
2	Abel, Wilhelm, Zimmermann, u. Frau, aus Wilsnack in Preussen
1	Boas, Rudolf, Barbier, aus Berlin in Preussen
1	Boer, C.S., Schmied, aus Langenbielau in Sachsen (Langenbrelau??)
6	Burmester, Wilhelm, Zimmermann, u. Frau u. 4 Kinder, 7 - 22 Jahre alt, aus Neukloster in Mecklenburg
3	Christiansen, J., Schneider, u. Frau u. Kind, aus Cramon in Mecklenburg
1	Daunker, Chr., Arbeitsmann, aus Krubbe in Preussen
	E -
1	Frisicke, Wilhelm, Stellmacher, aus Pritzabes in Preussen
1	Germer, Dietrich, Arbeitsmann, aus Wenddorf in Preussen
7	Graf, Joachim, Zimmermann, u. Frau u. 5 Kinder, aus Laaslich in Preussen
3	Hanson, H.F.(?), Schuhmacher, u. Frau u. Kind, aus Husum in Holstein
1	Hartwig, Gottl., Schachtm(eister?), aus Rosenthal in Preussen
1	Meintzky, Eugen, Oekonom, aus Muehlberg in Preussen
5	Mitscher, Michael, Arbeitsmann, u. Frau u. 3 Kinder, aus Wenddorf in Preussen
1	Hofmann, Wilhelm, Mueller, aus Magenow in Preussen
1	Hurtz, Wilhelm, Schmied, aus Kletzke in Preussen
	I -
6	Keiser, Fr., Gaertner, u. Frau u. 4 Kinder, aus Grube in Preussen
5	Kunst, Joachim, Arbeitsmann, u. Frau u. 3 Kinder, aus Wenddorf/Preussen
1	Ladage, Heinrich, Schneider, aus Hamburg
5	Michael, Johann(a?) u. Familie von 4 Personen, aus Perleberg i.Preussen
1	Paulson, Dorothea, aus Hamburg
2	Priest, Joachim, Arbeitsmann, u. Frau, aus Quitzow in Mecklenburg
	O,Q -
4	Regien, Carl, Arbeiter, u. Frau u. 2 Kinder, aus Gross-Gandern/Preussen
1	Roemmler, Chr. Wilhelm, Gaertner, aus Reudnitz in Preussen
7	Sander, August, Drechsler, u. Frau u. 5 Kinder, 5 - 17 Jahre alt, aus Perleberg in Preussen
1	Schenk, August, Tuchmacher, aus Perleberg in Preussen
1	Schmidt, Fr., (Schmied ?), aus Perleberg in Preussen
1	Schumacher, Heinrich, Zimmergeselle, aus Schoenfeldt in Preussen
1	Settgast, Chr., Knecht, aus Rependorf in Mecklenburg
2	Stechlich, Ed. u. Franz, Kaufleute, aus Tblau in Preussen
5	Steiness, Wilhelm, Schuhmacher, u. Frau u. 3 Kinder, aus Torgau in Preussen
2	Steinhagen, Schmied, u. Frau, aus Kroeplin in Mecklenburg
	U -
4	Viereck, Joachim, Maurer, u. Frau u. 2 Kinder, aus Webelin in Preussen
1	Wilde, Carl Eugen, Arbeitsmann, aus Frankfurt in Preussen
7	Winterfeldt, Friedrich u. Frau u. 5 Kinder bis zu 14 Jahren, aus Perleberg in Preussen
1	Wolff, Julius, Commis, aus Schlage in Preussen
	XYZ -

35 Eintraege mit 93 Personen.

From Hamburger Auswandererprotokolle ("Schiffslisten") im Staatsarchiv: From Hamburg Archives: Passenger list of ship Nr. 58, *Bassermann* which left Bremen, Germany on 15 August, 1851 for Galveston, Texas. List compiled and sent by Herr Karl Werner Klüber, Kulturhistoriker und Genealoge, of Hamburg-Altona.

Schiffsliste
der Hamburg, Bark „Texas"
Capt. ...., am 23. Oct.
von Bremerhaven gesegelt und
am 18. Dez. 1853 in Galveston
gelandet.

H. L. Conrads aus Niederbreisig. 4 Pers.
Friederike Arlitt aus Danzig, 3 Pers.
Minna Berwid, ebendas.
Marg. Seelhorst a. Bersmold, 2 Pers.
Helle Kollmann a. Winsen, 2 Pers.
Joh. Bruns a. Rastede, 6 Pers.
Cath. Nordhausen a. Neuenburg, 3 Pers.
Gerhard Büthe a. Rastede, 3 Pers.
Joh. Hilge, ebendf.
Gerh. Heye, ebend.
H. Mellinghoff a. Emmerich.
Berend Jansen a. Winsen.
Aler. Sendler a. Würtemberg.
Ferd. Guthe a. Andreasberg.
Helene Stoffers a. Rastede 2 Pers.
H. Lochstedt a. Holzminden, 7 Pers.
J. W. Linnenbrügger aus Bielefeld.
Anna Maria Kostrup a. Enger.
Cath. Ohlenmeyer a. Versmold.
Fr. Wilh. Lineweg a. Holzhausen.
A. Horn a. Goslar, 2. Pers.
F. Bergmann a. Schoulau.
Ch. Joh. Wattle a. Lulau.
August u. Elise Gloges a. Jacobsstadt.
H. Wicke a. Altenhausen.
Joh. Döhle a. Winningenhausen.
Jost Döhle, ebend.
Joh. Jegenhard a. Burghassungen. 2 P.
Heinrich Ritter, ebend.
J. H. Schwarz, ebend.
Joh. Koch, ebend. 6 Pers.
Gerh. H. Kraus, ebend. 7 Pers.
Fried. Bernhard a. Elshausen.
Ch. Laubengeier a. Plieningen. 2 Pers.
Israel Jöhrle, ebend.
Ferd. Wolfer, ebend.
Joh. Georg Koch a. Plieningen,
C. u. Henriette Dücker a. Burbach.
Carolina Wehrmann a. Gr. Elbe.
Franz Störes aus Crevelt.
Peter Heiligmann a. Lamboldshausen 2 P.

Wilh. Borchers a. Münster.
Marg. Senjel a. Neffenroth.
Heinrich Stock ebend.
Julius Berndt a. Kraschau.
Chr. Sattler a. Langesfeld.
Conc. u. Anna Hulsel ebend.
Louis Frede a. Möchern.
Helene Cath. Otholt a. Mohlberg.
Ed. u. Emilie Blankenfeld a. Langsberg.
Rudolph Müller a. Grafhorst, 3 Pers.
Wilh. u. Wilhelmine Graf a. Ludau.
Carl Krämer a. Halberstadt.
Friedr. Koch, ebend.
August Lange a. Krimmitschau. 4 Pers.
Wilh. Hest, ebend.
Carl Friedr. Rückert, ebend.
Carl Michel a. Traureith.
Fr. u. Frederike Piering a. Altenburg.
Therese Fischer ebend., 3 Pers.
Leonh. u. Wilhelmine ....
Chr. Gleich a. Hoppenstedt, 4 Pers.
Heinr. Hennecke a. Weghold.
Christian Schlage, ebend.
Heinrich Eberfeld a. Cappenberg, 4 Pers.
Adam Walter a. Bruletorf, 3 Pers.
Friedrich Dietrich a. Thoren. 3 Pers.
Steppon Wollen a. Forst, 7 Pers.
Peter Schaffers, ebend.
Gerhard Notten, ebend.
Albert Rippe a. Weghold, 9 Pers.
Elise Behnken, ebend.
Joh. u. Heinrich Blume, ebend.
Joseph Contrain a. Niederbruchter.
George Leuke a. Brownstorchen.
Albert Meytr a. Schwarme.
Peter Duffy a. Jachbach, 5 Pers.
Wilhelm Bomweg, ebend.
Gottlieb u. Louise Poble, a. Essen.
Wilh. u. Pauline Kruger a. Wongrovice.
Gottlieb Kuorth, ebend.
Carl Krüger, ebend.
Carl Kruger, ebend.
Franz Wenmeyer a. Hildesheim, 3 Pers.
Gottl. Kollad a. Briesen.
Carl Knaus a. Gemünd.
Edo Collmann a. Winsen.
Joh. Friedr. Kollmann, ebend.

From *Neu-Braunfelser Zeitung* dated 6 January, 1854: copy of passenger list of ship *Texas* which left Bremerhaven on 23 October, 1853 and arrived at Galveston, Texas on 18 December, 1853.

If one were to seek reasons for this change in the German immigrants' choice from 1847 to 1861 of an area in Texas on which to make a home, he might consider:

1) reports of the illness in the western part of Texas, especially New Braunfels and Fredericksburg where an epidemic of cholera had broken out in 1849 and diphtheria in 1851;
2) greater fertility of soil in Central and East Texas;
3) the fact that the counties of Austin, Fayette, Colorado, and Washington had been settled earlier and hence had more stores, blacksmith shops, and other industries that would make easier the adjustment to a new land;
4) there were more creeks and rivers to supply water for farming and other needs, and also a greater amount of rainfall.

As time passed, the German settlers and their children pushed the frontier of Texas farther north and west and claimed more land for farming and ranching. New counties were created both in West Texas and East Texas. By thrift and industriousness, the Germans in this new land thrived and no longer wished to return to Germany.

In 1861 war was imminent in the United States between the North and the South over the question of slavery, and those who had left Europe to avoid war found themselves involved. Although they did not believe in slavery, the cause of the conflict, they were willing to support the state in which they had found a home; hence most of the Germans served in the Confederate Army. With the beginning of this war, the ports on the Gulf of Mexico were blockaded, and therefore immigration ceased until peace was made in 1865. After this, immigrants began to come to Texas in large numbers.

NOTES

Chapter I
A. The Germans in Texas before 1836
   1. Moritz Tiling, **German Element in Texas**, p. 4
   2. R. L. Biesele, **History of Early German Settlements** in Texas, p. 42
   3. **Ibid.,** p. 42
   4. L. F. Lafrentz, **Deutsche-Texanische Monats-Hefte,** September 1906, p. 89

Chapter II
B. The Germans in the Texas War of Independence
   1. Hermann Ehrenberg, **With Milam and Fannin,** p. 14.
   2. **Ibid.,** p. 182
   3. **Handbook of Texas,** 704-705
   4. Moritz Tiling, **German Element,** p. 35
   5. **Ibid.,** pp. 34-35

Chapter III
C. German Colonization of Texas, 1836-1844
   1. Jerry Sadler, **History of Texas Land,** p. 9
   2. **Ibid.,** p. 7.

Chapter IV
D. The Adelsverein Immigration to Texas, 1844-1847
   1. R. L. Biesele, **History of German Settlements,** p. 83
   2. von Wrede, **Lebensbilder aus den Verengen Staaten von Nordamerika und Texas,** p. 317
   3. Chester W. and Ethel H. Geue, **A New Land Beckoned,** p. 25
   4. **Ibid.,** for copy of Contract, see Plate No. 10
   5. **Ibid.,** ship list, Plate No. 15
   6. **Ibid.,** p. 68
   7. **Ibid.,** p. 10.
   8. R. L. Biesele, **History of German Settlements,** p. 123
   9. A. Siemering, **Der Deutsche Pionier,** Vol. 10, pp. 57-62 "Die Latienische Ansiedlung in Texas," translated by C. W. Geue and published in **New Braunfels Herald,** August 6, 1963 and in **Texana,** Vol. V, No. 2, p. 129.
   10. Amon Carter Museum of Western Art, Fort Worth, Microfilm Newspaper Collection.

Chapter V
E. Aftermath of the Adelsverein
   1. Alwin Soergel, **Letters from an Emigrant,** p. 49
   2. Irene Marschall King, **John O. Meusebach,** p. 116
   3. Moritz Tiling, **German Element,** p. 112
   4. Irene M. King, **Meusebach,** p. 154
   5. Verein Collection, University of Texas Archives
   6. Frederick Olmsted, **Journey,** p. 132
   7. **Ibid.,** p. 142
   8. **Ibid.,** p. 144
   9. **Ibid.,** p. 177

Chapter VI
F. German Immigration to Texas, 1847-1861
   1.
G. Introduction to List of Immigrants
   1. Lillie Moerbe Caldwell, **Texas Wends,** pp. 46-50

II The List of Immigrants

NAMES OF SHIPS
from Bremen and Hamburg with Immigrants to Texas, 1847 - 1861

N.B.—Ports of departure and arrival are listed, with dates when known. In a date, Roman numeral indicates month.

ADOLPHINE—Bremen;
  Galveston, Fall 1859
ALEXANDER—Hamburg;
  Galveston, 4.III.1850
AMMERLAND—
  Galveston, 10.XII.1854
ANNA LOUISA—Bremen;
  Galveston, 30.VII.1857;
  80 days' journey
ANTOINETTE—Bremen;
  Galveston, 13.VI.1848
ANTOINETTE—Bremen;
  Galveston, XII.1854
ANTON GUNTHER—Bremen;
  Galveston, VI.1860
ANTON GUNTHER—
  Galveston, 2.I.1860
BASSERMANN— Hamburg,
  15.VIII.1851; Galveston
BRASILIAN—Hamburg, 2.IX.
  1850; Galveston, 13.XI.1850
E. von BEAULIEU or BRASILIAN
  —Bremen; Galveston, 1.I.1857
J. W. BUDDECKE—Bremen;
  Galveston, 1.I.1853
CANAPUS—Bremen;
  Galveston, 19.XII.1848
CANAPUS—Bremen;
  Galveston, 3.XII.1849
CHAS. N. COOPER—Bremen;
  Galveston, 23.X.1847
COLONIST—Hamburg;
  Galveston, 25.XI.1848
COLONIST—Hamburg, 28.III.
  1850; Galveston, 13.VI.1850
COPERNICUS—Hamburg, 15.IX.
  1852; Galveston and New
  Orleans
CREOLE—Bremen;
  Galveston, 8.VII.1852
ESTAFETTE—Bremen, 13.IX.
  1850; Galveston
FORTUNA—Bremen;
  Galveston, 8.VI.1858

FORTUNA—Bremen, ca 21.IX.
  1858; Galveston, 26.XI.1858;
  67 days' journey
FORTUNA—Bremen, 1860;
  Galveston, Oct. 1860
FRANKLIN—Hamburg, 3.IV.
  1852; Galveston and Indianola,
  31.V.1852
FRANKLIN—Hamburg, 1.IX.
  1853; Galveston
FRANZISKA—Bremen;
  Galveston, November 1847
FRANZISKA—Bremen;
  Galveston, 2.XII.1849
FRANZISKA—Bremen;
  Galveston, 20.XI.1854
FRIEDRICH GROSSE—Bremen;
  Galveston, 18.X.1853
GALLIOTT CONCORDIA— Brem-
  en; 75 days to Galveston, arr.
  25.XI.1854
GALLIOTT FLORA—Bremen;
  Galveston, 21.V.1849
GASTON—Bremen, 6.IX.1857;
  Galveston, 7.XI.1857
GASTON—Bremen;
  Galveston, 16.XII.1860
GESSNER—Bremen;
  Galveston, 30.IX.1854
GESSNER—Bremen;
  Galveston, 20.XII.1855
GESSNER—Bremen;
  Galveston, Fall 1860, 52 days'
  journey
GUTENBERG—Hamburg, 3.VIII.
  1855; Indianola, 2.X.1855
HAMBURG—Hamburg, 3.X.1849;
  Galveston, 15.XII.1849
HAMPDEN—Hamburg, 1.IV.1854;
  Galveston
HELEN AND ELISE—Galveston,
  7.XII.1847
HENRIETTE—Galveston, 14.VI.
  1843? ('1853)

HERMANN THEODOR—Bremen;
Galveston, 2.XII.1850
HERMANN THEODOR—Bremer-
haven, 15.IX.1853;
Galveston, 20.XI.1853
HERSCHEL—Galveston, 21.V.1849
HERSCHEL—Bremen;
Galveston, 24.I.1850
HERSCHEL—Bremen;
Galveston, 25.V.1851
HERSCHEL—Hamburg, 15.X.1855;
Galveston
IRIS—Bremerhaven, 6.X.1857;
Galveston, 29.XI.1857
IRIS—Bremen, 24.IX.1858;
Galveston, 7.XII.1858
IRIS—Bremen, 20.IV.1859;
Galveston, 5.VI.1859
IRIS—Bremerhaven, 18.X.1859;
Galveston, 25.XII.1859
IRIS—Bremen;
Galveston, 5.VI.1860
IRIS—Bremerhaven, 25.XI.1860;
Galveston, 19.I.1861
JEVERLAND—Bremen;
Galveston, 23.III.1858
JEVERLAND—Bremen;
Galveston, 18.XI.1860; 58 days'
journey
JOH. DETHARDT—Bremen;
Galveston, 2.I.1848
JOH. DETHARDT—Bremen;
Galveston, 15.XII.1848
JOHN FREDERICK—Hamburg,
12.X.1850;
Galveston, 21.XII.1850
JOH. ED. GROSSE—Bremerhaven,
27.IX.1853;
Galveston, 18.XII.1853
JOHN HOLLAND—Antwerp;
Galveston, 27.XI.1848
JUNO—Bremen, 23.XI.1852;
Galveston, 2.II.1853
JUNO (incomplete?) 4 passengers;
Galveston, 25.VI.1860
JUNO—Bremen;
Galveston, 19.XII.1860; 54 days'
journey
LEIBNIZ—Hamburg, 31.VIII.
1850; Galveston
LEO—Bremen; Galveston, 25.VI.
1848; incomplete: 6 entries, 23
persons
LOUIS—Antwerp;
Galveston, 20.XI.1848
LUCIE—Bremen;
Galveston, 7.XI.1854
MAGNET—Bremen;
Galveston, 2.II.1852
MAGNET—Bremen, 17.IV.1851;
Galveston, 25.VI.1851

MARYLAND—Bremen;
Galveston, 21.I.1859
MILES—Hamburg, 26.IV.1852;
Galveston, Indianola
MILES—Hamburg, 14.X.1852;
Galveston, 3.I.1853
MILES—Hamburg, 1.IX.1854;
Galveston
MILES—Hamburg, 14.IV.1855;
Galveston
MINNA—Galveston, 3.XI.1854
MISSISSIPPI—Bremen;
Galveston, 20.XI.1855; 73 days'
voyage
NATCHEZ—Bremen;
Galveston, Fall 1847
NEPTUNE—Bremen;
Galveston, 15.XII.1848
NEPTUNE—Bremen;
Galveston, 6.XI.1849
NEPTUNE—Bremen;
Galveston, 13.VI.1850
NEPTUNE—Bremerhaven, 1.X.
1853; Galveston, 28.XI.1853
NEPTUNE—Bremen;
Galveston, 3.XI.1854
REFORM—Bremen;
Galveston, 3.XII.1849
REFORM—Bremen;
Galveston, 29.XI.1850
REFORM—Bremen, 17.IV.1851;
Galveston, 25.VI.1851
REPUBLIC—Hamburg, 1.X.1851;
Galveston, Indianola
SARAH—Hamburg, 19.VIII.1851
Galveston
SOLON—Bremen;
Galveston, 29.XI.1850
SOLON—Bremen, 31.V.1852;
Galveston
SOPHIE—Bremen;
Galveston, 19.I.1852
SOPHIE—Hamburg, 28.VIII.1852
Galveston, Indianola
SUWA—Bremerhaven, 11.XI.1853;
Galveston, 23.XII.1853
TEXAS—Bremen;
Galveston, 12.VI.1853
TEXAS—Bremerhaven, 23.X.1853;
Galveston, 18.XII.1853
THERESE HENRIETTE—Ham-
burg, 3.XI.1853;
Galveston, 20.XII.1853
WASHINGTON—Hamburg,
17.VIII.1852
Galveston and New Orleans
WESER—Bremen;
Galveston, 23.I.1854
WESER—Bremen;
Galveston, 3.XII.1854
WESER—Bremen;
Galveston, 13.XI.1857

WESER—Bremen;
Galveston, 1.VI.1858

WESER—Galveston, 24.XI.1858;
slow journey, 75 days

WESER—Bremerhaven, 8.IV.1859;
Galveston, 3.VI.1859, 56 days'
journey

WESER—Bremen, 1859;
Galveston, Fall, 1859

WESER—Bremen;
Galveston, 2.VI.1860

WESER—Bremen;
Galveston, 23.XI.1860, 64 days

WILHELM—Bremen;
Galveston, 6.X.1858

List of Immigrants

Introduction to List of Immigrants

To the list of ships that brought immigrants to Texas between 1847 and 1861 should be added the *Ben Nevis*, which arrived in Galveston in December 1854. It sailed from Liverpool with 513 Wends from Lusatia (Lausitz, Saxony) and Rothenburg in the eastern part of Europe. There were 588 Wends who left their homes; but before they started their journey from Liverpool, tragedy struck in the form of an epidemic of cholera, and 75 of the 588 died. Eighteen died on the ship while on the trip overseas. Led by their pastor, John Kilian, after their arrival at Galveston, they went to an area in Lee County and established the town of Serbin. The Wendish culture was maintained for a number of years; but gradually as German families moved to Serbin, the German language was used.

That the listing of German immigrants from all available sources known to the compiler is far from complete will be evident in the following excerpt from the *Neu-Braunfelser Zeitung* of September 3, 1858, in a dispatch dated 20 August from New Orleans:

> The German organization, now in its 11th year, which was established to assist German immigrants who arrived there, gave the following information from 31 May, 1857 to the same date in 1858:
>
> From Bremen in 83 ships   9424 persons
> From Hamburg in 3 ships   352 persons
> From Havre in 28 ships   3980 persons
> From Antwerp in 1 ship   156 persons
>
> Of these 9796 went to St. Louis, 1259 to various places on the Ohio [River], and 111 to Texas. The rest stayed in New Orleans.

These 111 immigrants who came to Texas would be difficult to identify in New Orleans passenger lists as would also hundreds of others who came to Texas by the way of New Orleans in other years.

To give the location of the various towns in Germany from which the immigrants came was not considered feasible for several reasons. In the first place, the frequent wars in Europe changed boundaries of countries with the result that a town might be in Schleswig, for example, in one year and in Prussia the next; then after a period of time it would be in Denmark. The same thing would be true of such areas as Silesia, Bohemia, Poland, and others. Then, many towns of the same name are found in different parts of the country that is now known as Germany. In the 1850's it was still a group of kingdoms, duchies, and principalities which were then in the initial throes of unification under Bismarck. There were, for instance, twenty towns named Burg, thirty-one by the name of Münster, forty Schönfelds, sixty-two Hausens, thirty-seven Weilers, and 191 Neudorfs. Also some towns had dubious spellings caused by the pronunciation of the town as given by the immigrant at the port of entry (Galveston) and recorded by the clerk in this phonetic manner. In a good German gazetteer, most of the towns may be found.

Regarding the use of the umlaut (··), such as ä for ae, ö for oe, ü for ue, the umlaut has been retained in the spellings of towns since that is the manner in which these towns are printed on maps and in books. However, it has been changed to ae, oe, or ue in names, such as Mueller for Müller, Koehler for Köhler, or Gaertner for Gärtner.

Names of towns not easily found on a Texas map are located in counties as follows:

Cummins Creek, Austin County
Cypress, Harris County
Frelsburg, Colorado County
Harrisburg, Harris County
Hedwigs Hill, Mason County
Industry, Austin County
Latium, Washington County
Lexington, Lee County
Leon Springs, Bexar County
Meyersville, DeWitt County

Mill Creek, Austin County
Millheim, Austin County
Neighborsville, Comal County
New Ulm, Austin County
Quihi, Medina County
Richmond, Fort Bend County
Round Top, Fayette County
Shelby, Austin County
Spring Branch, Comal County
York's Creek, Comal County

A few places in Europe may possibly need identification, such as:

Kärnthen for Carinthia, now part of Austria;
Belgien for Belgium; Böhmen for Bohemia;
Pommern for Pomerania; Sachsen for Saxony;
"aus der Schweitz" for "from Switzerland"

A number of abbreviations were used for names of persons:

Aug. = August	Gust. = Gustav
Caro. = Caroline	Hein. = Heinrich
Cath. = Catherine	Herm. = Hermann
Charl. = Charlotte	Joh. = Johann
Dor. = Dorothea	Jos. = Joseph
Ed. = Eduard	Lud. = Ludwig
Elis. = Elisabeth	Marg. = Margaretha
Ferd. = Ferdinand	Nic. = Nicolaus
Fried. = Friedrich	Theo. = Theodor
Friedke = Friedricke	Val. = Valentine
Gerh. = Gerhard	Wilh. = Wilhelm
Gottl. = Gottlieb	Wilhme. = Wilhelmine

Other abbreviations used are: ch for child or children.

The name of the month of a year is listed in a ship list in Roman numerals, as, for instance: 3.IX.1854 = 3 September, 1854. Noblemen are indexed under *von*.

German Immigration to Texas, 1847-1861

........, Karl and Magdalena—Winterlingen to Victoria; Gaston, 1857

— A —

Abel, Aug.—arr. Nov. 1851; Austin Co.

Abel, J.—Krzeakatowoy ('Krzekotowo) now Kornfelde, Poland; wife and child; Lucie, 1854

Abel, Joh. — Cerewick (Cerevice, Poland); with famly, 5 persons; J. W. Buddecke, 1853; Washington Co.

Abel, Wilh. — Wilsnack, Prussia; with wife; Bassermann, 1851; Austin Co.

Abels, Peter—25, Koln; Cath. 25; Hein. 2/12; Franziska, 1849

Abels, Peter — from Galveston; Gessner, 1854

Abelt (Ahelt?) F. — Bohemia; 6 persons; Friedrich Grosse, 1853

Abendroth, C. and Engel—Wehdem to Brenham; Weser, 1860

Ackermann, J. and Barbara—Ludwigsburg to New Braunfels, Iris, 1858; Bexar Co.

Ackermann, L. with wife Bertha—Stettin, Prussia; Hampden, 1854

Ackermann, Peter — Herlefeld; 3 persons; Neptune, 1853

Ackert, And.—Orb; Lucie, 1854

Adam, C. — Prussia; Franziska, 1854; Kendall Co.

Adam, Fried.—Langenbielau, Prussia; Miles, 1854

Adamczeck (Adamczik), Franz—Austria; Rosalie, Veronica, Agnes, Pauline, Franz, Anna, Joh.; Jeverland, 1860

Adameck, Franz—Austria; Johanna, Carl, Anna, John, F.; Jeverland, 1860

Adameck, F —Austria; Jeverland, 1860

Adamnitz, Jacob and family — Prussia; Antoinette, 1854

Adler, Joh. — Cassel; 6 persons; Henriette, 1843 (1853)

Adolph, Aug.—42; Herschel, 1850

Aesch, F. — Gross-Salza; 7 persons; Neptune, 1854

Ahlefeldt, Ludwig—Hamburg; Copernicus, 1852

Ahlemann, Wilh. — Berlin; Henriette, 1843 (1853)

Ahlf, H.—Neuhaus, Prussia; Leibniz, 1850

Ahlhorn, Fried. — Jahrberberge (Jahderberg); Neptune, 1853

Ahrenbeck, B. — Hempstead to Hempstead; Gessner, 1860

Ahrenbeck, Bernh. — 52; Oldenburg; Wilhme. 57; Minna 27; Daniel 25; Bernh. 14; Franziska, 1847; Austin Co.

Ahrenbeck, Daniel—from Houston; Chr. and Maria; J. W. Buddecke, 1853

Ahrend, H. — Posen to Houston; Juno, 1860

Ahrends, Carl — 35; Hannover; Franziska, 1847

Ahrenke, Joh. — Garlitz, Mklbg; Copernicus, 1852

Ahrens, Anna — 22; Beidendorff, Mklbg; Copernicus, 1852

Ahrens, H.—to Round Top; Weser, 1859

Ahrens, J. F. W. — 29; Holstein; Natchez. 1847; Galveston Co.

Ahrnke, Hein.—Ammerland. 1854

Albert, C. C. H.—Seifertshain, Saxony; wife and 5 children. 4-14 years old; Miles, 1854; Austin Co.

Albert, Christine and Johanna—Altenbüthen; Gessner. 1854

Albert, Maria—Bergfreiheit; Gessner, 1854

Albert, R. — Bisse to Houston; Iris, 1859

Alberthal, A.—Belsch, Prussia; 4 persons; Estafette. 1850

Albrecht, Anton — Lauschenburg; wife and child; Weser, 1854

Albrecht, Bonrad (Konrad?) and Wilh.—Halle; Mississippi, 1855

Albrecht, Carl Hein.—32; Prussia; Louisa 23; Ferd.; Natchez. 1847

Albrecht, Carl Joh. — Wolgast, Prussia; wife and mother, 7

children 1 mo. to 10 yrs.; Copernicus, 1852
Albrecht, F. — Röhrig; Gessner, 1855
Albrecht, F.—to Brazoria; Weser, 1859
Albrecht, H. — 37; Halberstadt; Flortuna, 1858
Albrecht, Wilh.—Halle; Mississippi, 1855; Austin Co.
Albricht, Daniel—Miloslawitz (Milovice); Neptune, 1853
Alexander, B.—Rogoba (Rogowo, now Roggenau, Poland) to Houston; Weser, 1858
Alexander, S. — Kszorowkona, Poland; Miles, 1854
Alkier, E.—Fraustadt; Hamburg, 1849
Alladiencka, V.—Austria; Jeverland, 1860
Aller, Caro. — Bernstein; Minna, 1854
Allmeyer, Wilh. — 22; Cath. 24; Hermann Theodor, 1850
Almmelmann, Hein. and Anna Marg.—Joh. Ed. Grosse, 1853
Altenbrunn, Caspar and Anna Elis.—Weimar to San Antonio; Gessner, 1860
Altenbrunn, Caspar and Anna Maria — Weimar to San Antonio; Gessner, 1860
Altenkruger, F. M.—Berlin; 3 persons; Texas, 1853
Althaus, Hein.—38; Elis. 38; Hein. 7; Julius 2; Emilie 5; Sophie, 1852
Althaus, J. — Galliott Concordia, 1854; Fayette Co.
Althaus, Louise—Galliott Concordia, 1854
Altmann, A.—Bohemia; Franziska, 1854
Altmann, Anton—Neuchatel; wife, 8 persons; Mississippi, 1855
Altmann, Barbara — Neuchatel; Mississippi, 1855
Altmann, Carl—45; Frankenstein; Doro. 36; Ida 15; Bertha 14; Colonist, 1850
Altmueller, H.—Hesse; 2 persons; Friedrich Grosse, 1853
Ambrosius, Ernestine — Poland; Franziska, 1854
Ambrosius, Rudolph — Pena (Jena?), Sachsen-Weimar; Franklin, 1852
Amdohr, R. G. F.—32; John Frederick, 1850

Amsler, C. C.—Cat Spring (Texas) to Cat Spring; Gessner, 1860; Austin Co.
Amsler, J.—"Aus der Schweiz" to Houston; Gessner, 1860
Anders, Gottlieb — 32; Bunzlau, Prussia; Bertha 30; Miles, 1855
Anderwald, Franz and family—Kadlub; Weser, 1854; Bandera Co.
Andreas, Fried.—Meindorf to Austin; Weser, 1860; Fayette Co.
Andreas, G.—28 and lady 30; Herschel 1849; Austin Co.
Angerstein, Hein. — 21; Solon, 1850; Goliad Co.
Ankele, David—Scholldorf; Neptune, 1853
Antel, Gottl. — Kensendorf; Reform, 1849
Apenbrink, Gottlieb — Joh. Ed. Grosse, 1853; 3 persons
Apenbrink, Hanna — Joh. Ed. Grosse, 1853
Appe, Hein.—38; Hannover; Dorette 38; Dorette 6; Maria 4; Franziska 1847
Appel, Aug.—45; Hamburg; Elis. 45; Elis. 17; Caro. 14; Bernardine 12; Christoph 8; Bernard 6; Aug. 4; Colonist, 1850
Appelt, Franziska — B o h e m i a; Franziska, 1854; Lavaca Co.
Appman, Auguste — Bremen to New Braunfels; Gessner, 1860
Arlitt, Fr. Hermann—Danzig; Republic, 1851
Arlitt, Friedke — Danzig; Texas, 1853; 3 persons
Arlt, Carl Aug.—Lichtenau, Prussia; wife and son age 13; Franklin, 1853
Armerding, Joh. — 30; Mecklenburg; Franziska, 1847
Arnecke, Friedke—18; Creole, 1852
Arnim, Alex—Tretzdorf, Prussia; Albert and Christine; Franklin, 1852
Arnim, Edmund — 22; Kyritz, P r u s s i a; Joh. Ferd. 32; Joh. Friedrich, 1850
Arnold, Carl and Paul—Austria; Antoinette, 1854
Arons, Elize—27; Prussia; Colonist, 1848
Arzt, Georg and David—Waldeck; Franziska, 1854
Arzt, Wilhelmine — Waldeck to Houston; Anton Gunther, 1860
Aschen, F.—to Round Top; Iris, 1857

Aschen, Joh. — 32; Oldenburg; Franziska, 1847; Fayette Co.
Aschenbrandt, Conrad — Cassel; Leibniz, 1850
Aschermann, Charlotte — Wehdem to Brenham; Weser, 1860
Aschoff, Therese—Galo (Gallau); Iris, 1857
Ashorn, Christoph — 25; Solon, 1850; Austin Co.
Assman, Christian — 26; Joh. 23; John Holland, 1848
Assman, Peter—32; John Holland, 1848; Cath. 23; Joh. 3; Christian 11/12; Comal Co.
Aue, Friedrike — Werle, Mklbg; Therese Henriette, 1853; Bexar Co.
Auerochs, Joh.—21; Bavaria; Franziska, 1849
Aurich, A. F. — Norkoeping, Norway; Miles, 1854; Austin Co.
Aurich, Carl—Saxony; Friedrich Grosse, 1853
Aussenwinkler, Anna M. — Glochberᵒ· Jacob and Marie; Lucie, 1854
Austring, E.—Böhmen; Adolphine, 1859

— B —

Baarsch, F. with family; Falkenberᵒ to New Braunfels; Iris, 1860
Babels, August, 5 persons; Helmstädt; Juno, 1853; Guadalupe Co.
Bach, J. K.—43; Ernestine 30; Hermandine ½; Alexander, 1850; Fayette Co.
Bachel, L. — Geiersberg; Lucie, 1854
Bachke, W.—Bohemia; Friedrich Grosse, 1853
Bade, Wilhelm — Schluesselburg; Neptune, 1853; Austin Co.
Bademacher, Caroline—Prussia to Galveston; Anton Gunther, 1860
Baden, Josepha—Heinsberg to Victoria; Iris, 1858
Bader, A.—Quedlinburg to Galveston; Juno, 1860
Bader, Auguste — to Galveston; Weser, 1859
Bading, Fried—24; Neptune, 1850; Comal Co.
Baehr, C.—from Galveston; Weser, 1858
Baenfer, Leopold — 17; Württ; Franziska, 1847
Baenker, Joh.—Darmstadt; Magnet, 1851

Baer, Fried—26; Spandau; Brasilian, 1850
Baermann, Fr. — Arneburg, Prussia; Washington, 1852; Bexar Co.
Baethge, H.—Proistett (Proitze?); 4 persons; Neptune, 1854
Baettner, Hein. — Angelrode, Schwarzburg-Rudolstadt; Republic, 1851
Bagelmann, Herm.—27; Bremen; Joh. Dethardt, 1848
Bahle, Albert—Burg; 3 persons; Herschel, 1851
Bable (Bohle?), Aug.—29; Neptune, 1850; Galveston
Bahtke, C. and Louise—Blüthe to Hempstead; Weser, 1858
Baker, Hein.—22; Jeverland, 1858; to Louisiana
Balster, Doris — Weser, 1859; to Galveston
Baltus, Cath — Hollenhahn (Hollenhagen?); Henriette, 1843 (1853)
Balzen, Harms—Aurich, Oldendorf; Magnet, 1851; Medina Co.
Bammel, W.—Thülan to Industry; Fortuna, 1860; Austin Co.
Bandler, Fried.—Chemnitz; Minna, 1854
Bane, Heinrich—Berlin; Suwa, 1853
Banger, E. — Hesse; Friedrich Grosse, 1853
Banowsky, Charl. — Carlsruhe to Burnet; Weser, 1860
Banowsky, Friedke — Breslau to Burnet; Weser, 1860
Bantle, Louisa — Württemberg; Franziska, 1854
Barg, Carl — Beidendorf, Mklbg; wife and 5 ch., 14-23 years old; Copernicus, 1852
Bargfeldt, Fried. — 25; Stolpe; Brasilian, 1850
Barker, Hein.—22; Colonist, 1848; Bexar Co., 1860
Barnack, Carl — Birkenfeld; Hermann Theodor, 1853
Barres, Fr. W.—Erfurt; Reform, 1851
Bartels, Christ. — 25; Leinestedt; Joh. Dethardt, 1848
Bartels, Gottfried — Osterwieck; Henriette, 1843 (1853)
Bartels, Marie—Sermen, Mklbg.; Sarah, 1851; Galveston
Bartels, Maria—Ammerland, 1854
Bartels, Mary 68, Helene 23—Oldenburg; Franziska, 1849

Bartels, Wilh., 21 — **Solon,** 1850; Austin Co.

Bartha, E.—Böhmen; **Weser,** 1854; Austin Co.

Bartoszkiewitz, Johann—Pudewitz, Prussia; and family, 4 persons; Mississippi, 1855; Comal Co.

Bartoskiwiz, Rosh. — Weglewo to New Braunfels; **Gaston,** 1860

Bartram, Fried., 32 — Riga; Colonist, 1850

Barum, K. and A.—Hesse; **Friedrich Grosse,** 1853

Basaleger, Helen, 42—Oldenburg; **Franziska,** 1849

Basel, J. — Cassel to Galveston; **Juno,** 1860

Bass, Carl—Dillenburg; **Henriette,** 1843 (1853)

Bass, Hein—Reckenthien, Prussia; wife and 8 ch., 5-25 years of age; **Miles,** 1852

Batke, Christine and Rosalie — Aschner to Round Top; **Iris,** 1859

Battman, Carl Wilh. — Radeburg, Prussia; **Miles,** 1853

Batze, Fried. — Seidenburg; **Canapus,** 1849

Bauch, Madame D. W.—Schwerin; with 2 daughters, Elise and Caroline; **Hamburg,** 1849

Bauch, Eckardt and Wilhelm — Schwerin, Mklbg.; **Sophie,** 1852; Fayette Co.

Bauchenstein, Ida — "aus der Schweiz" to Cat Spring; **Gessner,** 1860

Bauchspiess, Th.—Rottdorf; **Neptune,** 1855

Bauck (Bauch?), Hein.—18; Mecklenburg; **Colonist,** 1848

Bauer, Aug. W. — 27; Dresden; **Galliott Flora,** 1849; Guadalupe Co.

Bauer, Carl 27, Emilie 29; Saxony; **Franziska,** 1847

Bauer, Carl and family; Saxony; **Neptune,** 1848; Fayette Co.

Bauer, Christoph 42, Johanna 44, Johanna 17, Jacob 14, Christoph 16, Cath. 8, Wilh. 5; **Herschel,** 1850; Guadalupe Co.

Bauer, Fried.—Friedeberg; 4 persons; **Neptune,** 1853

Bauer, Fried. — Burow; **Leibniz,** 1850

Bauer, Hen., 23 — **Galliott Flora,** 1849; Comal Co.

Bauer, Johann, Friedke, Maria; Württemberg to New Braunfels; **Gessner,** 1860

Bauerkamper, Chr., 20(?); **Canapus,** 1848

Bauermann, B.—Friesland; **Texas,** 1853

Bauermann, Wilhelm—Berlin; **Solon,** 1852

Bauhof, Franz—Rückersdorf; **Minna,** 1854

Baum, A.—**Estafette,** 1850

Baum, Ferdinand — Magdeburg; **Juno,** 1853

Baum, Gustav, 37; **Magnet,** 1852

Baumann, C. F. F., 22—Wittstock; **Hamburg,** 1849; Falls Co.

Baumann, H.—Spanish Flatt, California to Galveston; **Iris,** 1858 1858

Baumann, Jacob—Plieningen; and family, 5 persons; **Solon,** 1852

Baumann, Marie—Prussia; **Friedrich Grosse,** 1853

Baumann, R.—Duisburg to Galveston; **Iris,** 1858; Austin Co.

Baumgart, B. — Wittenberg to Brenham; **Fortuna,** 1860

Baumgarten, Christine — Madgeburg; **Mississippi,** 1855

Baumgarten, Fred—Gerldingberg, Prussia; arr. Galveston 1851; Bastrop Co.

Baumgarten, Joh. C.—Madgeburg; arr. Texas 1854; Fayette Co.

Baur, Johann, Rosina, Kate, Johannes, Ursula, Barbara, Johann, Samuel; Mähringen to New Ulm; **Fortuna,** 1860; Austin Co.

Bautsch, C. G. 45, Amalie 40, E. Reg. 18, A. F. 13, W. A. 11, H. M. 9, Emma 20; **Galliott Flora,** 1849; Galveston

Bautz, Fried.—Posen; **Juno,** 1853

Beban, H. — Madgeburg to Houston; **Fortuna,** 1860

Bebenroth, Hr. Chs., 21—Parsau; **Helen & Elise,** 1847

Bechner, Anna — Holzhausen to New Braunfels; **Iris,** 1860

Bechstedt, Ernst Theo. — Altenburg; **Lucie,** 1854

Beck, C. A. 38, Wilhme 32, Louis 7, Machen 5 (m), Theo 3, Helene 1½; **Galliott Flora,** 1849

Beck, Carl L.—Plieningen, Württ.; **Hermann Theodor,** 1853; Bexar Co.

Beck, Johannes and family, 5 persons—Dettingen; **Solon,** 1852

Beck, Siegfried and family—Steingrund, Silesia; **Gessner,** 1854

— 51 —

Beckendorf, Aug. 34; Carol 27, Emilie 7, John 4, Aug. 2—Apenburg; Helen & Elise, 1847

Becker, Auguste, widow, 30; Rudolpn 9/12 — Prussia; Colonist, 1848

Becker, Caroline — Burg; Weser, 1854

Becker, Eduard — Uhlau, Poland; Minna, 1854; Bexar Co.

Becker, Elise, Marianna—Wuctse (Wietze?) to Galveston; Fortuna, 1860

Becker, Franz — Glane; Reform, 1851

Becker, Hanne—Ohsen (Ohrsen?); Lucie, 1854

Becker, Hein., 24—Solon, 1850

Becker, Hein., Cath — Joh. Ed. Grosse, 1853

Becker, Johann and wife—Edena, Mklbg.; Copernicus, 1852

Becker, Louis—Hannover; Weser, 1854; Austin Co.

Becker, Martin 33, Marie 23, Jacob 3; Sophie, 1852; Bexar Co.

Becker, W(ilhel)m—Altona; Leibniz, 1850

Becker, Wilhme—Zeitz to Bastrop; Weser, 1860

Beckmann, A u g u s t, Elisabeth, Fried., Wilh.—Weimar to San Antonio; Gessner, 1860

Beckmann, Carl, Bertha and 1 ch. —Weimar to San Antonio; Gessner, 1860

Beckmann, Hein. with family, 10 persons—Oberg; Juno, 1853

Beckmann, Marie—Lemgo to Galveston; Weser, 1857

Beckmann, W.—Prussia; Friedrich Grosse, 1853

Bednarz, Anton, Ferdinand, Franz, Caro, Aloise, Magda, Anna; Jeverland, 1860

Behning, D.—Winebergen (Weinberge) to Galveston; Iris, 1859

Behnke, Carl, 32—Pudewitz, Prussia; Miles, 1855; Austin Co.

Behnke, Gottfried — Pudewitz, Prussia; 4 persons; Mississippi, 1855; Austin Co.

Behneken, Anna 23, Meta 20; Sophie, 1852

Behnken, Elise — Weghold (Wegholm?); Texas, 1853

Behrehns, Moritz 23, Pauline 26; Hamburg, 1849

Behrend F.—Mähren to Industry; Juno, 1860

Behrend, Friedrich, E m i l i e — Springberge to Houston; Iris, 1860

Behrend, Heinrichs, 24 — Felde; died at sea; Weser, 1857

Behrends, Ch.—Prussia; 4 persons; Friedrich Grosse, 1853

Behrendt, H.—Gaartz, Mklbg; wife and 3 daughters, 5-10(19?) yrs. old; Hampden, 1854

Behrens family — Ostfriesland; Adolphine, 1859

Behrens, Ch.—Oberg to Fredericksburg; Weser, 1858

Behrens, Fr.—Ga(a)rtz, Holstein; Hampden, 1854

Behrens, Friedrich—Dortmund; 3 persons; Herschel, 1851

Behrens, Henriette — Göttingen; Weser, 1854

Behrens, Joh. — Gaartz, Holstein; 6 ch., 2-17 yrs. old; Hampden, 1854; Austin Co.

Behrens, M. — Strelitz, Mklbg.; Moritz 23; Pauline 26; Hamburg, 1849; Fayette Co.

Behrenshausen, Anna Elise; Galliott Concordia, 1854

Behrenz, W.—Hannover to Galveston; Weser, 1860

Behring, Jacob, 28; Herschel, 1850

Behrmann, Rebecca — Galo (Gallau?); Iris, 1857

Behrns, R.—28; Herschel, 1849

Beihmann, A. and family—Blumenthal, Han.; Gessner, 1855

Beineck, M a t t h i a s — Schran (Schruns?); Texas, 1853

Belecke, G. — Wolgast, Prussia; wife and 2 ch., 2-6 yrs. old; Copernicus, 1852

Bellinger, Robert 32, Sophia 28— Hamburg; Alexander, 1850

Bellinger, Wm.—Hannover; Neptune, 1848; Bexar Co.

Bellmann, Sophie—Herrnhut, Saxony; Lucie, 1854

Beloh, Robert and family; Galliott Concordia, 1854

Below, Max, 19—Leipzig to Comfort; Iris, 1859

Belsche, Fried., Caro.—Fallersleben to Hempstead; Gessner, 1860

Bender, Anna—Breslau to Galveston; Fortuna, 1858

Bender, Edw., 32—Poland; Alexander, 1850

Bender, Jacob—Galliott Concordia, 1854

Benderath, H.—Buddern (Budin?, Bohemia) to San Antonio; Juno, 1860

Bendt, C. and Friedke—Prussia to Houston; Gessner, 1860
Bendt, Carl, Anna — Prussia to Houston; Gessner, 1860
Beneke, Joh., Joachim, 38—Brome, Han.; Dav. 28, Dor. 8, Fred 6, Wilh. 4, Carl 2—Helen & Elise, 1847; Fayette Co.
Benke, Ludwig, Anna, Emma — Pükeburg to Brenham; Weser, 1860
Benner, Jos. — Gross Bauden; 6 persons; Magnet, 1851
Bennewitz, Theodor — Liegnitz; with wife and child; Henriette, 1843 ('1853)
Bense, Louisa, 23 — Warmbeck to Galveston; Weser, 1859
Bentheim, C.—Meinhausen to Austin; Juno, 1860
Benze (Beirze?), William, 31— Magnet, 1852
Benzsch, Gottfried — Corbitz to Galveston; Fortuna, 1860
Berg, J.—Fallenda (Vallendar) to Fredericksburg; Iris, 1859
Berg J.—Nassau; Berg, Cath, and 2 ch.; Franziska, 1854
Berg, Peter—Iris, 1857; Fredericksburg
Berge, W.—Croppenstedt to La Grange; Iris, 1860
Bergelin, M i c h a e l — Bagenitz, Mklbg.; Therese Henriette, 1853
Berger, Caroline, 74; Reform, 1850
Berger, Carl—Quedlinburg; Iris, 1859
Berger, M. 31; Magdalene 35, Marie 9, Matthias 7, Johann 4, Georg 16—Seidenwinkel, Prussia; Herschel, 1855; Austin Co.
Berghaus, Friedr. — Bieckerfeld (Bickefeld); Hermann Theodor, 1853
Berghold, Fried. 45; Chrissine 20, Ludwig 18; Herschel, 1850
Berghold, Jacob, 28; Herschel, 1850
Bergmann, C.—Greifswald; Leibniz, 1850; Comal Co.
Bergmann, Christian — Bernstein; wife and 6 ch.; Minna, 1854
Bergmann, Ernst, 51 — Prussia; Maria 41, Julia 12, Mathilda 7, Otillie 5, Agnes 2; Alexander, 1850; Austin Co.
Bergmann, F.—Schonlau (Schondau?); Texas, 1853
Bergmann, Franz — Riggersdorf (Rückersdorf), Böhmen; Mississippi, 1855; Bexar Co.

Bergmann, Joseph — Reichenberg, Bohemia; 11 persons; Texas, 1853; Bexar Co.
Bergtold, J.—Zürich to Galveston; Iris, 1859
Berke, Louise, 23—Detmold; Franziska, 1847
Berkemeier, F.—Weser, 1854; Galveston
Berkenbusch, Theresa 22, Lisette 28; Reform, 1850
Berkenbusch, Th.—Ervitte, Prussia; 6 persons; Mississippi, 1855
Berkenhoff, August, 24—Prussia; Franziska, 1847; Colorado Co.
Berlitz, Adam and M.—Galveston to Galveston; Juno, 1860
Berlocher, Anna, 27 — Galveston; Solon, 1850
Berlacher, Anna and Louise—Galveston to Galveston; Jeverland, 1860
Berlocher, John and John—Galveston to Galveston; Jeverland, 1860
Berlocher, Mad. A. — Schweiz to Galveston; 2 ch.; Weser, 1857
Berlocher, William—Galveston to Galveston; Jeverland, 1860
Bernal, Kath. — Lamenstein to Fredericksburg; Iris, 1859
Berndt, Aug., 23; Herschel, 1850
Berndt, E. — Schweidnitz; Estafette, 1850
Berndt, Julius—Kraschau; Texas, 1853
Berne, August — Lamenstein to Fredricksburg; Iris, 1859
Berner, Chs. G. P., 20; Galliott Flora, 1849
Berner, Heinrich—Eldena, Mklbg. to New Orleans; wife and sister; Copernicus, 1852
Berner, H. — P r u s s i a to New Braunfels; Gessner, 1860
Berner, Robert—Wetzlar, Prussia to Indianola; Miles, 1852; Austin Co.
Bernert, Franz—Rendorf; 4 persons; Hermann Theodor, 1853
Bernhard, Amelia, 35—Galveston to Galveston; Iris, 1859
Bernhard, Carl—Galveston; Ammerland, 1854
Bernhard, Caroline — Dankersen; 2 persons; Neptune, 1853
Bernhard, Fried. — Elshausen, Württ.; Texas, 1853
Bernsteen, Bernhard — Merseburg; Minna, 1854
Bersser(?), Hein.—24; Hermann Theodor, 1850

Berthold, Margarethe — Hinters-
büren; **Solon,** 1852
Bertollot, Adolph, 26—Magdeburg;
Franziska, 1849
Bertram, H.(ein.), 44—Fallersleb-
en; **Hamburg,** 1849; Colorado Co.
Bertram, M a r i e — Madgeburg;
Adolphine, 1859
Bertram, Sophie — Hannover to
Hempstead; **Gessner,** 1860
Beschel, Friedrich, Antonio—Lim-
bach; **Solon,** 1852
Besdeker, Ignaz—Galliott Concor-
dia, 1854
Besselre, Carl 33 — Prussia; Au-
guste 29, Carl 8, Ernst 6—**Fran-
ziska,** 1848; Calhoun Co.
Bessig, Carl; **Ammerland,** 1854
Best, F. 31, wife 31, Gottfried 10,
Fried. 4—Anhalt Dessau; **For-
tuna,** 1858; Fayette Co.
Bethge, Carl, Clara — Berlin to
Galveston; **Iris,** 1860
Betke, Ch. F.—Landsberg, Prus-
sia; wife and 2 ch., 3-13 yrs.
old; **Miles,** 1854
Betzier, Charlotte—Oldenburg to
Fayettee Co.; **Gaston,** 1860
Beutel, Ernst—Eben to Houston;
Juno, 1860
Beutler, Friedrich — Jacobowe,
Prussia; wife and 2 ch., 1 and
3 ·rs. old; **Miles,** 1852
Beutler, Carl, wife of — Köslin;
Herschel, 1851
Bever, H.—Elberfeld; **Lucie,** 1854
Beversdorf, Ludwig—Seidel; with
family, 5 persons; Beversdorf,
Martin—Seidel; with family, 6
nersons; **J. W. Buddecke,** 1853;
Victoria Co.
Bewin, M. — Schmiedl; Michaellis
and Dorothea; **Leibniz,** 1850
Bey, Andreas — Milowo, Prussia;
wife and 4 ch., 1¼-11 yrs. old;
Miles, 1852
Bey, Hans Peter — New Orleans;
wife Martha; **Leibniz,** 1850
Beyer, Christian—28; **Creole,** 1852
Beyer, Friedr.—Golchen, Prussia;
and wife; **Miles,** 1852; Austin
Co.
Beyer, J.—**Jeverland,** 1860; Fayette
Co.
Beyer, Joh. Samuel—Golancz; 9
nersons; **Neptune,** 1853; Bas-
trop Co.
Beyer. W.—Wöckenstein; **Gessner,**
1854; Kendall Co.
Beyland, C. F.—Hamburg; **Leibniz,**
1850

Beyland, D. G.—Gardelegen; wife
and 4 ch., 3-7¾ yrs. old; **Leib-
niz,** 1850
Biddeck, Peter — Austria; Magda.,
Val.; **Jeverland,** 1860
Bieberstein, Aug. and family—
Eschwege; **Weser,** 1854; Fayette
Co.
Biek, H.—Hannover; **Franziska,**
1854
Biel, Carl—Norden; wife, Mathil-
da nee Hander, Christiansfeld,
Den.; **Magnet,** 1851; Austin Co.
Bierenbrok, Hein. 28, Wilh. 23—
Prussia to Alabama; **Joh. Det-
hardt,** 1848
Biering, F. and 2 sons — Alten-
burg; **Lucie,** 1854; Bexar Co.
Biermann, Alois, 19—Prussia; **Joh.
Dethardt,** 1848
Biermann, Joseph—Ervitte, Prus-
sia; **Mississippi,** 1855
Biesewig, Wilhelm — Hannover;
Juliane, Sophia; **Franziska,** 1854
Biesing, Sophie—Elsfleth to Gal-
veston; **Juno,** 1860
Bilau, F. and wife — Ollmütz;
Gessner, 1855
Bilgmann, Fried. and wife—Duder-
stadt; **Weser,** 1854
Billert, Georg—Duderstadt; **Wes-
er,** 1854; Colorado Co.
Billig, Heinr. — Bautzen, Prussia;
Miles, 1852; Galveston
Billineke, Andreas, Anna, Anna,
Rosalie, Magda, Aloise, Joseph,
Ferd.; **Jeverland,** 1860
Bilow, Fried., Josephine; Billow,
John—Schwerin, Mklbg; **Joh. Ed.
Grosse,** 1853; Austin Co. 1880
Binder, Carl, 24—Frankfort a/m;
Joh. Dethardt, 1848
Bindseil, Wilh.—Osterwieck; **Tex-
as,** 1853; Comal Co.
Bindseil, Wilh., Henrietta—Oster-
wieck; **Weser,** 1854
Binz, Nicolaus, 30—Baden; **John
Holland,** 1848
Birgal, A.—Austria; **Jeverland,**
1860
Birk, Andreas, Altingen—2 per-
sons; **Neptune,** 1853
Bischoff, Carl, 30—Mecklenburg;
Louise 34, Caro. 2; **Franziska,**
1847
Bischoff, Fritz, 25—Breslau; Col-
onist, 1850
Bischoff, J. F.. 20; H. Phil. 17, F.
Wilh. 14 — **Fortuna,** 1858; Aus-
tin Co.

Bittermann, R.—Prussia; Friedrich Grosse, 1853
Blaeker, Dor.—Landkamp to Houston; Fortuna, 1858
Blaha, Franz and family—Humpoletz, Bohemia; Weser, 1854
Blank, Carl—Perleberg, Prussia; wife and 2 ch. and mother; Franklin, 1852; Washington Co.
Blanke, H.—Fortuna, 1858
Blankenfeld, Ed, Emilie — Langsberg; Texas, 1853
Blaschke, Wenzel and family; Antoinette, 1854; Austin Co.
Blaser, Dorothy—Kensendorf; Reform, 1849
Blasienz, Johann—Lehmanshoefel, Bavaria; wife and 6 ch., 3-13 yrs. old; Hampden, 1854
Blecker, Chas., 36; Galliott Flora, 1849
Blegert, I—Wolfenbüttel; Neptune, 1854
Blei, W.—Perleberg; Hamburg, 1849
Bleicke, Theo., 58 — Hannover; Caro. 22, Fried. 18, Carl 14, Wilh. 61; Reform, 1850; Galveston
Blersch, G.—Ammerland, 1854; Bexar Co.
Blick, Joh. Fried., 37; Susanna 32, Justina 10, Johanne 7—Prussia; Chas. N. Cooper, 1847
Blick, Wilhelm, 24—Prussia; Henriette 18, Johanne ½; Chas. N. Cooper, 1847
Blieder, Joh. and wife—Eisenroth, Nassau; 5 persons; Mississippi, 1855; Comal Co.
Blohm, Christoph, 49—Wandsbeck, Holstein; mother, Cath., 70; Brasilian, 1850
Blome, Hanne—Stieghorst; Weser, 1854
Bluecher, F.—Düsseldorf; Weser, 1854
Blum, Ernst, 34—to Louisiana; Jeverland, 1858
Blumberg, Joh. Aug., 48—Velten, Prussia; 9 persons — Dor. 41, Joh. Fried. 17, Joh. Aug. 14, Carl Fried. 10, Fried. Wilh. 8, Herm. Jul. 6, Auguste 4, Maria ½; Hamburg, 1849
Blume, Joh., Heinrich — Weghold (Wegholm); Texas, 1853; Fayette Co.
Blume. Wilh.—Hannover; Franziska, 1854
Blumenreich. Ant. — Hegewald; wife and 3 ch.; Minna, 1854

Blumentritt, J. C.—Reudnitz, Saxony; Miles, 1854
Blunk, Johann—Hollenbeck, Holstein; Washington, 1852; Bexar Co.
Boas, Rudolf—Berlin; Bassermann, 1851
Boback, Geo., 45, Magda. 41, Joh. 10, Andreas 4—Weser, 1848
Bobzien, Fried.—Trendelberg, Denmark; and wife; Copernicus, 1852
Bochers, Hein. — Wolfenbüttel; and family; Weser, 1854
Bock, Adolph, 13 years old, and Auguste, 16 years old—Golchen, Prussia; Miles, 1852; Fayette Co.
Bock, Christine—Erfurt; Texas, 1853
Bock, Caspar—Schneidhain; Juno, 1853
Bock, Christel, 39 — Hannover; Franziska, 1847; Galveston
Bock, H.—Berlin; Gessner, 1854
Bock, Peter, 43—Bavaria; Peter 23, Maria 21; Chas. N. Cooper, 1847; Galveston Co.
Bock, S. W. and wife — Neptune, 1849
Bockelbrush, Hein., 22—Solon, 1850
Bocker, A.—Prussia; Franziska, 1854
Bodden, Querin, Peter, Lambert, Charlotte—Aachen to Victoria; Iris, 1861; Bexar Co.
Bode, C.—Prussia; Friedrich Grosse, 1853
Bode, Elise—Wehren; Adolphine, 1859
Bode, F.—Peine to Houston; Gaston, 1857
Bode, G. and Anna — Werden, Prussia; Bode, Wilhelmine—Wetter, Prussia; Hampden, 1854
Bode, Joachim—Berlin; Suwa, 1853
Bode, Joh.; Galliott Concordia, 1854
Bode, W.—Rosenthal to Galveston; Fortuna, 1860
Bode, Wilhelmine—Oldendorf; Neptune, 1853
Bode, Louise—Cassel; Solon, 1852
Bodecker, Aug., 23; Neptune, 1850
Bodemann, Rudolph, 17 — Hamburg; Chas. N. Cooper, 1847
Boecker, P.—Huelken to Victoria; with 3 ch.; Fortuna, 1858
Boeckler, M(ada)me Soph., 58—Schwerin; Hamburg, 1849
Boedecker. Otto, 21, Hein. 23; Creole, 1852; Austin Co.

Bo(e)hl, Joh. — Marlow, Mklbg; wife and 5 ch., 1½-9 years; Miles, 1853
Boehler, F.—Westrup; and wife; Gessner, 1855; Bexar Co.
Boehlmann, Gottfried—Zerbst; and family, 8 persons; Juno, 1853; Goliad Co.
Boehm, Jos.—Heida; Weser, 1854; Austin Co.
Boehm, Joseph, Rosina — Joh. Ed. Grosse, 1853; Austin Co.
Boehme, D. M., 32—Saxony; Colonist, 1848
Boehme, G.—Rogau to New Braunfels; with family; Iris, 1860
Boehme, Gottlieb—Erdeborn; and family; Weser, 1854
Boehme, H.(ieronymus), 34 — Löbau; Hamburg, 1849
Boehme, Hein., widow and 4 children—Dahlhausen, Prussia; Republic, 1851; Comal Co.
Boehmer, F.—Prussia; Friedrich Grosse, 1853
Boehnke, M. F. — Rahnwerder, Prussia; Therese Henriette, 1853; Fayette Co.
Boehr, F.—Bunzlau, Bohemia; Magnet, 1851
Boehse, C. and H.—Ostertimke to Galveston; Weser, 1858
Boelke, Sophie, 58—Schwerin; Hamburg, 1849
Boening, Christian—Atens to Galveston; Iris, 1861
Boer, C. S. — Langenbielau, Saxony; Bassermann, 1851
Boerner—see also Berner
Boesche, Dorothea—Hattorf; J. W. Buddecke, 1853
Boeschling, Hein. Fried.; Galliott Concordia, 1854
Boese, Johann—Barentin, Prussia; wife Doris; Franklin, 1853
Boesel, Ernst, Joseph — Lüneburg to Houston; Iris, 1859
Boethe, Wilh., 20; Creole, 1852
Boethger, Wilh. — Gwethan, Saxony; Franklin, 1852
Boettcher, Fried and wife — Gaston, 1860; Colorado Co. to Colorado Co.
Boettger, Hermann—Schleusingen; Neptune, 1853; Fayette Co.
Boettne, Wilhelm—Meiningen; Solon, 1852
Bogaschefsky, A., Marie, Elis.— Houston to Houston; Weser, 1860
Bohacz, Franz, Maria — Austria; Jeverland, 1860

Bohe, Heinz—Neptune, 1849
Bohenbach, Otto, 19—Prussia; Colonist, 1848
Bohl, Johann — Marlow, Mklbg.; wife and 5 ch., 1½-9 yrs. old; Miles, 1852; Gillespie Co.
Bohle, Aug.—See Bahle, Aug.
Bohle, Cath.—Joh. Ed. Grosse, 1853
Bohlen, Wilhelm—Hamburg; Copernicus, 1852
Bohm, Fred., 29—Prussia; Franziska, 1847
Bohms, Hein.—Rastederberg; Neptune, 1853
Bohne, J.—Gresen to La Grange; Iris, 1860
Bohnewitz, Wilh. — Berghardrode; and family, 11 persons; Juno, 1853
Bohning, Carl, 20—Desbel; Canapus, 1848
Bokenfohr, Wm., 27—Galliott Flora, 1849
Boker, Hein., 22—Germany; Jeverland, 1858
Bokohe, Hein., 42—Berlin; Henriette 47, Rudolph 13, Albertine 12, August 9, Albert 7, Adolph 3; Franziska, 1847
Boldbuck, H. and wife—Mecklenburg to Millheim; Juno, 1860
Boldt, Christian, 12—Moellenbeck, Mklbg.; Joh. Friedrich, 1850
Boldt, Gottfried — Neumark; 10 persons; Mississippi, 1855
Bolt (Bol(d)t), Fr., 30—Sophie, 1852; DeWitt Co.
Boleg, Louise, 29—Herman Theodor, 1850
Bolken, Auguste — Abbehausen to Galveston; Iris, 1859
Bollem, Tim—Siegfelder; Weser, 1854
Bollfrasz, Johanne—Bockhorn; Iris, 1857
Bolte, Joh.—Joh. Ed. Grosse, 1853
Bolting, Joh. Fr., 48—Helen & Elise, 1847
Bolz, Michael, 28—Prussia; Chas. N. Cooper, 1847
Bombe, C. Ed.—Dribitz; Canapus, 1849
Bonifah, Carl, 28—Silesia; Franziska, 1849
Bonnadgeck, J., 25—Prussia; Alexander, 1850
Boortz, Michael Fried.—Schwarzsee, Prussia; wife and 3 ch., 1¼-11 yrs. old; Miles, 1853
Boots, H.—Osnabrück; Neptune, 1854

Borchers, Hein. and family—Ammerland, 1854; Gillespie Co.
Borchers, Wilh.—Münster; Texas, 1853
Borga, A., and J.—Raab to San Antonio; Weser, 1858
Borga, F., and P.—Klempner; Weser, 1858
Borgemann, Helene — Pockborn (Bockhorn); Neptune, 1853
Borgfeld, Ch. and wife—Didderse; Neptune, 1854
Borgfeldt, Fried.—See Bargfeldt, Fried.
Borkhard, F., 38; Dor., 32—Fortuna, 1858
Borner, Carl—Ammerland, 1854
Borntraeger, F., 21 — Fiersen (Viersen) to San Antonio; Iris, 1859
Borsch, C.—Prussia; 4 persons; Friedrich Grosse, 1853
Borsmann, Fried., 25—Solon, 1850
Borsum, F.—Dungelbeck, Han. to Galveston; Gaston, 1857
Bortfeld, Hein, 27—Dittersen (Didderse); Joh. Dethardt, 1848
Bosetzny, F.—Austria; Jeverland, 1860
Boshe, Joh. Hr., 22—Sudweye; Neptune, 1850
Boss, Wilhelmine—Kappel to Galveston; Weser, 1860
Bosse, W. — Oppenwehe to Houston; Weser, 1858; Austin Co.
Bossoek, Franz — Austria; Marianne, John, Franz, Anna; Jeverland, 1860
Bosten, Maria—Buetzow; Leibniz, 1850
Bostian, Johann — Krabow (Krakau?); Leibniz, 1850
Both, J. Chr., 19—Galliott Flora, 1849
Bothe, E. and family—Ammerland, 1854; Bexar Co.
Bothmer, August, 23—Hannover; Franziska, 1847
Botsch, M.—Switzerland; Franziska, 1854
Bottcher, Auguste, 30—Saxony; Colonist, 1848
Bowe (Bome?), C.—Prussia; Neptune, 1848
Brabandt, Carl—Motzig, Mklbg.; Washington, 1852
Bracht, Felix, 40 — Düsseldorf to New Braunfels; Herschel, 1849
Bracht, Josephine and Felicia—Prussia; Neptune, 1849
Bracht, Victor, 27—Düsseldorf to New Braunfels; Herschel, 1849

Braden, Andreas 39, Cath. 37, Anton 42, Cath. 11, Andreas 10, Gertrude 8, Eva 6, Marg. 4, Anna Barbara 2, Barbara 3 wks. —John Holland, 1848; Colorado Co. 1850
Braden, Anton, 42—John Holland, 1848; Colorado Co. 1850
Braden, Josef, 43 — Hesse; Barbara 45, sister Barbara 22, mother Marg. 64, Georg Josef 20, Eduard 18, Adam 17, Magda 10, Marg. 3, Martin 6, Annie and Marie 4; John Holland, 1848; Harris Co.
Braeger, Carl—Torgau, Prussia; Miles, 1854
Braeschler, Jacob, Maria—Greifensee, Switz.; Lucie, 1854; Comal Co.
Braesike, A.—Pödeniss to Houston; Iris, 1860; Austin Co.
Braeuer, A. — Breslau, wife and ch.; Neptune, 1854
Brag. Joh. 37, Cath. 38, Johanna 15—Sophie, 1852
Brakeback, Heinr., 25—Galliott Flora, 1849
Bran, Eilert, 33—Helen & Elise, 1847
Brand, Chr.—Waldeck to Houston; Weser, 1860
Brand, Dorothea — Hannover to Galveston; Weser, 1860
Brandel, Caspar—Keltsch, Moravia; Weser, 1854
Brandes, Hein. and Johanna—Joh. Ed. Grosse, 1853; Fayette Co.
Brandes, Maria 50, Anna 10—Prussia; Colonist, 1848
Brandt, Bertha — Henisen; Hermann Theodor, 1853
Brandt, Adolph—Osnabrück; Neptune, 1853; Fayette Co.
Brandt, Christ—Bauersdorf, Holstein; Washington, 1852
Brandt, Fried., 22—Oldenburg; Solon, 1850
Brandt, F., 52, H. 29, Fr. 23, Christian 17 — Hannover; Fortuna, 1858
Brandt, H. — Allendorf to Mill Creek: Iris, 1859; Fayette Co.
Bransser, Leopold, 17—Württ.; Franziska, 1847
Brast, Christine—Stuttgart; Texas, 1853
Brathering, Hein. — Oberg; with family, 8 persons; Juno, 1853; Gillespie Co.
Braubach, Phil. 21 — Wiesbaden; Neptune, 1850; Bexar Co.

Braun, Carl — Röhrbruch to York-
town; **Fortuna,** 1860
Braun, Ernst, 29—**Reform,** 1850;
Fayette Co.
Braun, F.—Zansbruck; 9 persons;
Texas, 1853
Braun, Frank—Röhrbruck to York-
town; **Fortuna,** 1860
Braun, H.—Düsseldorf to San An-
tonio; **Weser,** 1860
Braun, Henry, Doris — Wedel to
Lexington; **Fortuna,** 1860
Braun, Johann—Wittenberg; **Wes-
er,** 1854; Comal Co.
Braun, Math.—Bacham (Bachheim,
Bockhorn?); **Lucie,** 1854
Braun, Philipp and family, 8 per-
sons—Bike, Prussia; **Mississippi,**
1855
Brecher, -—Cassel to Galveston;
Iris, 1858
Brecher, Henriette—Nassau; **Fran-
ziska,** 1854
Brecht, F.—Hannover; **Friedrich
Grosse,** 1853
Breidzeicke, Elis., 91—**Natchez,**
1847
Breihorn (Breihan?) f a m i l y—
Uppea; **Adolphine,** 1859; Aus-
tin Co.
Bremer, Dietrich, wife and 4 ch.—
Bruckhöfen to Brenham; **Weser,**
1857
Brenke, A. 34, Mariann 25, Julius
½—**Fortuna,** 1858
Brenke, M.—Schwidsowa to San
Antonio; **Fortuna,** 1858
Brenkatter, H.—to New Braun-
fels; **Weser,** 1859
Brenner, Jos. — Kärnthen; 2 per-
sons; **Reform,** 1851
Brenwald, Lisette — Meinedorf to
Galveston; **Iris,** 1859
Breslauer, M.—Falkenberg to Gal-
veston; **Iris,** 1860
Bretag, C. H.—Samter, Prussia;
Miles, 1854
Bretschneider, Karl 18, and Eg-
mont—Velpe to Galveston; **Wes-
er,** 1858; Austin Co.
Brettschneider, G., wife and 4 ch.—
Litzlingen to Galveston; **Juno,**
1860
Bretzke, Johann, and Wilhelm —
Sprinck, Prussia; **Therese Hen-
riette,** 1853; Comal Co.
Breuer, Carl—Scharzau, Prussia;
Mississippi, 1855
Breustedt, C. H. and wife, Gottl.
and Henr.—**Neptune,** 1849; Co-
mal Co.

Breversdorf—See Beversdorf
J. W. Buddecke, 1853
Brieger, W. — Scheidelwitz to La
Grange; **Iris,** 1858
Briesmy, H., Sophie, Fried., and
Henry—Hannover to Frelsburg;
Weser, 1860
Brill family — Burgdorf; **Adol-
phine,** 1859; Austin Co.
Bringmans, Leonore, 19—**Creole,**
1852
Brink, Carl—Mecklenburg; Marie,
Minna, Marie; **Franziska,** 1847;
Austin Co.
Brinkmann, Alexander and Carl—
Hausberge, Han.; **Mississippi,**
1855; Kendall Co.
Brinkmann, Fritz—**Galliott Concor-
dia,** 1854
Brock, J. G.—Galveston to Galves-
ton; **Weser,** 1860
Brockmann, H. W. — Buetzow,
Mklbg.; wife and 2 ch., 2-11 yrs.;
Sarah, 1851
Brodt, N.—Ostheim; **Estafette,**
1850; Guadalupe Co.
Brohn, C. and wife—Granzow;
Gessner, 1854
Brokmann, Hr., 20—Kohlstadt;
Canapus, 1848
Broks, Ferdinand; **Joh. Ed. Grosse,**
1853
Brook, Gotthelf, Rosalie—Görlitz
to Galveston; **Weser,** 1860
Brosde, H. and M.—Hagenburg;
Reform, 1849
Brosig, Auguste—Neisse; 5 per-
sons; **Reform,** 1851
Brosig, Theo. 28, Josef 30—Neisse;
Colonist, 1850; Austin Co.
Brotzell, Aug. 35, and Louise 33—
Galliott Flora, 1849
Bruck, H.—Greifensee, Switz.;
Lucie, 1854
Brucker, O.—Gotha to Galveston;
Weser, 1858
Bruckisch, W.—Prussia; **Friedrich
Grosse,** 1853; Comal Co.
Brueckner, A.—Bohemia; **Friedrich
Grosse,** 1854
Brueggeboose, Wilh.—**Galliott Con-
cordia,** 1854
Brueggenworth, -, 46—**Hermann
Theodor,** 1850
Bruhn, Hein. Chr., 22—Winterha-
gen, Schleswig; **Gutenberg,** 1855
Bruhn, Peter Nic.—Burg, Den-
mark; **Copernicus,** 1852
Brune, Wm.—Prussia; **Neptune,**
1848; Austin Co.
Bruner, Caro—Oppendorf to Hous-
ton; **Weser,** 1858

Brunkow, D.—Prussia; Franziska, 1854
Brunner, J.—Juhlede (Juhöhe); 7 persons; Lucie, 1854
Brunner, Joh.—Dresden; Suwa; 1853
Bruns, Conrad, 16—Minden; Franziska, 1849; Kerr Co.
Bruns, F., 28, and lady—Herschel, 1849
Bruns, Joh.—Rastede; 6 persons; Texas, 1853; Fayette Co.
Bruns, Maria, 26—Welda, Prussia; Gutenberg, 1855
Bruns, S.—Herschel, 1849
Buaas, J.—Trumsö; Hamburg, 1849; Austin Co.
Buch, J. D., 49—Galliott Flora, 1849
Buchener, Bertha—Zella; Juno, 1860
Buchholz, Johann — Schwaan, Mklbg.; wife and 2 ch., 4 and 8 yrs. old; Hampden, 1854; Milam Co.
Buchhorn, L., 23 — Magdeburg to LaGrange; Iris, 1859
Buchmeier, Philipp — Hesse to Fredericksburg; Weser, 1860
Buchtien, Chr.—Buetzow, Mklbg.; wife and 4 ch.; Leibniz, 1850; Austin, Co.
Buck, C.—to Brenham; Weser, 1859
Buck, C. and H. — Wehdem to Houston; Weser, 1858
Buck, Sophie and Wilhma—Winzlar; Reform, 1849
Buckert, Conrad—Waldeck; Franziska, 1854; Victoria Co.
Buckethal, Hein.—Breslau; Juno, 1853
Budde. Gerhard—Hannover; Anna, Kath., Anna; Jeverland, 1860
Budde, Ludwig—Hamburg; Minna, 1854
Buecking, F. and wife—Gruenberg to Coletto; Anton Guenther, 1860; Victoria Co.
Bueckskemper, Theodor, 40—Prussia; Elizabeth 29, Lucia 5, Elizabeth 3; Reform, 1850; Colorado Co.
Buehler, Franz and Max — Freyburg; Gessner, 1854
Buenger. Hein, 54, and Friedke, 54—Creole, 1852; Austin Co.
Buer. D.—Althagen; Leibniz, 1850
Buerge. Wilhelm — Erfurt, Prussia; Republic, 1851
Buergermeister, Caro—St. Johann; Hermann Theodor, 1853

Bues, Andreas—Galliott Concordia, 1854
Buescher, H.—Erfurt to New Ulm; Weser, 1860; Austin Co.
Buesen, Hans — Buettelerko(o)g, Denmark; Copernicus, 1852
Buesing, Reinhr., 30 — Langwarden; Canapus, 1848; DeWitt Co.
Buethe, Gerhard—Rastede; 3 persons; Texas, 1853
Buettner, A. and F.—Prussia; Friedrich Grosse, 1853
Buettner, Gustav — Frankenstein, Prussia; Copernicus, 1852
Bulling, Hein.—Jahderberg; Neptune, 1853
Bumann, Cl(aus), 40 — Walmersdorf; Hamburg, 1849
Bundnig, Mrs., and 2 daughters—Darmstadt to New Braunfels; Anton Gunther, 1860
Bunge, Carl—Falkenhagen, Prussia; wife and 4 ch., 2-9 yrs. old; Franklin, 1852
Bunge, Christian, 35 — Perleberg; Wilhme. 28, Wilh. 7, Wilhme. 3; Colonist, 1850; Austin Co.
Bunte family — Braunschweig; 7 persons; Suwa, 1853
Buntziel, Fr.—Bernstadt. Prussia; wife and 5 ch.; Republic, 1851; Austin Co.
Burde. H.—Obornik to Galveston; Iris, 1860
Burger. Aug. and family—Bavaria; Neptune, 1848
Burger, Bartholomä—Cöln; Franziska, 1849
Burkhorn. H.—Wehdem to Brenham; Weser. 1860
Burmeister, Claus — Hollenbeck, Holstein; Washington, 1852
Burmeister, Fried., 34—Holstein; Brasilian, 1850
Burmester, Fried., 30—Wandsbeck; see also Burmeister, Fried.; Brasilian. 1850
Burr, G.—Gebron; Weser, 1854
Bursa, Jos.—Friedland; Canapus, 1849
Bursing. Bernhard—Kirgenwies; Solon, 1852
Busch. Carl, Julia—Barmen; Solon, 1852
Busch, Louis—Hamburg to Indianola; Marie, Hein., Marie, Fried.; Iris, 1861
Buschick, Ad.—Posen; Texas, 1853
Buse, August—Schwarzsee, Prussia; Miles, 1852
Buse, F.—to Houston; Weser, 1859

— 59 —

Bussian, Cath., 70—Prussia; Chas.
N. Cooper, 1847
Butler, Jul.—Cöslin; Herschel, 1851
Butscher, F.—Blumenthal to Harrisburg; Fortuna, 1860; Harris Co.
Buttler, Christian — Mecklenburg to Millheim; wife and 4 ch.; Juno, 1860; Austin Co.
Buttner, Anna, 26—Natchez, 1847
Butzbach, Auguste, 26—Franziska, 1849
Buzeck, Georg — Austria; Marianne, Marianne; Jeverland, 1860
Buzeck, Philipp — Austria; Anna, John, Franz, Maria, Karl, Barbara, Johanna; Jeverland, 1860
Bzycha, Joseph — Böhmen; wife and 2 ch.; Weser, 1854

— C —

Callman, Mathilde—Inowrailau to Houston; Gaston, 1860
Cansieur, Chr. D. — Buechow, Mklbg.; Sarah, 1851
Carby, Gottfr.—Halberstadt; Reform, 1849
Carnatz, Joh., 48 — Mecklenburg; Franziska, 1848
Carney, W., Amalie and Louise—Friedeberg to Yorktown; Iris, 1858
Carsten, Wilhmine and Auguste—Bocklum (Böckum?); Texas, 1853
Carstens, Johann — Oldenburg; Suwa, 1853; Galveston
Caspar, Elis.—Joh. Ed. Grosse, 1853
Caspar, Johann and wife—Junnen, Prussia; 3 persons; Mississippi, 1855
Caspar, M.—Berlin to Galveston; Iris, 1859
Casparie, J. and family—Ammerland, 1854
Cassel, Christian, 34, Anne 36, John 9—Magnet, 1852; Galveston
Cattula, C. and wife — Zuronea (Zuromin); Gessner, 1855
Caufel (Coufal), Amalie—Vienna; Suwa, 1853
Centner, G.—Cincinnati (Ohio?); Adolphine, 1859
Chalupa, Ignaz — Austria; Marianne, Martin; Jeverland, 1860
Chasse, K.—Hannover to Houston; Weser, 1860
Chemmitz, Louis—Pegau, Saxony; Copernicus, 1852

Cheske, Fr. A. and wife—Schrodda, Poland; 8 persons; Mississippi, 1855
Chodorowsky, Meyer — Racky (Rackin?); Leibniz, 1850
Christensen, Paul — Sonderburg, Schleswig-Holstein to New Orleans; wife and 3 ch., ¾ to 5½ yrs. old; Washington, 1852
Christiansen, J.—Cramon, Mklbg.; wife and child; Bassermann, 1851
Christoph, George — Kittendorf, Mklbg.; 2 daughters, 32 and 33 yrs. old; Therese Henriette, 1853
Chrisoph, Joseph and family—Ammerland, 1854
Cjmarsch, Franz 42, Teresa 30, Anna 14, Marianne 10, Franz 6; Brasilian or E. von Beaulieu, 1857
Classen, H. and family—Brachelen to San Antonio; Iris, 1857
Claude, Louis—Leipzig, Saxony; Hampden, 1854
Claus, Gottfried—Bernburg; Neptune, 1854
Claus, Hein., 21 — Prussia; Joh. Dethardt, 1848; Kendall Co.
Claus, J.—to Independence; Weser, 1859
Clausewitz, Gustav, 55, Elise 50, Elise, 28, Fritz 20 — Fortuna, 1858
Clauvin, Chr. — Luhmannsdorf, Holstein to New Orleans; Washington, 1852
Clemens, Wilh. and wife—Prussia; Neptune, 1849; died New Braunfels, 1877
Cleve, Ottilia—Burg; Hermann Theodor, 1853
Cloppenburg, Bernhard, 24—Oldenburg; Franziska, 1847
Clothilde, W. — Dargun, Mklbg.; wife and daughter, W. 25; Hampden, 1854
Cloudt, Fred, 32—Hannover; Joh. Dethardt, 1848
Cloudt, W. — Ammerland, 1854; Wm. Cloudt died Indianola, 1867
Cluth, C. and wife — Tuchhein; Gessner, 1855
Cochoy. Louis—Neu-Ruppin, Prussia; Republic, 1851
Coenetius (Cornitius), W.—Prussia; Jeverland, 1860; Austin Co.
Cohn, Sophie, 18—Brasilian, 1857
Cohtmaull, H. and Dor.—Ammerland, 1854
Collmann, Edo—Winsen; Texas, 1853

Collmann, Sophie — Wetter, Prussia; **Hampden,** 1854
Collmeyer, Ammalie—Sippentrup; **Neptune,** 1853
Colmar, B.—Prussia; **Friedrich Grosse,** 1853
Commien, Joachim, 32 — Bordesholm, Holstein; **Marg.** 30, Christian 1½; **Gutenberg,** 1855
Commien, Joh. Hein, 37—Neumünster, Holstein; **Gutenberg,** 1855
Conger, Hch. 27, Julius 21—**Louis,** 1848
Conrad, Clements, 23—**Reform,** 1850; Comal Co.
Conrad, Carl — Liegnitz to La Grange; **Gessner,** 1860
Conrad, Ernst, 21 — Urschkau, Prussia; **Gutenberg,** 1855
C o n r a d, Jakob Chr. — Foehr, Schleswig; **Republic,** 1851
Conrad, Marie—Joh. Ed. **Grosse,** 1853
Conrade, Adolph, 22—Hamburg; **Chas. N. Cooper,** 1847
Conrads, H.—N(ieder) Breisig; 3 persons; ship? date?
Conrads, H. J.—Niederbreisig; 4 persons; **Texas,** 1853; Comal Co.
Conrads, Joseph—Breisig; **Juno,** 1853
Constant, A. — Prussia to Millheim; **Gessner,** 1860
Constant, Charlotte—Prussia; **Antonette,** 1855
Constant, Louis, 40 — Prussia; Charlotte 38, Mariann 10, Elis. 8, Armand 4; **Colonist,** 1848; Austin Co.
Contrain, Joseph—Niederbrüchter; **Texas,** 1853
Cordes, Cath. — Versmold to Galveston; **Iris,** 1859
Cordes, Hein., 20 — Oldenburg; **Solon,** 1850; Fayette Co.
Cordes, Hein., Henriette; Ammerland, 1854; Galveston
Cordes, Rudolph and family, 3 persons — Galveston; **Mississippi,** 1855
Cordes, Wilhme—Loxten to Galveston; **Fortuna,** 1858
Cordt, Fr. (paper water-stained); **Herschel,** 1849
Coreth, Count Ernst von — Maryland, 1859; New Braunfels
Coring, P.—Lafferde to Houston; **Gaston,** 1857
Cornelius, Albert, 35—Sonneborn; Emilie 24, Julius ¾; **Neptune,** 1850; Austin Co.

Cornitius—see Coenetius
Corssen, C. F., 45 — Oldenburg; **Galliott Flora,** 1849
Cortegass, Caroline, A l w i n e — Braunschweig; **Antoinette,** 1854; Galveston
Coufal—see Caufel
Crach, Gustav—Kassel; 5 persons; **Suwa,** 1853
Cramer, Carl, 27; Angelica 26, Rosalie ½—**Louis,** 1848
Cramer, E. — Schweinfurt to San Antonio; **Iris,** 1860
Cramer family—Gnesen to Brenham; **Iris,** 1859
Cramer, Fried., 41, Auguste 37—Prussia; **Joh. Dethardt,** 1848
Creuholz, Carl, 32, Maria 74—Danzig; **Hamburg,** 1849
Crivitz, Christ.—Parchim, Mklbg.; **Miles,** 1852
Cunze, C. and wife—Dubrau; **Gessner,** 1855
Custodis, Leopold, Johanna—Dusseldorf; **John Frederick,** 1850
Cuttner, Julius — W i t k o w o to Madsville (Madisonville?); **Fortuna,** 1860
Czirnoch, Marianne—Austria; **Jeverland,** 1860

— D —

Dackel, Joh., 27—Prussia; **Franziska,** 1849
Daen, Maria Johanna — Joerdensdorf, Mklbg.; **Republic,** 1851
Daenisch, Rudolf — Oppeln; **Herschel,** 1851
Dahlen, Sophie, 23 — Goericke, Prussia; **Miles,** 1852
Dahlgrün-, —Hameln; **Magnet,** 1851; Austin Co.
Dahms, Friedrich — Gross-Zarnewanz, Prussia; **Copernicus,** 1852
Dahne, Carl B., 24—Saxony; **Joh. Dethardt,** 1848
Dallahau, Joh. and family — Ammerland, 1854
Dallmeier, Arnold — Dissen, Hannover; **Mississippi,** 1855
Dambach, F.—Oggersheim; **Weser,** 1854; Gillespie Co.
Damke, Elis., 17 — Oldenburg; **Franziska,** 1847; Colorado Co.
Damm, Georg — Niedervellmar; 3 persons; **Hermann Theodor,** 1853
Danckwardt, Anna, 50 — Rostock, Mklbg.; **Herschel,** 1855
Dangers, Aug., 18—**Sophie,** 1852
Dangers, W. and family—Ammerland, 1854; Mason Co.

Daniels, S.—Osnabrück; Iris, 1857
Danielsen, Georg—Kiel, Holstein;
Miles, 1852
Danielsen, Hermann — Kiel, Holstein; wife and 4 ch., 16-22 yrs.
old; Miles, 1852
Dankert, Johann — Kahlenburg,
Mklbg.; and wife; Copernicus,
1852
Dannemann, Ferdinand — Züllichau; Solon, 1852
Dannemann, Friedke—Oldenburg;
Neptune, 1848
Dannenburg, August, Sophie — to
Houston; Weser, 1859
Dannhainer, Gabriel, 25—Bavaria;
Herschel, 1850; Fayette Co.
Dannhaeuser, M. — Stockelsberg,
Bavaria; Franklin, 1853
Dannhaus, Joachim—Breddin, Holstein; wife and 4 ch., 1-12 yrs.
old; to Galveston; Washington,
1852; Washington Co.
Darenbaumer, H. W., 29—Winkelshütten; Neptune, 1850
Darnus, Adolf, 30—Pr. Hollande;
Colonist, 1850
Daulchan, A. and wife—Landsberg
to Bastrop; Iris, 1857
Daum,. John Theodore — Görlitz,
Silesia; arr. Texas 1850, Austin
Co.
Daunker, Chr.—Krubbe, Prussia,
to Galveston; Bassermann, 1851
Deckel, Joh., 27—Prussia; Franziska, 1849
Degener, Edward — Braunschweig,
to Texas in 1850, Bexar Co.
Degenhardt, Alb.—Prussia; Friedrich Grosse, 1853
Degner, J. with family — Marlen
to Industry; Iris, 1860
Dehls. Elise—Vegesack; Neptune,
1853
Deinhart, Michael. 27 — Lauber
(Lauberg?); Joh. Dethardt, 1848
Delabarre, Franz—Bremen; Mississippi, 1855
Delff, Fried., 35—Witt(en); John
Frederick, 1850
Dellater, Daniel. Christine—Meissenheim; J. W. Buddecke, 1853
Demann, G. and lady — Herschel,
1849
Demke, Franz, Rosina—Prussia;
Jeverland, 1860
Denker, Ludwig — Winterfeld;
Weser, 1854
Dentler, J.—Steinbachen; Lucie,
1854

Deo, Johann, Mary—Preiritz (Prietitz) to Cunningham; Fortuna,
1860
Deppermann, W. — Werther to
Houston; Iris, 1858
Depperwin, W.—Heinebach; Leibniz, 1850
Depta, J.—Waldhäuser; Gessner,
1855
Dermhardt, Joh., 20—Bavaria;
Franziska, 1849
Descher, Ch.—Merschlitz; Gessner, 1854
Dessauer, Friedr.—Dresden; 7 persons; Reform, 1851
Detenhof, J.—to Galveston; Weser,
1859
Dethloff, Carl, 36; Behnkenhagen,
Mklbg.; Herschel, 1855; died in
Austin
Dettmer, Christ., 47 — Isenbüttel,
Han.; Joh. Dethardt, 1848; Austin Co.
Deubner, Johann—Creuzburg; with
family, 6 persons; J. W. Buddecke, 1853; Galveston Co.
Diagos, Joh. and family — Rojemirsch; Weser, 1854
Dick, Anton—Duderstadt; Weser,
1854; Austin Co. 1870
Diebel (Deibel?), Christian, 19,
Christoph 27—Solon, 1850; DeWitt Co.
Dieckmann, Auguste—Jerstedt;
Lucie, 1854
Dieckmann, Christ., Johanna —
Galveston; Franklin, 1853
Dieckmann, Hanna, Minna—Hamburg; Franziska, 1854
Diedlitz, Rich., 15; Herschel, 1850
Diederich, - —Kirchheim to Round
Top; Iris, 1858
Diederick, - — Frankfurt a/M to
Houston; Iris, 1858
Diedrich, Cath. — Odershausen;
Canapus, 1849
Diedrich, Maria—Cassel; Suwa,
1853
Diedrick, Hein. Fr. 59, Friedke 57,
Friedke 20, Hein. Wilh. 20 —
Solon, 1850
Diegelmann, Eugen—Böckels; Joh.
Dethardt, 1848
Diek, Reinhard, 34—Aachen; Josephine 27, Gustan ¾; Franziska,
1849
Dield. Joh. Aug.—Neptune, 1848
Dierke, Fritz—See Duerke, Fr.
Dierkes, Aug.—Dahlhausen; Herschel, 1851
Dierkes, Clemens, 25, Ina 26 —
Prussia; Joh. Dethardt, 1848

Dierkes, C.—to Galveston; **Weser,** 1859
Dierks, F. and family — **Ammerland,** 1854
Diesing, Elise, Karl, Dor.—Hackeborn to Columbus; **Juno,** 1860
Diesterweg, Caro, 24 — Siegen to Yorktown; **Iris,** 1859
Diesting, F.—Croppenstedt to La Grange; **Iris,** 1860
Dietert, Fr.—Prussia; wife and 5 ch.; **Franziska,** 1854; Guadalupe Co.
Dietrich, Cath. — Frankfurt a/M to Houston; **Iris,** 1861
Dietrich, Cath. — Odershausen; 2 persons; **Hermann Theodor,** 1853
Dietrich, E., 41; **Uhland,** 1851
Dietrich, Ferdinand — Bruehlingsdorf, Mklbg.; **Miles,** 1853
Dietrich, Friedrich — Thören; 3 persons; **Texas,** 1853
Dietrich, G., 28—**Uhland,** 1851
Dietrich, Johann—Breuhlingsdorf, Mklbg.; **Miles,** 1852; Fayette Co.
Dietrich, Moritz.—Saxony; Johanna; **Neptune,** 1848; Dietrich, Karl Ernst Moritz; Bastrop Co.
Dietrich, W.—Wollersleben; **Gessner,** 1854; Fayette Co.
Dietz. Anna Cath. — Neustadt; **Solon,** 1852
Dietz, Aug., 24—**Galliott Flora,** 1849; Guadalupe Co.
Dietz, Ferd., 19 — Wiesbaden; **Franziska,** 1849; Comal Co.
Dietzel, Charlotte, and 2 daughters — Heinrichs to Indianola; **Fortuna,** 1858
Dietzel, Edwill and Oscar—Marsfeld; **Gessner,** 1854
Dingethal, Georg, 22 — Einbeck; **Joh. Dethardt,** 1848
Dinker, A. and wife—Falkenberg to Galveston; **Iris,** 1857
Dionipius, P. and wife—Galo (Galau?); **Iris,** 1857
Dipp, Franz Jos., 26 — Neuhaus, Prussia; Dorothea, 22; **Gutenberg,** 1855
Dirkob, Johann 41; Elis. 25, Josef 5—**John Holland,** 1848
Discher, George, 30—**Jeverland,** 1858
Dischinger, Magda. 19, Wilhme 16; —**Herschel,** 1850
Disselhorst, Theo., 26 — Minden; **Franziska,** 1849; Comal Co.
Distel, E.—Labeschon; **Texas,** 1853
Ditert, Wilh.—Loböse; **Juno,** 1853; Austin Co.

Ditthardt, J. with family—Rehe to New Braunfels; **Iris,** 1860
Dittmar, Alex — Wiehe; **Gessner,** 1858; Fayette Co.
Dittmar, A.—Oranienburg to Cat Spring; **Juno,** 1860
Dittmar, Carl 46, Louis 44—**Louis,** 1848; Guadalupe Co.
Dittmar, Emilie and Amalie — Wiehe; **Gessner,** 1854
Dittmeyer, Maria—Schönau; **Lucie,** 1854
Dittreth, J.—Gleine to New Braunfels; wife and 4 ch.; **Juno,** 1860
Ditze, W.—Ziegenhain to Galveston; **Weser,** 1860
Dlugasch, F. and wife — Olmütz; **Gessner,** 1855
Dobelke, Michael and family — Prussia; Antoinette, 1854; Comal Co.
Doebel, Chr. — Harmsdorf, Holstein to New Orleans; **Washington,** 1852
Doebler, Henriette—Berlin; **J. W. Buddecke,** 1853
Doecke, Henriette—Prussia; **Neptune,** 1849
Doeckel, Dietrich, with wife and 5 ch. — Rehburg to Brenham; **Weser,** 1857
Doehle, Foh (Joh?) and Jost—Winnegenhausen; **Texas,** 1853
Doell, Christiane—Roda, Sachsen-Weimer to Galveston; **Republic,** 1851
Döppenschmidt, Jacob and family —Bavaria; Antoinette, 1854; Comal Co.
Doerk, Moritz—Prussia; **Neptune,** 1849
Doerning. Miss C.—Gleinau; **Neptune,** 1853
Doerr, Carl, 41—Schocken; **Canapus,** 1848; Fayette Co.
Doerr, Chrna (Christina) — Tscthocken (Schocken?); **Reform,** 1849
Doerr, Ludw., 22—Rogasen; **Canapus,** 1848
Dogelsang, Jacob and Hette—See Vogelsang, Jacob
Dohm, F.—Havelberg to Galveston; **Weser,** 1857
Dohm, Louise and ch.—Havelberg to Galveston; **Fortuna,** 1858
Dohme, Doctor Carl—Oberkirchen; 6 persons; **Henriette,** 1843 (1853)
Dolle, Fried.—Hannover to New Braunfels; Christine. Henry, Fried., Karl; **Weser,** 1860

Dollfuss, J.—Berlin to Houston; **Juno, 1860**

Dombrowa, Herman—Inowrailau to Houston; **Gaston, 1860**

Donarth, Joseph—Friedland; wife and 1 ch.; **Minna, 1854**

Donat, Carl—Breslau; **Reform, 1851**

Donnersberg, Heinrich—Rohden; 4 persons; **Texas, 1853; Comal Co.** sus, **Comal Co.**

Doreck, L.—Mannheim; **Weser, 1854; Galveston**

Dorendorf, G.—Barkentin, Mklbg.; wife Doris; **Hampden, 1854**

Dornhoefer, Frederic, 31—Feudingen; Mary, born Gerhard, 26, Elisa, 1; **Antoinette, 1848**

Dornhoefer, John, 27—Feudingen; **Antoinette, 1848**

Dornwell, Aug. and wife — Holstein; **Neptune, 1849**

Dosch, E., 26—**Louis, 1848; Comal Co.**

Dott, Eduard—Wiesbaden; **Reform, 1849**

Doubrawa, John, wife and 5 ch.—Delsch (Döltsch?) to Austin Co.; **Gaston, 1860**

Draeger, Henrietta and 2 ch.—Poland; **Franziska, 1854**

Drage, Claus, Magda. — Spitzendorf to LaGrange; **F o r t u n a, 1860; Washington Co.**

Dramand, 31—Germany; **Louis, 1848**

Drasdo, Georg—Dresden; **Reform, 1851**

Drave(?), Adolph, 24—**Canapus, 1848**

Drave, Aug., Maria—**Ammerland, 1854**

Drecke, Henriette—**Neptune, 1849**

Dregelmann, Eugen. 28—Bockels; **Joh. Dethardt, 1848;** see Diegelmann, Eugen

Dreger, Emilie—Pudewitz to Lockhart; **Iris, 1858**

Dreidoppel, Carl—Neu Wied; **Henriette, 1843 (1853)**

Dreithaler, Wm.—Gablonz; 3 persons; **Texas, 1853**

Drescher, Kaetchen — Vilbel to Houston; **Weser, 1860**

Dresel, Emil, 30—Wiesbaden; **Franziska, 1849**

Dresel, Julius, 32; **Louis, 1848; Kendall Co. 1850's**

Dresel, Rudolph, 18 — Wiesbaden; **Franziska, 1849; Kendall Co.**

Dreyer, Hein., 59—Lippe Detmold; Friedke 50, Louise 24, Friedke 22, Justine 14, Caro. 10, Ludw. 6, Dor. 34; **Joh. Dethardt, 1848; DeWitt Co.**

Dreves, Carl—Berlin; **Suwa, 1853**

Droste, Joh., 25; **Creole, 1852**

Drumm, Johann Martin, wife and 3 ch.—M. Friedland, Mklbg. to Galveston; **Republic, 1851;** Comal Co.

Dube, G.—Waldeck to Houston; **Weser, 1860**

Dube, Hein., 14—**Magnet, 1852**

Dubsky, Ferd.—Humpoletz; **Weser, 1854**

Dudensing, W., 33; Wilhme 27, Wilhme 7, Elise 6, Henriette 4, Marie ½—**Fortuna, 1858;** Austin Co.

Duderstadt, Andreas—**Ammerland, 1854; DeWitt Co.**

Duderstadt, Fr. and family—**Ammerland, 1854; DeWitt Co.**

Duebel, Johan, 29—Proettlin, Prussia; Dor. 24, Maria 4, Dor. 2; **John Frederick, 1850**

Duebeler, M.—Prussia; 5 persons; **Friedrich Grosse, 1853**

Duecker, E. and Henriette—Burbach; **Texas, 1853**

Duehlen, H. and wife—Hagen; **Gessner, 1855**

Duehm, Hans, 27; Christine 26—Holstein; **Brasilian, 1850;** see also Duehren, Hans.

Duehren, Hans, 27, Christine 26—Wandsbeck; **Brasilian, 1850;** see also Duehn, Hans

Duelberg, Franz Wilh., 53—Germany; Fried. Wilh. 15, Maria Elise 56, Hein. Wilh. ½; **Solon, 1850**

Duelm, Fried., 19, Louisa 24; Sophie, 1852; **Comal Co.**

Duer family — Warenberg; **Adolphine, 1859**

Duerke, Fr(ied.), 50 — Prussia; Cath. 49, Hermann 19, Joachim 17, Maria 14, Dor. 11; **Hamburg, 1849;** Austin Co.

Duester, L.—Schmuesen, Prussia; **Hampden, 1854**

Duesterding, F.—Hannover; **Franziska, 1854**

Duffy, Peter — Fachbach; 5 persons; **Texas, 1853**

Duhn, Gerhard — Elsenhain; **Neptune, 1853**

Dumeny, Maria—Hamburg to Galveston; **Sarah, 1851**

Dung, H.; Martin, John—Hof to Houston; Fortuna, 1860
Dungen, Jos., 25; Lise 26, Catharina 42—Reform, 1850
Dunkelstein, Carl—Breslau; Neptune, 1854
Durkhanner, 26 — Prussia; Colonist, 1848
Durkopp, Sophie, 25—Franziska, 1847
Durler, Carl, 26; and F. F., 29—Louis, 1848
Durst, Gottlieb — Scharnhausen; J. W. Buddecke, 1853
Dusch, Carl, 43—Lauenburg; Chas. N. Cooper, 1847
Dyanissinz, J. (I?) P., 29; Frederike, 25—Hamburg; Alexander, 1850

— E —

Ebeling, E. — Galveston; Weser, 1857; Ed. Ebeling, Fayette Co. 1858
Ebeling, Ernst—Galveston to Galveston; Weser, 1857
Ebeling, Ernst and Dor.—Elze to Galveston; Juno, 1860
Eben, Joh. Fr., 25; Solon, 1850; Austin Co.
Ebener, Philipp — Löcknitz, Prussia to Galveston; Washington, 1852
Eberfeld, Hein. — Cappenberg; 4 persons; Texas, 1853; Colorado Co.
Eberhard, Fried. — Greiffenau; John Frederick, 1850; San Antonio
Eberhard, W. — 2 persons; Estafette, 1850
Eberhardt, H.—Eisenach to Austin; Gessner, 1860; Austin Co.
Ebers, Dorothea and family—Berlin to Galveston; Iris, 1857
Ebert, Anna—Wustensachsen; Henriette, 1843 (1853)
Ebez, Anton, 38; Anna 41, Peter 13, Vincenz 9, Phillipp 6, Christian 2—John Holland, 1848
Echhard, G. Willib, 23—Saxony; Chas. N. Cooper, 1847
Eck, A.—Hesse; Friedrich Grosse, 1853
Ecke, M.—Fallersleben to Hempstead; Gessner, 1860
Eckelmann, J. H.—Westerwald to Industry; Caro., Charl., Louise, Christine, Henry; Fortuna, 1860
Eckermann, Anton — Ulzburg; Hampden, 1854; Bexar Co.

Eckermann, Aug. — Krebshagen; Canapus, 1849; Austin Co.
Eckermann, W.—Ulzburg; Hampden, 1854
Eckert, Aug., 41—Prussia; Theresa, 31; Reform, 1850
Eckert, Caro.—Burg.; Texas, 1853
Eckert, Friedricke — Burg.; Herschel, 1851
Eckerts, Fried.—New Wied; wife and 2 ch.; Henriette, 1843 (1853)
Eckhardt, Ludwig — Breslau; Reform, 1851; DeWitt Co. or Comal Co.
Eckhof, H.—Wedel to Lexington; Fortuna, 1860
Edlinger, Jos., 41; S. 46, Peter 6, Maria 5, Gertrude 2—Solon, 1850
Edwing, Thomas—Schulau to La Grange; Kate, Maria, Julius, Elise; Fortuna, 1860
Effinger family—Aldingen; Adolphine, 1859
Efsinger (sic) (Effinger?) ...., and family—Wittenberg; Adolphine, 1859
Egeling, Christ., 50—Gs Sch (illegible) perhaps Gross Schwülper?; Joh. Dethardt, 1848
Egers, Heinr., 40—Gs-Sch (illegible) perhaps Gross Schülper?; Joh. Dethardt, 1848
Eggeling, S. — Prussia; Friedrich Grosse, 1853; Comal Co.
Eggert, Fr., 44 — Brome, Han.; Soph. 27, Hr. 5; Helen & Elise, 1847
Eggert, Jac., 50—Steimke; Soph. 50, Hr. 17, Marg. 15, Elis. 12, Wm. 5; Helen & Elise, 1847
Eggert, Johann—Strehlen, Mklbg. to Galveston; Washington, 1852
Ehler, Christian, and wife—Württemberg; Weser, 1854
Ehler, Gottfried, and wife—Württemberg; Weser, 1854; Coleman Co.
Ehlers, Fried.—Hausberge, Han.; Mississippi, 1855; Colorado Co.
Ehlers, Hein., 25—Tweierhausendericke(?); Neptune, 1850
Ehmker, Joh.—Zweiborg; Neptune, 1853
Ehrenburg, Carl F. — Landsberg, Prussia; wife and 2 ch. ¼ and 1½ yrs. old; Miles, 1854
Ehrhard, David—Guxhagen; Herschel, 1851
Ehrig, Max—Klamp, Mklbg.; and wife; Copernicus, 1852; Gonzales Co.

Eichhoff, Fred., 21—Prussia; Franziska, 1847
Eichholz, W.—Schweidnitz to Bastrop; Fortuna, 1860; DeWitt Co.
Eichhorn, Peter, 33; 4 children—Leo, 1848
Eichler, A.—Gotha to New Braunfels; Iris, 1860
Eichler, J. and family — Saubernitz; Anton Gunther, 1860
Eichoorst, A.—Oderburg; Adolphine, 1859
Eicke, A.—Hemmingen to Lexington; Iris, 1857
Eickel, Joh.—Breissig; Juno, 1853
Eickenmeyer, Fried., 48; Lisette 26, Elis. 22, Wilh. 18, Carl 25; Reform, 1850
Eigendorf, C. F.—Berlin, Prussia; wife and son, 17; Hampden, 1854; Comal Co.
Eigenhorst, F. — Stalle to Brenham; Weser, 1860
Eigler, Marg., 35—Bavaria; Franziska, 1847
Eiler, Catharina, 21—Hermann Theodor, 1850
Eilers, ... — LaGrange to LaGrange; Iris, 1858
Eilers, Louis — Damme; Solon, 1852; Bastrop Co.
Einkauf, W.—4 persons; Estafette, 1850
Eisen, ...—Frankfurt to Houston; Anton Gunther, 1860
Eisen, Nic. and family — Linz/Rhein; Gessner, 1854
Eisenbart, Chr. — Lambsheim; Weser, 1854; Bastrop Co.
Eisenlohr, Elise — Carlsruhe to New Braunfels; Fortuna, 1860
Eismann, Johann and Johanna—Joh. Ed. Grosse, 1853
Eismann, Johann and Marie—Rödelwitz; Henriette, 1843 (1853)
Elbel, Chas. G., 22—Galliott Flora, 1849; Comal Co.
Elbel, J. E. C., 20—Galliott Flora, 1849
Elbert, ... and family—Galveston to Galveston; Iris, 1858
Elbrecht, Heinrich—Berlin; Suwa, 1853
Eldagsen, A., 29—Kiel to Galveston; Weser, 1858
Elers, Aug., 22—Herschel, 1849
Elisabeth, Caspar: see Caspar, Elisabeth—Joh. Ed. Grosse, 1853
Elkes, J.—Poland; Lucie, 1854
Elkes, Mathilda—Posen; Weser, 1854

Elkes, R. M.—Galveston; Weser, 1854
Ellenburger, Jos., 33—Lipspringe; Franziska 4; Canapus, 1848; Harris Co.
Ellendrup, H. A.—Bielefeld; Canapus, 1849
Ellerbusch, J. A., 40 — Hamburg; Gesche 36, Dor. 16, Nancy 8; John Frederick, 1850; Fayette Co.
Elmendorf, Carl, 28; Amalie 20, Pedramella 25, Heindrick 22; Louis, 1848; Bexar Co.
Elsner, Aug.—Liegnitz; 5 persons; Magnet, 1851; Bastrop Co.
Elsner family — Friedland; Adolphine, 1859; Comal Co.
Elsner, Johann and wife, 3 persons—Bullendorf, Bohemia; Mississippi, 1855; Lavaca Co.
Elstener, Anton—Friesland; Texas, 1853
Elsterer, J.—Bohemia; 5 persons; Friedrich Grosse, 1853
Elzner, Auguste and family — Zeitz; Weser, 1854
Emek, Jak. — Lühmannsdorf; 3 persons; Magnet, 1851
Emhoff, W. with family—Wehdem to Houston; Weser, 1858
Emler, R.—Brande to Galveston; Iris, 1860
Emmenhardt, Wilhelmine — Brake to Galveston; Weser, 1860
Emshoff—See Emhoff or Ernshoff
Engbrock, Michel, Wilhme—Joh. Ed. Grosse, 1853
Engelage family—to Brenham; Weser, 1859
Engelbrecht, H.—Prussia to Brenham; Weser, 1860
Engelhardt, Christian, 25—Creole, 1852; Fayette Co.
Engelke, Aug.—Duderstadt; Weser, 1854; Austin Co.
Engelke, Ernst — Hildesheim; Reform, 1851; Galveston 1859
Engelke, Hinrich—Halle to Fredericksburg; Weser, 1857
Engelke, Rud. Charles, 25—Magdeburg; Antoinette, 1848
Engelking, Ferd., 39 — Texas; Franziska, 1849; Austin Co.
Engelmann, Rosale—Mützyum to Houston; Fortuna, 1860
Engemann, Carl — Klein-Neuendorf, Saxony; Miles, 1854
Englemann, Andreas—Bühne; Weser, 1854
Engelmann, Mart.—Neudorf; 2 persons; ship? date?

Englemathe, Harvie, 29 — Lambforde (Lamferding); Neptune, 1850
Entred, L.—Gotha to Galveston; Weser, 1858
Eppers, Ferd.—Galliott Concordia, 1854
Erasmus, C. F.—Stralsund; 2 persons; Estafette, 1850
Erb, Elias—Waldfisch; Weser, 1854
Erb family—to Galveston; Weser, 1859
Erb, P.—Heismar (Geismar?) to Galveston; Fortuna, 1858
Erbe, C.—Gedern; Weser, 1854
Erfurt, Marius — Dessau; 4 persons; Hermann Theodor, 1853; Guadalupe Co.
Erich, Sophie, 38—Lübeck; Alexander, 1850
Erichson, Jul.—Breslau; Reform, 1851
Erler, H.—Lokenwalde; Estafette, 1850
Ermler, Gottfried — Langenbielau, Prussia; Miles, 1854
Ermler, H.—Frensdorf to Frelsburg; Iris, 1857
Ernshoff, Chr., 40; M a r i a 47, Christian 14, Christoph 4, and 3 daughters — Hermann Theodor, 1850; Christian Emshoff, Austin Co.
Ernst, C. J.—Torgau, Poland; Mississippi, 1855! Austin Co.
Ernst, Fr.—Ammerland, 1854
Ernst, Friedrich—Keetz, Mklbg.; Copernicus, 1852; Fayette Co.
Ernst, Johann—Mainz; Herschel, 1851; Comal Co.
Ertschjusch, E.—Buddern, Bohemia to San Antonio; with wife and child; Juno, 1860
Escher, Christian, 26—Creole, 1852
Esner, Moritz—Leibnitz; Neptune, 1854
Esperscheitz, Joh., 40; Carl 10—Franziska, 1847
Essinger—See Effinger; Adolphine, 1859
Eule, Adolph—Bautzen, Saxony; John Frederick, 1850
Evers, Ch.—Hallichter(?); 7 persons; Neptune, 1854; Llano Co.
Evers, Claus Hartwig, 38—Schiersensee, Holstein; Catharina 36, Christina 5, Christian 8; Gutenberg, 1855
Ewersberg, A. -- Remscheid to Houston; Juno, 1860

Ewert, Heinrich—Eisenberg, Prussia; wife and 7 children, 11-28 years of age; Sophie, 1852
Exoner, Fr. D. and wife; Exoner, Fr. Th. and wife Christine—Saxony; Neptune, 1848
Eye (Eyg?), Eva—Prussia; Franziska, 1854
Ezener, Philipp and family—Tost; Weser, 1854
Ezermak, Franz—Vienna; 3 persons; Suwa, 1853

— F —

Fabian, Marg. and 2 dau.—Suhl; Henriette, 1843 (1853)
Fackler, Mich., 40—Wilsdorf; wife Barbara, 35; Canapus, 1848
Faehler, Cath., 52—Louis, 1848
Faemer, Georg — Belzenberg to Neighbor's Creek; Iris, 1859
Faerber, Mart.—Hallgarten; 5 persons; ship? date?
Faerschmann, A.—Sobieschen (Sobieszyn, Poland) to Galveston; Iris, 1859
Fahne, Gertr., 25—Paderborn; Canapus, 1848
Fahrholz, Frd.—Königsberg, Prussia; wife Maria; Franklin, 1853
Faitisch, Anna—Achalm; Adolphine, Fall 1859
Falche, Carl, 26—Botzow (Boitzum?); Wm. Fr. 16, Carl 51, Sophie 49; Canapus, 1848
Falk, Heinrich—Schlierbach; Herschel, 1851
Falke, Andreas—Bakuth to Cunningham; John, Johanna, Mary; Fortuna, 1860
Falke, Fr.—Oldendorf; 4 persons; Magnet, 1851; died New Braunfels, 1852; Comal Co.
Falkenhagen, Fr.(ied.), 19—Goldbeck; Hamburg, 1849
Falkenhagen, Georg, 45 — Wittstock, Prussia; Sophie 47, Joh. 14, Dor. 5; John Frederick, 1850
Falkenhagen, Ludwig, 23 — Wittstock, Prussia; Wilhme 18; John Frederick, 1850
Fansch (Fausch?), ..., 26—Prussia; Joh. Dethardt, 1848
Faseler, Harm. H.—Felde to Quihi; wife and 2 ch.; Weser, 1857
Fatsch, J. W. and N. — Estafette, 1850; Austin Co.
Faubel, Johannes—Marburg; with family, 5 persons—Juno, 1853
Faussen, Robert, 26—Berlin; Antoinette, 1848

Fechner, Caroline — Pudewitz to New Braunfels; Iris, 1858
Fechner, Ed., 18; Brasilian, 1857
Fechner, Wilhelm — Coburg; with family, 6 persons; Juno, 1853
Feh, Joh. Baptiste, 35—Württ.; Colonist, 1848
Fehrenkamp, Joh. Gerh., 38—Faderberg; Helene 28, Joh. Hein. 8, Sophie 5, Joh. Gerh. 2½; Helen and Elise, 1847; Colorado Co.
Feigin, Chs., 18—Galliott Flora, 1849
Feinhals, Wilh.—Odendahl (Odendorf?); Solon, 1852
Felder, Gustav, 31 — Petschkau; Anna, 27; Colonist, 1850
Felix, Joh.—Gross Brogitsch (Broditz?); and family; Weser, 1854
Fellman, Jos., 26, Louise 32—Solon, 1850
Felter, F. and family — Lewin; Gessner, 1854; Austin Co.
Fenski, J. and Wilhme—Bagniewo to Fredericksburg; with family; Iris, 1860
Fenstedt, Christian, and Johanne—Hesse-Cassel to Houston; Gessner, 1860
Feuerstacke, Jungfer — Braunschweig; Hermann Theodor, 1853
Fiata, Johann—Böhmen; Weser, 1854
Fidken, Joh., 34 — Aschhausen; Helena 36, Luker 9, Helene 3; Neptune, 1850; see also Fiken, Gerd.
Fiebig, Carl — Petersdorf; 5 persons; Magnet, 1851; Fayette Co.
Fiedjen, Reinhard — Reckum to Harrisburg; Fortuna, 1860
Fiedler, G(eorg), 34 — Meiningen; Wilhme 23, Amelie, Fried.; Hamburg, 1849; Fayette Co.
Fieh, Hein., 25—Solon, 1850
Fier, F.—Gablonz; 5 persons; Texas, 1853
Fietze, Daniel, 32—Hannover; Franziska, 1847
Fiken, Gerd., 21—Aschhausen; Neptune, 1850
Filmer, Louise — Bodenwerder to Galveston; Iris, 1859
Findeisen, F.—Lengefeld; wife and 9 ch., and Johanna; Lucie, 1854; Austin Co.
Finger, O., 32—Fortuna, 1858
Finger, Wolbreth, 56 — Mecklenburg; Marie 58, Marie 27, Friedke 25; Franziska, 1847

Fink, Johann—Neubernitt, Mklbg.; wife and 6 children; to Galveston; Sarah, 1851; Fayette Co.
Fink, Peter—Wendtorf, Holstein; wife and 3 ch., 1¼-7 yrs. old; Hampden, 1854
Finke, W.—Brinkhausen; Gessner, 1854
Finn, Auguste—Sondershausen; Antoinette, 1854
Finser, Aug., 21; Cleve—Franziska, 1846
Finzel, ... (musician); Prussia to Galveston; Anton Gunther, 1860
Fischer, A.—Magdeburg; Neptune, 1854
Fischer, A.—Ostende to Galveston; Iris, 1859
Fischer, Adam—Pfieffe to San Antonio; Weser, 1860
Fischer, Adam, 27—Herschel, 1850
Fischer, Bernhard, 44—Friedland; Petramella 42, Regina 16, Anna 14, 6 small children; Colonist, 1848
Fischer, C. — Tfeilbach (Thalbach?) to Llano; Juno, 1860
Fischer, Carl; Joh. Ed. Grosse, 1853; Fayette Co.
Fischer, C. T. — Wünschendorf, Prussia; wife and 3 ch., ¾-11 yrs. old; Franklin, 1853
Fischer, Chr. Fr.—Saxony; Neptune, 1848
Fischer, Ferd.—Hilkers; Henriette, 1843 (1853)
Fischer, Franz, 49; Carl 13—Magnet. 1852; Austin Co.
Fischer, Franz; Galliott Concordia, 1854; Austin Co.
Fischer, F.—Neudorf; Neptune, 1853
Fischer, H. L. — St. Petersburg, Russia; wife and 2 sons, 2 and 6 yrs. old; Franklin, 1853
Fischer, Hein.—Sicke to Brenham; Weser, 1857
Fischer, Hein., 19—Solon, 1850
Fischer, Jurgen, 24—Oldenburg; Franziska, 1849
Fischer, Ludwig, Dr. med.—Torgau Sachsen; wife and 1 child, ¾ yrs.; Franklin, 1852; Galveston
Fischer, O. — New Braunfels to New Braunfels; Weser, 1860
Fischer, ... (tailor)—Burgdorf to New Braunfels; Iris, 1858
Fischer, Theo.—Menne to Houston; Juno, 1860
Fischer, Therese — Altenburg; 3 persons; Texas, 1853

Fischer, Wilhelm—**John Ed. Grosse,** 1853
Fischer, W., 43; Hermine 38, Wilhme 7, Albert 5, Franz 3, Max ½; **Fortuna,** 1858
Fisler, W.—Wildungen to Industry; **Iris,** 1859
Fisseler, Fried.—Gilsa, Kurhessen; wife and 6 ch., 9-21 yrs. of age; **Sophie,** 1852; Austin Co.
Fittu, Fr.—**Ammerland,** 1854
Fitz, J.—Pommern; **Adolphine,** 1859
Fitz, Philipine, 16—**Hermann Theodor,** 1850
Flache, Andreas — Saxony; arr. Galveston Nov. 1853; Gonzales Co.
Flack, Franz, 24—Hesse; **Joh. Dethardt,** 1848; Kendall Co.
Flake, Ferd., 26—Galveston; **Franziska,** 1849; Galveston
Flath, F.—Braunsdorf to Galveston; **Iris,** 1859
Fleckhammer, Charlotte — Fahingen; **Iris,** 1857
Fleger, Wilh.—**Galliott Concordia,** 1854
Floech (Floeck?), M.—Mühlhein/ Coblenz; 7 persons; ship? date?
Floericke, Heinrich—Wendrickendorf, Prussia to Galveston; wife and 3 children; **Republic,** 1851
Fluehr, Rosine — Sinzheim; **Gessner,** 1854
Focken, E.—Oldcnburg; **Reform,** 1851
Foehrle, Israel—Plieningen; **Texas,** 1853
Foerster, Ant. — Reckichsdorf (Rückersdorf?); wife and ch.; **Minna,** 1854; Fayette Co.
Forster (Foerster), Ant.—Bullendorf; **Minna,** 1854; Fayette Co.
Foerster, Leopoldine — Horstdorf to Frelsburg; **Iris,** 1857
Foite, Magda.—Prussia; **Jeverland,** 1860
Foler, Friedke, 19—**Louis,** 1848
Fonses, Sophie—to Frelsburg; **Weser,** 1859
Forster, Caro., 24—Prussia; **Franziska,** 1849
Forstmann, H., 25—**Fortuna,** 1858
Forzombeck, Anton and family— Brogitsch (Broditz?); **Weser,** 1854
Fost, Johanna—Magdeburg to La Grange; **Iris,** 1860
Foth, Caroline and son — Osnabrück to Austin; **Gaston,** 1857

Fraenkel, F. — Prussia; **Friedrich Grosse,** 1853
Frank, Carl, 23 — Cur Hessen; **Franziska,** 1847; Fayette Co.
Frank, Damian and wife — Sahl (Suhl); **Gessner,** 1854
Frank, Friedr., 30—Saxony; Rosine 28; **Joh. Dethardt,** 1848; Austin Co.
Frank, Mart—Ober-Walluf; 6 persons; ship? date?
Franke, Carl Gottlieb, 38—Adorf; **Hamburg,** 1849
Franke, Fried. and Mathilda — Braunschweig to Galveston; **Weser,** 1860
Franke, Heinrich, with wife and 2 ch.—Hannover Münden; **Minna,** 1854
Franke, Henry—Steinberge, Prussia; **Mississippi,** 1855
Franke, Louis—Berlin; **Solon,** 1852; Fayette Co.
Franke, Wilh. and Wilhme — Lippersdorf; **Lucie,** 1854
Franke, Wilh. and Louis — Herstelle; **Solon,** 1852
Frantz, Charles, 21—Frankenhausen; **Solon,** 1850; Fayette Co.
Franz, Fried.—Polenz, Saxony; **Miles,** 1854; Goliad Co.
Franze, Carl—Herrenhut, Saxony; **Lucie,** 1854; Fayette Co.
Franziska, Oceana, 19—**Franziska,** 1849; Falls Co.?
Franzmann, C.—Wehdem to Brenham; **Weser,** 1858
Frauenstein, Charlotte — Dresden; 3 persons; **Reform,** 1851
Freck, Anton — Essendorf; **Lucie,** 1854
Frede, Louis—Möchern; **Texas,** 1853
Freely, I. H., 43; John Christian 40, Aug. Cath. 11, Henriette 9, Johanne 6, Peter Hein. 4—**Hermann Theodor,** 1850
Frei, Moritz, and Julius—Kinten, Poland; **Solon,** 1852
Freitag, Hein.—Oberfeld; **Weser,** 1854
Freitag, Heinrich — S c h w e r i n, Mklbg. to Galveston or Indianola; **Franklin,** 1852
Freitag, Johann—Prussia; **Antoinette,** 1854; Comal Co.
Freks, Henriette, 27—Wehdem to Brenham; **Iris,** 1859
Frels, Fried.—Hahnenmoor; three persons; **Neptune,** 1853; Colorado Co.

Frels, Gerh., 28—Cummins Creek, Texas; Solon, 1860; Colorado Co.

Frels, Herm., 28 — Oldenburg; Franziska, 1847; Colorado Co.

Frels, Joh., 35—Solon, 1850; Fayette Co.

Frenkel, S.—Posen; Leibniz, 1850

Frentrup(?), Fried., 21—Detmold; Franziska, 1847

Frenz, Louise—Gewitzen; 3-year-old son and ¼-year-old daughter; Leibniz, 1850

Frenzel, Andrew—Oberscheibe; 7 p e r s o n s; Hermann Theodor, 1853; Fayette Co.

Freter, Heinrich and wife—Posen; Miles, 1853

Freter, Heinrich — Klein-Sorge, Mklbg.; wife and 2 ch., 1¼ and 6 years old; Miles, 1852

Freter, W. with family — Bergbruch (Bergenbrüch) to Galveston; Iris, 1860

Fresinia, H. and sister—Posen to Galveston; Iris, 1857

Fresinius, H., 23; Herschel, 1849; Gillespie Co.

Freuth, Mathilde — Wiesau; Hermann Theodor, 1853

Frever, Frances, 36—Antoinette, 1848; Fayette Co.

Frey, Fried., 19—to Louisiana; Jeverland, 1858

Frey III, Peter, 39; Justine 37, Magda 7, Jacob 5, Justina ¾— John Holland, 1848

Freytag, Mich.—Lohne; Solon, 1852

Freytag, Anna—Lohme to Helena (Karnes Co.); Justine, Eva; Iris, 1860

Fricke, Claus Joachim, 36 — Neumuenster, Holstein; Anna 42, August 13, Claus 9, Anna 6, Carl 9; Gutenberg, 1855; Indianola

Fricke, Georg, 27—American citizen; Louise 29, Fred 32—Hannover; Franziska, 1847; Austin Co.

Friebel, A. F., 26—Galliott Flora, 1849

Friedel, J.—Gacenka (Jasenka) to Industry; Juno, 1860

Friedel, Joh.—Landenhausen; Weser, 1854

Friedemann, W.—Oppendorf; Adolphine, 1859

Frieder, J.—Pommern; Adolphine, 1859

Friedlander, Bertha, 22—Wessecke (Weseke) to Houston; Weser, 1859

Friedlander, Carl, 38—Hamburg; Hamburg, 1849

Friedmann, G. and wife—Breslau; Gessner, 1855

Friderich, Aug. Ferd.—Landsberg; Neptune, 1853

Friedrichs, C.—Neu-Strelitz; Adolphine, 1859

Friedrichs family — Bodenwerder to Galveston; Iris, 1859

Friedrich, H. and M. — Föhr to Galveston; Juno, 1860

Friedrich, J. with family — Oelshausen to Houston; Iris, 1860

Friedrich, Rosine, 18—Creole, 1852

Friedrichs family—Bodenwerder to Galveston; Iris, 1859

Friedrichs, Louis—Galveston; Ammerland, 1854

Friedrichs, Ludwig and Minna—Neu-Strelitz; Mississippi, 1855

Friesmann, C. — Hesse; Friedrich Grosse, 1853

Frischmayer, Karl—Braunschweig; wife and 2 children; Republic, 1851; Gillespie Co.

Frisike, W i l h e l m — Pritzabes (Pritzerbe?), Prussia; Bassermann, 1851

Friske, J. — Wihtorava (Wiktorow?) to Independence; Fortuna, 1858

Fritsch, A. — Neustadt to Gatesville; Fortuna, 1858

Fritsch, Franziska—Neuchatel; Mississippi, 1855

Fritsch, Franziska — Neustadt to San Antonio; Fortuna, 1858

Fritsch, Josepha—Neustadt; Adolphine, 1859

Fritz, C. with family—Bergebruch to Richmond; Iris, 1860

Fritz, Jacob, 25—Magnet, 1852

Fritz, Johann—Kahrstadt, Mklbg.; Franklin, 1853; Gillespie Co.

Fritz, Louise, 32 — Wolfenbüttel; Auguste 10, Eduard 8, Carl 4; Canapus, 1848

Fritz, Simon—Hesse; Weser, 1854

Fritze, Gust.—Derenberg; Reform, 1849

Fritzsche, Jos.—Mittelwalde; Magnet, 1851; Fayette Co.

Frobese, Ferd.—Einbeck to Indianola; Juno, 1860; Galveston Co.

Frobese, Wilh. — Einbeck to Indianola; Juno, 1860

Froboese, Aug. — Rhoden; Weser, 1854; Comal Co.

Froehleich, Sibussa, 19(?)—Franziska, 1849

Froehner, Fr. G.—Annaberg; six persons; Hermann Theodor, 1853
Froelich, A.—Königsberg; Gaston, 1857; Fayette Co.
Frohner, J.—Potsdam; Gessner, 1855
Fromm, Wilhelm and E. — Mannheim; Juno, 1860
Fromme, A.—Blackede; Iris, 1859
Fromme, L.—Gestorf; Iris, 1859; Goliad Co.
Frosch, H.—Udenhausen; Neptune, 1853; Fayette Co.
Frost, Anna and Cath.—Prussia to Galveston; Anton Gunther, 1860
Frost, Dina — Rösebeck; Hermann Theodor, 1853
Frost, Carl—Bautzen, Saxony; John Frederick, 1850
Fruth, Georg, 24—Bavaria; Franziska, 1849
Fuchs, Adolph and family—Kettindorf; Joh. Dethardt, 1848; Austin Co.
Fuchs, Alex, 15 — Wittkowo to Galveston; Iris, 1859
Fuchs, Auguste—Düsseldorf; Neptune, 1853
Fuchs, Carl, 23—Chas. N. Cooper, 1847
Fuchs, David—Joh. Ed. Grosse, 1853; Guadalupe Co.
Fuchs, Fried, 60—Penzlin; Juliane 52, Otto 21, Wilh. 20, Carl 14, Fritz 9; John Frederick, 1850; Fayette Co.
Fuchs, J. C.(?)—Prussia; children, Jules, Carl, Emmy; Neptune, 1849; Austin Co.
Fuchs, L.—Ammerland, 1854; Fayette Co.
Fueler, H.—Prussia to Brenham; Weser, 1860
Fuer, Emil—Cologne (Köln); Juno, 1853
Fuettner, C.—Bärdorf to Galveston; Fortuna, 1860
Fukoether, Joh. Wilh.—Hilliganen; Solon, 1852
Fulauff, H., 21, and Caro.—Prussia; Neptune, 1849
Fulg (Fuig?), Joh.—Darmstadt; Magnet, 1851
Fultener, Helene, 24—Berlin; Joh. Dethardt, 1848
Funke, Gerh.—Sengwarden to Galveston; Fortuna, 1860
Fuss, Anna—Aldingen; Adolphine, 1859
Fuss, Mathias—Aldingen; Henriette, 1843 (1853)

— G —

Gabbert, Herm., 19—Franzthal; Weser, 1858
Gabczynski, Adam—Rogasen, Poland; Herschel, 1851
Gabitzsch, Gottfr. H.—Blosin; Magnet, 1851
Gabler, Joh. Ernst—Keidersdorf; Canapus, 1849
Gabrisch, Thomas, wife and child —Semetin (Sembtin) to Travis Co.; Gaston, 1860
Gade, Hein., 23—Oldenburg; Franziska, 1849
Gaebel, C. and wife—Kassel to La Grange; Gaston, 1857
Gaertner, Cath.—Eisenach; Henriette, 1843 (1853)
Gaertner, J.—Loish; Weser, 1854; Grimes Co.
Gaetjen, Gesina and Lina Charl. Marie — Aumund to Galveston; Iris, 1861
Gaetke, N. Wilhelm, and wife— from Texas; Sophie, 1852; Austin Co.
Galle family—to Yorktown; Weser, 1859
Gallia, Andreas — Austria; Marianne, Theresia, Jos., Carl, Clara, Val., Ignaz; Jeverland, 1860;
Gambel, Joh., 57—Werdorf; wife Elis. nee Sinz, 45; Jacob 24, Joh. 15, Fried. 11, Cath. 18; Antoinette, 1848
Gammelin, Christian—Rathenbeck, Holstein; wife and 7 ch., 3-27 years old; Washington, 1852
Ganze, Fr., 28 — Katte (Kalle?); Wilh. 26, Carol ¾; Helen & Elise, 1847
Ganzer, L.—Coswig to Galveston; Iris, 1860
Garenfloh, Jacob — Chitsborn(?); with family, 7 persons; Juno, 1853
Garlipp, Joh. C. (Carl), 47—Havelberg; Dor. Soph. 55, Joh. Carl 21, Sophia 19; Hamburg, 1849; Austin Co.
Garrels, Louis, 21 — Bremerhafen to Galveston; Weser, 1859
Gasch, F.—Schimnowitz; Gessner, 1855
Gassman, J. — Nordhausen, Prussia; Miles, 1854
Gastmann, Hein., 22 — Isenbüttel, Han.; Joh. Dethardt, 1848
Gastman, W.—Hannover to Houston; Weser, 1860

Gaetze, Joh. Fr. Cans — Feddelau (Federath?); Helen & Elise, 1847

Gaugler, Chrissina, 20; Elis. 19; Herschel, 1850

Gaugler, Jacob, 17; Magnet, 1852

Gebauer, Louis—Crina, Saxony; Miles, 1854

Gebhard, Urban—Bavaria; Antoinette, 1854

Gebhardt, Ferd. and family—Duderstadt; Weser, 1854; Austin Co.

Gebner, Joh. Hein.; Galliott Concordia, 1854

Geffert, Hein.; Ammerland, 1854

Gehner, Fried., 14; Magnet, 1852; Colorado Co.

Gehrcke, Daniel — Rojewer, Prussia; wife and 3 ch., ½-4 years old; Miles, 1853

Gehrcke—see also Goehrke

Gehring, Conrad—Detmold to Galveston; Gaston, 1860

Gehring, Joh. Herm. — Stughorst (Stieghorst); Solon, 1852

Gehrke, Gottl.—Bagenitz, Prussia; Therese Henriette, 1853

Gehrmann, Caspar, 18; Alexander, 1850

Geiger, C.—Ellhofen to Galveston; Iris, 1859

Geiger, L.—Darmstadt to Houston; Gaston, 1857

Geihring, Martin, 55 — Gurkow; Ann 45, Ferd. 15, Gottl. 14, Wilhme 9, Franz 3, Ludwig 12, Bertha 8, Herm. 6; Weser, 1858

Geimer, Anna—Buchhofen; Lucie, 1854

Geisler, Richard; Joh. Ed. Grosse, 1853

Geissmann, Ant. — Treikenhorst?; 2 persons; Magnet, 1851; Colorado Co.

Geistweit, Wilhme., Cath.—Joh. Ed. Grosse, 1853

Gelbke, Hein.; Galliott Concordia, 1854

Geldmacher, W., 21 — Adorf to Shelby; Iris, 1859

Geldmeyer, W. — Wehdem; Adolphine, 1859

Geles, Carl and C. Hch.—Bukbergen (Buchberg); Canapus, 1849

Gelhmann, J. G.—Warin; Leibniz, 1850

Geller, Johanna family — Friedeberg to Yorktown; Iris, 1858

Gelser, Anna, 31; Katharina. 12—Irmenach; Anna Louise, 1857

Gelzus, Maria and family—Joneiten, Poland to Yorktown; Iris, 1857

Gembler, Christian — Aurich; six persons; Neptune, 1853; Bexar Co.

Gembler, Ludwig, 75; Cath., 65; Herm. Theodor, 1850; Bexar Co.

Gentner, Ed.; Marie, 36—Liegnitz; Franziska, 1849; Fayette Co.

Gentsch, E. and wife—Freyburg; Gessner, 1854

Gen(t)sch, Fried. — Altenflies to Yorkton; Louise, Fried., Emilie, Auguste, Wilhme, Henriette, Louise, Bertha; Fortuna, 1860; Victoria Co.

Gentsch, H. and family — Freyburg; Gessner, 1854

Genz., Christ., 56; Charl. 54, Friedke 17, Alwine 12, Joh. 12, Carl Fried. 10, Carl Ferd. 6; Neptune, 1850

George, Aug., 34—Bockhorn; Franziska, 1849

Georg, C. — Oldenburg to Frelsburg; wife and 3 ch.; Juno, 1860

Gerber, H. A.—Lübeck; Weser, 1854

Gerber, Moritz, 24—Ottmanshausen to New Braunfels; Weser, 1859

Gerdes, A. — Bockhorn to Frelsburg; Fortuna, 1858

Gerdes, Grete M.—Sengwarden; Herschel, 1851

Gerdes, Heinr. with wife—to Quihi; Weser, 1857

Gerdes, J. M. Henrietta, 24; Helen Cath. Henr., 21 — Bockhorn to Galveston; Iris, 1859

Gerhard, Adelheid and Mary — Holzminden to Galveston; Fortuna, 1860

Gerhardes, Mehne — Sengwarden; Herschel, 1851

Gerhardy, Hein., 40—Düsseldorf; Solon, 1850

Gerkens, Adolph—Hamburg; Hampden, 1854

Gerlach, Julie—Böhmen; Adolphine, 1859

Gerland, Heinr. and Christine—Oedelsheim; Texas, 1853

Gerlitz, Chr. — Zicko (Zwickau?) to Austin; wife and 4 ch.; Juno, 1860

Gerloff, Georg. and Adelheid—Ottersberg; J. W. Buddecke, 1853

Gerlos, Ludwig — Beumsdorf (Boimsdorf); Neptune, 1853

Germer, Dietrich — Wenddorf, Prussia to Galveston; Basser- mann, 1851

Gerner, Ernst, 26—Kl. Biewende; Joh. Dethardt, 1848

Gernert, Stephen—Rendorf (Nen- dorf?); six persons; Hermann Theodor, 1853; Fayette Co.

Gerritz, Edo, 26 — Oldenburg to Galveston; Iris, 1859

Gerst, Carl and family—Lohausen; Weser, 1854

Gersch, P.—Buchwalde; Adolphine, 1859

Gerstenberger, Eduard — Langen- bielau, Prussia; Miles, 1854; Fayette Co.

Gersting, H.—Mackenbruch to Gal- veston; Iris, 1859

Gert, W.—Bromberg to Cypress; Fortuna, 1860

Gerth, Auguste—Leipzig to Gal- veston; Gaston, 1860

Gerves, G., 32, and lady; Herschel, 1849

Gesche, ... — Prussia to New Braunfels; Anton Gunther, 1860

Gesche, Margaretha, 46; Solon, 1850

Geschke, Carl—Stralsund, Prussia; wife and 3 ch., 5-14 years old; Therese Henriette, 1853; Colo- rado Co.

Gettwert, C. H., 58—Dresden; and Hedwig, 17; Canapus, 1848

Geu. Friedr.—Göricke, Prussia; Miles, 1852

Geu, W.—Vealgast to Houston; Iris, 1858

Geusch, Fried—see Gensch, Fried.

Geyer, Rudolph. 22; Galliott Flora, 1849; Comal Co.

Giesbers, H. and wife—Düsseldorf; Reform, 1849

Giese, Pauline—to New Braunfels; Weser, 1859

Giesel, Elis.—Pritzwalk, Prussia; 4 ch., 11-21 years old; Hampden, 1854; Austin Co.

Giesel. Herm.; Joh. Ed. Grosse, 1853; Austin Co.

Giescher, Dor. — Weinsbach to Lockhart; Juno, 1860

Giessel, J.—Posen, Prussia; wife, Marie; Franklin, 1853; Austin Co.

Giessen, Johann—Wisboe, Schles- wig to Galveston; Republic, 1851

Gigka. Joh.—Friedland; Canapus, 1849

Gildermann, Auguste — Hannover; Ernestine, Wilhme, Julie; Jever- land, 1860

Gimpel, Christian—Ungefar (An- zefähr) to San Antonio; J. W. Buddecke, 1853

Gindler, Friedricke — Braun- schweig; Texas, 1853

Gindorf, S.—Dusemond; Estafette, 1850

Glanz, L. C. F.—Penzlin; Leibniz, 1850

Glaser, Gottlieb and mother, Chris- tine — Flitzberg (Flischberg); Miles, 1854

Glaser, Louise — Golon Holaland? to Galveston; Gaston, 1860

Glass, Adolph, 32; Eduard, 31; Chas. N. Cooper, 1847; Austin Co.

Glass, Theo., 33; Anna 30, Hugo 28, Maria 30, Franz 1¼; Brasil- ian, 1850; Austin Co.

Glatz, F. and Ernestine—Breslau to Matagorda; Weser, 1860

Glauchie, Thomas, wife and child— Böhmen; Weser, 1854

Gleich, Chr.—Hoppenstedt; 4 per- sons; Texas, 1853

Gleinecke, Aug.—Hannover; Hen- riette, 1843 (1853)

Glett, Conrad, 24; Maria, 23; Gal- liott Flora, 1849

Glober, Jacob and Augustin—Dy- burg (Deibou?); Solon, 1852

Glockner. A.—Bohemia; Franzis- ka, 1854

Gloeckner, M.—to Fayetteville; Weser, 1859

Gloeckner, Therese — Neustadel (Neustädtl) to San Antonio; Iris, 1859

Gloges, Aug. and Elise — Jacob- stadt; Texas, 1853

Glueck, Franz — Kabuel, Prussia; wife and 5 ch., 0-11 years old; Therese Henriette, 1853; Austin Co.

Gmolla, Joh.—Rojamirsch; Weser, 1854

Gnigel, Heinrich, 33 — Wyscka, Prussia; Sophia, 28; Miles, 1855

Gnueske (Grueske(?), Fried., 36— Prussia; Joh. Dethardt, 1848

Gobe, Heinrich—Pritzwalk, Prus- sia; Hampden. 1854

Gober, Christoph — Reckenthien. Prussia; wife and 2 ch.. ¼ and 1¼ years old; Miles, 1852

Goebe, Franz—Werle, Mklbg.; wife and 3 ch.. 21-27 years old; Ther- ese Henriette, 1853

— 73 —

Goebel, Carl; **Joh. Dethardt, 1848;** Comal Co.

Goebel, H. — Hesse-Cassel to La Grange; **Gessner, 1860**

Goebel, Joh. and Cath.—**Joh. Ed. Grosse, 1853;** Austin Co.

Goebel, Joh. Peter, 26—Grossboch; **Antoinette, 1848;** Comal Co.

Goef, Edward, 28; Elis. 28, Emma 4, Louise 2—**Louis, 1848**

Goef, Hermann, 63; Johanna 54, Pauline 17; **Louis, 1848**

Goef, Hugo, 22; Barbara 21— **Louis, 1848**

Goehring, C. W.—Bielefeld; **Weser, 1854**

Goehring, Ferd. and family—Prussia; **Antoinette, 1854**

Goehring, Joh. — Garkau; 7 persons; **Texas, 1853**

Goehrke, Elis. — Pritzwalk, Prussia; **Hampden, 1854**

Goehrke—see also Gehrcke

Goentzel, D.—Kiebau; **Gessner, 1855**

Goessler, Herm.—Chemnitz; **Minna, 1854**

Goetel, Elis. — Lahmhof to Mill Creek; **Weser, 1858**

Goeth, Carl—Wetzlar, Prussia to Indianola; **Miles, 1852;** Fayette Co.

Goeth, Ernst—Wetzlar, Prussia to Indianola; wife and 2 ch., ½ and 1¾ years old; **Miles, 1852;** Fayette Co.

Goetz, Fried.—Buetzow, Mklbg.; **Franklin, 1852**

Goetzmann, Felix, 32; **Sophie, 1852**

Gohlke, Carl—Gurkow to Georgetown; **Weser, 1858**

Gohlke, Charles Fr.—Birkbruch to Clinton; **Fortuna, 1860;** De Witt Co.

Gohlke, J. S.—Garkau; 6 persons; **Texas, 1853;** Victoria Co.

Gohlke, Mathilde, 19 — Birkbruch to Yorktown; **Weser, 1858**

Gohlke, August, 33 — Gottschimbruch (Gottschimmerbruch), Prussia; Johann 22, Beata 63, Gottfried ¼; **Gutenberg, 1855;** De Witt Co.

Gohlke, Wilh., 9; Alwine, 7; with Schley. Wilh. family; **Weser, 1858;** De Witt Co.

Gohmert, Carl, 51; Landsberg a/ Warthe; Charlotte 56, Adolph 29, Rudolph 21, Berthold 15, Maria 13, Kobert 11; **Gutenberg, 1855;** De Witt Co.

Gohmert, Julius, 26; Wilhelm 21— Landsberg on the Warthe, Brandenburg; **Gutenburg, 1855;** De Witt Co.

Gohn, Christ.—Reckenthien, Prussia; **Miles, 1852**

Golbel, Carl—Prussia; **Neptune, 1848**

Gold, W.—Obercostenz; 6 persons; **Estafette, 1850;** Comal Co.

Goldbach, Carl—Jauer; **Colonist, 1850**

Goldberg, Christina, 31; Aug. 4— Saxony; **Joh. Dethardt, 1848**

Goldberg, Dor.—Wolfenbüttel; **Henriette, 1843 (1853)**

Goldberg, E. — Johndorf; Rosina and Anna; **Lucie, 1854**

Goldmann, Salomo—Burg Ebrach; **Solon, 1852**

Golke, Fried.; **Joh. Ed. Grosse, 1853**

Gollberg, G.—Berzdorf; 5 persons; **Neptune, 1854**

Golska, Apolonia—Gnesen; **Neptune, 1854**

Gorgass, Hein. — Schilde, Mklbg.; **Washington, 1852;** Austin Co.

Gormanns, family—Hückelhofen to Hempstead; 7 persons; **Iris, 1859**

Gormanns, Eva — Hückelhofen to Victoria; **Iris, 1858**

Gotsche, Fr. and wife; **Neptune, 1849**

Gottschald, Otto—Elterlein; **Hermann Theodor, 1853**

Gottschalk, Gottfried—Galveston; **Galliott Concordia, 1854**

Gotte, Caro., 21—Prussia; **Joh. Dethardt, 1848**

Grab family—Nassau; **Adolphine, 1859**

Graber, Meta and 3 ch.—Bremen; **Franziska, 1854**

Grabow. Ch., 28 — Reckenthin; **Hamburg, 1849;** Austin Co.

Grabow, Johann — Birkenfelde. Prussia; wife and 4 ch., 3-9 years; **Franklin, 1852;** Colorado Co.

Graeger, A.—Osterwieck to Fredericksburg; **Iris, 1860**

Graetz, C. with family—Rötgen to New Braunfels; **Iris, 1860**

Graf, A. — Wolkow to Fredericksburg; **Iris, 1860**

Graf, G.—to Fredericksburg; **Weser, 1859**

Graf, Joachim—Lasslich, Prussia; wife and 5 children; **Bassermann, 1851;** Austin Co.

Graf, Johann—Posen, Prussia; Franklin, 1853
Graf, Wilh. and Wilhme—Luckau; Texas, 1853; Fayette Co.
Grahan, Christian, 28; Hamburg, 1849
Graicher, Gottlieb—Frohburg; Henriette, 1853
Gramberg, ...—Kiel, Holstein; wife Henriette; Hampden, 1854
Grambrech, F. H.—Prussia; Neptune, 1848
Gratzen, Marie, 31; Auguste 11, Wilhme 6—Hannover; Joh. Dethardt, 1848
Graul, J.—Rohheim to Galveston; Juno, 1860
Graunhorst (Grannhorst?), Hein., 27; Solon, 1850
Graupner, Fr.—Saxony; Weser, 1860
Greis, Wilh., 45—Werdorf; Antoinette, 1848
Greisen, August, 35; Auguste 29—Landsberg on the Warthe, Brandenburg; Gutenberg, 1855
Grewe, Fred., 36, and Rosa 23—Holstein; Natchez, 1847
Griebel, Andreas, 40; Solon, 1850
Griesenbeck, Emil—Cöln; Juno, 1853; Guadalupe Co.
Griffenbeck (Griesenbeck), Carl—Cleve; Franziska, 1849; San Antonio
Grimm, J.—Bergfreiheit; Gessner, 1854; Guadalupe Co.
Grob, Auguste, 53—Perleberg; Ottilie 21, Charlotte 18; Brasilian, 1850
Grob, Georg, 33—St. Gallen; Joh. Dethardt, 1848
Grob, Regina—Offenbach, Prussia; Miles, 1854
Groben, John—Böckelheim (Bockenheim)to San Antonio; Gaston, 1860
Grodziel, P.—Grodzischko, Poland; Gessner, 1855
Groeger, Joh. and Minna—Prussia to Fredericksburg; Weser, 1860
Groff, Wilh., 24—Wolkow; Weser, 1858
Groll, Dorothea—Samter, Prussia; 2 children, 16 and 18 years; Franklin, 1852
Gronau, H. and family—Weissenfels to Fredericksburg; Gaston, 1857; Austin Co.
Groos, Hedwig—Ervitte, Prussia; Mississippi, 1855

Gross (Groos), Carl Wilh., 49; Frederick 20, Julie 19, Carl 18, Gustav 16, Emilie 14, Adolph 12, Hedwig 9, Wilhelm 6; Louis, 1848; Fayette Co.
Gross, Frederic, 33 — Werdorf; Marg. nee Gambel, 29; Wilhme 2, Fried. Carl, born on board ship; Antoinette, 1848; Austin Co.
Gross, ..., with family—Alberode to Marlin; Iris, 1858
Gross, Johann, 58 — Wünsche to Bastrop; Gertrude 58, Agnes 19; Iris, 1859
Grosse, Louis, 34—Auma; Julie 26, Ernst 4, Franz 2; Colonist, 1850
Grosselake (?) (illegible), Louis, 50; Emilie 43, Marianne 14; Solon, 1850
Grossgebauer, Dorothea, and son—Winterlingen to New Braunfels; Gaston, 1857
Grossman, Wilhelm — Kahrstadt, Mklbg; Franklin, 1853
Grote, Fried., 32 — Mackenbrück; Wilh. 22, Fritz 10, ... 8, Fried. 2; Canapus, 1848; Victoria Co.
Grote, F. W.—Berlin; Suwa, 1853; Comal Co., died before March 1855
Grote, Louis—Lobach; Reform, 1849
Grote, Moritz — Demold (Detmold?); 6 persons; Henriette, 1843 (1853)
Grote, W.—to Brenham; Weser, 1859
Groth, Doris, 25 — Wangelin, Mklbg.; Copernicus, 1852; Galveston Co.
Grothaus, Fried., 47; Charlotte 46, Auguste 14, Fritz 12, Herm 9, Louis 2, Mathilde 13, Emilie 5; Magnet, 1852; San Antonio
Grueckmaker, Louis—Havelberg to Galveston; Weser, 1857
Gruenbein, Fried. — Wittstock, Prussia; wife and 2 ch., 7 and 9 years old; John Frederick, 1850
Gruenhage(n), H. — Rehberg to Brenham; with wife, brother and 3 ch.; Weser, 1857
Gruenwald, H. — Busch, Holstein; Hampden, 1854
Gruenwald, J. F. and wife, Doris—Perleberg, Prussia; Franklin, 1853; De Witt Co.
Grueske—see Gnueske

Gruessmacher, L. — Havelberg to Galveston; Louis Gruetzmacher and family died in 1900 Galveston storm; **Weser, 1857**

Gruetzmacher, M., and 4 ch.— Spandau to Lavaca; **Fortuna, 1858**

Grupe, Friedr., 26, Friedke, 41— Borny (Borne); **Joh. Dethardt, 1848**; Comal Co.

Grussendorf, Andreas—Gifhorn; **Reform, 1849**

Grutschky, A. and wife—Königswill; **Gessner, 1855**

Guebel, Joh., 29; Dor. 24, Maria 4, Dor. 2; **John Frederick, 1850**

Guehne, Carl and family—Bautzen; 6 persons; **Mississippi, 1855**

Guelk, Claus—Nienhof, Schleswig-Holstein; wife and 1 ch., ½ yr. old; **Washington, 1852**

Guendel, M.—Bavaria; **Friedrich Grosse, 1853**

Guenther, Adolph and family (4)— Schlawinzitz (Schlawin), Pomerania; **Solon, 1852**

Guenther, Aug.—Breslau; **Neptune, 1854**

Guenther, Christiane; **Joh. Ed. Grosse, 1853**

Guenther, Ed.—Blechhammer; **Magnet, 1851**

Guenther, H.—Stuttgart; **Texas, 1853**

Guenthmann, A.—Frankfurt a/M **Franklin, 1853**

Guenzel, William — Langenbielau, Prussia; **Miles, 1854**

Guerner, Fried.—Roernitz; **Solon, 1852**

Guhl, Eduard—Pritzwalk, Schleswig; **Franklin, 1852**

Gurke, Peter, 36—Kanitz; **Canapus, 1848**

Gurken, Jos., 51; **Reform, 1850**

Gurlitz, J. C.—Bojanow, Prussia; wife and 2 ch.; **Sarah, 1851**

Gushen, Johanna—to Frelsburg; **Weser, 1859**

Guth, Carl, 26; **Louis, 1848**

Guthe, Ferd.—Andreasberg; **Texas, 1853**

Gutsu, Jos. and wife—Prussia; **Neptune, 1849**

Guttish, Johann — Böhmen; wife and son; **Weser, 1854**

Guttmann, Joachim — Kuddewar, Mklbg.; 6 persons; **Herschel, 1851**; Colorado Co.

Gutwasser, F.—Saalfeld to Frelsburg; **Fortuna, 1860**

— H —

Haafe, G.—Silesia; **Adolphine, 1859**

Haak, F.—Birkbruch to Yorktown; **Fortuna, 1860**

Haar, Joh. H.—Brockum; **Neptune, 1853**

Haase, Dorothea—Wittstock, Prussia; Ferdinand, age 15; **John Frederick, 1850**

Haase, E.—Breslau to New Ulm; **Weser, 1860**; Austin Co.

Haase, Fr. Wilh. — Zecklin, Prussia; **Washington, 1852**; Gonzales Co.

Habelmann, W.—Hamburg to Galveston; **Weser, 1858**

Habermann, Julius—Schlepuchowa, Saxony; **Franklin, 1852**; Comal Co.

Hackbell, Carl Aug.—Prussia; **Neptune, 1848**

Haeberle, Christian—Erligheim to Liverpool; **Gaston, 1857**

Haegemann, Augusta — Burgdorf; **Adolphine, 1859**

Haeneke, Jos.—Entrup; **Canapus, 1849**

Haerter, Eduard, 30—Crawinkel; **Neptune, 1850**

Haesejer (Haeseler?) Joh. P. — Wevenrode (Bevenrode or Wennerode?); **J. W. Buddecke, 1853**

Haesler, Ernst—Rothwasser, Prussia; **Therese Henriette, 1853**

Haeuseler, Lud. Theo.—Lockwinkel (Lockwinnen?) to Galveston; **Iris, 1861**

Hafer, H. with family—Oppendorf to Houston; **Weser, 1858**

Haferkorn, A. G., 46—Prussia; **Alexander, 1850**

Hagedorn, C.—Weibeck; 3 persons; **Neptune, 1853**; Austin Co.

Hagelseib, Wm., 20; **Sophie, 1852**

Hagemann, Fried., 34 — Detmold; Wilhme 39, Amalie 11, Caro., Carl; **Franziska, 1847**; Guadalupe Co.

Hagemann, Hein., 25 — Dinkelve (Dingelbe?); **Joh. Dethardt, 1848**; Galveston Co.

Hagemann, Hein., 55—Fraustadt; Dor. 49, Max 16, Rudolph 6 (died); **Hamburg, 1849**; Colorado Co.

Hagemeier, Wilh., 18; Herman **Theodor, 1850**

Hagemeister, Henriette—Lotte to Meyersfeld (Meyersville); **Weser, 1854**; De Witt Co.

Hagemeyer, C.—Sand; **Gessner,**
1854; Washington Co.
Hagen, Chr., 24, and Anton, 17—
Prussia; **Joh. Dethardt,** 1848
Hagenlocher, Rosina — Plieningen,
Württ.; **Hermann Theodor,** 1853
Hagerdorn, Ferd., 12—Hannover;
with Pastor Victor Witte; **Neptune,** 1850
Hahller (Hahler?), Fr.—Altingen;
Neptune, 1855
Hahn, Ad.—Lengefeld; wife and 4
ch.; **Lucie,** 1854; Fayette Co.
Hahn, Diedrich, 38 — Oldenburg;
Ann Marg., 38; **Franziska,** 1849;
Colorado Co.
Hahn, Heinrich—Parchim, Mklbg.;
Copernicus, 1852
Hahn, Hermann—Rühren, Mklbg.;
and family, 3 persons; **Mississippi,** 1855
Hahn, Joachim—Duepow, Mklbg.;
wife and 2 ch., ½ and 6 years
old; **Washington,** 1852; Austin
Co.
Hahn, Karl—Constanz (Konstanz),
Baden; wife and 4 ch.; **Republic,**
1851
Hahn, M.—Prussia; **Friedrich**
Grosse, 1853
Hahn, Matth.—Duebow, Prussia;
Franklin, 1852
Hahn, Selma, 19—Saxony; **Chas.**
M. Cooper, 1847
Hahn, Wilh., 14—Hannover; **Joh.**
Dethardt, 1848; De Witt Co.
Hahnel, A., 20; **Fortuna,** 1858
Hahnzog, Henriette and Julie —
Berlin; **J. W. Buddecke,** 1853
Hainhagen, A.— Corbach to Austin; **Iris,** 1859
Halberstadt, A., 23—Hamburg;
Hamburg, 1849
Halfmann, Hein., 25; **Solon,** 1850;
Colorado Co.
Halfmann, Joh. B., 26—Ludwigshausen; **Joh. Dethardt,** 1848;
Colorado Co.
Halfner, Gertrude, 19—**Louis,** 1848
Hallas, John; Theresa, Joseph;
Jeverland, 1860
Hamann. J.—Friedeberg to Yorktown; **Iris,** 1858
Hamann, Joachim — Gross-Laasch.
Mklbg.; **Hampden,** 1854; Comal
Co.
Hamann, Maria, 6 — Moellenbeck,
Mklbg.; **John Frederick,** 1850
Hamer, Carl Ludw., 16—**Hermann**
Theodor, 1850; Bexar Co.
Hamff—see Hampf

Hammerstein, Joh., 54; Cath. 50,
Annie Marie 14, Jacob 12—**John**
Holland, 1848
Hampel, G.—Prussia; 6 persons;
Friedrich Grosse, 1853
Hampf (Hamff), F. and F. —
Landsberg to Bastrop; **Iris,** 1857
Hander, Amalie Maria — Christiansfeld, Den.; **Gutenberg,** 1855;
San Antonio
Hander, Carl—Christiansfeld, Den.;
Gutenberg, 1855; Fayette Co.
Hander, Christian Wilhelm—Christiansfeld, Den.; **Gutenberg,** 1855;
Austin Co.; Falls Co. later
Hander, Julius — Christiansfeld,
Den.; **Gutenberg,** 1855; Washington Co.; McLennon Co. later
Hander, Maren, 50 (died in Comal
Co., 1856)—Christiansfeld, Den.;
Carl 22, Christian 21, Julius 18,
Maria 15, Charlotte 12; **Gutenberg,** 1855
Hane, Julius—Halberstadt; **Reform,** 1849
Hanisch, Anton—Grünwald; **Texas,** 1853; Bexar Co.
Hanitsch, ...—Moorburg; **Republic,** 1851
Hanke, Eduard, 37—Prussia; **Chas.**
N. Cooper, 1847
Hanke, Fried. Wilh.—**Joh. Ed.**
Grosse, 1853
Hanke (Hauke?), Wilh.—Burg;
Weser, 1854
Hankel, G.—Markoldendorf, Han.;
Reform, 1851; Comal Co.
Hann, Carl, 28, Christ., 24—Teichweider, Austria; **Joh. Dethardt,**
1848
Hannebal, Anton—Entrup; **Canapus,** 1849
Hannicky, Friedke, 46, widow—
Breslau; Robert 17, Adolf 13;
Colonist, 1850
Hanno, G.—Lausitz; **Weser,** 1854
Hans, Ludwig, 30—Prussia; **Chas.**
N. Cooper, 1847; Austin Co.
Hansding, J. W. and wife; **Neptune,** 1849
Hansen, Anna — Grube, Holstein;
2 ch., 7½ and 9 yrs. old; **Hampden,** 1854
Hansen, Lorenz—Sunderbord, Denmark; **Copernicus,** 1852
Hansen, H. F.(?)—Husum, Holstein; wife and child; **Bassermann,** 1851; Galveston Co.
Hanst, Anna—Wiesbaden; **Canapus,** 1849
Happes Maria, and family of 3—
Menzingen; **Solon,** 1852

Harask, Joh. Gerh., 29—Fadenberg (Fackenburg?); **Helen & Elise,** 1847
Harborth, Fried.—Dohnsen, Han.; **Neptune,** 1854; Guadalupe Co.
Harborth, W.—Dohnsen, Han.; 4 persons; **Neptune,** 1854; Guadalupe Co.
Harde, Ludwig — Bockhorn; **Magnet,** 1851; Colorado Co.
Harder, Anna—Schwetz, Mklbg.; **Sarah,** 1851
Hardtmann, Hein.—Wolfenbüttel; **Weser,** 1854
Harecke, Titus, 36—Grätz; Fanny 20, Adelms (?) 1½; **Franziska,** 1849
Harke, Peter—Mittelbreck, Prussia; **Franklin,** 1852
Harlfinger, C. with wife—Chappel Hill to Chappel Hill; **Iris,** 1858
Harms, Borchers — Sengwarden; 7 persons; **Herschel,** 1851
Harms family—to Galveston; **Weser,** 1859
Harms, John, 37; Auguste 29, Hermine 7, Doris 4; **Magnet,** 1852
Harnagel, Sophia — Holtensen, Han.; **Neptune,** 1854
Harold, Carl, 37; Louise 5, Louis 4, Hein. 3, Wilh. 26; **Reform,** 1850
Harpe, C.—Brunkhausen; **Gessner,** 1854
Harrer, C.—to Indianola; **Weser,** 1859
Harrigel family—to LaGrange; **Weser,** 1859
Harsch, Carl—Kupferberg; **Neptune,** 1853
Harsdorf. Fried., 45; Caro. 43, Louisa 18, Fried. 16, Christoph 14. Wilh. 9, Hein. 6, Emilie ½; **Solon,** 1850; Comal Co.
Hartenstein, C. A. and family—Plauen; **Weser,** 1854; Guadalupe Co.
Hartkemeier, Fried. — Destel to Brenham; Charlotte, L o u i s e; **Fortuna,** 1860
Hartmann, A. and family—Drehsa (Dreska?); **Anton Günther,** 1860
Hartmann. Fried.—Wendthagen; 4 persons; **Hermann Theodor,** 1853
Hartmann. H., 22—Solingen; **Wilhelm,** 1858; Calhoun Co.
Hartmann, Hch.—Wendthagen; **Canapus,** 1849
Hartmann. John — Koenigsborn, Schleswig; **Franklin,** 1852; Comal Co.

Hartmann, Ludwig—Wendthagen; **Herman Theodor,** 1853
Hartmann, O.—Wörlitz to Galveston; **Iris,** 1857
Hartmann, Sophia — Windhagen (Wendthagen); **Lucie,** 1854
Hartmann, W.—Hirzdorf; **Neptune,** 1854
Hartmann, Wilh. and Dor.—Hannover; **Suwa,** 1853
Hartwich, Emilie—Schwiningen; **Minna,** 1854
Hartwig, Gottl.—Rosenthal, Prussia; **Bassermann,** 1851
Hartwig, Louis, 22—Schraplau to Austin; Dor. Maria 58; **Iris,** 1859
Hartwig, Sophia; **Ammerland,** 1854
Harward, Joh.—Tholkemüt; **Herschel,** 1851
Harz, Eduard Ferdinand — Lommatsch, Bohemia; **Miles,** 1853; Kendall Co.
Haselbusch, Marie—Freiburg to Houston; **Weser,** 1860
Haselmann, Carl D.—Delmenhorst; **Neptune,** 1853
Haske, Cath., 31; Maria 4, Louise ⅗; **Creole,** 1852
Hasse. Joh.—Harzburg; **Canapus,** 1849
Hasselmann. Carl, 24 — Einbeck, Han.; **Joh. Dethardt,** 1848
Haster, Ferdinand — Landsberg, Prussia; family of 5 persons, ¼-30 years old; **Miles.** 1854
Hating. Ludwig, 24; **Brasilian,** 1857
Hattersen. James — Sunderbord, Denmark; **Copernicus,** 1852
Haubold. Herm.—Pösneck; **Neptune,** 1853; Austin Co.
Hauer. Gottfried. 34; Maria 32, Christian 10. Maria 6, Caro. ½; **Creole,** 1852
Hauke—see Hanke
Haun. Otto. 24—Mühlhausen; **Wilh.** 29; **Solon.** 1850; Fayette Co.
Haunig. Josef and Franz — Bärdorf; **Neptune,** 1853
Hausding, Emil—Sorau; **Juno.** 1853
Hauseler, Lud. Theo.—Lockwinkel (Lockwinnen?) to Galveston; **Iris,** 1861
Hauser, A.—Neustadt; **Adolphine,** 1859; Colorado Co.
Hauser, Ch. and J.—Altingen; **Neptune,** 1854
Hauser, Georg — Bruelingsdorf. Mklbg.; sister, wife. 4 ch. 2-16 years old; **Miles,** 1853
Hauser. Georg—Posen; with family of 6; **Miles,** 1853

Hauser, Joh., 33; **Magnet,** 1852
Hausmann, A.—to Galveston; **Weser,** 1859; De Witt Co.
Hausmann, A. and wife — Lippe Detmold to Meyersville; **Juno,** 1860
Hausmann, Fr.—Bohemia; **Friedrich Grosse,** 1853; De Witt Co.
Hausmann, Gottl., 50—Lippe Detmold; Louise 50, Gottl. 22, Caro. 17, Hein. 14, Wilh. 9; **Johann Dethardt,** 1848; De Witt Co.
Hausmann, J.—Bohemia; 2 persons· **Friedrich Grosse,** 1853
Haussen, Marie—Aldingen; **Adolphine,** 1859
Haverlot, W. — Upen to Schönau; **Gaston,** 1857; Comal Co.
Heber, Johanna—Wallersdorf; **Lucie,** 1854
Hecht, Carl—Grabow, Mklbg.; **Franklin,** 1853
Heckill, Charles — from New Orleans; wife and 1 ch. 3 years old; **Washington,** 1852
Heddich, G.—Heinewalde (Heimwalde?); **Neptune,** 1854
Heesch, M. Fr., 30—Bordesholm, Holstein; Maria 27, Margarethe 5, Anna 2; **Gutenberg,** 1855
Heft, Wilh—Krimmitschau (Kremetschau); **Texas,** 1853
Hegek (Hesek?), J o h a n n and wife, Joseph and Marie—Bohemia; **Weser,** 1854
Heger, F. and wife—Belgard to Galveston; **Iris,** 1857
Heger, Joh.—Wüstensachsen; **Henriette,** 1843 (1853)
Hegewalth, Rud., 25; **Fortuna,** 1858
Hegg, Fried., 34—Gebersdorf; **Colonist,** 1850
Hegmann, Albert — Wiesbaden; wife Marg. nee Rogge; Louise, daughter; Dietrich, E d w a r d; **Canapus,** 1849; Galveston
Heggemann, M. — Bardenfleth to Galveston; **Iris,** 1857
Hehr, Gottfried and Christine — Rohrdorf; **Neptune,** 1853
Hehr, W.—Langenbielau, Prussia; wife and daughter 2 years old; **Miles,** 1854; Fayette Co.
Heidemeyer, Fried.; **Herschel,** 1849
Heidenreich, Carl Henry — Dresden; **Galveston,** 1848
Heidenreich, H.; Heidenreich, J., wife and dau., age 2—Schwaan, Mklbg.; **Hampden,** 1854

Heidorn, H.—Siegfelder; **Weser,** 1854
Heilemann, J.—Oberwestnitz (Oberwestrich?); **Minna,** 1854
Heilers, Eilert, 19—Oldenburg; **Franziska,** 1849
Heiligmann, Peter—Lampoldshausen; 2 persons; **Texas,** 1853; Kendall Co.
Heilmann, Hein., 28—Saxony; **Joh. Dethardt,** 1848; Comal Co.
Heilsinger, M.—Undingen to Galveston; **Fortuna,** 1858
Heimann, J. G.—Prussia to Austin Co.; Elis., Ernst, Wilh.; **Gessner,** 1860
Heinatz, Fred., 27—Prussia; **Colonist,** 1848
Heine, A. — Hannover to New Braunfels; **Gaston,** 1857
Heine, Friedrich — Schönewitz, Prussia; **Miles,** 1854
Heine, Friedrich—Hannover; **Suwa,** 1853
Heine, Theodor—Galveston to Galveston; **Fortuna,** 1860
Heine, W.—Holzminden; **Deptune,** 1853
Heinecke, Gottfried, 38—Badersleben; **Joh. Dethardt.,** 1848; Fayette Co.
Heineke, H., 25 — Fallersleben to Houston; **Iris,** 1859
Heinemann, Caspar and Fr. Wilh.; **Joh. Ed. Grosse,** 1853
Heinemann, Friedr.—Eschwege; **Weser,** 1854
Heinemann, Fried.—Neudorf; **Texas,** 1853; Gonzales Co.
Heinemann, Wilh. and wife; **Neptune,** 1849
Heinemeier, H. — Lüridissen to New Braunfels; **Fortuna,** 1860
Heinemeyer, Johanna Soph., 52—Lüridissen; **Joh. Dethardt,** 1848; Comal Co.
Heinen, Th. — Boc(h)um to Comfort; **Fortuna,** 1860
Heinen, P. and family—Latum to New Braunfels; **Gaston.** 1857
Heinen, W. — Willig (Willich) to Comfort; Kate, Hein., Ferd., Jos., Joh.; **Fortuna,** 1860
Heinicke, Nicolaus, 39—Wentdorf; Elis. 34, Ferd. 8, Sophie 7. Fried. 6, Albertine 5; **Brasilian,** 1850; Austin Co.
Heinrich, J.—Altenhausen to Houston; **Iris,** 1860; Fayette Co.
Heinrich, Joh. Gottl.—Neuenkirch, 3 persons; **Herschel,** 1851; Colorado Co.

Heinrich, Joseph and Magda.; Jeverland, 1860; Fayette Co.
Heinrich, W., 45 — Mähren; Mrs. 40, Jos. 16, Ferd. 14; Fortuna, 1858
Heinrichs, H.—Felde to Quihi; Weser, 1857
Heinrichs, J.—Sillenstede to Galveston; Fortuna, 1860
Heinrichsen, G. and wife — Föhr to Galveston; Juno, 1860
Heins, Charles, 44; Johanne 38, Louis 14, Adolf 12, Theo. 11; Brasilian, 1850
Heinschow, F.—to Galveston; Weser, 1859
Heinsohn, Anton, 18—Faherburg; Helen & Elise, 1847
Heinsohn, Hein., 31 — Faherburg; Chaterine 33, Diedrich ¾; Neptune, 1850; Colorado Co.
Heinsohn, Wilh., 36; Meta 29, Cath. Marie 6, Dietr. Wilh. Fr. 4; Solon, 1850; Colorado Co.
Heintz, Elis.—Weppersheim (Weppersdorf?) to Indianola; Juno, 1860
Heintzky, Eugen—Mühlberg, Prussia; Bassermann, 1851
Heinz, Otto—Pforzheim to Indianola; Juno, 1860
Heinze, Friedr.—Reinerz; 4 persons; Reform, 1851
Heinzelberg, Emmerau and wife— Colbach (Calbach); Juno, 1853
Heinzelmann, J. F. A., 40; Wilhme 35, Wilh. 7, Gust. 6; Hamburg, 1849; Fayette Co.
Heinzelmann, J. F. A.—Round Top to Round Top; Wilhme, Karl; Weser, 1860
Heinzen, Johanna — Flitzberg, Prussia; Miles, 1854
Heise. Wilh., 34—Burg; Neptune, 1850; Comal Co.
Heisig. Carl—Landsberg; Texas, 1853; De Witt Co.
Heisler, Jacob. 24—St. Gallen; Joh. Dethardt, 1848
Heissig, Gottlieb; Marie—Landsberg to Yorktown; Iris, 1860
Helas. G(eorg). 43—Bautzen; Mathilde 40, Clara 12. Bernhard 6, Otto ¾, Maria 48; 8 persons; Hamburg, 1849
Helferich, Franz, 19, Marg. 61; Louis. 1848; Galveston Co.
Helferich. Paul. 23—Hesse; Chas. N. Cooper, 1847; Galveston
Hellendahl. Ludw., 35—Hannover; Dor. 36, Doris 10, Ludw. 8, Theo. 4, Georg ½; Franziska, 1847

Hell, Jac.—Hallgarten; 5 persons; ship? date?
Heller, Mathilde, 24—Oldenburg; Reform, 1850
Hellman, H. — Prussia to La Grange; Gessner, 1860
Hellman, Robt., 25; Galliott Flora, 1849; Guadalupe Co.
Hellmers, Madame Th. — Galveston; Gaston, 1857
Hellmuth, Herm., 30—Potsdam; Franziska, 1849; Fayette Co.
Helm, John — Latienne (Latien?) to Houston; Juno, 1860
Helm, J. V.—Oberbechstadt; Weser, 1854
Helmecke, Fr.—Schönebeck; Hermann Theodor, 1853
Helmers, Wm.—Bremen; Neptune, 1849; Comal Co.
Helms, Carl, 58 — Willershagen, Mklbg.; Herschel, 1855
Helms, Wilhelm—Warnow, Mklbg.; wife and son 0 years old; Therese Henriette, 1853
Helmrich, E.—Marsfeld; Gessner, 1854; Comal Co.
Helwig, Bh.—Kirchheim; Weser, 1854
Helwig, Carl — Lippe Detmold; Ammerland, 1854; Austin Co.
Hellwig, Caroline—Zirzone (Zirzow); Texas, 1853
Hellwig, Martin, 25; Galliott Flora, 1849
Hemmelmann. Elis.—Bremen; Neptune, 1854
Hemmelmann, Elis. — Bremen to Galveston; Iris, 1860
Hemmelmann. Hans C.—Prussia; Neptune, 1849
Hemmelmann. M.—Uelzen to Galveston; Gaston, 1857
Hempel. Gustav, 28; Herschel, 1849; Bastrop Co.
Henckel. Eduard and Mathilde; Brasilian. 1857
Hendrick. Carl. 25: Magnet, 1852
Hener. Gustave, 26; Wilhme 27, Bertha 2; Hener, Louis 22 and Carl 22; Louis. 1848
Hengst, Aug., 24: Herschel, 1849
Henke, Carl — Westerbrak; Neptune, 1854; Waller Co.
Henke. Fr.—Bertheim: 4 persons; Neptune. 1854; Waller Co.
Henkel, Eduard, Mathilde; Brasilian. 1857
Henkel. L.—Hesselbach to Lavaca; Iris. 1860
Henkel. P. and H.—Odenhausen to Seguin; Gaston, 1857

Henking family—to Galveston; **Weser, 1859**
Henking, Fried.—Krebshagen; five persons; **Hermann Theodor,** 1853
Henkurt, Wilh.—Wellentrup; **Weser,** 1854
Hennersdorf, August—Zwickau; **Mississippi,** 1855
Henney, Elis., 20; **Fortuna,** 1858
Hennig, August—Pulsbruch (Pulsberg?) to Yorktown; Wilhme, Carl, Emilie; **Fortuna,** 1860; Fayette Co.
Hennig, Caro.—Garkau; 3 persons; **Texas,** 1853
Hennig, H.—Hannover; **Friedrich Grosse,** 1853
Hennig, Julius—Posen; **Juno,** 1853
Henning, Fr. Wilh.—Hesse; **Solon,** 1852
Henning, Wilhelm—Roslau to Galveston; **Weser,** 1860
Henninger, Joh., 54 — Prussia; Friedke 38, Christian 20, Auguste 18, Herm. 9, Caro. 11, Pauline 6, Auguste ¼; **Franziska,** 1847; Fayette Co.
Hennings, F(riedri)ch. — Brackow (Brakau?); wife and 4 ch., 3-19 years old; **Leibniz,** 1850
Hennsmann, Fried., 28—Hamburg; Grassius 36; **Chas. N. Cooper,** 1847; Bexar Co.
Henrichs, Antoinette — Altona to Galveston; **Iris,** 1860
Henrichs, G., 44; Mario 45, 5 ch.; **Leo,** 1846
Henrichsen, H. C.—Föhr; **Leibniz,** 1850
Henrichsen, W. J., 27—Westindia (sic); **Colonist,** 1848
Henschel, Antonie—Neustadt; **Minna,** 1854
Henschel. Fr.—Neustadt; wife and 2 ch.; **Minna,** 1854
Henschel, Samuel, 20—**Hermann Theodor,** 1850
Hense, C., 35; Wilhme 39, Wilhme 7, Louise 5, Marie 2—**Fortuna,** 1858
Hensel, Aug., and wife, 3 persons —Schlieben, Prussia; **Mississippi,** 1855
Hensel, E.—to Indianola; **Weser,** 1859
Hensel, 'Samuel — Prussia to La Grange; Anna Rosina, Ernst Wilh.. C. Gottlob; **Gessner,** 1860
Hentzel, A. and J.—Friese (Friesen?) to Galveston; **Iris, 1857**
Henuber, G.—Hildesheim to Galveston; **Weser,** 1860

Henze, Andreas, 36 — Koselitz; Christiane 32, Wilh. ¾; **Weser,** 1858
Hanzel, Carl, 34—Breslau; Betty 49, Herm. 5, Emilie 8; **Colonist,** 1850
Herberhold, Joseph, 36 — Prussia to Ohio; **Joh. Dethardt,** 1848
Herbrig family—Weissenberg; **Adolphine,** 1859
Herbst, Carl—Hildesheim to Galveston, 1849; **Kendall Co.,** 1854
Herbt, Fr. Aug., 24—**Hermann Theodor,** 1850
Herburg, Dorothea—Jeinsen; **Reform,** 1851
Herdmann, Adam—Schmalkalden; **Henriette,** 1843 (1853)
Hergesell, Ch. — Thiemendorf, Mklbg.; **Franklin,** 1853; Galveston, 1859
Hergst, Joh.—Burg; **Weser,** 1854
Herle, L.—Oggersheim; **Weser,** 1854
Hermann, Aug.—Liegnitz; 6 persons; **Magnet,** 1851; Fayette Co.
Hermann, Conrad, 28; Anna 25; **Sophie,** 1852
Hermann, Julius and wife—Eisenberg; **Weser,** 1854
Hermann, Mar.; **Ammerland,** 1854
Hermann, Marianne—Heinrichsdorf; **Minna,** 1854
Hermann, Mathias, 28; Maria 29, Marg. 6, Mathias 2—**Sophie,** 1852
Hermann, Wm.—Petersdorf; 2 persons; **Magnet,** 1851; Fayette Co.
Hermann, Wilhelm—Schirstedt; **Solon,** 1852
Hermes, Wilh.; **Neptune,** 1854; Houston, Fayette Co. later
Hermischen, Cath., 58; Wilh. 3; **Franziska,** 1847
Herms, Herm — Pansin; **Reform,** 1849; Fayette Co.
Herms, Wilh., 52—Pansin; Christine 57, Adam 30, Caro. 26, Sophie 24, Friederike 22, Fried. 17; **Brasilian,** 1850; Fayette Co.
Herold, Joh. Georg, 39; Marg. nee Buchmann, 54; **Antoinette,** 1848
Herrer, G.—Baden; **Franziska,** 1854
Herrmann, Eugen, Anna; **Ammerland,** 1854
Hermann. Franz Xaver — Königgrätz; 7 persons; **Herschel,** 1851
Herrmann, F. — Gnadenfrei: wife, Benedicta nee Hander; **Magnet,** 1851; Comal Co.
Hermann. Sophia—Württ.; **Franziska,** 1854

Hersten, Adolph—Oberhausen; Solon, 1852

Hertzberg, F. — Blockwinkel to Fredericksburg; Iris, 1860

Herzberg, Michael—Broddin, Prussia to Galveston; Republic, 1851

Herzberg, Carl and Dr. Th.—Minden to San Antonio; Iris, 1858

Herzberg, T. — Minden; Texas, 1853; Bexar Co.

Herzberg, Theo, 31, Doctor—Halberstadt; Franziska, 1849; Bexar Co.

Herzger, Eduard—Dresden; Suwa, 1853

Herzig, F., 40—Mähren; Fortuna, 1858

Hesek (Hegek?), Joh., Jos., and Marie—Böhmen; Weser, 1854

Hesigelmann, J. A., 40; Wilhme 35, Wilh. 7, Gustav 6—Hamburg, 1852; see Heinzelmann, J. A.

Hess, Adam—Eisenach; Lucie, 1854

Hess, Elise—Bremerhafen to Shelby; Fortuna, 1860; Austin Co.

Hess, H.—Prussia to Galveston; Gessner, 1860

Hess, Johann and family, 9 persons—Tombach; J. W. Buddecke, 1853

Hesse, Carl—Samter, Prussia; and 2 children, 16 and 18 years; to Galveston or Indianola; Franklin, 1852

Hesse, Franciska, 25; Creole, 1852

Hesse, Michel, 29; Barbara 34, Georg 13, Michel 8, Marg. 5; Hermann Theodor, 1850

Hessig, Auguste — Michelstock (Michelstadt); Gessner, 1854

Hessler, Wilhme—Bernburg; Neptune, 1854

Hester, H. J.—Wedel to Lexington; Christine, Christiane, Louise; Fortuna, 1860

Hettmann, Anna — Hainau (Haina?) to Coleto; Iris, 1859

Heu, Peter — Heiligenhafen, Holstein; Hampden, 1854

Heuchling, Christian — See Huchting, C. Chr.

Heunecke, Heinr.—Weghold; Texas, 1853

Heunzel, Joh. F., 49—Dresden; Galliott Flora, 1849

Heur, Carol—Lobach; Reform, 1849

Heuse, Johann—Odersberg. Prussia; wife and 4 ch., 3-17 years old; Miles, 1852

Hevenig, Hein.—Herlidorf (Herlsdorf); Minna, 1854

Heyde, Christian — Berlin; Otto, Heinrich; Leibniz, 1850

Heydmann, Jost and Wilhelm — Sand; Gessner, 1854

Heydorn, J.—Driesen to Galveston; Gaston, 1857

Heyduck, Albert, and family — Gross Strelitz; Weser, 1854

Heye, Gerh.—Rastede; Texas, 1853

Heyer, F.—Torgau, Prussia; Therese Henriette, 1853

Heyer, Fritz, 53—Torgau, Prussia; Elis. 38, Mathilde 22; Herschel, 1855

Heyer, Hein, 28—Prussia; Emilie 24, Friedke 21; Colonist, 1848

Heyk, Theo. and Val.—Varel; Solon, 1852

Heyne, Fried., with wife — Rehburg to Brenham; Weser, 1857

Heyne, Ernst — Rehburg to Brenham; wife and 3 ch.; Weser, 1857

Heyne, Heinr. — Hagenburg to Brenham; Weser, 1857; Fayette Co.

Heyne, H. W., 49; Galliott Flora, 1849

Heyne, Ludwig — Rehburg to Brenham; wife and 5 ch.; Weser, 1857

Hezel, Ferd., 25—Sachsen; Franziska, 1847

Hfullmann (Pfullmann?), C. — Wingendorf; Neptune, 1854

Hilbert, Jacob — Wendtorf, Holstein; Hampden, 1854; Guadalupe Co.

Hildebrand, Edward — Podarwego; Gaston, 1860

Hildebrand, Hein.—Baderhorn (Paderborn); Franziska, 1849

Hilge, Joh.—Rastede; Texas, 1853; Grimes Co.

Hilgers, G.—Brachelen to San Antonio; Iris, 1857

Hilke, Carl — Hannover; Antoinette, 1855; Kendall Co.

Hill, Friedrich and family (6)— Dettingen; Solon, 1852

Hill, Friedrich—Weimar to Austin; Elis. and 1 child; Gessner, 1860

Hill, G. — Weimar to Austin; Christine, Julius, Eva; Gessner, 1860

Hill, Josef, 38; Marg. 36; John Holland, 1848

Hillenthal, H.—Fallersleben; with family, 5 persons; J. W. Buddecke, 1853; Harris Co.

Hiller, Friedrich—Jessnitz, Mklbg.; wife and 1 ch., ¼ year old; Copernicus, 1852; Victoria Co.

Hiller, Joh., 18; Creole, 1852

Hillert, ...—Neu-Ruppin; wife and son; John Frederick, 1850; Comal Co.

Hillert, Fried., 27—Stettin; Neptune, 1850

Hillmer, Carl Fr., 25 — Hermann Theodor, 1850; Colorado Co.

Hilscher, John — Austria; Marianne, Pauline, Veronica, Franz; Jeverland, 1860

Himer, Franz—Ollgut; Neptune, 1854

Himmelmann, Hans C.—Prussia; Neptune, 1849

Hingst, Fr. W., 40—Stralsund; Hamburg, 1849

Hinke, Hein.; Ammerland, 1854

Hinkel, Conr. and Anna — Langefeld; Texas, 23.X.1853

Hinkel, H.—Saxony; Weser, 1860

Hinkel, W.—Lengefeld; Lucie, 1854; Austin Co.

Hinkennis, Herm., 21—Baden; Franziska, 1849

Hinrichs, Ancke—Felde to Quihi; Weser, 1857

Hinrichs, Behrend, 24—Felde (died at sea); Weser, 1857

Hinrichs, Harm—Felde to Quihi; Weser, 1857

Hinrichs, Mrs. W.—Felde to Quihi; Weser, 1857

Hinselman, Hans, 32 — Schönbeck, Holstein; Maria 35, Johanne 6; Gutenberg, 1855

Hinselmann, Jacob, 36—Schönbeck, Holstein; Anna 36, Lena 14, Cath. 12, Joh. 9, Marg. 7, Henrich 5, Hans 2; Gutenberg, 1855

Hinterwinkler, Thekla—Endach; Lucie, 1854

Hintge (Hintze), Engel—to Independence; Weser, 1859

Hintz, Jochen, 36 — Brockhusen, Mklbg.; Jette 30, Sophie 12, Maria 5, Ludwig ½; Herschel, 1855; Austin Co.

Hinze, Andreas—Walle to Austin; Weser, 1857

Hinze. Franz. — Prussia to Independence; Dor., Sophie, Wilh., Christine; Weser, 1860

Hinze, G. with family—Croppenstedt to LaGrange; Iris, 1860

Hirsch, Adolph, 18 — Gonsewo (Ganzow?) to Eutaw (Utah?); Weser, 1859

Hitscher, Michael — Wenddorf, Prussia to Galveston; wite and 3 children; Bassermann, 1851

Hitz, Babette—Hausen to Austin; Iris, 1859

Hitze, Joh. Fr., 29; Solon, 1850

Hitzelmann, C.—Württemberg; Weser, 1854

Hobein, Andreas and Mathias—Ostharingen to Houston; Gaston, 1860

Hoch, A. and F.—Genf (Göns? or Gönz?)—Gessner, 1855; Fayette Co.

Hochen, Hein.—Hannover; Suwa, 1853

Hodlicka (Hrdliczka), Johann and wife—Mähren; Weser, 1854

Hoecker, Carl and Alois — Rosenthal; Neptune, 1853; Cameron Co.

Hoecker, Henriette; Ammerland, 1854; Cameron Co.

Hoefer, Fried.—Wissen; Solon, 1852

Hoehne, Fried., 24 — Kosultze to Austin; Christiane 22, Friedke 2½; Weser, 1858

Hoelscher, Wilh.—See Holscher, Wilh.

Hoerling, Anton and wife—Galveston; Weser, 1854

Hoermann, F.—Winzlar, Han.; six persons; Estafette, 1850; Fayette Co.

Hoerning, A.—Dresden to Galveston; Weser, 1858; Austin Co.

Hoertle, J.—Württ.; Franziska, 1854

Hoeser, A., 40—Prussia; Joh. Dethardt, 1848

Hoeser, Emilie — Springberg to Houston; Iris, 1860

Hoesse, Joh. and Marie; Joh. Ed. Grosse, 1853

Hofbauer, J.—Windorf; Lucie, 1854

Hofbecke, J.—Rudertshofen; Lucie, 1854

Hoff, Johann, 35 — Willershagen, Mklbg.; Caroline 27, Carl 3, Lischen ½; Herschel, 1855

Hoffers, C.—Marton (Marten?) to Houston; Weser, 1858

Hoffman, Andreas — Bergebruch, Mklbg.; son August, 23; Miles, 1853

Hoffman. Aug., 26 — Darmstadt; Chas. N. Cooper, 1847; Guadalupe Co.

Hoffman. Carl — Prussia; 4 persons; Friedrich Grosse, 1853

Hoffman, Caroline — Riggersdorf (Riegersdorf); **Mississippi**, 1855
Hoffman, E., 47; Ernestine 40, Auguste 17, Ernestine 8, Minna 4; **Fortuna,** 1858
Hoffman, Elis. — Ungefar (Anzefähr?); **J. W. Buddecke,** 1853
Hoffman, G. and family—Wolkenried (Wolkering?); **G e s s n e r,** 1854
Hoffman, Gustan, 30—Etats Unis; Urich his servant, 35; **John Holland,** 1848; Comal Co.
Hoffman, Hein.—Glogau; **Herschel,** 1851
Hoffman, Hein.—Prussia; **Antoinette,** 1854; Guadalupe Co.
Hoffman, H. and family—Liegnitz; **Gessner,** 1854
Hoffmann, Heinrich — Seedorf, Mklbg.; wife and 1 ch., age 4; **Miles,** 1852
Hoffmann, Heinrich — Posen; 4 persons; **Miles,** 1853
Hoffmann, J.—Bavaria; **Franziska,** 1854
Hoffmann, J. — Missisco (Mysdzkow?) to Houston; **Juno,** 1860
Hoffmann, John—Pudowitz to Galveston; **Gaston,** 1860
Hoffmann, J. F.—Galveston; **Neptune,** 1849
Hoffmann, Marie, 54; **Brasilian,** 1857
Hoffmann, Michael, 32; **Magnet,** 1852
Hoffmann, Peter—Prussia; **Antoinette,** 1854; Guadalupe Co.
Hoffmann, Simon — Minutsdorf, Mklbg.; wife and 4 ch., 5-17 yrs. old; **Miles,** 1852
Hof(f)meister, C.—Hildesheim to Galveston; **Juno,** 1860
Hoffmeister, Mathias, 48—Magdeburg, Prussia; Catharina 39, Minna 13, Wlhelm 7, Maria 5; **Gutenburg,** 1855
Hofmann, A. — Prussia; **Friedrich Grosse,** 1853
Hofmann, H.—Hockenau to Houston; **Weser,** 1858
Hofmann, Wilhelm—Kletzky, Prussia to Galveston; **Bassermann,** 1851
Hofring, Joh., 39; Cath. 34, Frd. 10, Christian 7—**Sophie,** 1852
Hohenberger, Ferd. — Burg; and wife; 6 persons; **Mississippi,** 1855; Gillespie Co.
Hohl. ...., (Bookbinder)—Marburg to Houston; **Iris,** 1858

Hohlt family—to Harrisburg; **Weser,** 1859
Hohlt, H., 20—Wehdem to Brenham; **Iris,** 1859
Holderbaum, Elis., 28; Carl 2— Enkirch; **Anna Louise,** 1857
Hollandson, Christine — Sörup to Galveston; **Weser,** 1860
Hollas, C., 24—Mähren; **Fortuna,** 1858
Holle, Fr. H.—Brockum; 2 persons; **Neptune,** 1853
Hollkaemner, Hein. Ludw. — See Nollkaemper, Hein. Lud.; **Solon,** 1850
Holly, Jacob, and wife—Böhmen; **Weser,** 1854
Holmeister (Hofmeister?), W., with family — Heiligendorf to Houston; **Weser,** 1858
Holscher (Hoelscher?), Wilh. and Charlotte; **Joh. Ed. Grosse,** 1853; Fayette Co.
Holst, J. A., 27—Norway; Colonist, 1848; Galveston
Holstein, H.—Galveston; **Ammerland,** 1854
Holtermann, Herm., 70; Joh. B., 26 —Ludwigshausen; **Joh. Dethardt,** 1848
Holtopp, Wilh., 33—Oldenburg; **Franziska,** 1847
Holtropp. Franz, 29—Prussia; **Franziska,** 1847
Holub, J.—Austria; **Jeverland,** 1860
Holzanfel, Eduard, 28; Louisa, 25; **Magnet,** 1852; De Witt Co.
Holzanfel, Gustav, Herm—Paderborn; **Franziska,** 1849; De Witt Co.
Holzheimer, Rudolph — Posen; **Texas,** 1853; Comal Co.
Holzinger, Friedrich — Barmen; **Weser,** 1860; De Witt Co.
Hombloch, T.—Flittard; **Weser,** 1854
Homburg, Hein., 21; Caro. 18— Wehdem to Brenham; **Iris,** 1859
Homburg, J. H., 65; F. W. 20— Westruh, Prussia; **Fortuna,** 1858
Homnighausen, Louise — Ruppershausen to Yorktown; Peter, Marie, Wilh.; **Fortuna,** 1860
Homuth, Heinrich — Freienstein, Saxony; wife and 6 ch., ¾-11 yrs. old: **Washington,** 1852; Fayette Co.
Honir Cath.; **Joh. Ed. Grosse,** 1853
Honir Dor.—Laaslich to Brenham; **Fortuna,** 1860

Honig, P.—Prussia; Friedrich Grosse, 1853
Honig, Reinhold; Galliott Concordia, 1854
Honig, Simon and Sophia; Joh. Ed. Grosse, 1853
Hook, Fried.—Erfurt; Mississippi, 1855
Hoppe, ...—Moorburg to Galveston; Republic, 1851; Bastrop Co.
Hoppe, Emilie, 45—Prussia; H. 18, A. 13, Joh. Wm. 24; Colonist, 1848; Bastrop Co.
Hoppe, Heinrich. — Samter, Prussia; wife, 4 ch., ½-8 years; to Galveston or Indianola; Franklin, 1852; Bastrop Co.
Hopper, Hein.—Hannover; Suwa, 1853
Horling, Ant., wife of—Galveston; Canapus, 1849
Hormann, Ferd., 24—Hannover; Colonist, 1848
Horn, A.—Goslar; 2 persons; Texas, 1853; Bexar Co.
Horn, Jacob—Schlierbach; Herschel, 1851; Colorado Co.
Horn, P.—to Galveston; Weser, 1859
Horning, Joh.—Sodendeck (Sodenberg?); 3 persons; Hermann Theodor, 1853; Colorado Co.
Horst, Joh., 30—Bodenhausen; Joh. Dethardt, 1848
Horstmann, Th. — Preuss Minden; Weser, 1854
Hosig, Joh. Frz., 49; Joh., 50—Lobau; Neptune, 1850
Hotte, W., with family — Oppenwehe to Houston; Weser, 1858
Hotz, Barbara — Gomaringen to San Antonio; Iris, 1858
Houchold, F.—Lengefeld; wife and 3 ch.; Lucie, 1854
Hoyer, Richard, 23—Posen; Brasilian, 1850
Hrdliczka, Joh. — See Hodlicka, Joh.
Hrnizirz, Joseph—Austria; Anna, John, Anna, Rosalie, Joseph; Jeverland, 1860
Huber, Andreas and wife—Lanzing; Lucie, 1854
Huber, Christian—Wittenberg; Suwa, 1853
Huberich, H.—Vorbeck to Houston; Weser, 1860
Huberich, Wilh., 18—Vorbech to LaGrange; Weser, 1859
Hubricht, Herm.—Oberhausen; Solon, 1852

Huchling Christian, 30 — Bockhorn; Franziska, 1849; Galveston
Huchling, Christian — Ebersbach; wife and 3 ch.; Minna, 1854; Galveston
Huchting, C. Chr. — Galveston to Galveston; Christina, Erna; Gessner, 1860
Huchting, Christine—Oldenburg; 4 persons; Texas, 1853
Hudgitz, Magdalene—Jacobswalde; and family (5); Solon, 1852; Freestone Co.
Hudner, Herm. — Gablonz; 7 persons, Texas, 1853
Huebener, E.—Prussia; Friedrich Grosse, 1853; Galveston
Huebener, Johann — Rostock, Mklbg.; Copernicus, 1852
Huebener, J. F., 19—Galveston; Galliott Flora, 1849
Huebner, Adam—Rothenberg; 3 persons; Neptune, 1853
Huebner, August—Sprinck, Prussia; dau. Johanne 17; Therese Henriette, 1853
Huebner, Christine—Sprinck, Prussia; dau. Johanne 17; Therese Henriette, 1853
Huebner, Christiane — Gros-Heinersdorf (Gross-Hennersdorf?) to San Antonio; Juno, 1860
Huebner, F.—Gablonz; 3 persons; Texas, 1853; Colorado Co.
Huebner, G.—Bautzen to La Grange; Fortuna, 1858
Huehne, Wilh., 24—Hamburg; Antoinette, 1848
Huellenthal, Henriette—Fallersleben to Houston; Fortuna, 1858 See Hillenthal, H.
Huels, Joh.—Sommersell; Canapus, 1849
Huelswede, J. H., 29; Galliott Flora, 1849
Huenich, C. Ed., 48—Dresden; Galliott Flora, 1849
Huesemann, H.—Brokum; Neptune, 1853
Hueter, Kate — Oberkaufungen to Washington (on-the-Brazos); Fortuna, 1860
Huette, Joseph—Böbervörde; Juno, 1853
Huettemann, Fried.—Johannesberg; Texas, 1853
Huhn (Kuhn), Amalie, 43—Burg; Neptune, 1850
Huhr (Huhs?), Bertha, 13; Magnet, 1852
Huick, A., 28; Herschel, 1849

Hummer, C.—Spremberg to Galveston; **Weser,** 1858
Hunsch, Carl Gottl., 39; Christiane 38, Carl Gottl. 17, Aug. 10, Ernst 8, Wilh. 7, Gottlieb 5; **Joh. Dethardt,** 1848
Huppe, Chr., 36; Lizette 30—Merschede ('Meschede); **Canapus,** 1848
Hupperts family—Battheim to San Antonio; 10 persons; **Iris,** 1859
Hurccack, J. and wife—Gacenka to Industry; **Juno,** 1860
Hurtting, Robert—Prussia to Brenham; Caro., Louise; **Weser,** 1860
Hurtz, Wilhelm—Kletzke, Prussia to Galveston; **Bassermann,** 1851
Hussmann, Jacob and Marg.— York to Frelsburg; **Fortuna,** 1860
Huth, Christian and Johanna—to LaGrange; **Weser,** 1859
Huth C. H., 30—West Prignitz to Houston; **Iris,** 1859
Huth, Gottfried, 28; Wilhme 25, Louisa ¾; **Magnet,** 1852
Huth, Louis—arrived before 1851; married Sophie Louise Kühlman Medina Co. 1851; Bexar Co. 1875
Huth, Peter, 33; Marienwörder; Julie 25; **Brasilian,** 1850
Huttel, Herm., 29; **Reform,** 1850; Fayette Co.
Hutter family—to Houston; **Weser,** 1859

— I —

Ickert, Charlotte, Amalie; Prussia to Galveston; **Anton Gunther,** 1860
Idens, Joh. and wife — Wrisse to Meyersville; **Weser,** 1857
Ideus (Idens?) family — to Maisville (Meyersville?); **W e s e r,** 1859
Idstein, H.—Oestrich; 2 persons; ship? date?
Ifatzing (Pfetzing), Conrad—Sterkelshausen; **Texas,** 1853; Galveston Co. See Pfetzing, Conrad
Ihle, F.—Serno; **Adolphine,** 1859
Ilgen. Wilhme — Schmalkalden to Galveston; **Fortuna,** 1860
Illek, Joh.; **Galliott Concordia,** 1854
Illig, Carl—Weiler; **Neptune,** 1855; Comal Co. or Colorado Co.
Immke, G.—Schweiberg to Frelsburg; **Iris,** 1858

Ingenueth (Ingenhuett?), H.— Nassau; **Franziska,** 1854; Kendall Co.
Ingermann, Petronella—Aachen to Galveston; and Metzger, Daniel (listed together on ship list); **Weser,** 1860
Inholt, Elizabeth, 24—Ludwigshausen; **Joh. Dethardt,** 1848
Isenbuehl, L.—Landon (London?); **Gessner,** 1855
Iske, W.—Heiligenrode; **Gessner,** 1854

— J —

Jacke, Michael — Lüneburg; and family, 5 persons, 3-27 yrs. old; **Hampden,** 1854
Jacoby, Hein.; **Galliott Concordia,** 1854
Jacoby, Lina, 14; **Magnet,** 1852
Jaeckel, F.; **Adolphine,** 1859; San Antonio
Jaeckel, Math.—Friedland; **Canapus,** 1849; Bexar Co.
Jaeger family, 4 persons — Versmold to Galveston; **Iris,** 1859
Jaeger, Franc—Neudorf to Richmond; Euphosine, Hulda, Fried.; **Fortuna,** 1860
Jaeger, Fried. and H.—Mecklenburg to Lexington; **Fortuna,** 1860
Jaeger, John—Leipzig to Galveston; **Iris,** 1860; John Jaeger and wife died in Galveston storm, 1900
Jaeger, Johann—Landsberg, Prussia; wife Anna; **Miles,** 1854
Jaeger, Michael—Dettingen; and family (6); **Solon,** 1852
Jaeggli, Pastor R. — Switzerland; **Juno,** 1860; Fayette Co. 1870
Jaehnke, Carl — Friedrichsberg; and wife—4 persons; **Mississippi,** 1855
Jaeker, Therese—Ervitte, Prussia; **Mississippi,** 1855
Jahn, Carl, 23; Jahn, G(ottlieb), 48, died; Maria, 35, died; Maria 14, Wilhme 12, Emelia 5/6; **Hamburg,** 1849
Jahn, J. C., 17; **Galliott Flora,** 1849
Jain, H(er)r A.—Adorf; **Hamburg,** 1849
Janda, C.—Austria; **Jeverland,** 1860; Fayette Co.
Janda, John—Austria; Anna, Veronica, John, Pauline, Veronica; **Jeverland,** 1860

Janda, Veronica—Austria; Jeverland, 1860
Janecek, Wenzel, Anna — Vienna; Suwa, 1853; Austin Co.
Janeczeck, E. — Böhmen; Weser, 1854
Jangsen, A.—East Friesland to San Antonio; Gessner, 1860
Janick (Janicek), Vincenz and son Austria; Jeverland, 1860
Janisch, Aug., 29—Mecklenburg; Alexander, 1850
Janisch, C. Theo, 33—Mecklenburg; Alexander, 1850
Janke, Ernestine—Altendorf to Richmond; Iris, 1860
Janke, Fr. — Lenzen to Brenham; Kate, Albertine, Aug., Rudolph, Caro., Herm., Theo.; Fortuna, 1860
Janke, J. with family—Grosswerdenhausen to Richmond; Iris, 1860
Janowsko, Anna—Velgast to Houston; Iris, 1858
Jansen, Anna and Gesine—Oldenburg to Galveston; Iris, 1859
Jansen, Berend—Winsen; Texas, 1853
Janson, C.—Falkenberg to Galveston; Iris, 1860
Janssen, D. — Jeggeborn (Jägerborn?) to Galveston; Iris, 1858
Janssen, G. with family — Kniphausen to Round Top; Iris, 1857
Janssen, H. with family — Bretewalden to Industry; Weser, 1858
Janssen, Hein., 36—Holstein; Maria 24, Ludw. 4, Hein. 1; Colonist, 1848
Januecke, Otto—Neustadt to Galveston; Weser, 1860
Japhen, Joh., 65—Oldenburg; Jüinke 50, Joh. 34, Jüinke 32, Marie 23, Anna 20; Franziska, 1847
Jarhof, Joh., 42—Oldenburg; Franziska, 1849
Jarigegeke, Joh., 38; Rosina 38, Catarina 6; Brasilian, 1857
Jegel family—to Petersburg; Weser, 1859
Jenander, Charles — Strömstadt, Sweden; Mississippi, 1855
Jende, J. C.—Sagan to Galveston; Fortuna, 1860
Jenull, Jos.—Kärnthen; 2 persons; Reform, 1851
Jepp. Detlev Heinrich—Rönnfeldholz, Holstein; wife and 4 ch., 3-17 yrs. old; Copernicus, 1852
Jeremia, J.—Belgien; Adolphine, 1859

Jeremias, Carl; Ammerland, 1854
Jessen, Joh. Henrik, 36 — Svendborg, Denmark; Gutenberg, 1855
Jirasch family, 3 persons—Vienna; Suwa, 1853
Jochem, G. with family—Köselitz to New Ulm; Iris, 1860
Joelke, G.—Klein Johnsdorf; 6 persons; Neptune, 1854
Joglowik, A.—Borisch (Boritz) to Galveston; Iris, 1860
Joffe (Jaffe?), Caro., 21—Prussia; Joh. Dethardt, 1848
Johanss, Heinrich—Zühr, Mecklenburg; Copernicus, 1852
John, Mrs. Anna — Bohlendorf, Prussia; Therese Henriette, 1853
John, H. A. F., 41—Hamburg; Dor. 39, Aug. 8, Hein. 7, Johanne 5, Bertha 5; Brasilian, 1850; Austin Co.
John, Wm., 24—Prussia; Colonist, 1848
Jonischkies, J. — Rabkahven to Yorktown; Iris, 1857
Jordan, Carolina—Bremen to Galveston; Iris, 1860
Jordan, Ernst — Prussia; Franziska, 1854; Mason Co.
Joska, Vencent and family—Prussia; Antoinette, 1854
Josting, F.—Holsen; Lucie, 1854; Colorado Co.
Juelfs, Carl—Jever to Galveston; Weser, 1857
Juelfs, Karoline and daughter—to Galveston; Iris, 1858
Juelfs, Otto—Galveston to Galveston; Juelfs, Otto—Oldenburg to Galveston; Fortuna, 1860
Juenemann, Franz—Duderstadt; Weser, 1854
Juenemann, Louis—Galveston; Weser, 1854
Juengst, Ferdinand, 24; Frederike 13, Hermann 10; Sophie, 1852
Juengst, Joh., 55; Henriette 45, Ferd. 24, Johanna 20, Amalia 18, Friedke 13, Herm. 10, Aug. 6; Sophie, 1852
Juergen, H.—to Galveston; Weser, 1859
Juergens, Fried. — Hannover; Suwa, 1853; Colorado Co.
Juergens, Joh. H. — Moorburg to Galveston; Republic, 1851; Austin Co.
Juergens, W.—Hannover; Jeverland, 1860
Juhl, August and mother, Henriette — Swinemuende, Prussia; Miles, 1854

Junck, Gustav with family, 8 persons—Cöln (Köln); **Juno,** 1853
Juncke, Georg, 20; Henriette 24—Einbeck; **Joh.** Dethardt, 1848
Jung, Anton and family; **Ammerland,** 1854
Jung, Elise and family—Burg to San Antonio; **Iris,** 1857
Jungmann, Mathias, 28; Gertrude 26, Mathias 2, Cath. 54, Joh. 17, Peter 15, Nic. 12; **Sophie,** 1852, Medina Co.
Jungmichel, G.—Wallersdorf; **Lucie,** 1854
Junk, Sigismund—Berlin; **Suwa,** 1853
Junker family, 3 persons, and Cath. — Riechenbach; **Iris,** 1859; De Witt Co.
Jureck, Rosalie—Austria; **Jeverland,** 1860
Jurgens — See also Juergens
Jurgens, W.—Wehdem to Galveston; with family; **Weser,** 1858
Jurgensen, H. A., 26 — Holstein; Elise 21; **Colonist,** 1848
Jurt, C.—Welzin to Indianola; **Juno,** 1860
Jury, Carl — Havelberg, Prussia; wife and 2 ch., ¾ and 3 years old; **Washington,** 1852
Jusina, Marianne—Austria; **Jeverland,** 1860
Juspann, Gottl.—Hannover; **Canapus,** 1849
Justy, L. — Giseldorf to San Antonio; **Weser,** 1860
Jutte, Christian—Ervitte, Prussia; **Mississippi,** 1855

— K —

Kaatz, J.—Templeburg; **Neptune,** 1854
Kabella, Franz — Neponek (Nepomuk?) to Cat Spring; wife and 2 sons; **Iris,** 1861
Kachler, Albert, 22—**Louis,** 1848
Kadgchen, Otto and wife — Riga, Prussia to Galveston; **Sarah,** 1851
Kadlescheck, Rosina — Gacenka (Jasenka) to Industry; **Juno,** 1860
Kadner, Karl — Ramenau (Rappenau?); **Minna,** 1854
Kaemmlein, Auguste—Gurkow to Yorktown; **Fortuna,** 1860
Kaese, H.—Halle; **Neptune,** 1854

Kaesse, Andreas — Bernburg to New Ulm; Dorothea, Friedke, Franz, Karl, Albert, Ernstine, Caro.; **Weser,** 1860
Kahl, Carl Fr.—Roenfeldholz, Holstein; **Copernicus,** 1852
Kahlbau, Friedrich and wife—Reckenzien, Mecklenburg; **Copernicus,** 1852
Kahlbau, F. — Perleberg, Prussia; wife and daughter, Mine 19; **Franklin,** 1853
Kahn, Andreas, 56; **Brasilian,** 1857
Kailing, Barbara; **Galliott Concordia,** 1854
Kaiser, ...—Moorburg to Galveston; **Republic,** 1851
Kaiser, Ernst; **Galliott Concordia,** 1854
Kaiser, Joh. Georg.—Irringenhausen; **Hermann Theodor,** 1853; Fayette Co.
Kalbaar, Alvin, 38; — Elberfeld; Gertrude 30; **Franziska,** 1849
Kalbau, Friedrich—Dalmin, Mecklenburg; **Copernicus,** 1852 See also Kahlbau, F.
Kaleb, Mathias and wife—Böhmen; **Weser,** 1854
Kalina, Jos. — Neponek (Nepomuk?) to Cat Spring; with wife and 2 children; **Iris,** 1861
Kaling, Ludwig, 24; **E. von Beaulieu,** 1857
Kalker, Caspar and family—Kadlup; **Weser,** 1854; Bandera Co.
Kalthof, Anton—to Frelsburg; **Weser,** 1859
Kaltwasser, A.—Seebergen· to Austin; **Iris,** 1860
Kalzben, Peter, 30; **Anna Louisa,** 1857
Kamann, H.—Mannheim; **Iris,** 1857
Kammann, Wilh., 42—Burg See Kammerer, Wilh.
Kammer, H.—Alt-Gebhardt, Mecklenburg; daughter Anna, 2 years old; **Franklin,** 1853
Kammerer (Kammann?), Wilh., 42—Burg; **Neptune,** 1850
Kamp, F.—Tempelburg; **Neptune,** 1854
Kampe, Karl and Mathilde—Weferlingen to Galveston; **Weser,** 1860
Kampe, W., 24; **Fortuna,** 1858; Austin Co.
Kampert, Bernhardt, 23; **Solon,** 1850
Kanneman, Johanna—Suhl; **Gessner,** 1854

Kanter, ...—Duisburg to Galveston; **Iris,** 1858
Kanti, Simon—Jacobswalde; **Solon,** 1852
Kaper, Marie—to Galveston; **Weser,** 1859; August Kaper, wife and 1 child died in Galveston storm, 1900.
Kapke, Ed, 17—Berlin; **Helen and Elise,** 1847
Kapke, Helene Sophie — Rastederberg; **Helen and Elise,** 1847
Kapke, Joh. Hr., 35—Jübar; Wilhme 32, Fr. 9, Wm. 5; **Helen and Elise,** 1847
Kapp, Ernst, 41—Minden; Ida 41, Antonie 14, Alfred 12, Eulie 9, Hedwig 6, Wolfgang 3; **Franziska,** 1849; Sisterdale, Kendall Co.
Kapp, Otto, 17—Hannover; **Franziska,** 1849
Karbisch, Agnes—**Joh. Ed. Grosse,** 1853
Karflang, Cath., 24—Langwarden; **Canapus,** 1848
Karger, G. with family—Falkenberg to New Braunfels; **Iris,** 1860
Karney, Aug., 24—Lübeck to Yorktown; **Weser,** 1858
Karsch, Caro.. 35; Auguste 15, Carl 10 — Wistawallersdorf to Galveston; **Iris,** 1859
Karstens, Maria, 31—Holstein; **Alexander,** 1850
Karsten. Widow—Oppendorf; **Adolphine,** 1859
Kartel, Abertine; **Joh. Ed. Grosse,** 1853
Kartlang, Cath.. 24—Langwarden; **Canapus,** 1848
Kasemacker, Aug.. 45—Hannover; **Joh. Dethardt,** 1848
Kasser, F.—Bernburg; **Neptune,** 1854
Katt, Ernst and Louise; **Joh. Ed. Grosse,** 1853; Guadalupe Co.
Katting. G.—Mileslobitz (Milostowitz) to Galveston; **Weser,** 1852
Kattman, Fried., 29; Julie 22; **Magnet,** 1852
Kattner, Aug., 30; Robert 28—Breslau; **Colonist,** 1850
Katzmann, Christ., 33 — Bordesholm, Holstein; Marg. 33, Auguste 5, Wilhme 2; **Gutenberg,** 1855
Kauffer family—to Frelsburg; **Weser,** 1859
Kaufmann, Ad.. 27—Breslau; **Colonist,** 1850; Fayette Co.

Kaufmann, Madame C. and child—Galveston; **Neptune,** 1853; Mrs. Charles Kaufmann died in 1900 Galveston storm.
Kauffmann, Christian, 28—Galveston; **Creole,** 1852
Kauffman, J.—Galveston; **Neptune,** 1848
Kaule, Gotthelf—Berlin; **Suwa,** 1853
Kaup, Carl, 25; **Galliott Flora,** 1849
Kaupert, Lorenz—Wustensachsen; **Henriette,** 1843 (1853)
v. d. Kauss, Joh. Chr., 29—Oldenburg; Helene 28; **Joh. Dethardt,** 1848
Kayser, Frederic, 57; Gesina nee Kanning, 55, Gesina 16; **Antoinette,** 1848
Keidel, Moritz, 39 — Cahla; Johanne 40, Moritz 14½, Carl 13, Caro. 12, Franz 8, Adolf 10, Ernst 6, Jos. 4; **Hamburg,** 1849
Keim, Gertrude—Schlierbach; **Herschel,** 1851
Keiser, Fr.—Grube, Prussia; wife and 4 ch.; **Bassermann,** 1851; Medina Co.
Keitmann, Ludwig, and wife — Greifswalde, Prussia to Galveston; **Sarah,** 1851
Keitz, Johann—Landenhausen; **Weser,** 1854; Galveston
Kellenbeck, W., 27; **Herschel,** 1849
Keller, Carl, 20; **Louis,** 1848; Mason Co.
Keller, J.—Greifensee, Switz.; **Lucie,** 1854; Fayette Co.
Keller. S.—Muncyfey?; **Neptune,** 1854
Kellermann, Fr., 59—Hanniar?; **Canapus,** 1848
Kellermann, H., 25, and lady; **Herschel,** 1849
Kellers, John—Galveston; **Neptune,** 1854
Kellersberger, H(er)r Julius, 28—Baden; **Hamburg,** 1849
Kellner, Eduard and family—Hannover; **Weser,** 1854; Austin Co.
Kempe, F.—Gros Eder to Houston; **Juno,** 1860
Kemper, Franz—Ervitte, Prussia; **Mississippi,** 1855
Kemper, Theo. B., 40; Elis. 29, Lucia 3/6; **Reform,** 1850
Kendler, Carl—Saxony; **Friedrich Grosse,** 1853
Keneweg. Joh.—Centaver; **Weser,** 1854
Kenna, Mathilde, 24 — Hannover; Hermine 3; **Franziska,** 1847

Kennecke, Carl—Burg; Herschel, 1851
Kennecke, Heinrich—Fallersleben; J. W. Buddecke, 1853
Kensling, Fr. Wilh.—Mackenbrüch; Reform, 1849
Kentz, Carl, 28—Prussia; Maria 24; Colonist, 1848
Kerbs, B.—San Antonio; Gessner, 1855
Kertzell, Joh.—Mausbach to Houston; Weser, 1857
Kesiling, Carl, 31—Frankenstein; Colonist, 1850
Kessel, Friedr.—Prussia; Antoinette, 1854
Kessig, Sophia; Ammerland, 1854
Kessler, Albert—Hannover; Solon, 1852
Kessler, Caroline and Emilie — Hannover; Texas, 1853
Kessler, Kuno—Hannover; Solon, 1852
Kessler, V.—Saxony; Lucie, 1854
Kessling, Franz, 24; Solon, 1850
Kestel, Joh. Gust., 46; Charl. 48, Caro. 18, Auguste 14; Hermann Theodor, 1850
Kettenburg, Marie — Lübeck to Galveston; Iris, 1861
Kettmann, C.—Koethen to Austin; Weser, 1860
Kettmann, Wilh. and Friedke — Meindorf to Austin; Weser, 1860
Kettner, Franz (Francis)—Baden to Galveston, 1848; Gillespie Co.
Keuffel, Wilh. — Koenigsborn, Schleswig to Galveston or Indianola; Franklin, 1852; Austin Co.
Keylich, Franz — Detmannsdorf; Reform, 1849
Keyser, Charlotte, 26—Engter; Antoinette, 1848
Kieche, Aug., 25—Schilde; Brasilian, 1850
Kiecke, August and Christ.—Wittenburg, Prussia; Therese Henriette, 1853
Kiefer, Cath. and Fz (Franz?)—Mülheim; Estafette, 1850
Kiefer, Hermann, 27; Louis, 1848
Kiehl, Julius, 30—Vorbrück; Weser, 1858
Kieler, Cor., 29—Rastedeburg; Helen & Elise, 1847
Kielholz, Hein., 26; Magnet, 1852; Austin Co.
Kielmeyer, Carl, 30; Sidonia 23; Solon, 1850
Kieschna, Wilh. — Varrup (Vorhup?) to Austin; Gaston, 1860

Kiesel, Joh. Hr., 34—Langwarden; Cath. 27, Henriette 4; Canapus, 1848; Colorado Co.
Kiesel, Wilhelm; Wilhme — Frelsburg to Frelsburg; Weser, 1860
Kiess, Joh. Gottl.—Plieningen; Solon, 1852
Kilbride, Sophie, 32 — Walsrode, Han. to Galveston; 2 ch., 2 and 6 years old; Miles, 1852
Kilian, Ferd.—Cothen (now Kothen); Canapus, 1849
Kilmer, Ch.—Landau; Neptune, 1854
Kinbel, Franz; Anna Louise, 1857
King, Frederick, 42 — Detmold; Wilhme 37, Fried. 17, Wilh. 13, Aug. 11, Pauline 10, Herm. 6; Franziska, 1847
King, Hein., 30—Breslau; Colonist, 1850
Kinne, Gottfried—Osterwik; wife and ch.; Henriette, 1843 (1853); Austin Co.
Kipling, Johann, 20; Herschel, 1850
Kirchner, Carl, 45 — Thomasdorf, Prussia; Johanna 43, Auguste 22, Ernestine 20, Carl ½; Gutenberg, 1855
Kirchner family—to Galveston; Weser, 1859
Kirchner, W(ilh)., 36 — Prussia; Hamburg, 1849; Bandera Co.
Kirke, Wilh., 27; Natchez, 1847
Kirlinche, A. with wife—Jonaiten to Yorktown; Iris, 1857
Kirschner, Henriette; Ammerland, 1854
Kiselint, Andreas, 31—Klein-Saubernitz to Houston; Johanna 25, Marie 6, Johann 3, Helena 1; Iris, 1859
Kitschke family — Falkenburg; Adolphine, 1859
Kittel, Herm. and Christiane—Berlin; Suwa, 1853
Kittlemann, Otto — Torgau, Saxony to Galveston or Indianola; Franklin, 1852
Kittner, Franz, 33—from France; Louis, 1848. See Kettner, Franz.
Kittrer, A.—Württ.; Franziska, 1854
Kitzfelder, Leonhard, 26; Barbara, his wife, 26; John Holland, 1848
Klaffke, Fried., 44 — Gottschimmerbruch, Brandenburg; Wilhme 38, Ernestine 10, Joh. 8¼; Gutenberg, 1855
Klancke, Louise and Sophie; Brokum (Brockum); Neptune, 1853

Klanke, H.—Hannover; wife and 2 ch.; **Franziska, 1854**
Klappenbach, Friedricke and Minna — Lehburg (Lehbach?) to Fredricksburg; **Iris, 1859**
Klatt, H., 30; **Herschel, 1849**
Klatte, Hanna—Callies to Austin; **Weser, 1857**
Klebe, Carl Fr.—Landsberg; five persons; **Neptune, 1853**
Kleben, K.—Haselberg; **Gessner, 1855**
Kleibring family—Oppendorf; **Adolphine, 1859**
Kleid, Niklas—Heinzenbach; wife and 7 ch.; **Minna, 1854**
Kleien, Louis—to New Braunfels; **Weser, 1859**
Klein, Adam, 18; **Brasilian, 1857;** Gonzales Co.
Klein, Elis.—Hesse; **Friedrich Grosse, 1853**
Klein family—Berlin; 5 persons; **Suwa, 1853**
Klein, F.—Burg; with family, 5 persons; **J. W. Buddecke, 1853;** Kerr Co.
Klein, Wilhelmine and child—Callies to Austin; **Weser, 1857**
Kleine, Aug. and Fried.—Prussia; **Franziska, 1854;** Gonzales Co.
Kleine, Wilh., 15—Münster; **Franziska, 1849**
Kleinecke, Auguste. 17; Christiane 14; **Reform, 1850**
Klement, Aug. — Guz, Prussia to Indianola; **Miles, 1852**
Klengechman, Louis, 15—Bremen; **Franziska, 1849**
Klenger, M.—Prussia; **Friedrich Grosse, 1853**
Klettner, Marie—Neustadt; **Adolphine, 1859**
Kleugebeil, Herm.—Merseburg; **Minna, 1854**
Kliemt, Joh. Traugott—Derschka (Drescha?); 6 persons; **Herschel, 1851**
Klier. William—from Gillespie Co. to Gillespie Co.; **Gaston, 1860**
Kliever, Wilh.—Meschede; **Neptune, 1854**
Klint, Johann — Nienhoff, Schleswig-Holstein; **Washington, 1852**
Klitzing. F.—Havelberg to Galveston; **Fortuna, 1858**
Klitzing family—to Galveston; **Weser, 1859**
Klober, Susanna—Darmstadt; five persons; **Suwa, 1853**
Klockmann, C. — Croppenstedt to La Grange; **Iris, 1860**

Klockow, Hein.—Klinken, Holstein; wife and 3 ch. ¾-14 years old; **Washington, 1852**
Kloepper, Antoinette, 43—Hannover; Jacob 20, Hein. 13, Johanne 9, Ernst 7; **Franziska, 1847;** Comal Co.
Klopmann, H.—Granzin; **Leibniz, 1850**
Klopp, Fr., 27; **Helen & Elise, 1847**
Kloppenberg, G. and family—Kniphausen to Round Top; **Iris, 1857**
Kloppstock, Fredrich — Callies to Austin; wife and 4 ch.; **Weser, 1857**
Klose, Ernst, 24—Meisse(n?) (or Neisse?); **Colonist, 1850**
Klostermann, B.—Oldenburg to Galveston; **Gessner, 1860**
Kloth, Wilhelm — Penwick, Mecklenburg; **Copernicus, 1852;** Colorado Co.
Klotz, Detlev, 25—Neumuenster, Holstein; **Gutenberg, 1855**
Kluge, Wilh.—Langenbielau, Prussia; wife and 1 ch. 4 years old; **Washington, 1852**
Kluge, G.—Welzin to Indianola; **Juno, 1860**
Kluick, Asmus, 28 — Holstein; **Chas. N. Cooper, 1847**
Klumm, Carol (Carl?)—Saxony; **Neptune, 1849**
Klump, Aug., 24—Bavaria; **Chas. N. Cooper, 1847;** Austin Co.
Klungers, Wilhelmine and family —Prussia; **Antoinette, 1854**
Klunker family — Berlin; 3 persons; **Suwa, 1853**
Kluth, Hein. — Klinken, Holstein; **Washington, 1852.** See Knuth, Dor.
Kluts, J.—Foehr to Galveston; **Juno, 1860**
Knacker, Christine — Wüstensachen; **Henriette, 1843 (1853)**
Knacksuss, Charles Louis, 22 — Prussia; Hein. Etzel (his domestic), 23; **John Holland, 1848;** Bexar Co.
Knacksuss, Gustav. 36 — Sachsen; Babette, 35, Sophia 8; **Chas. N. Cooper, 1847**
Knapp, Alwin and Carl; Prussia; **Neptune, 1849**
Knapp, H.—Eilborn; 5 persons; ship? date?
Knauer, D. and G.—**Gessner, 1855;** San Antonio.
Knaumpkan. Louis, 19—Prussia; **Colonist, 1848**
Knaus, Carl—Gemünd; **Texas, 1853**

Knebel, K.—Boehmen; **Friedrich Grosse,** 1853

Knierim, G.—Rückeburg (Rüggeberg?) to Marlin; **Iris,** 1858

Knipscheer, Joh., 31 — Elberfeld; Johanna 41, Friedke 13, Clement 7, Johanne 4, Carl 11, Helene 11; **Joh. Dethardt,** 1848; Fayette Co.

Knobloch, Aug.—Jaulsdorf; **Neptune,** 1854

Knoche, Joh.; **Joh. Ed. Grosse,** 1853

Knoche, Joh.; **Galliott Concordia,** 1854

Knoedel, J.—Maulbronn; **Neptune,** 1854

Knoerth, Gottl.—See Kuerth,Gottl.

Knolle, Fr. and Philipine—Krebshagen; **Canapus,** 1849; Austin Co.

Knopflauch, A.—Wernitz to Bastrop; **Iris,** 1857

Knoppick, Jos. and family—Tost; **Weser,** 1854

Knoth, Wilhelmina 42, and Wilhelme 12; **Herschel,** 1850

Knueppel, Joh., 61—Lassan; Louise 50, Ferd. 26, Ernst 24; **Neptune,** 1850

Knuesli, Konrad—Uster, Switz.; **Lucie,** 1854

Knuetter, Eduard—Gartz, Prussia; wife and 4 ch., ¾-6 years old; **Washington,** 1852

Knuth, Dorothea, 21 — Kiel, Holstein to Galveston or Indianola; **Franklin,** 1852. See Kluth, Hein.

Knuth, Friedrich — Gross-Klonid ('Gross-Klonia), Prussia; **w i f e** and 3 ch., 0-14 years old; **Theresa Henriette,** 1853

Kobs, Fr., 47—Kalbe; Friedke 17, Carl Fr. 15, Friedke 11; **Canapus,** 1848

Kober, H. and Sophie — Breddin, Prussia; **Franklin,** 1853

Koch, Barbara—Hintersbüren; **Solon,** 1852

Koch, Carl — Breddin, Prussia; wife and 2 ch., 1½ to 6 years old; **Washington,** 1852

Koch, Carl—Coswig; **Neptune,** 1853

Koch, Carl, 23; Dor. 25, Ludwig ¾; **Herschel,** 1850

Koch, Carl, 24 — Hamburg; **John Frederick,** 1850; Austin Co.

Koch, Christian, 18 — Hamburg; **John Frederick,** 1850; Austin Co.

Koch, Christian, 20—Hamburg; **Creole,** 1852; Austin Co.

Koch, Christ. — Breddin, Prussia; Christoph and wife and 2 ch., 1 and 3 years old; **Franklin,** 1853

Koch, Christoph, 26; **Sophie,** 1852

Koch, Emil and Bertha; **Neptune,** 1849; Austin Co.

Koch, Ernst—Cassel; **Neptune,** 1854

Koch, Fried.—Halberstadt; **Texas,** 1853; Fayette Co.

Koch, Fried., 48—Lassan; Aug. 34, Ernestine 28, Auguste 12, Alwine 6, Fried. 5, Peter 2, Christian ¾; **Neptune,** 1850

Koch, G. — Mengershausen to Round Top; **Weser,** 1857; Austin Co.

Koch, Henriette and Emilie — Bromberg to Richmond; **Iris,** 1859

Koch, J., 48 — Hintersteinau to Brazoria; Marg. 19, Elisa. 15; **Iris,** 1859

Koch, Joh.—Burghassungen; six persons; **Texas,** 1853

Koch, Johann—Hamburg; **Sophie,** 1852

Koch, Johannes—Hundshausen; **Herschel,** 1851

Koch Joh. George — Plieningen, Württ.; **Texas,** 1853; Galveston Co.

Koch, Julie; **Hamburg,** 1849

Koch, Karl—Wildungen to Industry; **Iris,** 1859

Koch, Louis, 40—Osnabrück; **Colonist,** 1850

Koche, Gustav and Amalie—Saxony; **Neptune,** 1849

Kochen family—to Richmond; **Weser,** 1859

Koegler, Daniel and family (4)— Schauenhausen; **Solon,** 1852

Koegler, Ignaz.—Glatz to Industry; Josephine. Theodor. Hyronimus, Alnif; **Fortuna,** 1860

Koehl, Chr.—Kosolof (Kosolup?); **Magnet,** 1851; Walker Co.

Koehl, Frau Emilie (died on the way): **Solon,** 1852

Koehl, Wilhelm—Hoslof (Haslhof?); **Solon,** 1852

Koehler. Aug., 29; **Solon,** 1850; Comal Co.

Koehler, ... and family—Darmstadt to New Braunfels; **Anton Gunther,** 1860

Koehler F. and wife—Hagen; **Gessner,** 1855; Galveston

Koehler, Seph.; **Hermann Theodor,** 1853; Galveston

Koehn, Johann—Cumblosen, Prussia; Franklin, 1852; Austin Co.
Koehmicke, M.—Burg to Fredericksburg; Weser, 1858
Koehncke, Fritz—Wangelin, Mecklenburg; Copernicus, 1852
Koehncke, Johann—Krabow (Krackow?); wife and 2 ch., ½ and 2 years old; Leibniz, 1850
Koehnke, Anna—Hannover; Jeverland, 1860
Koell, G. N.—Rudolstadt, Thuringia; wife and 4 ch., 5-14 years old; Therese Henriette, 1853
Koenig, ...—Wittenberg to San Antonio; Iris, 1858
Koenig, August—Schwarzsee, Prussia; wife and 1 ch., 6 years old; Miles, 1852; Fayette Co.
Koenig, Auguste—Neustadt to Austin; Gaston, 1860
Koenig, F.—Oldenburg; Friedrich Grosse, 1853
Koenig, Fried.—Ober Neukirch to Austin; Gaston, 1860
Koenig, Friedke—Lobach; Reform, 1849
Koenig, G.—Oldenburg; Friedrich Grosse, 1853; Galveston
Koenig, Hch.—Nordeln (Nordel or Norden); Reform, 1849
Koenig, Hein. — Zella, Prussia; wife and 2 ch., 3 and 9 years old; Miles, 1852
Koenig, Joseph—Lemförde; Herschel, 1851
Koenig, L.—Althagen; wife and 2 daughters, ¾ and 4 years old; Leibniz, 1850
Koenig, Lina and Sarah—Galveston to Galveston; Weser, 1860
Koenig, Maria—Prussia; Franziska, 1854
Koenig, Salomine and child—Broderode (Brotterode); Nepune, 1854
Koenigsberger, Eduard, 43—Grottkau; Anna Louise, 1857
Koenitz, Fr., 33—to Houston; Herschel, 1849
Koennecke, August — Burg, Prussia; Republic, 1851; Gillespie Co.
Koepcke, Hedwig — Altenhof, Schleswig; 2 sons, 11 and 13 years; Franklin, 1852
Koepke (Kolke?), Christian—Buchwerder to Yorktown; Weser, 1858
Koepke, Fr.—Burow; wife and 2 ch., 9 and 16 years old; Leibniz, 1850

Koeppe, Heinrich — Magdeburg, Prussia; and family, 6 persons; Copernicus, 1852
Koerner, Hein., 21—Bautzen; Hamburg, 1849
Koerner, J.—Greene to Galveston; Weser, 1860
Koerth, G. — Lapienne (Leppin or Lappin?) to Houston; Juno, 1860
Koester, Henriette—Prussia to Frelsburg; Weser, 1860
Koester, J.—Rehebeck (Rehbeck); Adolphine, 1859
Koester, P(eter) J. H., 36 and A. Cath., 24; —Ritzenbüttel; Hamburg, 1849
Kohblank, Johann — Perleberg, Prussia to Galveston or Indianola; Franklin, 1852
Kohl, Joh. Christ., 40; Anna Dor. 37, Joh. Christ. 5; Hamburg, 1849
Kohl, L.—Steinnefel (Steinenfeld) to Yorktown; Iris, 1858
Kohl, Louis and Wilhme—Altenburg; Suwa, 1853
Kohlenberg, Fr. and family; Ammerland, 1854; Comal Co.
Kohler, Geo.—Albershausen; Canapus, 1849
Kohler, J.—Bohemia; Franziska, 1854
Kohlfahr, Maria—Ungefar (Anzefähr?); J. W. Buddecke, 1853
Kohlhoff, Hein. Fried. Joh. — Schwarzsee, Prussia; Miles, 1853; Austin Co.
Kohlhoff, Ida—Gross-Schwarza; Neptune, 1854
Kohlmetz, Ludwig — Blandikow, Holstein to Galveston; Republic, 1851
Kohmecke, Victor, 27—Burg; Neptune, 1850
Kohn, Bernard—Polzin, Prussia; John Frederick. 1850
Kohn, R. J. G.—Friedland; Herschel, 1851
Kohn, Simon, 26; Galliott Flora, 1849
Kohrt, Aug.—Springfeld (Sprengersfelde?); Lucie, 1854
Kolar, Jos.—Neponek (Nepomuk?) to Cat Spring; with wife and 2 ch.; Iris, 1861
Kolb, Fredrick, 43—Sachsen; Johanna Regina 36, Emilie 16, Pauline 15. Eduard 11. Fried. 8; Chas. N. Cooper, 1847
Kolb, Georg and wife—from New York; Juno, 1853

Kolbe, Carl, 31 and Maria, 31; **Galliott Flora,** 1849; Colorado **Co.**

Kolbe, W.—Salzbrunn; **Gessner,** 1854; Austin Co.

Kolbow, Carl, 25 — Moellenbeck, Prussia; Maria 29, Carl 10, Joh. 6, Wilhme ½; **John Frederick,** 1850

Kolik, J. — Mähren to Industry; wife and 2 ch.; **Juno,** 1860

Kolke, Christian, 32—Buchwerder; **Weser,** 1858. See Koepke, Chris.

Kollad, Gottl.—Briesen; **Texas,** 1853

Kollasch, Anton and Anna—Austria; **Antoinette,** 1855

Kollatschny, Gottl. and Joh.—Bukowina; **Weser,** 1854; Austin Co.

Kolle, F. — Polshausen (Pohlhausen) to Victoria; **Iris,** 1857; Victoria Co.

Kollhoff, Johann—Stuttgart; **Texas,** 1853; Austin Co.

Kollman family—Posen; **Adolphine** 1859; Colorado Co.

Kollmann, Heike—Winsen; 2 persons; **Texas,** 1853; Fayette Co.

Kollmann, Joh. Friedr.—Winsen; **Texas,** 1853; Fayette Co.

Kolodzet, Jos. and family—Prussia; **Antoinette,** 1855

Komalz, Bernhard, 17; **Creole,** 1852

Konwiczka (Konvicka), Martin — Austria; Genovena, Genovena, Agnes; **Jeverland,** 1860

Konyr, Georg—Goericke, Prussia to Indianola; **Miles,** 1852

Kopcke. C. Hein, 28—Holstein; Colonist. 1848; Colorado Co.

Kopke, Ed—Berlin; **Helen and Elise,** 1847

Kopke, Joh. Hr., 31 — Rastederberg; Wilhme 24, Fr. 4½, Wm. 2½, Helen Soph. ¼; **Helen & Elise.** 1847; Colorado Co.

Kopp. A. and wife—Nieder-Neuendorf; **Gessner,** 1855

Kopp. Ad.—Nieder-Neuendorf; **Gessner,** 1855

Kopp. Christoph, 25 — Württ.; Anna, 27—Hannover; both from Kressbach; **Brasilian,** 1850

Kopp, F.; **Herschel,** 1849

Kord. Wilhme. 36 and Hein.. 8— S t e i g h o r s t (Steighaus?) to Houston; **Weser,** 1859

Korff. Carl and Marie—Oldendorf; 7 persons; **Neptune,** 1853; Austin Co.

Korner, Heinrich. 21—Bautzen; **Hamburg,** 1849

Korns, Joh. and family—Tost; **Weser,** 1854

Korte, Fried., 35—Buetzow; **Brasilian,** 1850

Korte, Marie—Rehburg to Brenham; **Weser,** 1857

Kortegas, Emma — Braunschweig to Galveston; **Weser,** 1860

Korth, C. — Schönlanke to Yorktown; **Iris,** 1859

Korth, C., with wife—Wildforth; **Weser,** 1857; Austin Co.

Korth, Ch. with wife and 5 ch.— Wildforth; **Weser,** 1857; Austin Co.

Korth, Ernestine and child—Viereichen; **Mississippi,** 1855

Korthamer, Hch.—Winzlar, Han.; **Reform,** 1849

Kortzick, D., wife and 3 ch.—Sobiechen (Sobieszyn) to Indianola; **Juno,** 1860

Koschel, Samuel. 35—Breslau; **Brasilian,** 1850

Kosewitz, C., B., Marie—to Houston; **Weser,** 1860

Kosewald, Wilhelm—Flitzberg, Prussia; **Miles,** 1854

Kosine, Franz, with wife and Oswald; **Neptune,** 1849

Koster, C.—Westrup to Houston; **Weser,** 1858

Kostrup, Anna Maria—Enger (Engter?); **Texas,** 1853

Kosts, Fried.—Braunschweig; **Juno,** 1853

Koth, Joachim — Schwerin, Mecklenburg; wife and 1 ch.; **Sophie,** 1852

Kotulla, Joseph, 11; Amalie, 36; **Brasilian,** 1857; Atascosa Co.

Kotulla, Maria—Himlowitz (Humpolitz); **Weser,** 1854; Atascosa **Co.**

Kotz. Juliana—Württ.; **Franziska,** 1854

Kovajan, Jann. and family—Humpolitz; **Weser,** 1854

Kowitz family—Braunsdorf to Galveston; **Iris,** 1859

Kox, Wilhelmine — Altona, Denmark; 2 daughters, 16 and 21 years old; **Copernicus,** 1852

Koy, Nathalie — Kalueb, Prussia; 3 ch., 0-6 years old; **Therese Henriette,** 1853; Austin Co.

Kozisch (Kopisch), Franz—Strasseney (Strassengel?), Austria; **Minna,** 1854

Kraeger. Hein., 39; **Brasilian,** 1857

Kraehe. Auguste—Magdeburg to La Grange; **Iris,** 1860

Kraemer, Carl—Halberstadt; Texas, 1853
Kraemer, Christian, 27—Oldenburg; Reform, 1850
Kraemer, Hein.—Lemförde; Neptune, 1853
Kraemer, J.—Altenflies to Yorktown; Fortuna, 1860
Kraenke, Carl, 32—Hannover; Alexander, 1850
Kraetze, Appolonia — Bullsdorf (Bullendorf?), Boehmen; Mississippi, 1855
Kraetzer, Fr.—Hannover; Friedrich Grosse, 1853
Kraft, Hein.—Hassleben, Prussia; Washington, 1852; Comal Co.
Kraft, Johann—Bresch, Prussia to Galveston; Miles, 1852
Kraft, Joseph—Brunstadt; Minna, 1854
Kraft, W., 17—Arolsen; Fortuna, 1858
Kraft, Wilhelm and Marie—Waldeck to Galveston; Weser, 1860
Krahn, F. — Bergbruch (Bergenbrüch) to Cypress; Anna, August, Ephensina; Fortuna, 1860
Krambeck, Marg., 20 — Nienhoff, Schleswig-Holstein; Washington, 1852
Kramer, Bernh., 34; Solon, 1850; Galveston. See Kremer, Bernh.
Kramer, Carl—Prussia; Chas. N. Cooper, 1847; Comal Co.
Kramer, Christian, 54—Ostcrode; Caro. 24, Albertine 18; Joh. Dethardt, 1848; Grimes Co.
Kramer, Fried., 24—Baden; Chas. N. Cooper, 1847; Washington Co.
Kramer, Gottfried, and wife, five persons—Grona, Anhalt; Mississippi, 1855
Kramer, Hermann — Wildenshausen, Oldenburg; Mississippi, 1855
Kramer, Jos.—Kärnthen; 2 persons; Reform, 1851
Kramer, Marie—Prussia to Brenham; Weser, 1860
Kramer, W. and Wilhme—Wehdem to Brenham; Weser, 1860
Kranich, Carl Fried. — La(n)genwiesen; Solon, 1852; Gillespie Co.
Kranzmann, H. — Bielefeld to Houston; Iris, 1857
Krapf, W.—Torgau; Juno, 1860; Victoria Co.
Kraus, Gerh. H.—Burghassungen; 7 persons; Texas, 1853
Kraus. Heinrich — Niedenstein, Prussia; Franklin, 1853

Kraus, Joh.—Anzefähr; J. W. Buddecke, 1853
Krause, Anton—Lussdorf; Lucie, 1854
Krause, Bernhard and wife, 4 persons — Riggersdorf, Boehmen; Mississippi, 1855
Krause, C.—Gross-Posena (Gross-Posna), Saxony; wife and 8 ch. ½-17 years old; Miles, 1854
Krause, Caroline; Hamburg, 1849
Krause, Christian, 29—Hamburg; Chas. N. Cooper, 1847
Krause family—Weissenstein; Adolphine, 1859
Krause, Ernest William—Breslau, Silesia; arr. 1853; Waco, Texas
Krause, Gustav—Wachsdorf, Saxony to Galveston or Indianola; Franklin, 1852
Krause, J. (Rrause, sic) — Günthersleben; Gessner, 1854
Krause, J.—Bohemia; Franziska, 1854
Krause, Joh., 31; Emilie 28, Wilh. 3, Hulda ¾; Creole, 1852
Krause, J. H., 27; Galliott Flora, 1849
Krause, Leopold, 29; John Holland, 1848
Krause, W. — Niederwaltersdorf, Mecklenburg; Franklin, 1853
Krauss, D., 32; Wilh. 24. Julius ¼; Fortuna, 1858; Washington Co.
Krawitz, Leopold — Himlowitz (Humpolitz?), Bohemia; Weser, 1854
Krebs, Hein., 53 — Braunschweig; Dor. 40, Wilh. 21, Franz 18. Marie 15, Otto 12, Theo. 8, Edw. 6. Herm. 4, Julius 2; Franziska, 1847; Austin Co.
Krehmeyer, Christ., 23 — Lippe Detmold; Joh. Dethardt, 1848; Victoria Co.
Kreikenbohm. Sophia — Braunschweig; Franziska, 1854; Comal Co.
Kreiker. Thomas—Laubach: 2 persons; Henriette, 1843 (1853)
Kreis. Johann—Burghausen to Houston; Weser. 1857
Kreischelt. C. F. W., 37. and Louisa — Clausthal to Galveston; Iris, 1859
Kremer, Bernhard. 22—Prussia; Chas. N. Cooper, 1847
Kremer, Peter, 26—Traben; Anna Louise, 1853
Kremkau. C.—Salzwedel. Prussia; son, Otto. 16; Hampden. 1854; Bexar Co.

Kremp, Conrad, 30—Gross-Lafferde; Joh. Dethardt, 1848
Krengel, Joh.; Galhott Concordia, 1854
Kretschma, Camilla—Dresden to Indianola; Weser, 1860
Kretchsmann, Emilie, 40—Prussia; Emily 15, Mina 14, Alfred 13; Colonist, 1848
Kretzschmar, C. G.—Glasten, Saxony; wife and 2 sons, ¼ and 3 years old; Miles, 1854; Austin Co.
Kretsdronen, D. H., 29—Havelberg to Galveston; Weser, 1859
Kreuz, W.—Lohme to Helena; Iris, 1860; Karnes Co.
Kreuzkamp, H.—Warge(n); Adolphine, 1859
Kriebel Franz—see Kruebel, Fr.
Krieg, C. F. G.—Marwitz, Prussia; wife and son, 3 years old; Therese Henriette, 1853
Kriegel, M. — Bagenitz, Prussia; wife and 5 ch., 5-23 years old; Therese Henriette, 1853; Wharton Co.
Kriegel, Rosina; Therese Henriette, 1853
Krinn, J. G., 20—Berkheim to Galveston; Iris, 1859
Kroalik, Johann and Anna—Vienna; Suwa, 1853
Kroeger, Carl—Beidendorf, Mecklenburg; wife and child, age 20; Copernicus, 1852
Kroeger, Wilh.—Gollanz, Prussia to Indianola; Miles, 1852
Krohme, Joh. Adam, and family (3)—Dettingen; Solon, 1852
Krohn, Peter—Holstein; Antoinette, 1855
Kroll, Aug., 24—Rogasen; Hamburg, 1849
Kroll, Charlotte, 45—Hamburg; Washington, 1852
Krone, Jane—Luther am Berge to Houston; Gaston, 1860
Kronkoska, Rosalia—Poland; 2 ch.; Franziska, 1854
Kronkowsiky, Lorenz, 24 — Kirschowa? to Galveston; Weser, 1859
Krosch, Chr. and wife — Mainscholz(?) to New Braunfels; Gaston, 1857
Kroschel, Joh.—Gurkow to Yorktown; Eva, Emma. Auguste, Hein., Joh.. Minna. Ferd.. Aug.; Fortuna, 1860; De Witt Co.
Kroschel, L.—Altenflies to Yorktown; Fortuna, 1860

Kroschel, Ludwig — Gurkow to Yorktown; Juliane, Henriette, Ludwig, Julie, Marie, Gustav, Louise; Fortuna, 1860
Krotzben, Peter—Prossen; Anna Louise, 1857
Krubel, Franz, 26—Friedland; Anna Louise, 1857
Kruegel, Martin—See Kriegel, M.
Krueger, Carl and Carl—Mongrovice; Texas, 1853
Krueger, Chr., wife and 4 ch.—to Hempstead; Gaston, 1860
Krueger, Emilie—Falkenburg; Neptune, 1854
Krueger, F.—Ottendorf; 7 persons; Neptune, 1854
Krueger, Ferd.—Prussia; Franziska, 1854
Krueger, Ferd(inand)—Hamburg; Leibniz, 1850
Krueger, Fr.—Breddin, Prussia; Franklin, 1853
Krueger, Fried., Friedke, Fritz—Roskau to Austin; Weser, 1860
Krueger, H., with family — Rohburg (Rohrberg?); Weser, 1858
Krueger, Joh., 38—Springberge; Antoinette, 1848
Krueger, Julius—Prussia; Franziska, 1854
Krueger, Robert and Cath.—Prussia; Franziska, 1854
Krueger, Sophie—Weitenhagen to New Braunfels; Weser, 1858
Krueger, W. and Caro.—Westrup to Houston; Weser, 1858
Krueger, Wilh., Pauline—Mongrovice; Texas, 1853
Kruese, F. — Hannover to New Braunfels; Sophia, Fried., Henry; Weser, 1860
Krueser, F.—Friedeberg to Yorktown; Iris, 1858
Krug, G.—Streetz to Houston; Iris, 1860
Kruger, Conrad, 24; Fried. 18; Solon, 1850
Kruger, Hein., 21—Hannover; Joh. Dethardt, 1848; Austin Co.
Kruger, W., 23—Birkbruch; Weser, 1858
Krunke, F. and wife — Segefeld (Secenfelde) to Lexington; Iris, 1857
Kruse, Bernhard, 46; Carl 22, Aug. 20, Christian 10; Solon, 1850; Austin Co.
Kruse, Christian and Christine—Hannover to New Braunfels; Weser, 1860

— 96 —

Kruse family—Ostfriesland; Adolphine, 1859
Kruse, Fried.—Twietfarth, Mecklenburg; Washington, 1852; Colorado Co.
Kruse, H.—Heilenbach; 4 persons; Reform, 1851
Kubala, Andreas—Austria; Veronica, Stephan, John, Marianna; Jeverland, 1860
Kubala, C.—Austria; Jeverland, 1860
Kubala, Theresia, Carl, Vincenz, John—Austria; Jeverland, 1860
Kubitz, Aug.—Neumark; Mississippi, 1855
Kubitz, Christoph, 18—Kaschel; Hamburg, 1849
Kuchel, August—Oldenburg, Holstein; wife and 3 sons, 5-12 yrs. old; Hampden, 1854
Kuck, Albert, 61; Marie 55; Reform, 1850
Kuck, W.—Oldenburg; Adolphine, 1859
Kuebel, Charles Aug., 27; John Holland, 1848
Kuebler, Doris, 4 yrs. old—Schoenkirchen, Holstein; (with August Küchel); Hampden, 1854
Kuebler, Gottlieb—Dresden; Reform, 1851
Kueche, August, 25—Schilde; Brasilian, 1850
Kueckert, Carl Friedr.—Krimmitschau; Texas, 1853
Kuechler (Kuebler?), Gottlieb—Dresden; Reform, 1851
Kuechler, Jacob — Unter-Sensbach in Odenwald; arr. Gal. 1847; Gillespie Co.
Kuehn, Daniel, 30—Kiel Gotha; Antoinette, 1848
Kuehl, Chr. Hinrich—Kems, Holstein; Copernicus, 1852
Kuehn, Juliane—Gr. Groele (Grossgolle) to Washington (on-the-Brazos); Weser, 1860
Kuehn, V.—Rückersdorf; Minna, 1854
Kuehn, W. — Posen to Galveston; Juno, 1860
Kuehne, Friedrich — Wensickendorf, Prussia; wife and 2 ch.; Republic, 1851; Fayette Co.
Kuehne, Hein.—Bottmersdorf; Weser, 1854
Kuehne, Jacob and Christine—Gail-(s)dorf; J. W. Buddecke, 1853
Kuehnel, E.—Burgstädt to Galveston; Fortuna, 1860

Kuehnle, J. and B. — Eichenlamberg; Gessner, 1855
Kuencke, H. and wife—Suesfeld (Sulzfeld?); Gessner, 1855
Kuenkel, Joh. and wife, 4 persons —Strotchenchollam?; Mississippi, 1855
Kuester, H., wife and ch.—Pattensen; Neptune, 1854
Kugel, Johanne, 36—Prussia; Fibbe(?) 34, Caro. 7, Wilhme, Carl ¾; Chas. N. Cooper, 1847
Kugler, Johann—Tschmanschwitz, Prussia; mother, wife, daughter age 4; Miles, 1854
Kuhl, Joh.; Galliott Concordia, 1854
Kuhlae, Friedka, 23; Brasilian, 1857
Kuhlbohn, Marie, 27 years old—Barkow, Mecklenburg; Washington, 1852
Kuhlfahl, G.—Burg to Fredericksburg; Weser, 1858
Kuhlmann, Fr.—Hannover; Franziska, 1854
Kuhly, Joh.; Joh. Ed. Grosse, 1853
Kuhmann, Franziska, 24; Franziska, 1849
Kuhn, Amalie, 43—Burg; Neptune, 1850
Kuhn, Frederick, 28—Thunningen (Thuringia?); Franziska, 1847
Kuhnel, J. H. R., 29; Ernestine 23; Galliott Flora, 1849; Karnes Co.
Kuhrt, Jochen, 29; M a r i a 25— Brockhusen, Mecklenburg; Herschel, 1855
Kunath, Ludwig—Ocslmettingen (Oest Mettingen?); Reform, 1849
Kunde, Johann — Polzen, Prussia; wife and 6 ch., ages 6-12; John Frederick, 1850
Kunger, Wm., 32; Friedke 24 — Rosser?; Canapus, 1848
Kunkel—See also Kuenkel
Kunkel, Caro.—Pudewitz to San Antonio; Gaston, 1860
Kunkel, Gottlieb, and wife—Weglewo to San Antonio; Gaston, 1860
Kunshe(?), George, 30—Louis, 1848
Kunst, Joachim—Wenddorf, Prussia; wife and 3 children; Bassermann, 1851
Kunst, Sophie — Lalendorf, Mecklenburg; Sarah, 1851

Kuntz, Louis, 55—Dresbach; Mary nee Stoffers 50, Elis. 25, Henry 21, Wilh. Hein. 18, Frederic 12, Joachim 10, Conrad 4½; Antoinette, 1848
Kunz, Christian — Grabow, Mecklenburg; wife Marie; Franklin, 1853; Comal Co.
Kunz, Thomas—Boehmen; wife and 3 ch.; Weser, 1854
Kuoerth, (Knoerth?), Gottlieb—Mongrovice?; Texas, 1853
Kupperschmidt, Peter, 46; Christine 42, Christine 9, Hein. 7; Solon, 1850
Kurdie, Clara—to New Orleans; Gutenberg, 1855
Kurschner, Carl, 43—Saxony; Colonist, 1848
Kurten, Heinrich—Odendahl; Solon, 1852
Kurz, Joseph and family—Prussia; Antoinette, 1854; Ausin Co.
Kusch, Joh.—Brujenitz?; Weser, 1854
Kuske, Michael—Ascherode; Solon, 1852
Kuss, August—Hannover; 3 persons; Henriette, 1843 (1853); Comal Co.
Kuss, F.—Hannover to New Braunfels; Weser, 1860
Kuster, Dor., 22—Mühlhausen; Solon, 1850
Kutscher, Hein., 24; Sophie, 1852; Guadalupe Co.
Kutter, Michael—Krähenbach; Juno, 1853
Kutzendorf, Marg., 30—Bavaria; Franziska, 1849
Kutzer, Carl and family—Schilda; Gessner, 1854; Kendall Co.
Kutzer, R.—Schilda; Gessner, 1854; Kendall Co.
Kwintel, H.—Ottendorf; Neptune, 1854
Kysella, C., 28; Fortuna, 1858

— L —

Laas, Gottfried, 50—Kosultze (Koselitz?); Friedke 48, Gottl. 20, Fried. 18, Henriette 13; Weser, 1858; Fayette Co.
Labisch, Johann, 37 — Tarnau, Prussia; Maria 39, Barbara 7, Mariane ½, Florentine 1½, Franziskau 17; Miles, 1855
Labohm, J. G.—Astrup; Weser, 1854
Lackner, Anna — Unterwatsdorf (Unterwaltersdorf?); Lucie, 1854

Lacroir, J. and wife—Oggersheim; Weser, 1854
Ladage, Heinrich — Hamburg to Galveston; Bassermann, 1851
Ladendorf, Friederike—Penzlin; Leibniz, 1850
Ladehof, Wilh.—Klamp, Mecklenburg; Copernicus, 1852
Laesch, Herm., 22; Hermann Theodor, 1850
Lafin, Ernst—Polzin, Prussia; John Frederick, 1850
Lage, Anna, 20 — Gaedersdorf, Schleswig Holstein; Washington, 1852; Bexar Co.
Lagershausen, A., 20; Fortuna, 1858
Lages, Mathilda—Braunschweig; Antoinette, 1855
Laging, W.—Wehdem to Brenham; Weser, 1860
Lakenmacher, Daniel and Johanne —Hattorf, Han.; J. W. Buddecke, 1853
Lakenmacher, W. and wife, 5 persons—Fallersleben; Lakenmacher, Doris; J. W. Buddecke, 1853
Lamb, Jean Hermann, 27; John Holland, 1848
Lambeck, Dor., 36 — Beligheim (Bellheim?) to Bastrop; Wilh. 14, Louis 12, Aug. 9; Weser, 1859
Lamby, Adam, 34 and Marg. 23—Hesse; John Holland, 1848
Lamers(?), Anna, 17; Solon, 1850
Lamp, Lena, 27 — Stackendorff, Schleswig-Holstein; Washington, 1852
Lampe, ...—Schöningen to La Grange; Iris, 1858
Lampe, Fried. H.—Brockum; Neptune, 1853; Washington Co.
Lampe, Wilh.— Prussia to Brenham; Wilhme, Wilh., Henriette, 1860
Langbein, Andr.—Prussia; 7 persons; Friedrich Grosse, 1853; Comal Co.
Lange, ... (Blacksmith) and family — Prussia to Bellville; Anton Gunther, 1860
Lange, Amalie, 7 years old—Golchen, Prussia; Miles, 1852
Lange, August—Kremmitschau; 4 persons; Texas, 1853; Washington Co.
Lange, C.—Berlin to Galveston; Iris, 1857

Lange, Carl, 44—Hamm by Hamburg; Wilhme 34, Julius 6, Carl 1; **John Frederick,** 1850; Fayette Co.
Lange, Franz, 45 — Nackenheim; Catarina 35, Ludw. 11, Lena 8, Eva 5, Joh. 4, Carl 3; **Neptune,** 1850
Lange, Franz — Friedland; wife and 2 ch.; **Minna,** 1854; Bastrop Co.
Lange, J. — Kiel, Holstein; wife and 2 daughters, 7 and 9 years old; **Franklin,** 1853
Lange, Johann—Papenhagen to New Braunfels; **Weser,** 1860
Lange, Ludwig — Gehrden; 8 persons; **Magnet,** 1851
Lange, Maria—Perleberg, Prussia; 2 daughters, 22 and 28 years; **Franklin,** 1852; to Galveston or Indianola
Lange, Sophie — Neuschlemmin, Mecklenburg to Galveston; **Sarah,** 1851
Lange, Val.—Friedland; **Minna,** 1854; Fayette Co.
Lange, W.—to Industry; **Weser,** 1859
Langen, Ferd.—Mildenau; **Hermann Theodor,** 1853
Langen, Joh. and Therese; **Galliott Concordia,** 1854
Langenhennig, H.; **Ammerland,** 1854
Langer, Ad.—Tarnowitz; **Leibniz,** 1850
Langhammer, Maria — Austria; Bertha, Maria, Fanny, Toni, Josephine, Carl Hein.; **Neptune,** 1849; Austin Co.
Langhein. Bernhard, 28—Bavaria; **Chas. N. Cooper,** 1847
Langlob, Carl Aug.—Prussia; **Neptune,** 1848
Langmaak, Heinrich — Boenhusen, Schleswig-Holstein; **Washington,** 1852
Lanlé, Alexander, 34; **John Holland,** 1848
Lantschek, M.—Grodzischka; **Gessner,** 1855
Lashe, Esther — Roernitz (Koernitz); **Solon,** 1852
Laske, Magda., Susanne — Roessnitz to New Braunfels; **Weser,** 1860
Lasman, J. Ehrenfried — Heitersdorf (Heilgersdorf?); **Neptune,** 1854
Laubengeier, Ch. — Plieningen; 2 persons; **Texas,** 1853

Lauritz, Cath., 63 and daughter 21—Sondersburg, Schleswig-Holstein; **Washington,** 1852
Lausen, Christian — Schleswig to Galveston; Marg., Marg., Doris, Hans, Christian, Andreas, Cath., Peter; **Weser,** 1860
Lausen, C. H. — Schleswig in Schleswig; **Hampden,** 1854
Lauterbach, Clara—to Galveston; **Weser,** 1859
Lautrich, Christian, 27; Constanze 27 — Sachsen-Meiningen; **Chas. N. Cooper,** 1847
Laux, Christian—Berlin; wife and 4 ch.; **Minna,** 1854
Lechner, Ant.—Prussia; 2 persons; **Friedrich Grosse,** 1853; Fayette Co.
Lede, Marie L.—Brockum; **Neptune,** 1853
Lederer, Rossine — Birkach to Fredericksburg; **Iris,** 1859
Lehde, Caro., 24—Wehden to Brenham; **Iris,** 1859
Lehde, F.—Wehdem to Brenham; **Weser.** 1860
Lehde, Henriette—to Brenham; **Weser,** 1859
Lehmann, A.—Birkbruch (Birkenbruch) to Yorktown; **Fortuna,** 1860
Lehmann, Andreas, 51 — Weigersdorf to Shelby; Anna 49, Joh. 21, Andreas 18, Aug. 16, Ernst 14, Carl 10, Maria 5; **Iris,** 1859
Lehmann, C. and wife — Königsberg to York's Creek; **Iris,** 1857
Lehmann, Carl — Grossen-Mütze, Hannover; 2 persons; **Mississippi,** 1855
Lehmann family—Friedland; **Adolphine,** 1859
Lehmann, G.—to Independence; **Weser,** 1859
Lehmann, G.—Dessau; **Weser,** 1858
Lehmann, H.—Stalle to Brenham; **Weser,** 1860
Lehmann, Joh., 53 — Weissenberg to Galveston; Johanna 55, Magda. 22, Ernst 14; **Iris,** 1859
Lehmann, Joh.—Janowice; **Lucie,** 1854; Austin Co. or Bastrop Co.
Lehmann, Ludwig, 55—Hamburg; Caro. 45, Ludwig 24, Adolph 22, Julius 18, Herm. 14, Therese 75 (Died); **Hamburg,** 1849
Lehmann, M.. wife and child—Bernburg; **Neptune,** 1854; Austin Co.

Lehmann, Moritz and wife, 5 persons—Lewa, Saxony; Mississippi, 1855; Mason Co.
Lehmann, Susette—Uster, Switz.; Lucie, 1854
Lehmann, Wilhelmine and Louise —Schilda; Gessner, 1854
Lehmbach, J.—Waldberg; Weser, 1854
Lehmberg, J. — Proistett; 5 persons; Neptune, 1854; Mason Co.
Lehms, Christian—Ganzlin, Mecklenburg; wife and son; Washington, 1852
Lehms, Friedrich and wife—Ganzlin, Mecklenburg; Washington, 1852
Lehnz, Wilhelm — Rostock, Mecklenburg; Copernicus, 1852
Lehrmann, Wilh.; Galliott Concordia, 1854
Lehst, R.—to Galveston; Weser, 1859
Lehsten, Aug.—Rostock, Mecklenburg; Washington, 1852
Leib (Leis?), Wilhelmine, 47, Henriette 26; Brasilian, 1850
Leibrand, Jacob and Caroline—Ilsfeld; Solon, 1852
Leiche, George—Brownskirchen (Bromskirchen); Texas, 1853
Leiding, Hein., 28; Solon, 1850
Leidner, Fried. and Charlotte — Bremen; Mississippi, 1855
Leiveste, Christ., 32 — Bruggen; Leifeste, Christoph—Mason Co.; Joh. Dethardt, 1848
Leinberg, Lisette and son—Stetterling (Stötterlingen); Weser, 1854
Leining, Christian, Christiane and Caro. — Saxony to Mill Creek; Weser, 1860
Leis — See Leib
Leissner, Mr. and Mrs. [sic]— Freyburg; Gessner, 1854
Leist family—to Galveston; Weser, 1859
Leist, Fried. Wilh. and family, 12 persons — Altwerder, Prussia; Mississippi, 1855
Lembcke, Maria and 3 daughters, 11-17 yrs. old—Hamburg; Hampden, 1854
Lemke, H.—Rombergen to Houston; Juno, 1860; Colorado Co.
Lemmel, Johann—Rohrbach, Saxony; wife and 4 children, ½-8 years old; to Galveston or Indianola; Franklin, 1852

Lemp, Wilh.—Reckenthien, Prussia; with son 1¼ years old; Miles, 1852
Leng, Magnus, 26, Friedke 24— Böckels; Joh. Dethardt, 1848
Lenssen, H. A.—Rheydt; Neptune, 1853; Comal Co.
Lenth, Joh. Fr., 56—Moellenbach, Mecklenburg; Jurgen 27, Magda. 25, Maria ½; John Frederick, 1850
Leonhard, W.—Schneeberg; Neptune, 1854
Leorenz(?), Maria, 27; Solon, 1850
Leschick, Joh. and family—Kadlup; Weser, 1854
Leschikar (Lesikar) family—Vienna; 11 persons; Suwa, 1853; Austin Co.
Leseberg, Cath., 32—Hamburg; Washington, 1852
Leser, Caspar — Broderode (Brotterode); Neptune, 1854
Letsch, Joh. Aug., 39—Thalheim to Meyersville; Maria Anna 34, Georg 9, Wilh. 7, Maria Cath. 3; Weser, 1859
Leu, Peter, Marg., Marg., Doris, Elise—Flensburg to Galveston; Weser, 1860
Leuchner, Aug., 47—Torgau, Prussia; Emilie 40, Carl 9, Aug. 3; Herschel, 1855; Victoria Co.
Leverkoehne, Dorothea, W., F., C. —Lafferde to Houston; Gaston, 1857
Leverkoehne, H.—from Houston; Gaston, 1857
Lewing, Anton and Hein.—Duderstadt; Weser, 1854
Lex, Christian and wife, 6 persons and Lex, Conrad — Offenbach, Nassau; Mississippi, 1855
Ley, Adam, 29; Sophie, 1852
Ley, Susanna E.—Kaltenlengsfeld; Magnet, 1851
Libke, Maria, 25; Brasilian, 1857
Lichthorn, J. — Prussia to La Grange; Weser, 1860
Lidecke, Th., Claerchen, and Alice —to New Orleans; Gutenberg, 1855
Lidiack, Jos. — Austria; Anna, John, Franz, Johanne, Jos.; Jeverland, 1860
Lieb, Therese—Kaltenwestheim to Lockhart; Juno, 1860
Lieb, Wilhme. 47, Henriette 26— Perleberg; Brasilian, 1850
Liebenow, E.—Greifswald; Leibniz, 1850

Liebscher, Joh. Gottl. — Neuenkirch; 5 persons; Herschel, 1851; Comal Co.

Liefert, W. — Birkbruch (Birkenbruch) to Yorktown; Fortuna, 1860

Liek, G.—Württemberg; Franziska, 1854

Liek, Gottfried—Prussia; wife and 7 ch.; Franziska, 1854

Lier, J. — Prussia; Friedrich Grosse, 1853

Liermann, Joh.—Nemerold (Nemerow?); 3 persons; Texas, 1853; Austin Co.

Lietsch, H i n r i c h — Gneusdorff, Mecklenburg; Washington, 1852

Lilie,Carl—Braunschweig; Texas, 1853

Lilie, Joh., 22—Gr. Schwuspen; Joh. Dethardt, 1848

Lilienthal, Hans—Klamp, Mecklenburg; wife and 4 ch. ½-10 years of age, and Margarethe, 62; Copernicus, 1852

Lillie, Marx Fr. and wife—Hohenfelde, Holstein; Copernicus, 1852

Lincke, Wilhelm and wife Caroline—Eilau, Prussia; Miles, 1854

Lindborn, A.—to Galveston; Weser, 1859

Lindemann, A. and wife — Bernburg; Neptune, 1854; Austin Co.

Lindemann, And. — Bernburg; 5 persons; Neptune, 1854; Austin Co.

Lindemann, Joh.—Schuelp, Schleswig-Holstein; Washington, 1852

Lindemann, Johann Val. and family (4)—Meiningen; Solon, 1852

Lindenburg, wife, 37 — Denkle (Demker?); Canapus, 1848; Bastrop Co.

Lindmuller, Dorothe, 22 — Brome, Han.; Helen & Elise, 1847

Lindner, Ann. and family; Ammerland, 1854

Lindner, Carl — Blechhammer; Magnet, 1851; Comal Co.

Lindner, Charlotte—Blechhammer; Solon, 1852

Lindstein, Auguste and 3 ch.— Prussia; Franziska, 1854

Lindvoight, George, 23; Caro. 22; Fannin Co., Texas; Joh. Dethardt, 1848

Lineweg, Fr. Wilh.—Holzhausen; Texas, 1853

Lingnau, F.—Rastadt, Prussia; Franklin, 1853; Austin Co.

Link, Joh. and Anna—Altingen; Neptune, 1854; Medina Co.

Link, Johannes—Reinhart(s); Solon, 1852

Linke, O.—Weissenfels to Galveston; Gaston, 1857

Linnenbruegger, F. W.—Bielefeld; Texas, 1853

Liphardt, H. C.—Honigsee, Schleswig-Holstein; Washington, 1852; Colorado Co.

Lipke, Christoph and family— Prussia; Antoinette, 1855

Lippel, Joh. M., 50—Grossenrode, Han.; Joh. Dethardt, 1848

Lippke, Albertine—Burg; Weser, 1854

Lipscher, Carl Wilh.—Kl. Borthen to New Ulm; Weser, 1857

Lipstran, Frd. and family, 4 ch. 6-31 years old — Footenkopf, Prussia; Franklin, 1853

Lissow, Andrew, Friedke, Hein.— Meindorf to Austin; Weser, 1860

Listich, Englehard—Polzin, Prussia; wife and family. ages 10-15; John Frederick, 1850

Locke, Johann — Alt-Grochwitz, Schleswig to Galveston or Indianola; Franklin, 1852

Locker, A., with wife—Ottmachau to Bastrop; Iris, 1857

Lockstedt, H.—Holzminden; 7 persons; Texas, 1853

Loebning, H.—Bettmer; Weser, 1854

Loeffler, Gottlieb, 19 — Württ.; Natchez, 1847; Bexar Co.

Loeffler, Johann and wife—Württ.; Weser, 1854

Loehmann, F. W. J.—Rehburg to Brenham; with wife and 3 ch.; Weser, 1857; Kendall Co.

Loehn, Hein. and wife — Gross-Lasch, Mecklenburg; Copernicus, 1852

Loehr, Christ., 28—Leinestedt, Württ.; Joh. Dethardt, 1848

Loehr, Heinrich—Kuwinkel, Mecklenburg; wife and children, 10-27 years old; Copernicus, 1852; Fayette Co.

Loehr, Joh., 32; John Holland, 1848

Loehse, Amalie A.—Lengefeldt to Boerne; Weser, 1860

Loehse, Carl Aug.—Lommatzisch, Saxony; arr. Galveston 1860; Comal Co.

Loeper, Caroline and Doris—to Galveston; Weser, 1859

Loesch, Fried., Friedke, Caro. — Papenhagen to New Braunfels; Weser, 1860

Loescher, F. — Wehdem to Houston, with family; **Weser,** 1858
Loeschmann, J. and F.—Pudewitz to Austin; Iris, 1857
Loeser, C. G.—Lengefeld; **Lucie,** 1854
Loew, Hirsch; **Ammerland,** 1854
Loewensohn, Paul—Posen to Gonzales; **Weser,** 1860
Loewensohn, Sophie — Posen to Gonzales; **Weser,** 1860
Loewison, ... (Merchant) — Posen to Gonzales; Iris, 1858
Loewissohn, L.—Posen; **Weser,** 1854
Loff, Fr. Wm., 31—Bismark; Dor. 22, Wm. 2½; **Canapus,** 1848
Lohfeld, Anna—Moorburg; **Republic,** 1851
Lohl, Christ., 26—Leinestedt; **Joh. Dethardt,** 1848; Comal Co.
Lohl, Christian, 29 and Wilhme, 19—Braunschweig; **Solon,** 1850; Comal Co.
Lohl, Conrad, 25; Lucia, 21; **Solon,** 1850; Comal Co.
Lohlott, L.—Ziegenhain to Galveston; **Weser,** 1860
Lohmann, Friedke—Berlin; **Suwa,** 1853
Lola, Johan and wife—Böhmen; **Weser,** 1854
Londers, Clara—Hamburg; ch. 3 years old; **Hampden,** 1854
Lonn, P. and Dor.—Schleswig to Galveston; **Weser,** 1860
Loose, Carl Aug.; Amalie, Carl Theo.; **Neptune,** 1849; Galveston
Lorentzen, Max — Schwabstedt, Schleswig-Holstein; **Washington,** 1852
Lorenz, A.; **Estafette,** 1850; Bastrop Co.
Lorenz, Caro.—Hannover; **Franziska,** 1854
Lorenz, Christine — Parbi(?) to Galveston; Iris, 1860
Lorenz, J.—Friedland to San Antonio; Iris, 1860
Lorenz, Traugott—Wriesa (Wrisse); 2 persons; **Neptune,** 1853
Lorenz, W., with family—Breslau to Bastrop; Iris, 1860
Lossnitzer, Mrs. Christine — Görlitz, Prussia; **Therese Henriette,** 1853
Lott, Fr. Wm., 31—Bismark; Dor. 22, Wm. 2½; **Canapus,** 1848; Galveston
Lott, Joh. Henry, 22; **Canapus,** 1848

Lottmann, C. A., 30; Charl. 24—Hamburg; **Hamburg,** 1849; Bastrop Co.
Lotz, H.—Emden; **Gessner,** 1854
Loubitz, Ernestine—Friedeberg to Yorktown; Iris, 1858
Lubbert, Wilhelm—Detmold; **Suwa,** 1853
Lubinsky, J. and wife—Schurowitz(?); **Gessner,** 1855
Luck, Adolph and wife—Granzow; **Gessner,** 1854
Lucke, Aug., 20; **Reform,** 1850
Luckfil, Johan—Kieritzsch; **Leibniz,** 1850
Luckhard, Wilh.—Ziegenhain; **Juno,** 1853
Ludwig, ... (roofer)—Prussia to Galveston; **Anton Gunther,** 1860
Ludwig, Aug., 24; **Herschel,** 1849; Gonzales Co.
Ludwig, H. and family; **Ammerland,** 1854
Ludwig, Julius and Wilh.—Bern to Richmond; Iris, 1859
Ludwig, Otto—Halle, Prussia; **Miles,** 1854
Luebicke, C. with family — Birkbruck to Georgetown; **Weser,** 1858
Lueck, Fr., wife and child—Krzeakatowoy (Krzekotowo) (n o w Kornfelde); **Lucie,** 1854
Luecke, Anna and Caro.—Breitenstein to Independence; **Fortuna,** 1858
Lueckemeyer, Wilh. — Oppenwehe to Washington (on-the-Brazos); **Weser,** 1857
Lueckemeier family—to Independence; **Weser,** 1859
Lueckendiers, J.—Osterdieps? to Galveston; Iris, 1858
Lueckner, Wilhme—Plauen; **Weser,** 1854
Lueddecke, Charl., Joachim, Wilhme — Prenstin (Prenzing?) to Houston; **Juno,** 1860
Luedecke, E.—Neuhütten; **Neptune,** 1854
Luedeke, Henriette, Emilie, Emilie —Meindorf to New Ulm; **Weser,** 1860
Luederitz, A.—Bratz to Galveston; Iris, 1857
Lueders, Claus—Uetersen; **Weser,** 1854
Luedtke, Fried., 21—Perleberg; **Colonist,** 1850; Austin Co.
Luehken, J.—Varel to Galveston; Iris, 1857

Luehrs, Joh. H.—Sengwarden; Herschel, 1851; Austin Co.
Luelben, H.—Hannover to Galveston; Weser, 1860
Luenzel, Marie—Hamburg to Bexar Co.; Gaston, 1860
Luenzel, Max—Hildesheim to Bexar Co.; Gaston, 1860
Luerssen, Hein., 34—Helsdorf; Sophia 34, Hein. 9, Aug. 6, Wilh. 4, Wilhme 2; Solon, 1850
Luetgering, Conrad—Oberg; Juno, 1853
Lueth, J. F. and 2 children—Neukloster, Mecklenburg; S a r a h, 1851
Luettig, Jos.—Webersburg; Herschel, 1851
Luetzen, Heinrich—Tondern, Denmark; Washington, 1852
Luetzenbarger, C. W. — Grossenberkel; Leibniz, 1850
Luhm, Jacob and Anna—"Aus der Schweiz" to Houston; Gessner, 1860
Luhring, Ernestine, 18—Hannover; Joh. Dethardt, 1848
Luhrsen, Aug. and Chr.; Ammerland, 1854
Luk, Joh.—Bremersberge; Canapus, 1849
Luke, Friedke and Elis.—Bernburg; Neptune, 1854
Luke, Louise — Prussia to New Braunfels; Gessner, 1860
Lukhardt, W.—Ziegenhain to Galveston; Weser, 1860
Lummer, Wilh., 22—Prussia; Joh. Dethardt, 1848
Luscher, Joh., Rud.—Dürenasch to Leon Springs; Weser, 1860
Lutter, Fr.—Bayreuth, Bavaria; Washington, 1852
Lux, A.—Prussia; Friedrich Grosse, 1853

— M —

Maak, Dor.—Berlin; Suwa, 1853
Maas, M.—Mannheim; Iris, 1857
Maassen, H. — Aachen to Galveston; Weser, 1860
Maassen. Peter—Schuelp, Schleswig, Holstein; Washington, 1852
McCarty, Henry—Philadelphia; Mississippi, 1855
Machala, Paul; Ammerland, 1854; Fayette Co.
Macheleidt, Georg — Rohrbach, Saxony to Galveston; Franklin, 1852

Machemehl, Joh. and E. A.—Annaburg; Canapus, 1849; Austin Co.
Machemehl, Michael with wife—Wilthen; Machemehl, Michael with wife and ch. — Wilthen; Canapus, 1849; Austin Co.
Mack, Carl, 28—Garz; Brasilian, 1850
Mackel, Conrad, 23—Nassau; Franziska, 1849
Maclawezick, Mathias and family —Kroschnitz; Weser, 1854
Maczegemba, Anton — Kotullien?; Weser, 1854
Maczegemba, Aug.—Gross Kroznitz; Weser, 1854
Maczegemba, Jos. and family— Kotulien?; Weser, 1854
Maczegemba, Mathias — Gross Krognitz; Weser, 1854
Maczegemba, Joh. and family— Lagnitz; Weser, 1854
Maddaus, Charlotte, 62—Berlin; Copernicus, 1852
Maeckel, Carl, wife and 4 ch.— Russia; Lucie, 1854
Maedel, H(einri)ch—New Orleans; Maedel, Helene — Glueckstadt; Leibniz, 1850
Maertz, C. with family—Ost-Pieretz to Galveston; Iris, 1858
Maetze, Ernst Gustav — Glogau, Silesia to Millheim, Austin Co. in early 1850's
Maetze, Gottlieb, 48 — Landsberg a/W in Prussia; Amalie 45, Louis 16, Bertha 9, Gustav 7, Georg 5; Gutenberg, 1855
Magel, H. and family—Odenhausen to Seguin; Gaston, 1857
Magnus, Aug. and wife, 5 persons —Offenbach, Nassau; Mississippi, 1855
Magnu(s). Johann Ph. and wife, 3 persons — Offenbach, Nassau; Mississippi, 1855
Mahler, Friedr.—Prussia; Antoinette, 1855
Mahler, Ludwig, 21—Westenfeld; Anna Louisa, 1857
Mahlmann, Ernst with wife and 4 ch. — Rehburg to Brenham; Weser, 1857; Austin Co.
Mahlmann, H. with wife—Rehburg to Brenham; Weser, 1857
Mahlstedt, Antoinette, 25 — Ludwigslust; Solon, 1850
Mahlstedt. Sophia — Hamburg to Industry; Weser, 1860
Mahncke, H.. 27, Doris 28—Rövershagen, Mecklenburg; Herschel, 1855; Austin Co.

Mahrhoff, Hein.—Neustadt; Henriette, 1843 (1853)

Mahring, J. W.—Osterburg, Prussia; Hampden, 1854

Maimaldt (Maiwaldt?), Fr., 18—Krapkow (Krackau?); Solon, 1850

Malcomes, ... (merchant)—to Galveston; Anton Gunther, 1860

Malezak (Halescheck?), Adalbert, Josepha, Johann — Bohemia to Cat Spring; Weser, 1860; Austin Co.

Malustik, Marie—Gacenka (Jasenka) to Industry; Juno, 1860

Malz, Marg. E., 43; Joh. M. 18, Peter 16, Wilh. 11; Anna Louisa, 1857

Mandel family—Hannover; 5 persons; Suwa, 1853

Mandue, Franz and family; Ammerland, 1854

Maniko, Franz and family—Humpoletz; Weser, 1854

Mann, Anna Marie, 44; Reform, 1850

Mann, Ernst, 30—Muckerehne; Hamburg, 1849

Mann, Ferd.—Gau Böckelheim to San Antonio; Gaston, 1860

Mann, J. A., 24—Prussia; Colonist, 1848

Manshaar, Franca (died)—Rastadt; Reform, 1849

Maraun, Julius—Lübeck; wife and 5 ch., ½-8½ years old; Miles, 1852

Marburger, Joh. Hry., 27—Laasphehütte; Christine nee Bote; Antoinette, 1848; Austin Co.

Marburger, Ludwig and family; Galliott Concordia, 1854; Fayette Co.

March, Jos., Therese—Schönwald; Minna, 1854

Maresch family, 6 persons—Vienna; Suwa, 1853; Austin Co.

Margraf, ... and family—Altenburg; Gessner, 1854

Mark, Carl, 20; Creole, 1852

Mark, Carl Friedr., 5 persons—Bischofswerder; M a r k, Carl Gottl. — Bischofswerder; Herschel, 1851

Markmann, Carl Ludw.—Everhauserholz; Reform, 1849

Markmann, Georg, 32—Hamburg; F. born Huend, 27; Anna 3, Georg 4; Antoinette, 1848; Fayette Co.

Markmann, N.—Oldenburg to La Grange; Fortuna, 1858

Markwarden, F. D., 22; Galliott Flora, 1849

Markworth, H., 5 persons—Prussia; Friedrich Grosse, 1853

Marlmann, Sophie, 19; Hermann Theodor, 1850

Marnitz, Carl—Lasslig (Laaslich); wife and 5 ch., 12-22 years old; Copernicus, 1852

Marohn, Gottfried—Alt-Ponowow, Prussia; wife and 3 ch., ½ to 13 years old; Miles, 1852

Marold, Georg Theodor — Altenburg; Herschel, 1851

Maronde, Fried. with family, 5 persons—Cerewick (Cerekvice); J. W. Buddecke, 1853

Marschall, C.—Marburg to Houston; Anton Gunther, 1860

Marschall, F.—Hesse; Friedrich Grosse, 1853

Mart, Claus—Bargfeld, Holstein; Republic, 1851

Marte, G.—to Galveston; Weser, 1859

Martens, Fried.—Schilda, Prussia; Miles, 1852

Martin, ... (farmer)—Meschede to Hedwigshill; Fortuna, 1858; Mason Co.

Martin, ...—Bavaria to Galveston; Anton Gunther, 1860

Martin, Anna—Ungefar (Anzefähr or Unghvar?); J. W. Buddecke, 1853

Martin, Aug., wife and son—Rohrbach, Saxony; Franklin, 1852

Martin, Carl—Meschede; Neptune, 1854

Martin, Carl—Eisenroth; Mississippi, 1855; Austin Co.,

Martin, Ernst, 25—Meschede to Galveston; Weser, 1859

Martin, Galeo, 28—Baden; Joh. Dethardt, 1848

Martin, Jacob, 24; Peter, 59—Hannover; Antoinette, 1848

Martini, Hein.—Wittenberg, Prussia; Washington, 1852

Martins, Henry—Prussia to Harrisburg; Henriette, Wilh., Caro.; Weser, 1860

Martzahn. Chr.—Karbow; wife and 4 ch., 12-20 years old; Leibniz, 1850

Marwitz, Herm. and Wilh.—Burg.; Magnet, 1851; Galveston

Marx, Jacob—Umstadt to Galveston; Iris, 1861

Marxen, Phil.—Marne, Denmark; Copernicus, 1852

Maser, Georg Ludwig—Plieningen; Solon, 1852
Maser, Joh. M.—Plieningen; Hermann Theodor, 1853
Maske, Friedr. and family—Prussia; Antoinette, 1855; Comal Co.
Masser, Regina—Bertheim (Berkheim?); Neptune, 1854
Mast, Maria—Schildfach, Baden to Galveston; Republic, 1851
Masur, Gottfried—Polzin, Prussia; John Frederick, 1850; Guadalupe Co.
Matajowski, Wenzel — Nechanitz; arr. at Galveston 1850, Bastrop Co. 1852
Matchotka, Joseph and family—Humpoletz, Bohemia; Weser, 1854
Mateus, A.—Hesse; Friedrich Grosse, 1853
Mathaei, ... (farmer)—Hamburg to Austin; Anton Gunther, 1860
Matheas, M. with family—Burg to Liberty: Weser, 1858
Mathissen, G.—Middlefarth, Denmark; Washington, 1852
Mathner, Amandus—Carlau (Carlow), Prussia; Miles, 1854
Matijevsky, Wenzel—Königgrätz; Herschel, 1851
Matschke, Gustav, Caro., Auguste —Karlsruhe to La Grange; Weser, 1860
Matschke. Sam'l, 76; Elise 32, Louise 34; Baden; Reform, 1850
Matsen, Ch.—Oesterbye, Denmark; Washington, 1852
Matson, V.—Quintana (Spain?); Weser, 1854
Matthias. Jacob—Prussia; Neptune, 1848
Matting family—to Yorktown; Weser, 1859
Matuschezick, John. Veronica, Philipp — Austria; Jeverland, 1860: Austin Co.
Matz. Margaretha, J. P. and W.— Lötzbeuren: Anna Louisa, 1857
Matzdorff. Carl and Robert — Gartz. Prussia; Washington, 1852; Bexar Co.
Mauer. Geo., 38; Emilie 9. Georgie 58—Liegnitz; Reform, 1850; Fayette Co.
Mauermann, Bernhard, 17; Solon, 1850
Mauermann, Franziska — Bullendorf; Minna, 1854
Mautz. Elis—Berkheim; Neptune, 1854

Mautz, J. J., 20—Berkheim to Galveston; Iris, 1859
Max, George, 26; Sophie, 1852
Maxfeld, Heinrich, 34 — Bordesholm, Holstein; Maria 35, Detlef 7, Lena 5, Anna 3, Sophia 1; Gutenberg, 1855; Bexar Co.
May. Fr. Aug.—Bilmsdorf; Herschel, 1851
May, Gottl.—Förstgen; 4 persons; Herschel, 1851; Austin Co.
Mayer, A.—to Industry; Weser, 1859
Maywald, A.—Prussia; Neptune, 1848
Maywald, R.—Grüneberg; Neptune, 1854
Mebis, Fred, 38; Cath. 34, Carl 7, Dor. 4, Eliz. 2; Natchez, 1847
Mebus, Henriette, with 5 children — Solingen to Fredericksburg; Iris, 1858
Mechels, J. S.—Prussia; Friedrich Grosse, 1853
Mecker, Carl, 25—Perleberg; Colonist, 1850
Medinger, J.—Württ.; Franziska, 1854
Mehrens. Henrich, 38—Neumuenster, Holstein; Magda. 32, Christian 3; Gutenberg, 1855; Comal Co.
Mehrmann. Wilh.—Beckum to Galveston: Weser, 1857
Meier, August—Hannover to New Braunfels: Weser. 1860
Meier, C., 28; Herschel, 1849; Gillespie Co.
Meier, Christian — Hannover to New Braunfels; Weser. 1860
Meier, F.. 21; Fortuna. 1858
Meier, Fried., Marg., Wilh.—Wehdem to Brenham; Weser, 1860
Meier. Fried., Christine, Henry, Christine — Hannover to New Braunfels: Weser. 1860
Meier. Fried., Charlotte, Henry— Hannover to Frelsburg; Weser, 1860
Meier. Hein. — Hannover; Suwa, 1853; Comal Co.
Meier, Henry, Caro.. Louise. Sophie — Wehdem to Brenham; Weser. 1860
Meier, Joh., 28—Bavaria; Franziska, 1847
Meier, Th.—Bohemia; 7 persons; Friedrich Grosse, 1853; Austin, Texas
Meier, W. — Bohemia: 6 persons; Friedrich Grosse, 1853

Mein, Claus, 26—Prussia; Natchez, 1847
Meincke, Ernst, 28—Lauenburg or Gueltzen; Julie 24, Carl 3, Brasilian, 1850
Meinecke, Fried., 43—Prussia; Sophia 41, Carl 17, Fried. Wilh. 15, Joh. Fried. 12, Maria Emilie 10, Wilhme 5, Eduard 3; Natchez, 1847; Austin Co.
Meinen, ...—Clausthal to Gieseke's Platz (Place); Fortuna, 1858; Washington Co.
Meiner, L. — Hannover to New Braunfels; Weser, 1860
Meinert, Adolph — Berlin; 2 persons; Neptune, 1853
Meinhold, Jos., 29—Silesia; Joh. 11, Christ. 6; Franziska, 1849
Meinig, M. — Chemnitz to La Grange; Iris, 1860
Meirhof, Joh., 58 — Mecklenburg; Marie 58, Joh. 29, Minna 22, Sophie 18, Friedke 16; Franziska, 1847
Meissen, August, 22; Fortuna, 1858
Meissner, C. W. and family, 4 persons — Z w i c k a u; Mississippi, 1855; De Witt Co.
Meissner, Carl and Henriette — Züllichau; Solon, 1852; Austin Co.
Meister, Carl and Maria—Prussia; Antoinette, 1855; Austin Co.
Meisterlin, Friedr. — Schleswig; Miles, 1853; Austin Co.
Meitzen, Laura, 27—Königsberg; Brasilian, 1850
Meitzen, Otto, 39; Franz 31, Otto 9, Ida 2, J. E. W. ¼; Herschel, 1850; Fayette Co.
Meitzen, Wilh., 30—Breslau; Antonie 28, Marie 5, Max 4; Franziska, 1849; Fayette Co.
Melcher, Cath., 16—Hamburg; Chas. N. Cooper, 1847
Melcher, Christian, 34; Lisette 37, Mina 5, Lena ½; Creole, 1852; Fayette Co.
Melchior, M., R., and W.—Burg; Hermann Theodor, 1853; Fayette Co.
Melgian, Fr., 27—Hudelsen; Helen and Elise, 1847
Melitz, C. and W. — Theesen to York's Creek; Iris, 1857; Comal Co.
Melhanse, H.—Klabow; Leibniz, 1850
Mellinghoff, H.—Emmerich; Texas, 1853

Mendel, Justus—Salzburg; Weser, 1854
Mendelsohn, M. — Schneidemühl to Galveston; Weser, 1858
Menemacher, J.; Herschel, 1849
Menil, Rudolph du, 27; Hermann Theodor, 1850; Comal Co.
Menk, Johann—Posen, Prussia; Franklin, 1853
Menke, Hein., 25; Solon, 1850; Austin Co.
Menne, Ernst, Henriette, Caro., Johanna, Anna—Hillegossen to Galveston; Fortuna, 1860
Mennik, G. A.—Houston to Houston; Gessner, 1860
Mensch, Caro.—Sobiechen (Sobieszym) to Fredericksburg; Juno. 1860
Mensing, Aug.—Derenburg; Reform, 1849; Fayette Co.
Menze, Adolphe, 19—Schlangen; Canapus, 1848
Menzel, Caroline—Lichtenau, Prussia; Franklin, 1853
Menzel, Ernst, 25 — Wünschke to Bastrop; Christiane 23, Iris, died age 1 day; Iris, 1859
Menzel, Gottfried (Priest)—Neustadt, Bohemia; Canapus, 1849: New Braunfels, Comal Co.
Menzel, Michael and wife, 5 persons — Bullsdorf, Böhmen; Mississippi, 1855
Merherper, H.--Striegen; Gessner, 1855
Merrem, Theo. and 2 sisters—Witzenhausen, Hesse; Mississippi, 1855
Merseburger, Ed. and wife—Havelberg, Prussia; Fayette Co.; Merseberger, Hein.—Havelberg; Colorado Co.; Washington, 1852
Mertens, Fr.—Birkenfeld; 5 persons; Hermann Theodor, 1853
Mertens, Friedrich—Nielitz, Prussia; Copernicus, 1852; Austin Co.
Merz, Joh. Hch., 32; Anna Marie 31, Joh. Wilh. 6, Elis. 4, M.... 2; John Holland, 1848
Merz, Peter, 27; Cath. 43, Marie 17, Marg. 15, Jacob 11, Ottillia 8, Elis. 6; John Holland, 1848
Messinger, Herm., 26—Gottschimm to Yorktown; Weser, 1859
Messner, Anna, 26—Sophie, 1852
Methner, H.—Reinersdorf to Galveston; Iris, 1859
Metzger, Daniel—Aachen to Galveston; Weser, 1860; Austin Co.
Metzger, G. W.; Joh. Ed. Grosse, 1853

Metzger, J.—Galveston to Galveston (died on journey beyond Cuba and was buried at sea); **Fortuna, 1860**
Meuckhof, Sophie and Dorothea—Luessow, Mecklenburg; **Sarah, 1851**
Meussel, Georg—Kunzendorf; **Weser, 1854**
Mewes, Carolina — Waldenburg, Prussia; daughter Alwine, age 3; **Miles, 1854**
Mews, Johann and wife — Havelberg, Prussia; **Washington, 1852**
Mey, Johan, 35—**Sophie, 1852**
Meyer, Ahlert, Juliane, Marg.—Bremen; **Solon, 1852**
Meyer (Meytr?), Albert—Schwarme; **Texas, 1853;** Comal Co.
Meyer, Andreas, 20; **Solon, 1850;** Bexar Co.
Meyer, August—Neubrück; **Weser, 1854**
Meyer, Carl, 14; **Magnet, 1852**
Meyer, Carl, wife and 4 ch.—Rostock to Austin; **Gaston, 1860**
Meyer, Carol; **Reform, 1849**
Meyer, Ch.—Dohnsen; **Neptune, 1854**
Meyer, Chs., 18; **Sophie, 1852**
Meyer, Christian and wife—Helgoland to Bexar; **Gaston, 1860**
Meyer, Chr. F. and wife—Württemberg; **Weser, 1854**
Meyer, Christ., 42—Vordorf, Han.; **Joh. Dethardt, 1848**
Meyer, Christine—Berthelsdorf; **Neptune, 1853**
Meyer, Christine and Juliane—Nassau; **Antoinette, 1855**
Meyer, F.—to Brenham; **Weser, 1859**
Meyer, F.—Croppenstedt to La Grange; **Iris, 1860**
Meyer, F.—Rückeburg to Marlin; **Iris, 1858**
Meyer. F. F.—Theesen to York's Creek; **Iris, 1857**
Meyer, Ferd. Wm., 21—Ehlentrup (Ehlenbruck); **Antoinette, 1848**
Meyer, Frd.—Damlach, Prussia; **Franklin, 1853**
Meyer, Fried., 28—Buttersteig, Han.; **Brasilian, 1850**
Meyer. Fred. Daniel, 22; **Louis, 1848;** Guadalupe Co.
Meyer, Georg—Langensalza, Prussia; **Copernicus, 1852**
Meyer, Gerhard, 21; **Solon, 1850**
Meyer, Gesche and child—Sengwarden; **Herschel, 1851**

Meyer, Hans, with family, 4 persons—Kleinensiehl; **J. W. Buddecke, 1853**
Meyer, Herm. Hein., 47, and Caro., 34; **Solon, 1850**
Meyer, Hinrich—Passade, Holstein; **Hampden, 1854**
Meyer, J.—Hesse; **Franziska, 1854**
Meyer, J. with wife—Bromberg; **Weser, 1857**
Meyer, Joachim and wife—Schwerin, Mecklenburg; **Sophie, 1852**
Meyer, Joh. Chr., 35 — Jübar; Marg. 32, Hr. 9, Marg. 5; **Helen & Elise, 1847**
Meyer, Joh. Georg, 71—Hohnsen; Wm. 38, Carol 23, Dora 8; **Canapus, 1848**
Meyer, Julius, 24 and Henriette 26 —Koenigsberg; **Brasilian, 1850**
Meyer, L.—Liebenburg; **Adolphine, 1859**
Meyer's, Londorf wife, 43—Gross Lafferde; **Joh. Dethardt, 1848**
Meyer, Louise, 23—Nordheim; **Joh. Dethardt, 1848**
Meyer, Ludwig—Seehausen, Prussia; wife and 2 ch., ½ and 6 years old; **Washington, 1852;** Galveston
Meyer, Sophia—Neustadt; **Henriette, 1843 (1853)**
Meyer, W., 18—Wehdem to Brenham; **Iris, 1859**
Meyers, Wilhme, 32—Königsberg; Adolbert 12, Richard 10, Emil 8, Franziska 6, Betty 4; **Neptune, 1850**
Meyer, Wilh., 20; **Hermann Theodor, 1850**
Meyer, Wolfgang, 43; Cath. 13, Barbara 10; **Sophie, 1851**
Michael (Michel), Andreas, 31; Anna Marie 20; **Brasilian, 1857**
Michael, Auguste—Saxony; **Friedrich Grosse, 1853**
Michael, Joh.; **Galliott Concordia, 1854**
Michael, Johann(a?) — Perleberg, Prussia; family of 4 persons; **Bassermann, 1851**
Michalk, Carl, 16—Sandoverschagen? to Bastrop; **Iris, 1859**
Michaus, Herm. 24, Franz 19—Offelten; **Canapus, 1848**
Michel, Carl — Traureith (Traunreid); **Texas, 1853**
Michel, H.—to Corsicana; **Weser, 1859**
Michels, Elis.—Gross an/Eder to Houston; **Iris, 1859**

Michna, Wenzel — Austria; Marianne, Marianne, Johanna, Clara, Joseph; Jeverland, 1860
Micholsky, Jos. and family—Rojemirsch?; Weser, 1854
Micksch, E.—Reichenberg; Texas, 1853. See Mitschk
Middelegge, Louise—Lassbrück; Texas, 1853; Galveston
Mielke, A u g u s t — Schmielacke, Prussia; Republic, 1851; Cameron Co.
Mielke, Wilhme—Berlin; Weser, 1854
Mier, Hein., 25—Prussia; Franziska, 1849
Miers, Carl, 26; Margaretha 22— Neumuenster, Holstein; Gutenberg, 1855
Mikalachlik, Joh., 34; Brasilian, 1857
Mikau, Marie with 3 ch.—Weigersdorf to Bastrop; Fortuna, 1858
Mikesch, Jacob and family; Galliott Concordia, 1854
Mikeska, F. and wife—Mähren to Industry; Juno, 1860
Mikosch, Franz and wife—Wilkowitz; Weser, 1854
Milatz, Joachim—Wenddorf, Mecklenburg; wife and 3 ch., ¾-7 years old; Copernicus, 1852
Milatz, Joh., 62—Perleberg; Brasilian, 1850
Milatz, John, 63 — Prussia; Hein. 27, Dor. 21; Colonist, 1848
Milhusen, Carl—Wolgast, Prussia; wife and 6 ch., 6-24 years old; Copernicus, 1852
Miller, Carl—Burg; Mississippi, 1855
Miller, Gerhard, 45 — Oldenburg; Anne Elis. 44, Meta 29, Joh. 19, Herm. 17, Gerhard 15, Elisa 10; Franziska, 1849
Miller, Wilh., 57; Elis. 52, Theo. 27, Carl 18, Netta 16, Joleph 14; Joseph 14; Franziska, 1847
Mimbrauen, H. and Fried.; Ammerland, 1854
Mingegramm, Fr.—Ballenstedt; Leibniz, 1850
Minke, Christiane—Holzminden; John Frederick, 1850
Mischaleck, V. and wife—Schimnowitz (Schimmerwitz); Gessner, 1855
Mischer, Fritz, wife and brother— Schönemark; Weser, 1854; Fayette Co.

Mitschau, John — Austria; Anna, Franz, Agnes, John, Marianne, Joseph, Szueril, Ignaz; Jeverland, 1860
Mitschk, Maria — Baruth to Bastrop; Fortuna, 1858
Mitschke, Johanna and Marie — Görlitz to Bellville; Iris, 1860
Mittank, D. — Probsthagen, Prussia; Miles, 1854
Mittel, W.—Weiler; Gessner, 1854
Mittelberg, Fried. Wilh. — Stughorst (Stieghorst); Solon, 1852
Mittendorf, Christian and family— Wolfenbüttel; Weser, 1854; De Witt Co.
Mittler, Heinrich—Munich; Suwa, 1853
Mitze, Maria—Hesse; Franziska, 1854
Mobes, L., 19; Fortuna, 1858; Colorado Co.
Mockel, Joh.—Saxony; Friedrich Grosse, 1853
Moebus, ...—Solingen to Round Top; Fortuna, 1858
Moecke, H.—Breslau; 4 persons; Neptune, 1854
Moehl, Carl—Gifhorn; Reform, 1849
Moehl, Otto with wife—Breslau, Prussia; Miles, 1852
Moehrenberg, Joh.—Oldenburg; Henriette, 1843 (1853)
Moehrer, Christ.—Werle, Mecklenburg; wife and 3 ch., 19-29 years old; Moehrer, Wilhelm, wife and son, 0 years old; Therese Henriette, 1853
Moehrig, Christian, 43 — Braunschweig; Christiana 42, Maria 9, Christian 8, Fritz 4; Solon, 1850; Comal Co.
Moelhusen, Wilh. — Moelschow, Prussia; Miles, 1852. See also Milhusen.
Moeller, C. H. — Heiligenhafen, Holstein; Hampden, 1854
Moeller, Mrs. Emilie and daughter age 20—Hamburg; Therese Henriette, 1853
Moeller, Ferd. and Elisa—Wallen; 4 persons; Hermann Theodor, 1853
Moeller, Friedrich — Schwerin, Mecklenburg; wife and 3 ch. ¼-6 years old; Sophie, 1852
Moeller, Gotth. — Karbow; H(einri)ch, Johann, W(ilhel)m 3 yrs. old; Leibniz, 1850
Moeller, H.—Rehbeck; Adolphine, 1859

Moeller, Joh. F.—Berlin; Suwa, 1853
Moeller, J. H.—Sütel; wife and 3 ch. ½-6 years old; Hampden, 1854; Galveston
Moerer, Franz—Panckow, Prussia; wife and 7 ch. ½-13 years old; Franklin, 1852
Moerer, Fritz, 28 — Moellenbeck, Prussia; John Frederick, 1850
Mohmann, Anna, 14; Solon, 1850
Mohrhoff, Diedrich—Hannover; 7 persons; Henriette, 1843 (1853); Comal Co.
Mohrmann, A.—Altenburg; Weser, 1854; Bastrop Co.
Mohrmann, Ch.—Altenburg; Gessner, 1855
Moje, Gustav—Freiburg, Han.; Republic, 1851
Moll, H. and J.—Millich to San Antonio; Iris, 1857
Mollenbehrend, Adolph, 18 — Kolstadt; Canapus, 1848; Fayette Co.
Moller, Edward, 50; Josephine 46, Elise 20, Josephine 16, Witgarde 14, Clara 12, Herm. 8, Karl 8, Terese 6; Natchez, 1847
Moller, Joh., 26 and Friedke, 26—Mecklenburg; Chas. N. Cooper, 1847
Mollert, Jos., 45—Mähren; Mrs. W. 43, John 15, Franz 12; Fortuna, 1858
Monde, Carl A. and wife, 6 persons — Biscupiee?; Mississippi, 1855
Montag, R.—Angstedt; Weser, 1860
Morbach, Joseph and family, 6 persons—Breissig; Juno, 1853
Moreck, Franz—Vienna; Suwa, 1853
Morer, Fritz, 28; John Frederick, 1850
Morf, Rud.—Rindhausen; Lucie, 1854
Morgenroth, Georg — Schwarzenbronn to Frelsburg; Fortuna, 1860
Morgenstein, E. Lebrecht—Annaberg; 2 persons; Neptune, 1853
Moritz, Barbara—to Galveston; Weser, 1859
Mosebach, W.—Mühlhausen; 2 persons; Magnet, 1851; Bastrop Co.
Moser, Conrad, 20; Magnet, 1852
Moser, J. F.—Neugebhardsdorf; Franklin, 1853
Motzer, Barbara — Gomaringen to San Antonio; Iris, 1858

Moureau, Franz, 24—Weiburg; Franziska, 1849; Comal Co.
Moureau, Julius, 22—Wiesbaden to New Braunfels; Weser, 1858
Mross, V.—Rohsmiritz; Gessner, 1855
Muchow, Louise, 29 — Molnitz, Prussia; Franklin, 1852
Mucke, Jos.; Neptune, 1849; Austin Co.
Muckerd, J. G. C., 30—Mittlareid (Mitterreit?) to San Antonio; Iris, 1859
Muegge, Karl—Schnackenburg; Iris, 1859
Muehe, W.—Hannover; Franziska, 1854
Muehlenberg, C a r l — Bielefeld; Weser, 1854; Guadalupe Co.
Muehlenbruch, Friedrich; Muehlenbruch, Gottlieb, wife and 2 children — Biedendorff, Mecklenburg; Copernicus, 1852
Muehlenfeld, Charles, 36—Prussia; John Holland, 1848
Muehler, Gebhardt, 21; Solon, 1850
Mueller, ... and Marie—Warmbrunn('en) to Latium (Washington Co.); Juno, 1860
Mueller, A.—Buchmannsdorf to Lockhart; Gaston, 1857
Mueller, A.—Prussia; Friedrich Grosse, 1853
Mueller, Anna — Mühlhausen to Galveston; Iris, 1860
Mueller, Anna A., 29; Hermann Theodor, 1850
Mueller, Anna Elis.; Galliott Concordia, 1854
Mueller, Anna Marg. and Christine—Weimar to Austin County; Gessner, 1860
Mueller, August—Perleberg, Prussia; Franklin, 1853; Austin Co.
Mueller, Barbara, 24—Ungerndorf; Joh. Dethardt, 1848
Mueller, C. Fred. 50—Frohnau; Neptune, 1850
Mueller, Carl; Joh. Ed. Grosse, 1853
Mueller, Carl August—Braunschweig; Herschel, 1851; Fayette Co.
Mueller, Caro. 38, Jacob 15, Caro. 13, Hein. 11, Fried. 9 — Bergbruch to Houston; Weser, 1859
Mueller, Charlotte E.—Blankenese to Galveston; Iris, 1861
Mueller, Chas. F., 23; Galliott Flora, 1849
Mueller, Conrad—Spenge; Neptune, 1853

— 109 —

Mueller, E.—Baden; Franziska, 1854
Mueller, E. Herm.—Prussia; Neptune, 1849
Mueller, Emilie—Neudorf to Richmond; Iris, 1860
Mueller, Ephraim — Bergbruch, Mecklenburg; and family, 3 ch. ⅛-4 years old; Miles, 1852
Mueller, Ferd. and family—Nordhausen; Weser, 1854
Mueller, Fr., 27; Fortuna, 1858
Mueller, Franz and John—Brecke, Han.; Texas, 1853
Mueller, Fried.; Joh. Ed. Grosse,.. 1853
Mueller, Fried., 25; Louis, 1848
Mueller, Friedrich — Schmielacko, Prussia to Galveston; Republic, 1851
Mueller, Fried. Lud.; Galliott Concordia, 1854
Mueller, Friedke and Wilhelm—Laaslich to Brenham; Fortuna, 1860
Mueller, Gerhard, 24 and Lina, 23 —Oldenburg; Franziska, 1849; Fayette Co.
See also Miller, Gerhard
Mueller, Gerh., 34; Solon, 1850
Mueller, Gerhard—Heibuelt (Heidbühl); Neptune, 1853
Mueller, Herm. and Caro.—Serno to New Ulm; Fortuna, 1860
Mueller, Jacob—to Gonzales; Henriette, 1843 (1853)
Mueller, Johann and son 17 years old — Schwerin, Mecklenburg; Miles, 1853
Mueller, Johann—Schwerin, Mecklenburg; Sophie, 1852
Mueller, Joh. Fried.—Hannover; Miles, 1853
Mueller, Julie Ch.—Lippersdorf; Lucie, 1854
Mueller, Ludwig — Bergbruch, Mecklenburg; Miles, 1853
Mueller, Ludwig and Dorothea—Posen; Miles, 1853
Mueller, Louise. 19—Perleberg, Prussia; Franklin, 1852
Mueller, M., wife and child—Malberg; Neptune, 1854
Mueller, Marie—to New Braunfels; Weser, 1859
Mueller, Maria—Oldesloe; Neptune, 1854
Mueller, Max—Hörter; Juno, 1853
Mueller, Michael, Elis., Marg. — Eisenach to Austin; Gessner, 1860

Mueller, Otto, 29, Mathilde 26—Crossen; Solon, 1850
Mueller, Ottocar, 38 — Schönburg; Elis. 28, Jenny 3; Colonist, 1850; Gillespie Co.
Mueller, P.—Halberstadt to Galveston; Gaston, 1857
Mueller, Phillip, 34; Emma 37, Emilie 8, Gustav 4, Dor. 3, Marie 1; Louis, 1848; Comal Co.
Mueller, T.—Brake to Galveston; Fortuna. 1858
Mueller, Val. and family (5)—Zühernische; Solon, 1852; Goliad Co.
Mueller, Wilh. with family, 4 persons—Schweidnitz; J. W. Buddecke, 1853
Muench, Ad.—Neudorf; 4 persons; ship and date?
Muench, Carl; Galliott Concordia, 1854
Muench, Ernst—Petersdorf; Magnet, 1851
Muench, M. and Hunchminda—Oggersheim; Weser, 1854
Muenich, J., wife and child—Niedertimmend; Neptune, 1854
Muenter, Johann — Schleswig, Schleswig; wife and daughter ½ year old; Hampden, 1854
Mueschke, Wilhelmine and family—Prussia; Antoinette, 1855
Mueste, D.—Köln to San Antonio; Iris, 1860
Muhe, Friedr. and Hein—Söhlde, Han.; Minna, 1854
Muhl, C. A.—Lichtenau, Prussia; Franklin, 1853
Muhlke, Johann, 34 — Oldenburg; Maria 26, Gestina F. 1; Franziska, 1847
Muller, Joh. Fried., 28—Holstein; Colonist, 1848
Muller, Jos., 23 — Prussia; Joh. Dethardt, 1848
Muller, Rudolph—Grafhorst, Han.; 3 persons; Texas, 1853
Munch, Kunigund, 25 — Bavaria; Franziska, 1849
See Muench also.
Mundt, Albert—Tempelburg; Neptune, 1854
Munn, L. H. G., 44; Marie 45, Theo. 12, Ferd. 9; Hermann Theodor, 1850
Munnsen, M.—Föhr to Galveston; Juno, 1860
Munsch, Carl Fried.—Neustadt; Solon, 1852
Muri, J. — "Aus der Schweiz" to Austin Co.; Gessner, 1860

Murk, Emma—Prussia; Franziska, 1854
Muschke, Gustav — Berlin; Suwa, 1853; see also Mueschke
Muse, Wm., 18; Canapus, 1848
Muss, C.—Poland; wife and 3 ch.; Franziska, 1854
Muss, Hartwig—Sodendeck; 3 persons; Hermann Theodor, 1853
Muss, Joh.—Gülitz; Neptune, 1853; Fayette Co.
Muth, Ludwig, 35; Creole, 1852
Muts, Franz and family—Schemisal; Weser, 1854
Myros, Georg—Hannover; Weser, 1854

— N —

Nabel (Nebel?), Fried. — Galliott Concordia, 1854
Naeser, Aug.—Altenburg; Lucie Bremen, 1854
Nagel, Charlotte—Oldendorf; Neptune, 1853; Bexar Co.
Nagel, Julius and wife, 1 ch. age 2; Spitowa, Prussia; Miles, 1853
Nagel, Thies., wife and 4 ch. ¾-7½ years old—Buchholtz, Denmark; Copernicus, 1852
Nahl, Wilh. with 2 daughters—to New Braunfels; Fortuna, 1858
Napiorsky, E., 3 persons—Bromberg; Texas, 1853
Naravold (Nasswold?), Carl, 20—Burg; Neptune, 1850
Nauert, C. — Meindorf to Galveston; Weser, 1860
Nauert, Louise and Antonia — Meindorf to Galveston; Weser, 1860
Naumann, F. W.—Prussia; Neptune, 1848
Naumann, Ferd.—Wetter, Kurhessen; Sophie, 1852
Naumann, Rob.—Lumbach (Rumbach?); Reform, 1849
Nebring (Nehring?), A.—Prussia; Franziska, 1854; Colorado Co.
Necker, Carl, 25—Perleberg; Colonist, 1850; Austin Co.
Neich, C.—Posen to Houston; Juno, 1860
Neils, Hans, 25—Bordesholm, Holstein; Gutenberg, 1855
Neitzel, W. and wife—Belgard; Iris, 1857
Nelson, D.—Kniphausen to Round Top, Fayette Co.; Iris, 1857
Nemcke, J. H., 37; Galliott Flora, 1849

Nessel, J.—Bohemia; Franziska, 1854
Nessie, Fried. and wife—Casberg (Kasberg); Juno, 1853
Netzel, Edward, 54, Louise 14, Fr. Edw. 18—Danzig; Iris, 1859; Austin Co.
Neubauer, Carl—Bernstein; Minna, 1854
Neubuhr, Henry, 41—United States; Chas. N. Cooper, 1847
Neuenburg, Max—Berlin; Texas, 1853
Neuendorf, E. F., 28—Hamburg; Hamburg, 1849; Fayette Co.
Neuendorf, Eleanore—Linda (Leuda?); Neptune, 1854
Neuhardt, A. — Landenbeck to Lockhart; Juno, 1860
Neumann, Ad.—Neugebhardsdorf; Franklin, 1853
Neumann, B.—Friesland; Texas, 1853
Neumann, C.—Braunsdorf to Galveston; Iris, 1859
Neumann, Caro. and 2 ch.—Cereckwitz (Zerekwitz) to Post Oak Hill; Iris, 1858
Neumann, C. F., wife and 7 ch. ¼-15 years old—Landsberg, Prussia; Miles, 1854
Neumann, F., 25; Fortuna, 1858
Neumann, F.—Schönbach to Round Top; Weser, 1858
Neumann, Ferd., wife and 7 ch.—Bullendorf; Minna, 1854; Colorado Co.
Neumann, H.—Görlitz to Bellville; Iris, 1860
Neumann, J., wife and 3 ch. 15-22 years old—Fodtenkopf, Prussia; Franklin, 1853
Neumann, Joachim and family, 7 adults, 2 children — Kuwinkel, Mecklenburg; Washington, 1852
Neumann, Sigmund, Friedke, Wilh., Adolph, Hermine — Lenzen to Brenham; Fortuna, 1860
Neumeyer, August, wife and 1 ch. age ¼ yr. — Werdershausen, Mecklenburg; Miles, 1852
Neurenberg, F. L. H., 42, Christiane 36, Auguste 8, Wilhme 6, Maria 5, Johanna 3, Emilie ¾— Hamburg; Brasilian, 1850
Nicht, Wilh.; Ammerland, 1854
Nicolai, Carl L. with family, 4 persons—Labyschon? (Lobischau); J. W. Buddecke, 1853; Victoria Co.
Nicolai, J.; Ammerland, 1854

— 111 —

Nicolaisen, Nils—Oesterbye, Denmark; **Washington,** 1852
Nicolaus, Ferd. — Meseritz (Merschlitz?); **Gessner,** 1854
Niebler, Marg.—Stockelsberg, Bavaria; **Franklin,** 1853
Niebling, Charles and Eleonore— Galveston to Galveston; **Fortuna,** 1860
Niebour, G.—see Niedour, G.
Niederhoefer, Jost and family— Grundhausen; **Weser,** 1854
Niedermann, Carl — Middelfarth, Denmark; **Washington,** 1852
Niedermeyer, Josef, 22, Ida 17; **Louis,** 1848
Niediela, John, Anna—Austria; **Jeverland,** 1860
Niedl, Heinrich—Landsberg, Prussia; **Miles,** 1854
Niedour (Niebour?), G. and wife —Zwischen to Galveston; **Iris,** 1857
Niehn, Peter, 35; **Magnet,** 1852
Nielsen, Cornel — Röming, Denmark; **Washington,** 1852
Niemann, Conrad, 42, Maria 44, Fried. 16, Carl 10, Sophie 6; **Creole,** 1852; Fayette Co.
Niemann, Frederick, 32, Elise 28— Texas; **Franziska,** 1849; Galveston
Niemeyer family—Oppendorf; **Adolphine,** 1859
Niemeyer, Gustav — Detmold to Kerr Co.; **Gaston,** 1860
Niemeyer, W., wife and 3 ch.— Hannover; **Franziska.** 1854
Nienaber, Elis.; **Joh. Ed. Grosse,** 1853
Niens, Fried., 26—Klein Elbe; **Joh. Dethardt,** 1848
Niess. Christiane—Nassau; **Franziska,** 1854; Comal Co.
Niess, ... — Weilburg, Nassau; **Franziska,** 1854; Comal Co., then Mason Co.
Niller, F.—Heilsberg to Galveston; **Fortuna,** 1860
Nirsche, Mich.—Kunzendorf; **Texas,** 1853
Nitsche. L.—Buckau to Lynchburg; **Juno,** 1860
Nitzsche. A.—Görlitz; **Gessner,** 1854; Austin Co.
Nizze, Christian and family. 9 persons—Schweidnitz; **J. W. Buddecke,** 1853
Noak, A.—Prussia; **Franziska,** 1854; Austin Co.
Nocker. Ph., 4 persons—Hallgarten; arr. Galveston. Ship? date?

Nodark (Noark?), J. — Poland; **Franziska,** 1854; Colorado Co.
Nohe, Louis and Henriette—Prussia; **Nepune,** 1849
Nohl, Johann 31, Adam 56, Juliane 66, Christina 26, Maria 6, Cath. 5, Carl 4, Phil. 2½, Sophie 1; **Herschel,** 1850
Noll, W.—Eltville; 8 persons; Ship? date?
Nolle (Nolte?), Aug., 26; **Herschel,** 1849; Guadalupe Co.
Nollkaemper, Hein. Rud., 23, Chatarine 24, Hein. 1½—Urswoldt; **Solon,** 1850; Fayette Co.
Nolte, Aug.—See Nolle, Aug.
Nonn, W.—Brohl; 2 persons; ship? date?
Nordhausen, Cath., 3 persons — Neuenburg; **Texas,** 1853; Fayette Co.
Normann, H.; **Ammerland,** 1854
Norrmann, Carl, 55, Adolf 8— Perleberg; **Brazilian,** 1850; Comal Co.
Nose, Henry and Wilhme—Prussia to Brenham; **Weser,** 1860
Nowotny, Wenzel and family; **Galliott Concordia,** 1854; Comal Co.
Nuernberg, H.—Braunrod(e) to Galveston; **Juno,** 1860
Nuesse, Lorenz, 27; **Reform,** 1850
Nuessmann, Engelika and 2 ch.— Hannover; **Franziska,** 1854
Nuetze, Christian — Schwerin, Mecklenburg; **Sophie,** 1852
Nytra, Hedwig—Austria; **Jeverland,** 1860

— O —

Obelgonner, Maria, 14; **Magnet,** 1852; Lavaca Co.
Obenhaus, Lisette—to Columbus; **Weser,** 1859
Ober, Philipp—Berlin; **Suwa,** 1853
Oberlaender, Carl—Saxony; **Friedrich Grosse,** 1853
Obermann, Elise, 29—Engter; **Antoinette,** 1848
Obermeier, Joh. H.—Berlin; **Suwa,** 1853
Oberpriller, Apolonia—Wartenberg; **Lucie,** 1854
Oberwettam, Carol—Bohrenburg? (Dohrenburg?) **Canapus,** 1849;
Oberwetter, P. H.—Kendall Co.
Obrendorf (Ohlendorf?), Carl and family — Wöckenstein (Wolkenstein?); **Gessner,** 1854
Obst, Gotts. (Gottl.?)—Helsch; **Reform,** 1849; Bexar Co.

Ochs family, 4 persons—Cassel; Suwa, 1853
Ochs, Nic., 4 persons; Estafette, 1850
Ochse, Auguste, 4 ch.; Ochse, Wilhelmina — Prussia; Franziska, 1854; Bexar Co.
Ochsmann, Gottl. and family— Prussia; Antoinette, 1855
Ockhardt, Adolphine—Wiehe; Gessner, 1854
Oefinger, Paulus—Aldingen; Neptune, 1853; Medina Co.
Oeft, Friedr., 28—Wittmarshagen; Joh. Dethardt, 1848
Oehler, Fried.—Kleebrand (Kleebronn, Württ); Weser, 1854
Oelenik, Georg, 47, Rosina 37, Anna 10, Thomas 5; Brasilian, 1857
Oember, Carl, 19—Schwartzburg; Magnet, 1852; Fayette Co.
Oensch, Rud. D., 40, Adelheid 40, Oscar 11, Fried. 13, Richard 7; Reform, 1850
Oeser, Chr. and family; Ammerland, 1854
Oeser, Chr. Fr.—Oberscheibe; Hermann Theodor, 1853
Offenbade, Henriette, 24; Franziska, 1849
Offinger, Christian—Plieningen; Solon, 1852; Medina Co.
Offingen (Ossingen?), Maria—Aldingen; Henriette, 1843 (1853)
Ofinger, J.—Aldingen; Adolphine, 1859
Ofinger, V.—Achalm; Adolphine, 1859
Ohde, Ludwig Georg—Wattmannshagen, Mecklenburg; Republic, 1851
Ohl, Johann, 46; Adolphine, 1850
Ohldog (Ohldag?), Phillippine, 22, Sophie 16; Creole, 1852
Ohlenberger family — Nassau; Adolphine, 1859
Ohlendorf, J.—Braunschweig; Gessner, 1854
Ohlenmeyer, Cath.—Versmold; Texas, 1853
Oldejohann, Gerh.—Wohnbeck; Texas, 1853
Olendorf, Widow, 50—Hainengen; Joh. Dethardt, 1848
Oligslager, Marg., 70—Cöln; Franziska, 1849
Olland, Carl, 44, Maria Dor. 27, Elise 36—Brome; Helen & Elise, 1847
Olle, Aug., 25—Coswig; Weser, 1858

Olle, Christoph, Frederike, Fritz— Coswig to New Ulm; Weser, 1860
Olnagel, Miganese(?), 24; Solon, 1850
Opitz, Christian—Zwickau; Mississippi, 1855; Austin Co.
Oppermann, Caro.—Dölme; Reform, 1851
Oppermann, Christoph, 28—Gröningen; Joh. Dethardt, 1848
Oppermann, Mary and Amanda— Galveston to Galveston; Weser, 1860
Oprozenski family—to Galveston; Weser, 1859
Orken, Joh. Fr., 46, Soph. 42, Alb. 16, Joh. Fr. 11, Marg. 9, Reinh. Gehr. 6, Helene 3, Joh. A. 3— Schweiburg; Helen & Elise, 1847
Ort, J.—Hamburg; Minna, 1854; Guadalupe Co.
Orts, Georg—Schwartau; Minna, 1854; Bastrop Co.
Ortz, Georg—Schwartau; Minna, 1854; Bastrop Co.
Osburg, Friedke—Duderstadt; Weser, 1854
Osburg, Georg—Plauen; Weser, 1854
Osk, Kuenig and L.—Halberstadt; Reform, 1847
Oske, Hugo—Langenhausen to St. Bernhardt; Weser, 1860
Ostendorf, Hein. A., 27; Hermann Theodor, 1850
Ostermann, Dor.—Srave; Lucie, 1854
Ostermeyer, Hch., 60, Richard 19, Mathilde 24; Louis, 1848; Galveston
Ostlick, Fried., 21 (26?); Herschel, 1850
Oswald, Carl—Prussia; Antoinette, 1855
Oswald, Wilhelmina and ch.—Bexar Co. to Bexar Co.; Gaston, 1860
Otheld, Anton—Wahren; Neptune, 1853
Othold, Helene, 23; Solon, 1850
Othold, Helene Cath. — Mohlberg (Mahlberg?), (Mohrberg?); Texas, 1853
Ott, Haver—to Galveston; Fortuna, 1860
Ott, Maria—"Aus der Schweiz" to Houston; Gessner, 1860
Ott, Nepomne—Sigmaringen to Galveston; Fortuna, 1860
Otte, Carl — Suhlfeld (Sülfeld?) to Houston; Juno, 1860

Otte, Claus, 31—Neumuenster, Holstein; **Gutenberg,** 1855
Otte, Wilh. and wife—Glandorf (Glendorf?); **Neptune,** 1854
Otten, Johanna—Kosdorf to Spring Branch; **Iris,** 1859
Otten, Zct. (sic); **Ammerland,** 1854
Ottmann, Diedrich, 41, Helene 39, Meta 7, Auguste 3—Hannover; **Reform,** 1850
Ottman, Joh. Hein., 29; **Solon,** 1850
Otto, Elis.; **Joh. Ed. Grosse,** 1853
Otto, Wilh., Anna, Gottl.—Springberg to Brenham; **Juno,** 1860
Otto, Wilhelm—Polzin, Prussia; **Republic,** 1851; Guadalupe Co.
Ousta, Julius, 20, Ernestine 24—Gottschmerbruck; **Wilhelm,** 1858
Ovelgoenner (Obelgonner), H.—Holsen; **Lucie,** 1854
See Obelgonner, Maria
Overhage, Wilh., 27; **Franziska,** 1848

— P —

Paa(s)che, Dor., 66, and Dor., 21—Nemenhaldenrleben? (Neuhaldersleben); **Helen & Elise,** 1847
Paasche, Fr., 36—Nemenhaldenrleben? (Neuhaldersleben); **Helen & Elise,** 1847
Paasche, Joh. E. Chr., 45; Marie 44, Marie 17, Frields 12, Elise 9, Dor. 7, Hein. 3—Steimke; **Helen & Elise,** 1847; Colorado Co.
Pacoir, Aug.—Danzig; **Juno,** 1853
Paerl, Carl—Thuringia; **Weser,** 1854
Paetz, Fried., 37—Prussia; **Chas. N. Cooper,** 1847
Paezenskv, A., 45—Baden; **Reform,** 1850
Pagel, Gottfried, 54, Friedke 44, Wilh. 16, Carl 14, Aug. 12, Friedr. 6, Emilie 4, Franz 4—Kortenhagen; **Brasilian,** 1850; Lavaca Co.
Pahl, Caroline—Holzhausen to New Braunfels; **Weser,** 1860
Pahl, Isaac—Wolfshagen; **Reform,** 1851
Palm, Dorothea — Rostock, Mecklenburg; **Sarah,** 1851; Austin Co.
Palsow, Fr.—Sermon, Mecklenburg; **Sarah,** 1851
Palsow, Joachim and wife—Mecklenburg-Schwerin to Austin; **Gaston,** 1860

Pamfer, Ma(?), 24; **Nachez,** 1847
Pankonin, F. — Springberg to Brenham; **Iris,** 1860; Austin Co.
Pankonim, Ludwig and wife—Nieswiastrowic? to Brenham; **Iris,** 1861
Pantermuehl, Joh.; **Ammerland,** 1854; Comal Co.
Pape, A. — Hackeborn to La Grange; **Iris,** 1860; Comal Co.
Pape, Christian — Almke; **J. W. Buddecke,** 1853; Austin Co. or Comal Co.
Pape, Ferd., Mathilde, Ernst—Wetzlar to La Grange; **Fortuna,** 1860
Pape, H.—Prussia to Brenham; **Weser,** 1860
Pape, Ignaz—Duderstadt; **Weser,** 1854
Pape, Sophie—Hackeborn to Columbus; **Juno,** 1860
Papemann, Christian, 35; **Neptune,** 1850
Park, Maria — Freesenbrugge, Mecklenburg; **Franklin,** 1853
Paschen, Carl—Breddin, Prussia; **Franklin,** 1853
Pathe, Peter and wife; **Neptune,** 1849
Patow, Minna—Grabow, Mecklenburg; **Therese Henriette,** 1853
Patstrick, Hanna; **Joh. Ed. Grosse,** 1853
Patzing, Jacob and daughter—Rodenberg; **Weser,** 1854
Pauen, P.—Unterbrück to San Antonio; **Iris,** 1859
Paul, C. Fred., 36—Prussia; **Natchez,** 1847
Paul, F.—Buckau to Lynchburg; **Juno,** 1860
Paul, Fried., 46, Friedke 47, Herm. 19, Eduard 14, Reinhard 13, Clara 10, Auguste 8—Prussia; **Colonist,** 1848
Paulmann, Moritz, 19; **Hermann Theodor,** 1850
Paulicec, Franz—Vienna; **Suwa,** 1853
Paulsen, Dorothea—Hamburg; **Bassermann,** 1851
Paulsen, Gustav — Tramsbüttel, Holstein; **Miles,** 1854; Colorado Co.
Pawliczeck, Ignaz, Veronica, Johanna, Vincenz, John, M.—Austria; **Jeverland,** 1860
Pech, Georg—Bautzen; 5 persons; **Herschel,** 1851
Pechack family, 9 persons—Vienna; **Suwa,** 1853

Pechner, Christoph, wife and 2 ch.—Pudewitz to New Braunfels; **Gaston,** 1860
Pecht, Th., Al—Alberstedt; Hamburg, 1849; Travis Co.
Peden, Wilhme, 30—Machenbach; **Antoinette,** 1848
Pegelou, Jacob, 40—Moddenpfuhl? **Wilhelm,** 1858
Peglich, Joh.—Cassel; **Suwa,** 1853
Peltzer, Clara, 18—Dusseldorf; **Weser,** 1858
Penberg, Paul, Christine—Crefeld; **Lucie,** 1854
Peper, H.—Oppenwehe to Houston; **Weser,** 1858
Peplan, Martin, 33, Ottilie 25—Marienwärder; **Brasilian,** 1850
Pepper, Johannes—Hamburg; **Hampden,** 1854
Perfuhn, A.—Braunschweig; Hermann **Theodor,** 1853
Perlitz, Fried., 38, Caro. 37, Carl 12, Ana 10, Caro. 5, Werner 1—Prussia; **Colonist,** 1848
Pest, Friedrich—Eschberg, Schleswig; **Franklin,** 1852
Peter, Charl.—Burg; **Texas,** 1853
Peter, Gottfried and family—Lutzendorf; **Weser,** 1854
Petermann, Cath, 27; **Solon,** 1850
Peters, C.—Upen to Schönau; **Gaston,** 1857; Goliad Co.
Peters, Fr.—Zeplin, Mecklenburg; **Sarah,** 1851; Fayette Co.
Peters, Friedrich and wife—Wittenborge, Prussia; **Franklin,** 1852
Peters, Johann, and wife—Wolfshagen, Schleswig; **Franklin,** 1852
Peters, Johan, 21—Oldenburg; **Franziska,** 1847; Fayette Co.
Peters, L., and wife—Oggersheim; **Weser,** 1854
Peters, P C.—Foehr; **Leibniz,** 1850
Petersen, A. J. C.—Klockenhagen, Mecklenburg; **Hampden,** 1854
Petersen, F. W., A. F., Christian—Cismar, Mecklenburg; **Hampden,** 1854
Petersen, Johann—Schleswig, Schleswig; **Franklin,** 1853
Peterson, Kath.—Flensburg to Galveston; **Weser,** 1860
Petri, A.—Bremen; **Juno,** 1860
Petri, Adam—Neuhütte; **Reform,** 1851; Comal Co.
Petri, Lina—Giessen to Galveston; **Iris,** 1861
Petrich, Elis.—Posen; **Miles,** 1853

Petrich, Ferdinand, wife and 3 ch. 1¼-7 years — Bruehlingsdorf, Mecklenburg; **Miles,** 1853
Petsch, **Anna**—Weigersdorf to KleinBautzen; **Fortuna,** 1858
Petschke, G., 28; **Herschel,** 1849
Petz, Georg, wife and 5 ch.—Schönau; **Minna,** 1854
Petzold, Conrad E., 46; **Solon,** 1850
Petzsch, Ed A., 20—Aachen; **Weser,** 1858
Pfaehler, Louis, with family, 4 persons—Gaildorf; **J. W. Buddecke,** 1853
Pfalzmg, Jacob—Sterkelshausen; **Texas,** 1853
 See Pfetzing, Jacob
Pfannenschmidt, Christina; **Galliott, Concordia,** 1854
Pfeffer, Johann, wife and 7 ch.—Kussow, Mecklenburg; **Sarah,** 1851
Pfefferkorn, W., 6 persons—Krzeakatowoy (Krzekotowo?); **Lucie,** 1854
Pfeifer, A., 6 persons — Gablonz; **Texas,** 1853; Kendall Co.
Pfeifer, Friedr. Wilh, 47—Gross-Waltersdorf, Sachsen; **Gutenburg,** 1855; Kendall Co.
Pfeiffer, Cath., 36; **Neptune,** 1850
Pfeiffer, Gottl. and family—Schilda; **Gessner,** 1854
Pfetzing, Conrad—Sterkelshausen; **Texas,** 1853; Galveston
Pfetzing, Jacob, and dau. A. Elizabeth, 25—Sterkelshausen; **Texas,** 1853; Galveston
Pflueger, J. — Altenhasungen to Austin; **Fortuna,** 1858
Pflughaupt family—to Brenham; **Weser,** 1859; Washington Co.
Pfullmann, C.; **Neptune,** 1854
Phillip, George—Prussia; **Neptune,** 1848
Phillip, J., 17; **Fortuna,** 1858
Philippi, Wilh. Fr.—Bremen to Galveston; **Iris,** 1861
Pichard, Olympia — Galveston to Galveston; **Gessner,** 1860
Picos, Franz — Rosimirs?; **Weser,** 1854
Pielingen, Ignatz, 32, Sophia 30, Juliana 2; **Sophie,** 1852
Pieper, Bertha, 29, Albert 3, Iris (born on board ship)—Chemnitz to Port Sullivan(?); **Iris,** 1859
Pieper, Jacob, 57, Eva 46, George 24, Joh. 21, Ludwig 17, Martha Juliane 12, Hein. 3 (2?); **Creole,** 1852

Piering, Mrs. and Friedke—Altenburg; Texas, 1853
Pierstorff, Chr. — Beidendorf, Mecklenburg; Copernicus, 1852
Pietrucher, Josef, 32, Caro. 29, Anka 4, Thomas 2 — Lenz to Matagorda; Weser, 1859
Pietsch, Fried., wife and 4 ch.— Gross Schönbeck to Washington (on-the-Brazos); Gaston, 1860
Pietzke, Ludwig—Tost; Weser, 1854
Pillwitz, F. A., Helene, Emilie— Saxony to Galveston; Weser, 1860
Pimbach, J. J.—Modlich; Leibnitz, 1850
Pingel, Heinrich, wife and 3 ch. 8½ - 12 years old — Penwick, Mecklenburg; Copernicus, 1852
Pirdolla, Martin, and wife—Rojemirch(?); Weser, 1854
Pittrop, Christ. and wife Margaretha — Muenchberg, Bavaria; Hampden, 1854
Piwonka, M. and wife—Mähren; Weser, 1854
Plambeck, Heinrich, 42, Catharina 40, Christian 14, Heinrich 11, Anna 9, Catharina 7—Neumuenster, Holstein; Gutenberg, 1855
Plasmann, Johann—Stieghorst; Solon, 1852
Plasmann, Louise and 2 ch.—Berlin; Suwa, 1853
Platt, Emma—Sobiechen to Fredericksburg; Juno, 1860
Plattner, Martin—Riggenbach; Solon, 1852
Plauschan, Joachim, 34—Neumuenster, Holstein; Gutenberg, 1855
Pleny, Marg.—Galveston; Juno, 1853
Ploeger, Adolphine—Minden, Prussia; Mississippi, 1855
Plonsky, Fr(ied.), 45, Maria 46, Adolph 3, Henriette 26 — Hamburg; Hamburg, 1849
Plucker, E., 42; Herschel, 1849
Plueckhahn, Joh., 3 persons— Reetz; Neptune, 1853
Plueckhahn, Dorothea, 22—Reetz, Prussia; Franklin, 1850
Plumell, Herm.—Saxony; Neptune, 1848
Plumeyer, Hein. and family—Rhoden; Weser, 1854; Comal Co.
Pochila, Franz—Austria; Jeverland, 1860
Pochmann, Cölestine — Bullsdorf, Böhmen; Mississippi, 1855

Pockmann, Fried., 7 persons—Neudorf; Neptune, 1853
Poehler, Fried., Christine, Minna, Caro., Henry—Pükeburg to San Antonio; Weser, 1860
Poeter, Gottlieb—Friedeberg; Neptune, 1853
Poethig, Wilhelmine, 21—Bautzen, Prussia; Miles, 1852
Pogado, Joh.—Ruda; Magnet, 1851; Walker Co.
Pohl, Anton, 2 persons—Berndorf; Texas, 1853; Fayette Co.
Pohl, C., 4 persons; Pohl, Carl and wife — Maltschau (Malzow?); Neptune, 1854; Galveston Co.
Pohle, Gottlieb and Louise; Texas, 1853
Polack (Polak), Jacob, Rosalie, Marianne, Maria—Austria; Jeverland, 1860
Poland, Chr. — Niedervellmar; Ed Poland and sister died in 1900 Galveston storm; Hermann Theodor, 1853
Poldberg, Louise, 40—Prussia; Colonist, 1848
Polh, Richard, 45, Constantia 44, Anna 18, Elis. 8, Jacob 5; John Holland, 1848
Poll, Fritz, 6—Moellenbeck, Mecklenburg; John Frederick, 1850
Pollock, Caspar and family—Grodzeska (Grodzisko); Weser, 1854
Polmar, Herrmann—Leipzig, Saxony; Republic, 1851
Polzin, Ernestine—Nieswiastrowic(?) to Brenham; Iris, 1861
Pommervenke, Wilh.—Dresden; Suwa, 1853
Poppe, Minna, 30; Franziska, 1849; Fayette Co.
Poppert, Hugo, 24, Adelheid 25; Hermann Theodor, 1850
Potthoff, Wilh.; Joh. Ed. Grosse, 1853
Poudewitz, Ernestine—Ponig(1) to La Grange; Iris, 1851
Prager, Wilh., 3 persons; Joh. Ed. Grosse, 1853; Victoria Co.
Prallwitz, Gustav, 30—Insterburg to New Braunfels; Iris, 1859
Prange, Fried., 33 and Louise— Berlin; Brasilian, 1850
Prange, Gustav, 30—Mecklenburg; Franziska, 1847
Pranzin, Eduard, 26; Colonist, 1848
Praus, Arnold, wife and 4 ch. 9-15 years old; Prause, Arnold—Waldenburg, Prussia; Miles, 1854; Fayette Co.

Prause, Alois, Marianne—Schönthal; Minna, 1854; Fayette Co.
Preibisch, A.—Friedland to San Antonio; Iris, 1860; Austin Co.
Preisig, Robt., 27; Galliott Flora, 1849
Prellop, G.—Trschelle (Trechel) to Cunningham; Fortuna, 1860
Prentzel, Anton, 26; Solon, 1850; Colorado Co.
Presler, Paul—Torgau, Prussia; Republic, 1851; Austin, Texas
Pressler, C. W.—Prussia; Neptune, 1849
Pressler, Franz; Neptune, 1849
Preuss, Catharina — Kahlsendorf, Holstein; Hampden, 1854
Preuss, Eduard—Hoslof; Solon, 1852
Preuss, J. C., wife and 2 daughters, ¼ and 7 years old—Neukirchen, Holstein; Hampden, 1854
Preuss, Josef, 36—Nassau; John Holland, 1848
Preuss, M. and child—Röhrig; Gessner, 1855
Prien, Georg—Beidendorf, Mecklenburg; Copernicus, 1852
Priesemult, Fried., 29, Caro. 24, Bertha ½—Gurkow to Georgetown; Priesmuth, Fritz—Victoria Co.; Wilhelm, 1858
Priesemult, Henriette, 22—Sebenitz to Galveston; Wilhelm, 1858 See also Prisemuth, Henriette
Priest, Joachim and wife — Quitzow, Mecklenburg; Bassermann, 1851
Priester, C., 21; Neptune, 1850
Priester, Simon, 19, Emil 17; Creole, 1852
Prievus, Christine — Langburkersdorf to Neuweler(?); Fortuna, 1858
Prill, Fritz, 33—Zierzow; John Friedrich, 1850
Princel, Doris; Ammerland, 1854
Prinz, Conrad—San Antonio to San Antonio; Gaston, 1860
Prisemuth (Priesemult?), Henriette — Sebenitz to Galveston; Weser, 1858
Proehl, Elis.—Oplop?; J. W. Buddecke, 1853
Proekopde, Anton—Friedland; Minna, 1854
Proger, Bertha, 16—Torgau, Prussia; Herschel, 1855
Protzel, Wilh., 37—Fallersleben; Neptune, 1850
Prowelsky, G.—Königswille; Gessner, 1855

Pruessler, Sophia—Darmstadt; Neptune, 1853
Prutz, F. A., 23—Gräfenhagen; Anna Louisa, 1857
Przibisch, Philipp—Contawa (Kontenau?); Weser, 1854
Pubelskh, A. — Schimnowitz (Schimmerwitz?); Gessner, 1855
Pueschel, Robert—Spengeberg; 2 persons; Magnet, 1851
Puls, F. and Friedke—Berlin; Suwa, 1853
Puls, Friedrich, wife and 2 ch., 3 and 8 years old—Jessnitz, Mecklenburg; Copernicus, 1852; Comal Co.
Punsel, Joh., wife and 5 ch.—Trübenbach; Minna, 1854
Pupille, Fr.—Hannover; Friedrich Grosse, 1853
Pyka, Joh. and family—Suchedemjitz?; Weser, 1854
Pytel, Lorenz, and family—Boritz; Weser, 1854

— Q —

Quast, A.—Friedeberg to Yorktown; Iris, 1858
Quast, Julius, 21, Ernestine 24— Gottschimerbruch to Yorktown; Weser, 1858
Queke, Ludwg—Callies to Austin; Weser, 1857
Querin, Peter—Aachen to Victoria; Iris, 1861
Quistorf, L. A., 4 ch., 7¾-15 yrs. of age—Neudorf; Leibniz, 1850

— R —

Raabe, Caroline, 24—Klehst, Prussia; Miles, 1852
Raale. Anna—Bremen; Franziska, 1854
Rabbe, Henry—Brenham to Galveston; Weser, 1860
Rabe, J. A.—Breddin, Prussia; Franklin, 1853; Fayette Co.
Rabe, Johanna—Braunschweig; Suwa, 1853
Rabel, A.—Austria; Jeverland, 1860
Rabenau, Cath. — Darmstadt to Galveston; Weser, 1858
Rachug, L. and wife—Woczyanowo; Lucie, 1854
Rachup, J.—Tapowke(?) to Brenham; Fortuna, 1860
Radefeld, Fried.; Joh. Ed. Grosse, 1853
Radke, J.—Labychen (Labischau?) Texas, 1853

Rahe, Fried., 44, Cath. 35, Dor. 2, Christoph 2, Fried. Wilh. 22, Joh. Wilh. 4; **Hermann Theodor,** 1850; Comal Co.

Rake, Hermann, 44, Fritz 11— Winsmold(?); **Franziska,** 1849

Rakedorf, Carolina, 11, with Harsdorf group; **Solon,** 1850

Rakowitz, J., wife and 6 ch.—Poland; **Franziska,** 1854; Blanco Co. 1868

Ramakers, Theo.—Ervitte, Prussia; **Mississippi,** 1855

Ramowsky, F., 23; **Herschel,** 1850

Ramschutz, Carl, 54, Amelia 50, Carl 20, Maria 14, Alexander 8, Maximus 5 — Silesia; **Natchez,** 1847

Ramsel, Hch.—Heepen; **Canapus,** 1849; Colorado Co.

Ramsel, Wm. and wife—Hillighausen; **Canapus,** 1849; Washington Co.

Ranf, H.—Odenhausen to Seguin; **Gaston,** 1857

Ransky, Fried., 45, Maria 46, Adolph 3, Henriette 26 — Hamburg; **Hamburg,** 1849

Rasch, Alb.—Penzlin; **Reform,** 1851

Rasch, Aug., 5 persons—Penzlin; **Herschel,** 1851

Rasche, Gesche Marg., 27; **Canapus,** 1848

Raschke, August and Anna—Falkenberg to La Grange; **Iris,** 1860

Rast, Eduard, 37—Prussia; **Chas. N. Cooper,** 1847

Rast, Gottlieb, 29—Leipzig; **Solon,** 1850; Fayette Co.

Rathke, Michael — Ostatkowo, Prussia, or Bromberg; **Miles,** 1852

Ratje, Johann—Prussia; **Antoinette,** 1854

Ratz, Christian, wife and 3 ch. 2-5 years old—Bergbruch, Mecklenburg; **Miles,** 1852

Ratzburg, Jacob and wife—Preetz, Holstein; **Washington,** 1852

Rau, Louis—Galveston; **Gessner,** 1854

Rau, Louis, Mary, Leonore—Galveston to Galveston; **Fortuna,** 1860

Raube, H., 4 persons—Gadelte(?); **Neptune,** 1854

Rauch, Christiane—Görlitz to Galveston; **Weser,** 1860

Rauch, Eva, 21; **Sophie,** 1852

Rauch, Friedrich—Flechdorf: **Weser,** 1857; Comal Co. 1860

Raupe, Christian—Hannover; **Weser,** 1854

Raupe, F. with family—Neusitz to Fredericksburg; **Weser,** 1858

Rausch, Heinrich and Cath.—Kassel; **Suwa,** 1853

Rauschenberg, L.—Friedrichsrode; **Neptune,** 1854

Rause, J.—See Krause, J.

Rautsch, C.—Rosenhain; **Anton Günther,** 1860

Rebentisch, C. F.—Kassel; **Suwa,** 1853

Rebi, Ludwig, 35—Hungary; **Joh. Dethardt,** 1848

Reczeck, C.—Austria; **Jeverland,** 1860

Redlich, A., 4 persons — Justa (Justrup?); **Lucie,** 1854

Reese, Friedr.—Hannover; **Antoinette,** 1854; Lavaca Co.

Regien, Carl, wife and 2 children— Gross-Gandern, Prussia; **Bassermann,** 1851

Regenbogen, August—Kassel; **Neptune,** 1853

Regenbrecht, Georg, 23; **Fortuna,** 1858; Austin Co.

Reger, Marie—Braunschweig to Galveston; **Weser,** 1860

Rehmann, C. with family — Hadmersleben to La Grange; **Fortuna,** 1858

Rehberg, J.—Prussia; **Friedrich Grosse,** 1853

Reib, J. A., 27—Norway; **Colonist,** 1848

Reibenstein family—Burgdorf; **Adolphine,** 1859; Austin Co.

Reibherzer, H.—Rinteln; **Magnet,** 1851

Reich, J.—Poland; **Franziska,** 1854; Comal Co.

Reichardt, C. and wife—Plauen; **Weser,** 1854; Austin Co.

Reichard, Wilhelm and Friedke— Krewitz; **J. W. Buddecke,** 1853

Reiche, Ottelie M., Ida Camilla— Saxony; **Miles,** 1853

Reiche, W.—Friesland; **Texas,** 1853

Reichel, Gustav, Hermann, Robert, Amalie—Liegnitz to La Grange; **Gessner,** 1860

Reichenbach, H., 23; **Herschel,** 1849

Reichert, Auguste—Gomern; **Adolphine,** 1859

Reichinger, J.—**Herschel,** 1849

Reifer, Emil—Kassel; **Suwa,** 1853

Reifert, C.—Herrfeld to Indianola; **Juno,** 1860

Reiffert, H.—to Indianola; Weser, 1859; De Witt Co.
Reige, Fr.—Tempelburg; Neptune, 1854
Reimann, Heinrich—Sagern, Prussia; Washington, 1852
Reimers, Carl, 30, Christiane 24, Johann ¾—Bordesholm, Holstein; Gutenberg, 1855
Reimers, E. G.—Oldenburg; Leibniz, 1850
Reimershofer, J. and family—Ammerland, 1854; Austin Co.
Rein, Joh.—Sophie, 1852
Reinbach, Max, 26—Köln; Franziska, 1849; Bexar Co.
Reineck, C.—Salzbrunn; Gessner, 1854
Reinecke, L., 27—Uessinghausen; Wilhelm, 1858
Reineke, Christian, Henriette—Tapowke? to Brenham; Fortuna, 1860
Reiners, Marie—Oldenburg; Adolphine, 1859
Reinhard, Selly and son—Dresden to Dallas; Weser, 1858
Reinhardt, Christian, 62; Solon, 1850
Reinhardt, Christian, 64; Sophie, 1852
Reinhold, Caroline, Alwine, Wilhelm, Adolphe, Minna — Birkbruch to Clinton; Fortuna, 1860
Reinhorn, Doris—Oplop? J. W. Buddecke, 1853
Reinländer, J. and D.—Roehrig; Gessner, 1855
Reinlich, A.—Prussia; Friedrich Grosse, 1853
Reinoczeck, Franz, Johanna, John, Aloise—Austria; Jeverland, 1860
Reinold, Dorothea—Kehrenbach to Mengersville; Gaston, 1860
Reinschirk, Henriette — Freienhagen; Hermann Theodor, 1853
Reip, Carl, 31—Alt-Batkof; Brasilian, 1850
Reippert. J. — Juliusburg to Millheim; Juno, 1860; Austin Co.
Reis, G.—Billesheim (Billigheim?) Neptune, 1854
Reisner, Louis, 41, Auguste 11; Reform, 1850
Reissig, Jul.—Ziegenrück; Reform, 1851; Austin Co.
Reissner, Auguste and Ida—Falkenberg to La Grange; Iris, 1860
Reitz, H., wife Cath.—Meltzuhn; Hampden, 1854
Reitzel, A.—Pomerania; Adolphine, 1859

Remmin, Christian, 25—Moellenbeck, Prussia; John Frederick, 1850
Renheust?, Ernst, 26—Prussia; Colonist, 1848
Renken, Gerd., 37; Galliott Flora, 1849
Renken, Heinrich and Elise—Sengwarden to Galveston; Fortuna, 1860; Medina Co. 1865
Rethke, J. C. F.—Freienstein, Saxony; Washington, 1852; Guadalupe Co.
Reue, Henry, Caro., Fried., Lucie, William, Louise — Hannover to Brenham; Weser, 1860
Reusch, Ferdinand—Bromberg; Juno, 1853
Reusch, Georg, 24; Magnet, 1852
Reuss, Gottl.—Saxony; Friedrich Grosse, 1853; Calhoun Co.
Reuss, Joh. Ad., 28, Cath. 27, Fr. Adam 6, Joh. Ludw. 4, Anna Cath. 2; Hermann Theodor, 1850; Bexar Co.
Rexroth, A. — Schellenbach to Friedrichsburg; Iris, 1857
Rham, Friedke—Pomerania; Adolphine, 1859
Rhein, C., Barbara, Elis., P., Christine—Flinsbach to Houston; Weser, 1858
Rhenchard, Marg., 61, Jacob 27, Henriette, 20, Marie 9; Louis, 1848
Rhode, Hch.—Penzlin; Leibniz, 1850; Galveston
Rhodius, Aug.—Prussia; Neptune, 1849; Guadalupe Co.
Rhodius, Hugo—Prussia; Neptune, 1849
Rhodius, Hugo—Düsseldorf; Texas, 1853
Rhodius, Ottilie, 27; Herschel, 1849
Ribbel, Franziska—Vienna; Suwa, 1853
Richardz, F., 33; Fortuna, 1858
Riche, Carl, 29—Ahnebeck; Helen & Elise, 1847
Richert, Hein. and Engel—Sachsenhagen; Lucie, 1854
Richter, A. — Heinewalde (Heimwald?); Neptune, 1854
Richter, A.—Rudolstadt; Friedrich Grosse, 1853
Richter, August, 25, Wilh. 19, Henriette 18, Auguste 15, Hermann 13—Dresden; Antoinette, 1848
Richter, August — Bürkersdorf; Herschel, 1851; Austin Co.
Richter, Charles, 40—Wersdorf; Hamburg, 1849

Richter, C. G., 35—Beyersdorf;
Neptune, 1850
Richter, Carl Ernst — Viereichen,
Prussia; Mississippi, 1855; Aus-
tin Co.
Richter, Caro., Helene, Juliane,
Wilhelm — Wildenau to La
Grange; Weser, 1860
Richter, Christ. and wife, 5 per-
sons — Viereichen; Mississippi,
1855; Austin Co.
Richter, Eliesse, 24; Franziska,
1849
Richter, Gottfried and wife, 8 per-
sons—Kassel; Mississippi, 1855;
Austin Co.
Richter, Gustan—Hannover; Wes-
er, 1854; Colorado Co.
Richter, H.—Wehdem to Brenham;
Weser, 1860
Richter, Heinrecht, 28—Minden;
Franziska, 1849
Richter, J.—Prussia; Jeverland,
1860
Richter, Johann, Carl, Johanne—
Gross-Hennersdorf to San Anto-
nio; Juno, 1860
Richter, J. Carl and Charlotte;
Joh. Ed. Grosse, 1853
Richter, Joh. Samuel, 55, Christine
nee Wagne,r 56, Joh. Frederic,
26; Antoinette, 1848
Richter, Jos.—Wildenau; Minna,
1854
Richter, Kath.—Oppeln to Galves-
ton; Iris, 1859
Richter, Reinh.—Oschatz; Nep-
tune, 1854
Richtor, Traugott, 27—Saxony;
Natchez, 1847; Galveston
Richwardt, R.—Heilsberg; Lucie,
1854
Ricke, A. and M.—Rosebuck (Rose-
burg?) to Galveston; Weser,
1858
Ricksen (Ruecksen?), Wilhme—
Wandsbeck; Brasilian, 1850
Riebe, Peter, 56, Wilhme 47 (died),
Wilhme 21, Wilh. 18, Erdmann
13, Fried. 10, Ferd. 7; Hamburg,
1849
Riebel, Cath. 53, Lucia 24, Lazar-
us 15; Baumann, Caro., ¾ yr.;
Herschel, 1850
Rieck, Joh., 33; Alexander, 1850
Rieck, Theodor — Buetzow, Meck-
lenburg; Sarah, 1851
Riecken, Christ., wife and child 1¼
years old — Stolpe, Holstein;
Washington, 1852
Riedel, Minna, 25, Fritz 3, Emma
4; Reform, 1850

Riedel, Moritz, 39, Johanna 40,
Moritz 14½, Carl 13, Caro. 12,
Franz 8, Adolph 10, Ernst 6,
Joseph 4—11 persons from Cah-
la; Hamburg, 1849; De Witt Co.
Rief, Anton, 31; Galliott Flora,
1849
Rief, Josepha—Grehn (Gröbn); Re-
form, 1851
Riefkoch, Carl August—Hannover;
Solon, 1852
Riegenbahn, Johann — Oermelin-
gen; Solon, 1852
Rieger, Wilh., 28—Langenbielau;
Joh. Dethardt, 1848
Rieke, Joh.—Berlin; Suwa, 1853
Riemenschneider family, 2 per-
sons—Hainau to Coleto (Bexar
Co.); Iris, 1859
Riemenschneider, Lorenz, 25—Alt-
Morschen to Coleto; Iris, 1859
Riemenschneider, Valentin — Kas-
sel; Suwa, 1853
Riemer, Gottlieb—Callies to Gal-
veston; Weser, 1857
Riese, Aug., 27—Bismark; Cana-
pus, 1848
Riessling, Chr.—Hoppenstedt;
Weser, 1854
Rilling, Anna — Gomaringen to
San Antonio; Iris, 1858
Rimpel, Johann, 4 persons—Offen-
bach, Nass.; Mississippi, 1855
Rinik, Johannes, 25—Hannover;
Natchez, 1847
Rinn, Ludwig—Hesse; Antoinette,
1854; Austin Co.
Ripke, Emilie, 27, Ulrich 14—Min-
den; Solon, 1850
Ripke, Hein.—Galliott Concordia,
1854
Rippe, Albert, 9 persons—Weghold
Wegholm); Texas, 1853
Rippe, Christian, Dor., Marie—
Hofa; Franziska, 1849
Rippel, Franz—Vienna; Suwa,
1853; Austin Co.
Ristan, Julius and Wilh.—Cama
(Canna); J. W. Buddecke, 1853
Risters, C.—Gerderath to San An-
tonio; Iris, 1859
Rittel, Hermann and Christiane—
Berlin; Suwa, 1853
Ritter, Adam, 64, Magda 30, Chris-
tiana Rachel 18, Adam 9—Rode-
wig to Repserek(?); Iris, 1859
Ritter, Hein.—Burghasungen;
Texas, 1853
Ritzlof, Bernhard—Trziecziewcz,
Poland; Mississippi, 1855
Riwolzki, Wm. A., 19—(Prussia?);
Alexander, 1850

Rix, Daniel F., wife and daughter ¾ years old — Altona; **Leibniz, 1850**

Robensburg, Jacob—Waldeck; **Minna, 1854**

Robert, Ludwig, 5 persons—Wreseen (Wrietzen?); **Neptune, 1853**

Rochow, Johann, 58, Dorothea 54, Maria 26, Wilhme 21, Wilhelm 20, August 18, Joseph 16—Neu-Strelitz, Mecklenburg; **Miles, 1855**

Rock, Anton, 26, Ignaz 35, Helena 32, Ignaz 13, Mariana 8, Cath. 4, Elis. 2—**Sophie, 1852**

Rodden, Gerhard—Forst; **Texas, 1853**

Rodefeld, C.—Berchefeld? to Galveston; **Weser, 1858**

Rodefeld, F. and family—Wigkelshutten to Galveston; **Weser, 1858**

Rodefeld, H.—Bocholzhausen to Galveston; **Iris, 1860**

Rodenbusch, A., 4 persons; **Estafette, 1850**

Roebrich, F.—Niederwildungen; **Gessner, 1854**

Roecker, Sophia—Dettingen; **Solon, 1852**

Roeder, Anna—**Jeverland, 1860**

Roeder, Ernst—**Wilhelm, 1858**

Roeder, H., with family—Czernian (Czernice?) to Fredericksburg; **Weser, 1858**

Roeder, W., Caro., Herman—Gurkow to Yorktown; **Fortuna, 1860**

Roeder, Wm.—Hannover; **Magnet, 1851; De Witt Co.**

Roehl, J.—Berlin to Galveston; **Iris, 1860**

Roehl, Joh. C. Christ, 40, Anna Dor. 37. Joh. Christ 5—**Hamburg, 1849**

Roehl, J. F. H.—Sternberg; **Leibniz, 1850**

Roehling, Hr., 20, Louise 30—Oppendorf; **Canapus, 1848**

Roehling. Joh. Fr. W., 53, Henrietta 23, Wilh. 10: **Hermann Theodor, 1850;** Washington Co.

Roehling. Joh. H., 3 persons—Oppendorf; **Neptune, 1853;** Washington Co.

Roemhild, Emil—Neisse, Prussia; **Miles, 1854**

Roemmler, Chr. Wilhelm — Reudnitz, Prussia; **Bassermann, 1851**

Roenane, Carl, 30, Fredericia 30, Edouard 5. Amelia 3. Augusta—Prussia; **Natchez, 1847**

Roensch, Ed. and Clara—Bunzlau to Bellville; **Iris, 1861**

Roerner, Hein. and family—Hannover; **Antoinette, 1854**

Roesch, Carl, Hermann, Amalie—Gaildorf; **J. W. Buddecke, 1853;** De Witt Co.

Roese, Jacob, Christine, Margaretha—Altendorf to San Antonio; **Weser, 1860**

Roeser, A. and family—Wolkenstein; **Gessner, 1855**

Roesing, ...—Herrfeld to Indianola; **Juno, 1860**

Roesler, J.—Friedland to San Antonio; **Iris, 1860**

Roesler, Johanna—Lussdorf; **Lucie, 1854**

Roesler, V., 4 persons—Gablonz; **Texas, 1853**

Roessler, C. and family—Lawalde; **Anton Günther, 1860**

Roessler, H.—Lawalde; **Anton Günther, 1860**

Roessler, J. and family—Lawalde; **Anton Günther, 1860**

Roessner, Adam—Rödelwitz; **Henrietta, 1843 (1853)**

Roettcher, J. C., wife and 2 ch., 18 and 19 years old — Pritzwalk; **Leibniz, 1850**

Roettschaefer, F. and wife — Erlingshausen to Galveston; **Iris, 1857**

Roger, Hermann — Tempelberg, Prussia; **Therese Henriette, 1853** See also Royer. Th.

Rogge. Chr. — Damlack, Prussia; **Washington, 1852;** Washington Co.

Rohde. C.—Prussia; **Franziska, 1854;** Comal Co.

Rohde. Christe. 4 persons—Brenken; **Herschel, 1851**

Rohrbach, G.—Hesse; **Friedrich Grosse, 1853**

Roitsch. C. and family—Maltitz; **Anton Günther, 1860**

Roldt. Joh. R., 22 — Neitzwitz (Nietschitz); **Wilhelm, 1858**

Roling. Henriette—Prussia to Independence; **Weser, 1860**

Romaum. Fr. (Frau?), Maria and Rosa (her children) — Prussia; **Neptune, 1849**

Rommel, Ph.—Texas; **Franziska, 1854**

Rorsch. J., 8 persons — Prussia; **Friedrich Grosse, 1853**

Rosamka, W.. 5 persons—Maglin (Maglern?)—**Neptune, 1854**

Roscher, D.—Lengefeld; Lucie, 1854
Rose, Anna, Carl and Juliane—Thiemendorf, Mecklenburg; Franklin, 1853
Rose, F. and wife—Remlingen to New Braunfels; Iris, 1857; Comal Co.
Rose, Jacob, 32—Remlingen; Joh. Dethardt, 1848; Comal Co.
Rosekranz, Johann, Johanne—Rhoden; Weser, 1854; Galveston
Rosenbaum, F., 40—Galliott Flora, 1849
Rosenbaum, Wilhme—Wehdem to Brenham; Weser, 1860
Rosenberg, Friedricke — Niederwaldungen(?) to Galveston; Iris, 1859
Rosenberg, Heinrich and Amalie—Posen to Brenham; Juno, 1860
Rosenberg, Ulrich—Poland; Lucie, 1854
Rosenblatt, P.—Annaberg; Hermann Theodor, 1853
Rosenfeld, Jacob, 22, Alex 17, Ernestine 22, Herm. 18, Michaelis 18—Wesecke to Houston; Weser, 1859
Rosenfelt, Josef, 19 — John Holland, 1848; Harris Co.
Rosenow, Auguste — Fröbisch to Galveston; Fortuna, 1860
Rosenthal, Ad., 23—b. Berlin 1827; Galliott Flora, 1849; Kendall Co.
Rosentreter, Wilhme — Nieswiastrowic(?) to Brenham; Iris, 1861
Rosky, Joh., 54, Magda 53, Aug. 24, Anna 14, Albert 10—Prussia; Chas. N. Cooper, 1847; Austin Co.
Rosler, Doretha, 26—Schlaupitz; Joh. Dethardt, 1848
Ross. Joh.—Lut(h)au; Herschel, 1851
Rossbach. Peter—Gefell; Weser, 1854; Comal Co.
Rossbult, Elise—Krabow; Leibniz, 1850
Rost, Louise—to Galveston; Weser, 1859
Roth, Anton, 25—Amorbach; Neptune, 1849; Comal Co.
Roth, Aug.—Lasperbuth; Weser, 1854
Roth. Barbara, 16—Hammern; Antoinette, 1848
Roth, Eliza and child—Neptune, 1849
Roth. Ferdinand, 30—Chas. N. Cooper, 1847

Roth, Joh. Phillipp, 41, Anna Marie 30, Marie 17, Joh. 15, Christian 6, Cath. 4, Elis. 2, Peter 3/12; John Holland, 1848
Roth, Joh. Martin and family (8)—Dettingen; Solon, 1852
Rothe, A.—Thuringia; Gessner, 1855
Rothe, Anton, 34; Galliott Flora, 1849; Comal Co.
Rothe, Christian, 27, Caro. 25, Ernst 12—Hermann Theodor, 1850
Rothe, H., 7 persons—Warmenstein; Lucie, 1854
Rothhand, J. D.—Sachsenhausen; Herschel, 1851; Victoria Co.
Rothmann, August — Probsthagen, Prussia; Theresa Henriette, 1853
Rottinghaus, Elis., 22—Damme; Antoinette, 1848
Roy, Joseph—Grodzisko; Weser, 1854
Royer, Franz, Louis, Otto—Tempelberg; Neptune, 1854 See Roger, Herm.
Royer, Th. with family—Tempelberg; Neptune, 1854 See also Roger, Herm.
Ruchart, Carl, 28, Maria 24—Prussia; Colonist, 1848
Ruckhahn, Friedrich and wife—Perleberg, Prussia; Franklin, 1852
Rudi, C.—Wilsbach to Galveston; Juno, 1860
Rudniakowsky, A., wife and 6 ch. —Poland; Franziska, 1854
Rudolph, Franz—Ziegelhain; Solon, 1852
Rudolph, Hein., 3 persons—Marktsuhl; Henriette, 1843 (1853)
Rudolph, Joseph and family—Ammerland, 1854
Ruecksen — See Ricksen
Ruefer, Johann—Alsfeld; Weser, 1854
Ruegner, Joh.. 19. Chrisiana 26; Herschel, 1850; Mason Co.
Ruehl, Alexander — Prussia; Antoinette, 1854; Galveston
Ruehring. Wilh.—Osterwald; Hermann Theodor, 1853
Ruengener, Aug., 25—Schlangen; Canapus, 1848
Ruengener, Chr., 20—Schlangen; Canapus, 1848
Ruessing. L.—Prussia; Franziska, 1854; Fayette Co.
Ruff. Wm.—Braunschweig; Texas, 1853

Ruhland, H. — Prussia; **Friedrich Grosse,** 1853; Fayette Co.
Ruhle, Carl—Lehe; **Neptune,** 1853; Galveston
Rummel, C. W. and family; **Neptune,** 1848; Fayette Co.
Rummler, Ernest Rob(ert), 29— Freiberg in Sachsen; **Gutenberg,** 1855
Rump, Friederike—Galveston; **Weser,** 1860
Rump, J. E.—Galveston; **Neptune,** 1848
Rumpel, Joachich — Klockow; 5 persons; **Neptune,** 1853
Rumpf, Aug.—Blantikow, Schleswig; **Franklin,** 1852
Rumpf, Wilh. with family, 3 persons — Orewitz (Orlowitz?); **J. W. Buddecke,** 1853
Rumpke, Hein.—Klockow, Prussia; **Miles,** 1852
Runge, Carl and family, 6 persons—Schiefelbein; **Juno,** 1853; Austin Co.
Runge, Wm., 7 persons—Stuttgart; **Texas,** 1853
Rungener, Conrad, 27—Lippe Detmold; **Joh. Dethardt,** 1848
Rungener, Hermann—Schlangen; **Solon,** 1852
Ruppertsbly (Ruppertsberg?), Andr.—Sondershausen; 6 persons; **Neptune,** 1853; Fayette Co.
Ruprecht, Robert—Berlin; **Suwa,** 1853
Ruprecht, Rud., 24—**Herschel,** 1849
Rusche, Nicolaus — Hindenburg, Prussia; **Washington,** 1852; Gillespie Co.
Ruschek, Franz, Mariane—Vienna; **Suwa,** 1853
Rusen, Elisa—Köln to San Antonio; **Iris,** 1860
Russdeutscher, Ernst, Anna Auguste; **Joh. Ed. Grosse,** 1853
Rust, M.—Hesse; **Friedrich Grosse,** 1853
Ruthenberg, Carl—Wolgast, Prussia to Galveston; **Miles,** 1852

— Sa —

Saage, W.—Seest (Senst?) to New Ulm; **Fortuna,** 1860
Saager, Johann, wife and 3 ch. 12-22 years old; Zechlin, Prussia; **Franklin,** 1853
Saathoff, F. P.—**Herschel,** 1849; Medina Co.

Saathoff, Martin, wife and 3 ch.— Felde to Quihi, Texas (Medina Co.); **Weser,** 1857
Saathoff, S. T., 27 and E., 2 ch.; **Leo,** 1846
Sabbau, Fr., wife and 2 sons, 1¼ and 4 yrs. old — Gross-Laasch, Mecklenburg; **Hampden,** 1854
Sabo, Dorothea, 15—Hamburg; **Washington,** 1852
Sachasch, Joseph—Vienna; **Suwa,** 1853
Sachtleben, C. G., 50—Hadmersleben; **Weser,** 1859
Sachtleben, Doro., 6 persons—Saxony; **Friedrich Grosse,** 1853
Sachtleben, F., 3 persons—Prussia; **Friedrich Grosse,** 1853; Fayette Co.
Saeling, Albert—Friedeberg, Silesia; **Neptune,** 1853
Saettler, Carl—Lengefeld; **Lucie,** 1854
Sagebihl, August, wife and ch.— Lenzen to Fredericksburg; **Weser,** 1857
Sager, Christoph Adam — Dettingen, Württ to Texas, 1850; De Witt Co.
Sahse, J.—Altenflies to Yorktown; **Fortuna,** 1860
Saisick, Roja — Howesi (Howies) to Fayette Co.; **Gaston,** 1860
Salomon, F.—Quedlinburg to Indianola; **Juno,** 1860
Salomon, Fr.—**Ammerland,** 1854
Salomon, Joh., 37—**Alexander,** 1850; Austin Co.
Salsmann, Carl—Rosenberg; **Reform,** 1849; Galveston
Samuelson, B.—Schneidemühl to Austin; **Weser,** 1858
Sander, August and wife—Perleberg, Prussia; **Bassermann,** 1851
Sander, Bernhard—to La Grange; **Iris,** 1859
Sander, Chr.—Hof-Allenburg; **Weser,** 1854
Sander, Christian—**Galliott Concordia,** 1854
Sander, Christian. 26—Hesse; **Franziska,** 1847
Sander, Engel—Brockum; **Neptune,** 1853
Sander, Fr., Friedke—Hannover; **Franziska,** 1854; Austin Co.
Sander, Fried. Wilh., 31, Marie Elise 30, Fried. Wilh. 2; **Solon,** 1850; Fayette Co.
Sander, Ludwig. 26—Württ.; **Chas. N. Cooper,** 1847
Sanders, Emil and Hulda—**Ammerland,** 1854

Sannert, Clara, 26, Minna 2—Reform, 1850
Santer, C.—Diepoldshofen; Estafette, 1850
Sarasin, Louis, 22, Josefine 20—Butzbach; John Holland, 1848; Comal Co., 1849
Sasky, John and Rosalie—Austria; Jeverland, 1860
Sass, Joh. C. F., 33—Neu Strelitz, Mecklenburg; Gutenberg, 1855
Sasse, Heinrich, 53, Dorothea 48, Heinrich 22, Friedr. 20, August 18, Ludwig 15, Carl 11, Ottilie 10, Maria 5—Gurkow, Prussia; Gutenberg, 1855; De Witt Co.
Sassen, Anna, 21—Dreftsede to Galveston; Weser, 1859
Sassmanhausen, Henry, 51—Laasphehütte; Antoinette, 1848
Sassmanshausen, Hein. — Galliott Concordia, 1854; Guadalupe Co.
Sasmanshausen, Ludwig and family—Galliott Concordia, 1854
Satoni, Jos., 2 persons—Oestrich; arr. Galveston; ship? date?
Satter, Fried., 43, Joh. 32, Hein. 8, Fried. 3, Carl 44—Blankenburg; Neptune, 1850
Sattler, Chr.—Langefeld; Texas, 1853
Sattler, E.—Langefeld to Houston; Gessner, 1860
Sattler, Heinrich, Magda., Cath.—Wallendorf to Fredericksburg; Gessner, 1860
Sattler, Wilhelm — Berlin; Suwa, 1853; San Antonio
Saue, Conrad, Dorothea, Conrad, Maria, Dorothea, Conradine, William, Sophie, Minna—Hannover to Spring Branch; Weser, 1860; Comal Co.
Sauer, Christ., 33—Parnow, Prussia; Miles, 1852
Sauer, Ed. R.—Landsberg; Neptune, 1853
Sauer, Ida—Prittisch to Galveston; Iris, 1860
Sauer, Johann, 28—Parnow, Prussia; Miles, 1852; Fayette Co.
Sauer, Joh. Joach., 8 persons—Varnow ..(Parnow?); Neptune, 1853; Fayette Co.
Sauer, Julius, 32, Babette 23—Louis, 1848
Sauer, Wilhelm—Coblenz, Prussia; Miles, 1854
Sauerling. Louis—Frankfurt-on-the-Oder; Washington, 1852
Saur, Carl—Klein-Nemerow, Mecklenburg-Strelitz; Sophie, 1852; Guadalupe Co.

— Sch —

Schaadle, Eva—Schlawinzitz; Solon, 1852
Schabel, R.—Brätz to Houston; Iris, 1857
Schabusch, Christophe, 42, Ena 32, Wilhme 12, Auguste 9, Fried. 7, Vincent 5, Johanne ¾—Prussia; Chas. N. Cooper, 1847
Schachte, Gertrude — Gross an/ Eder to Houston; Iris, 1859
Schachten, Anna—Gross an Eder to Galveston; Juno, 1860
Schadewitz, Em., Ed—Stolpe; Magnet, 1851; Fayette Co.
Schadry, Michael, 23—Baden; Reform, 1850
Schaedlich, Emil—Heyde, Holstein to Galveston; Republic, 1851
Schaefer, A. G.—Grundhausen; Weser, 1854
Schaefer, August—Striegau, Prussia to Galveston or Indianola; Franklin, 1852; Milam Co.
Schaefer, Ernst—Prussia; Antoinette, 1854; Comal Co.
Schaefer, Fr.—Bohemia; Friedrich Grosse, 1853
Schaefer, Fried., 2 persons—Wildungen; Neptune, 1853; Comal Co.
Schaefer, Friederike, 29; Creole, 1852
Schaefer, J.—Raboldshausen; Estafette, 1850
Schaefer. K., 2 persons—Bohemia; Friedrich Grosse, 1853
Schafer, Sibilla, 35—Franziska, 1849
Schaeffer, Ferd., 23; Reform, 1850
Schaffer, Fr. and family—Ammerland, 1854
Schaffer, Friedricka, 21—Detmold; Franziska, 1847
Schaffner, Christian—Anweg (Umweg?); Solon, 1852
Schaffner, F.—"aus der Schweiz" (Switzerland) to Austin County; Gessner, 1860; Austin Co.
Schaffner, Jacob with 6 children—Switzerland to Austin Co., 1856
Schalfirt. Louis, 37—Saxony; Chas. N. Cooper, 1847
Schalk, G.—Bolanden to Galveston; Fortuna, 1858
Schalleck, Carl—Posen, Prussia; Franklin, 1853
Schalupka, Jacob, wife and child—Böhmen; Weser, 1854
Schalupka, Martin—Böhmen; Weser, 1854

Schamknecht, Friedr.—Lobach;
Reform, 1849; died
Schaper, Christian—Hannover;
Suwa, 1853
Schaper, Joh., 39—Gross Lafferde;
Canapus, 1848
Schare, Christine, and 2 daughters—Wolfenbüttel; Henriette,
1843 (1853)
Scharg, Gottlieb, Fried.—Bornitz;
Minna, 1854
Scharne, Hein., 49, Cath. 45, Maria
21, Augusta 19, Hein. 14, Maria
Louisa 9, Adolph Aug.; Natchez,
1847
Scharnhorst, Fr. and wife—Hannover to Galveston; Republic,
1851; died Gillespie Co. 1871
Schaub, Johann and family—Sand;
Gessner, 1854
Schaeublen, Johann—Gotteskinder;
Solon, 1852
Schauer, Joh. Friedr., 30—Perleberg; Colonist, 1850
Schauer, Stephan, wife and 6 ch.
0-7 years old—Strilewo, Prussia;
Therese Henriette, 1853
Schawe, Joachim Fr., wife and 4
ch. ¼-9 years old—Havelberg,
Prussia; Washington, 1852
Schedelbauer, C., with family—
Greifswalde to Galveston; Weser, 1858
Scheel, Detlev, wife and 3 ch. 3-7
years old, and Schell, Hans Chr.
—Wentdorf, Holstein; Copernicus, 1852
Scheel, R.—Michelsrombach to
New Braunfels; Iris, 1857
Scheel, Wilh., Eugen, and Philippina—Michelsrombach to New
Braunfels; Juno, 1860
Scheerer, Georg A.—Neptune, 1849
Scheferkoerper, Fr., 39, Cath. 40,
Fried. 8, Lisette 3; Creole, 1852;
Comal Co.
Scheffel, Gottfried, 3 persons—
Friesland; Texas, 1853; Comal
Co.
Scheffer, Ernst, 28, Louis 22—
Brasilian, 1850
Schehr, M.—Freyburg; Gessner,
1854
Scheib, A.—Wehren; Adolphine,
1859
Scheide, Barbara—Bielefeld;
Weser, 1854
Scheide, Peter—Schilda, Prussia;
Miles, 1852
Scheidel, Ferd—Bullendorf;
Minna, 1854
Scheiner, Franz Ludmille—Ludwigsdorf; Minna, 1854

S(c)hel, J. Peter and wife—Nassau; Weser, 1854
Scheler, Barbara, 21—Hannover;
Antoinette, 1848
Schelewa, Aug., 32—Modderpfuhl
(?) to Galveston; Wilhelm, 1858
Schelewa, Emilie, 7 ch.—Modderful(?) to Yorktown; Iris, 1858
Scheller, Carl, Wilhelm, and mother — Perleberg, Prussia; Mrs.
Charles Scheller and 4 ch. died
in 1900 Galveston storm; Franklin, 1852
Schellhaas, Maria, 3 persons—Joh.
Ed. Grosse, 1853; Kerr Co.
Schellhard, Jacob—Joh. Ed.
Grosse, 1853
Schenck, Fried. 32, Friedke 24—
Magnet, 1852
Schenck, Leopold, 30, Caro. 30—
Louis, 1848
Schenk, August—Perleberg, Prussia; Bassermann, 1851
Schenk, J. C. T., 17—Wandsbeck;
Hamburg, 1849
Schenken, Rudolph, Amalie —
Quedlinburg to Indianola; Juno,
1860
Schenken family, 4 persons—
Quedlinburg to Indianola; Iris,
1859
Schepper, Louis—Gueltzow; Brasilian, 1850; Bastrop Co.
Scherff, Elise—Göttingen; Maryland, 1859
Scherf, W., Friedke — Göttingen;
Adolphine, 1859; Comal Co.
Scherpetz, J. J.—Penzin or Pintzin,
Mecklenburg; Sarah, 1851
Schert, A. — Dritles (Drittel) to
Turkey Creek (Washington Co.);
Iris, 1857
Scheurich, August — Bernstadt,
Prussia; Sophie, 1852
Scheske, Georg, Henriette, Daniel,
Julie—Poland; Franziska, 1854
Schrick, David, 53—Quedlinburg;
Franziska, 1849
Schickedanz, Elis.—Hildesheim;
Juno, 1853
Schickentanz, Fr.—Ammerland,
1854
Schiefer, F.—Herschel, 1849;
Guadalupe Co.
Schieffer, Peter—Elberfeld; Minna, 1854; Guadalupe Co.
Schiele, Carl, 3 persons—Coswig;
Herschel, 1851
Schiffer, A.—Neustadt; Gessner,
1855
Schiffers family—Laffelde to San
Antonio; Iris, 1859

Schiffers, P.—from San Antonio; Iris, 1859
Schiffers, Peter—Forst; Texas, 1853
Schilde, J. G.—Berlin; Suwa, 1853
Schildknecht, Aug., 25 — Louis, 1848; died Gillespie Co. 1871
Schildkneckty, Christ., 19—Minden; Franziska, 1849
Schiller family, 38 persons—Wien, Austria; Suwa, 1853; Austin Co.
Schiller, Hein., 38—Oldenburg; Franziska, 1847
Schillhab, Ferd., Johann, John, Magda., Beata; Jeverland, 1860
Schilling, Diedrich L., 46, Helena 32, Ferd Theo. Fried. 15, Maria 9, Diedrich 7, Elisa 4; Solon, 1850; Austin Co.
Schilling, Ernst Fr., 6 persons—Gössitz; Reform, 1851; Kendall Co.
Schilling, H.—Sondershausen to La Grange; Gaston, 1857
Schilling, Heinrich, wife and child —Gössitz, Prussia; Republic, 1851
Schilling, Johannes, 20—Creole, 1852; Victoria Co.
Schilling, Joh. Gottf., 51—Saxony; Joh. Dethardt, 1848
Schimos, Carl and Raphael—Keltsch; Weser, 1854
Schimpke, Ernst, 24—Prussia; Franziska, 1847
Schindle (Schindler), Wenzel, Theresia, Barbara, Franz, Magda., John—Austria; Jeverland, 1860
Schipke, Aug., 41—Magnet, 1852
Schirmer, Aug.—Wurzen; Solon, 1852; Galveston
Schlaeger, Lottchen — Vegesack (Vegesank); Herschel, 1851
Schlaeger, Metta—Vegesack (Vegesank); Herschel, 1851
Schlage, Christian—Weghold; Texas, 1853
Schlahube, Franziska—Fürth; Adolphine, 1859
Schlanz. D. Detlev Chr., 27, Christine 32, Marg. 5. Juliane 2, Hein. ½—Preetz, Holstein; Gutenburg, 1855
Schlap. J. and S.—Kudlup; Gessner, 1855
Schlatten, Adam and family—Ammerland, 1854
Schlecht, Frederic, 32 — Bunzlau, Prussia; Antoinette, 1848; Austin Co.
Schlecht, Fritz, 39—Bunzlau, Prussia; Herschel, 1855

Schlecht, Henriette, 39, Clara 13, Anna 10—Hermsdorf; Wilhelm, 1858
Schleicher, F.—Bolkenhain to New Braunfels; Weser, 1860
Schleicher, Gustav—Darmstadt to Texas, 1847; San Antonio
Schleicher, M. — Meiningen to Frelsburg; Iris, 1857
Schleid, ... from ? (probably Darmstadt) to New Braunfels; Anton Gunther, 1860
Schleier, C.—Anzefähr; J. W. Buddecke, 1853
Schleiter, Albert, 29—Baderhorn ('Paderborn?); Franziska, 1849
Schlemmer, F. L. and widow, and J. C. and wife Doris—all from Goertz; see Sehlmer, W. from Goertz; Hampden, 1854
Schlesinger, Edward, 24—Hamburg; Colonist, 1848
Schleuter, Johann, wife and 2 sons 2 and 4 years old—Siggen, Holstein; Hampden, 1854
Schley, Wilh., 52, Marie 44, Wilh. 22, Louise 19, Franz 17, Wilhme 15, Julius 12, Mathilde 10, Herm. 8, Emilie 6, Albert 4, Auguste ¾—Gurkow; Wilhelm, 1858; De Witt Co.
Schley, W. — Friedeberg to Yorktown; Iris, 1858
Schleyer, Christian, 32, Lisette, his wife 28, Pauline 11, Franziska 25, Julius 26—Louis, 1848; Bexar Co.
Schleyer, Emil, 17—Brasilian, 1857
Schleyer, H. F., 32—Louis, 1848
Schleyer, Wilh. Georg Ernst—Hannover; Miles, 1853
Schlichting, Gustav, 19—Brasilian, 1857
Schlickum, Ferdinand — Bergen, Han.; Texas, 1853
Schlickum, Julius, 24—Münster; Franziska, 1849
Schlickum, Therese and 2 ch.—Bexar to Bexar Co.; Gaston, 1860
Schliedman, Friedr., 29—Prussia; Franziska, 1849
Schlimms, J. H., wife and 4 ch., 7-18 years old—Zerrinn; Leibniz, 1850
Schlomann, Adolph, 27—Hannover; Franziska, 1847
Schlome, Benjamin and wife; Leser and Louise — Inowrailau to Houston; Gaston, 1860
Schlomer, Fr., 29—Schlangen; Canapus, 1848

Schlomer, Otto, 27—Berlin; Antoinette, 1848; Austin Co.
Schlomer, Pauline, 22—Herschel, 1849
Schlotterbeck, Christina—Württ.; Franziska, 1854
Schlotz, C.—Galo; Iris, 1857
Schlucker, Aug., 19, Wilhme 21—Louis, 1848
Schluens, Fritz, wife and 5 ch.—Rostock; arr. Cat Spring, Austin Co., in 1850
Schluens, Johann, 23—Czermin; Hamburg, 1849; Austin Co.
Schluenz, John—Austin to Austin; Gaston, 1860
Schmalkoke, W. and wife—Dohnsen; Neptune, 1854
Schmeisterla, F r a n z, Marianne, Rud., John, Franziska—Austria; Jeverland, 1860
Schmelz, Heinrich, Kate, Phillipine, Carl, Trine, Hein.—Oberkaufungen to Washington (onthe-Brazos); Fortuna, 1860
Schmelz, Louise—Galliott Concordia, 1854
Schmib, Gustav—Joh. Ed. Grosse, 1853
Schmidkamp, Bernhard—Berlin; Suwa, 1853
Schmidt, ... and wife—Prussia to Fayetteville; Anton Gunther, 1860
Schmidt. A.—Michelsrombach to Victoria; Juno, 1860
Schmidt, Adam—Hofheim; Juno, 1853
Schmidt, Alb. and family—Rudolstadt; Gessner, 1854
Schmidt, Albert—Zittau, Saxony; Neptune, 1854
Schmidt, Anna W(?), 53—Hermann Theodor, 1850
Schmidt, Anton—Westphalia; Weser, 1854
Schmidt, August, 4 persons—Jonitz; Hermann Theodor, 1853
Schmidt. C.—Estafette, 1850; Galveston
Schmidt, C.—Friedland (Böhmen) to San Antonio; Gaston, 1860
Schmidt, C. C., wife Doris, 2 ch. 4 and 8 years old—Barentin, Prussia; Franklin, 1853
Schmidt, Carl, 50, Friedke 58—Perleberg; Colonist, 1850; Kendall Co.
Schmidt, Carl, 28—Saxony; Natchez, 1847
Schmidt, Carl and Charlotte—Burg; Mississippi, 1855

Schmidt, Caro.—Zicho (Zwichau?) to Austin; Juno, 1860
Schmidt, Christian, wife and 6 ch. —Steinburg to Victoria; Juno, 1860
Schmidt, Christian and Cath. — Steckigt (Stöckigt); Weser, 1854
Schmidt, Christiane, 48, with 3 ch. 4-21 years old—Tangedorf, Prussia to Galveston; Miles, 1852
Schmidt, Christoph—Barentin, Prussia; Franklin, 1853
Schmidt, D. H.—Lehmden; Estafette, 1850
Schmidt, Emil—Oppeln to Galveston; Iris, 1859
Schmidt, F.—Wehdem to Brenham; Weser, 1860
Schmidt, F.—Dettersbach; Texas, 1853
Schmidt, F. and C.—from Galveston; Weser, 1858
Schmidt, Focke, 3 persons—Aurich, Oldendorf; Magnet, 1851
Schmidt, Fr., Dorothea, Ernst, Emilie—Flensburg to Galveston; Weser, 1854
Schmidt, Franz, 22—Fortuna, 1858
Schmidt, Fried.—Galliott Concordia, 1854
Schmidt, Friedrich—Uenze, Prussia; Miles, 1852
Schmidt, G., wife and 2 ch.—Prussia; Franziska, 1854
Schmidt, G.—Niederbeisheim; Reform, 1851
Schmidt, Georg, wife and 5 daughters, 1½-24 years old—Fresenbrugge, Mecklenburg; Franklin, 1853
Schmidt, H.—Teichenau to Galveston; Iris, 1859
Schmidt, H. and 2 daughters, 17 and 14—Herschel, 1849
Schmidt, Hch., 26—Louis, 1848
Schmidt, Hein., 24—Zichaw (Zwickau) to Austin; Weser, 1858
Schmidt, Hein., 17—Hermann Theodor, 1850
Schmidt, Heinrich—Benz, Denmark; Copernicus, 1852
Schmidt, H. and Joh.—Ammerland, 1854
Schmidt, Johann and wife—Neu-Fresenbruegge, Mecklenburg; Copernicus, 1852
Schmidt, J. C. with family, 3 persons — Anzefähr; J. W. Buddecke, 1853

Schmidt, J. G.; Schmidt, Johann and Pauline 5, Julius 2—Lichtenau, Prussia; **Franklin,** 1853; Comal Co.

Schmidt, Joh. Fred., 46, Gesche Margaretha 43, Fried. Christoph 14—**Solon,** 1850; Austin Co.

Schmidt, J. M. T.—Gevezin; **Leibniz,** 1850

Schmidt, L.—to Round Top; **Weser,** 1859

Schmidt, Maria—Anzefähr; J. W. **Buddecke,** 1853

Schmidt, Pet.; Vilmor, 6 persons; ship? date?

Schmidt, Philipp, wife Louise nee Wagner—Darmstadt, Hesse; arr. Texas ca. 1852, Comal Co.

Schmidt, Sophia, 25—Willershagen, Mecklenburg; **Herschel,** 1855

Schmidt, T.—Mellrichstadt to Indianola; **Juno,** 1860

Schmidt, W.—Prussia to Galveston; **Jeverland,** 1860

Schmidt, Wilh. and wife—**Neptune,** 1849

Schmidt, Wilh., 27—Korsenz; **Colonist,** 1850

Schmidt, Wilhelm, wife and 5 ch. ¾-14 years old — Caminbrod, Prussia; **Miles,** 1853

Schmidz, Jos., 26, Anna 28, Marie 20; **Herschel,** 1850

Schmiedekamp. Wm.—Prussia; **Neptune,** 1848; Colorado Co.

Schmietmeyer, G., wife and 3 ch.—Lanzing; **Lucie,** 1854

Schmipff, Joh.—Schraplau; **Weser,** 1854

Schmitten, Sophie—Marlen to Industry; **Iris,** 1860

Schmitzen, M. — Berncastel to Frelsburg; **Iris,** 1860

Schmohk, J. C., wife and 2 daughters 0 and 2 years old—Studewick, Mecklenburg; **Franklin,** 1853

Schmuecklich. Maria—Marbach to Galveston; **Iris,** 1858

Schnackenbach. C., 28—Hannover; **Alexander**. 1850; Galveston

Schnachenwalte, Wilh.. 25—Eichwerder; **Wilhelm,** 1858

Schneider. A.—Neustadel to San Antonio; **Iris, 1859**

Schneider, Adam J., 24—**Hermann Theodor,** 1850

Schneider. Albert. Johanne—Sommerfeld to Goliad; **Iris,** 1859

Schneider. Anna—Friedland; **Minna,** 1854

Schneider. Aug.. 38. Anna 30 died, Ullrich 7, Sophie 6. Aug. 4, Marie 2; **Hamburg,** 1849

Schneider, Carl, 28—Ristedt; Colonist, 1850; Austin Co.

Schneider, Cath.—Udorf; **Henriette,** 1843 (1853)

Schneider, Christ., 4 persons—Ubbedessen; **Texas,** 1853; Guadalupe Co.

Schneider, Dorothea—Burg; **Herschel,** 1851

Schneider, F.—Friedland to Bastrop; **Iris,** 1857

Schneider, F. A., 37—Fegersheim to New Braunfels; **Iris,** 1859

Schneider family, 8 persons—Berlin; **Suwa,** 1853

Schneider, Gust., 34—Plauen; **Canapus,** 1848

Schneider, H.—Prittisch to Galveston; **Iris,** 1860

Schneider, J.—Neustadt; **Adolphine,** 1859

Schneider, J.—Sobieschen (Sobieszyn) to Galveston; **Iris,** 1859

Schneider, J. G.—Darmstadt; **Neptune,** 1853

Schneider, Jacob—Hesse; **Antoinette,** 1854; Gillespie Co.

Schneider, Joh., Elis.—**Joh. Ed. Grosse,** 1853; De Witt Co.

Schneider, Jul.—Hettstedt; **Reform,** 1849

Schneider, Julie—Friedland; **Adolphine,** 1859

Schneider, Louis, 14—**Magnet,** 1852

Schneider, Ludwig—Meiningen; **Solon,** 1852

Schneider, M. and family—Michelsrombach to New Braunfels; **Iris,** 1857

Schneider,.Philipp, 6 persons—Dillenburg; **Henriette,** 1843 (1853)

Schneider, W.—Irmenach; **Estafette,** 1850; Austin Co.

Schnelle, H., Friedke, Louise—Hannover; **Franziska,** 1854

Schnill, Bertha—Schleiz; **Weser,** 1854

Schnoor, Claus, wife and 4 ch. 1-13 years old — Kuden, Denmark; **Copernicus,** 1852

Schnoor, Heinrich, wife and 8 ch. 1¾-23 years old; **Copernicus,** 1852

Schnutz, Hein., Maria—Waldeck; **Franziska,** 1854

Schobert, J. and wife—Rudelzhofen; **Neptune,** 1854

Schobesta (Schebesta), Ignaz, Marianne, John, Anna, Theresia, Barbara, Veronica, Marianne—Austria; **Jeverland,** 1860

Schoebitz, Ch., 43, Jacob 68, Jacob 18, Johanna 19, Cath. 12, Philip 5, Fried. 43; **Herschel, 1850**

Schoel, Henrich—Ratjan, Holstein; **Copernicus, 1852**

Schoeler, Jacob, 2 children, 3 and 6 years—Rohrbach, Saxony; to Galveston or Indianola; **Franklin, 1852**

Schoenberg, Marie, 28—**Galliott Flora, 1849**

Schoenemann, Gottlieb—Schmalenberg, Mecklenburg; **Washington, 1852**

Schoenenberger, C.—Tescherthal, Switz.; **Lucie, 1854**

Schoenert, A.—Wolfenbüttel; **Neptune, 1854**

Schoenfeld, Henriette—Loewenberg, Prussia; **Miles, 1854**

Schoenher, Michael, 28—**Creole, 1852**

Schoke, Wilh.—Hannover; **Suwa, 1853**

Scholl, Georg, 48, Jacob 15—**Sophie, 1852;** Comal Co.

Scholmomer, Wilh., 38, Eva 21, Carl 3, Anna 10 mo.; **Louis, 1848**

Scholtz, Joh. G.—Saxony; **Neptune, 1848**

Scholz, A. and Marte—Falkenberg to La Grange; **Iris, 1860**

Scholz, Emma—Liegnitz; **Adolphine, 1859**

Scholz, J.—Bohemia; **Franziska, 1854**

Scholz, Theo., 34, Pauline 33, Hch. 5; **Reform, 1850**

Scholz, W.—Brande to Galveston; **Iris, 1860**

Schome, Julius, 25 and Mad., 22—Coleto Creek, Texas; **Herschel, 1849**

Schonhof, Aug.—Braunschweig; **Canapus, 1849**

Schonsling(?), John Hein., 35, Marie 5; **Herman Theodor, 1850**

Schontze, Martin — Schwarzenberg; **Neptune, 1853**

School, Jacob—Offenbach, Nassau; **Mississippi, 1855**

Schoppe, Louise—Wustroff (Westrup) to Galveston; **Juno, 1860**

Schorch, Amalie and Pauline—Alt. Gebhardt, Mecklenburg; **Franklin, 1853**

Schornstein, H. R.—Landsberg, Prussia; **Miles, 1854**

Schorr, Cath. and Georgine — Frankfurt a. Main to Houston; **Iris, 1861**

Schorr, George—Frankfurt a.M. to Houston; **Iris, 1861**

Schorr, Leo A.—Frankfurt/M to Houston; **Iris, 1861**

Schorre, Ed—Rinteln; **Canapus, 1849**

Schostalla, Johanne, 15 — Gurkow to Lexington; **Weser, 1858**

Schott, Christoph — Frankfurt to Houston; **Weser, 1860**

Schottman, Wilh., 22—Prussia; **Franziska, 1847**

Schoverling(?), Ernst H., 36, Marie Elise, 34; **Herman Theodor, 1850**

Schrader, Gust.—Celle; **Mississippi, 1855**

Schrader, Hein.; **Ammerland, 1854**

Schrader, Joh.—Sommersell; **Canapus, 1849**

Schrader, Theodor, with family, 9 persons—Helmstedt; **J. W. Buddecke, 1853**

Schrader, Wilh.—Braunschweig; **Chas. N. Cooper, 1847**

Schramm, C.—to Independence; **Weser, 1859**

Schram, F., wife and 2 ch. — Bohemia; **Franziska, 1854;** Austin County

Schreck, David, 53—Quedlinburg; **Franziska, 1849**

Schreen, F.—Weimar to San Antonio; **Gessner, 1860**

Schreiber, Adam—Albershausen; 8 persons; **Hermann Theodor, 1853**

Schreiber, C., wife and ch.—Risbeck (Risenbeck?); **Lucie, 1854**

Schreiber, C.—Hannover; **Weser, 1854**

Schreiber, Cath.—Albershausen; **Hermann Theodor, 1853**

Schreiber, Edmund—Meiningen; **Solon, 1852**

Schreiber, Ignaz and Marg.—Orb; **Henriette, 1843 (1853)**

Schreibage, Wilh., 49; Dor. 51, Lud. 21, Henriette 18, Theo. 16, Carl 11 — Hannover; **Franziska, 1847**

Schreyer, J. C. F., 21; **Galliott Flora, 1849**

Schriebel, C.—Tost; **Gessner, 1855**

Schrieber, Heinr. — Fockerode (Vockenrod?); **Herschel, 1851;** Comal Co.

Schroede, Amalie, 23—Damme; **Antoinette, 1848**

Schroder, Christian, 54; Wilhme 47, Fried. 20, Christian 17, Gottlieb 14, Wilhme 9, Franz 3—**Reutern; Wilhelm, 1858**

— 129 —

Schroder, Franz, 30—Prussia; Natchez, 1847
Schroeder, Aug.—Hannover; Weser, 1854; Washington Co.
Schroeder, C. — Altona Hamburg; Leibniz, 1850
Schroeder, Christ., 27; Magnet, 1852
Schroeder, Christoph, 41; Anna 27, John 7, Georg 2—Sophie, 1852; Washington Co.
Schroeder, Dorette—Suderburg to Galveston; Iris, 1859
Schroeder family—Oppendorf; Adolphine, 1859
Schroeder, F.—Prussia to Houston; Gessner, 1860
Schroeder, Gottlieb — Jesnitz to New Ulm; Weser, 1860
Schroeder, Gustav—Quedlinburg to Indianola; Juno, 1860
Schroeder, H.—Neustadt, Holstein; Hampden, 1854
Schroeder, H.—Bülow; Leibniz, 1850
Schroeder, Jacob, 37, Cath. 22; Sophie, 1852
Schroeder, Joh. A., 25, Albert 19; Anna Louisa, 1857
Schroeder, J. and U.—Augustendorf; Anna Louisa, 1857
Schroeder, K., 2 persons—Prussia; Friedrich Grosse, 1853
Schroeder, L. — Amthäven to La Grange; Iris, 1858
Schroeder, Wilhelm—Garz, Holstein; Hampden, 1854
Schroeder, Wilh., 27, Ferd. 18— Detmold; Neptune, 1850
Schroeke, H.—Oppendorf to Houston; Weser, 1858
Schroeter, Carl, 31, Wilhme 29, Wilhme 4, Carl 2, Friedke 1; Magnet, 1852
Schroeter, O.—Hamburg to Industry; Weser, 1860
Schrub('?), Joachim, 40, Dor. 31, Siegfried 10, Cluni(?) 8, Rosalind 7, Christian 28; Alexander, 1850
Schrudt, Heinr. — Wietendorf, Mecklenburg to Galveston or Indianola; Franklin, 1852
Schube, Joh., 24—Sachsen; Franziska, 1847
Schube, Wilh., 40—Neu-Ruppin; Solon, 1850
Schubert, A.—Breslau to New Ulm; Weser, 1860
Schubert, Chs.—Alvensleben; Reform, 1849

Schubert, Eduard — Hörter (Hörster); Neptune, 1853; Fayette Co.
Schubert, Emil—Prussia; Joh. Dethardt, 1848
Schubert, Jos., 67; Solon, 1850
Schubert, Maria with 2 ch.—Prussia; Franziska, 1854
Schuchard, Wolfgang, 22 — Louis, 1848
Schuchmaker, Conrad, 29, Cath. 26, Marg. 2—Germany; Natchez, 1847
Schuck, Moritz — Hildburghausen, Meiningen; Copernicus, 1852
Schuckmeyer, H. — Oppenwehe to Houston; Weser, 1858
Schuecke, Helene with 4 ch.—Posen to Galveston; Juno, 1860
Schueke, L.—Cadderfeld (Kälberfeld?) to Seguin; Gaston, 1857
Schuelke, August—Posen to Galveston; Juno, 1860
Schuenemann, August and Henriette — Bergbruch to Cypress; Fortuna, 1860
Schuerer, Christian—Joh. Ed. Grosse, 1853
Schuerer, Marie and Marie Therese; Joh. Ed. Grosse, 1853
Schuerre, F.—Nassau; Weser, 1854
Schuett, Hein.—Ottenwiesen; J. W. Buddecke, 1853
Schuett, Joachim — Hohenfelde, Holstein; 3 ch. 22-29 years old; Copernicus, 1852
Schuett, Johann, wife Caroline— Techentin, Mecklenburg; Franklin, 1853
Schuette, Carl, wife and 2 ch., 3-7 yrs.; Franklin, 1852; Austin Co.
Schuett, Chr.—Birkenfeld; 4 persons; Hermann Theodor, 1853
Schuette, Marie, Elise—Birkenfeld; Hermann Theodor, 1853
Schueter, ... —Paderborn to Collet (Coleto?); Iris, 1858
Schuetz, Chr., 3 persons—Hannover; Friedrich Grosse, 1853
Schuetz, G.—Hainewalde; Neptune, 1854
Schuetze, Julius—Dessau, Anhalt; arr. Texas 1852
Schuetze, Wilhelm, wife and son, age 8—Hannover; John Friederick, 1850
Schuhmann, Carl—Oberscheibe; 3 persons; Hermann Theodor, 1853
Schumann, Christian, 6 persons— Oberscheibe; Hermann Theodor, 1853; Fayette Co.

Schumann, Fried., 5 persons —
Oberscheibe; Hermann Theodor,
1853; Fayette Co.
Schula, C., wife and ch.—Gacenka
(Jasenka) to Industry; Juno,
1860
Schulack, Ernst, 40, Wilhme 36,
Auguste 6, Ida 4—Prussia; Col-
onist, 1848
Schuler, L.—Göttingen; Weser,
1854
Schult, Franz, wife and son age
17—Werle, Mecklenburg; Ther-
ese Henriette, 1853
Schulte, Chr. Fr., 26; Hermann
Theodor, 1850
Schulte, Joh.; Galliott Concordia,
1854
Schulte, Otto; Galliott Concordia,
1854
Schultz, A., 41—Hamburg; Alex-
ander, 1850
Schultz, Carl—Reichwalde; Missis-
sippi, 1855
Schultz, Cath.—Königgrätz; Her-
schol, 1851
Schultz, Christ., wife and 4 ch. 12-
21 years—Reckenthien, Prussia
to Galveston, Texas; Miles, 1852
Schultz, Friedrich, wife Maria—
Pritzwalk, Prussia; Hampden,
1854
Schultz, Fried., 54, Sophie 44, Au-
guste 24, Gottlieb 22, Franz 16,
Gusav 1/6—Werle; John Freder-
ick, 1850; Colorado Co.
Schultz, Joh., 46 — Moenkhagen,
Meck.; Herschel, 1855; Bastrop
Co.
Schultz, Maria, widow with 3 ch.—
Neu-Ruppin; Republic, 1851
Schultze, H., 28; Fortuna, 1858
Schulz, A.—Böhmen; Adolphine,
1859
Schulz, A., 40—Hamburg; Alex-
ander, 1850
Schulz, A.—Prussia; Franziska,
1854
Schulz, Albert, Auguste, Marie—
Friedeberg to Yorktown; Juno,
1860
Schulz, Aug., 21 — Franzthal to
Yorktown; Weser, 1859
Schulz, Carl, 48, Johanne 46, Carl
19, Louise 16, Fritz 12, Herm.
11, Robert 5—Derenburg; Nep-
tune, 1850; Guadalupe Co.
Schulz, Carl—Havelberg, Prussia;
Washington, 1852
Schulz, Fried.—Bohemia; Fried-
rich Grosse, 1853

Schulz, Fried.—Wusterhausen;
Reform, 1849
Schulz, Gottlieb—Friedeberg;
Neptune, 1853
Schulz, Hein., 31, Pauline 34—
Reichenbach; Colonist, 1850;
Comal Co.
Schulz, J.—Friedland to Bastrop;
Iris, 1857
Schulz, Joachim—Kletzke, Prussia
to Galveston with wife and 3 ch.
12-17 years old; Miles, 1852
Schulz, Joh.—Reetz; Neptune, 1853
Schulz, J. H. F.—Gevezin; Leibniz,
1850
Schulz, Johann, wife and son 17
years — Perleberg, Prussia to
Galveston or Indianola; Frank-
lin, 1852
Schulz, Martin, wife and 1 ch. 7
yrs.—Klein-Sorge, Meck.; Miles,
1852
Schulz, Martin, with family, 3 per-
sons—Posen; Miles, 1853
Schulz, W.—Bretz; Gessner, 1855
Schulze, Andreas, 43 — Grönhude,
Holstein; Louise 37, Hein. 14,
Amalie 12, Christophe 7, Adolph
6, Sophie 4, Louise 2; Hamburg,
1849
Schulze, C. and A.—Memphis;
Gessner, 1855
Schulze, Carl—Brome to Industry;
Sophie, Aug., Charl, Carl, Rud.;
Fortuna, 1860
Schulze, Dor. with 3 ch.—Bergzow
to Comfort; Fortuna, 1858
Schulze, E. with family—Theessen
to Galveston; Iris, 1860; Bas-
trop Co.
Schulze, Friedrich and wife —
Perleberg, Prussia to Galveston
or Indianola; Franklin, 1852
Schulze, Hermann, Wilhme—Oster-
wieck; Solon, 1852; Fayette Co.
Schulze, J. F. C.—Klein-Posena,
Saxony; Miles, 1854
Schulze, Johanna—Berlin; Suwa,
1853
Schulze, Johanne—Bratz to Hous-
ton; Iris, 1857
Schulze, Mary—Annaburg to Gal-
veston; Fortuna, 1860
Schumacher, Ahlert, 36 — Olden-
burg; Helena 40, Hein. 14. Anna
12. Meta 9, Diedrich 7, Joh. 5,
Esie(?) 1; Franziska, 1847
Schumacher, H.—Sinzheim; Gess-
ner, 1854
Schumacher, Heinrich—Schönfeld,
Prussia; Bassermann, 1851;
Austin Co.

Schumacher, Hinrich, 25—Seeland, Denmark; Gutenberg, 1855
Schumacher, M.—Rosdorf; 2 persons; Estafette, 1850
Schumack, W., 25; Herschel, 1849
Schumak, Hein., 15, Sabina 18—Mecklenburg; Franziska, 1847
Schumake, Gottfried, 29—Neusalz; Colonist, 1850
Schumaker, Joh., 23—Prussia; Franziska, 1847
Schumann, Adolph, 27—Hannover; Franziska, 1847
Schumann, C.—Oggersheim; Weser, 1854
Schumann, Wilh., 22, Traugott 30; Chas. N. Cooper, 1847
Schumme (Schamme?), Theo, Wilhme—Lohbau; Texas, 1853
Schunck, Auguste, 20; Louis, 1848
Schunemann, F.; Herschel, 1849; Comal Co.
Schunemann, Hein., 36—Braunschweig; Franziska, 1847
Schunka, Franz, wife and ch.—Bohemia; Weser, 1854
Schunka, Wenzel and wife—Bohemia; Weser, 1854
Schunta (Schonta), J.—Austria; Jeverland, 1860
Schuppe, A.—to Victoria; Weser, 1859
Schurig, Ad.—Elstra; Magnet, 1851; Bexar Co.
Schuster, C., with family—Neugersdorf to Washington (on-the-Brazos); Fortuna, 1858
Schuster, Caro.—Nassau; Weser, 1854
Schutti, C.—Seegraben, Switz.; Lucie, 1854
Schutz, Ed.—Breslau, Prussia to Indianola, Texas; Miles, 1852
Schutz, Wilh. — Goericke, Prussia to Indianola; Miles, 1852
Schutze, H.—Oranienbaum; Gessner, 1854
Schuwirth, J.—Brachelen to San Antonio; Iris, 1857
Schuwirth, J. and W.—Brachelen to San Antonio; Iris, 1857
Schwab family, 3 persons—Bernhards to Austin; Iris, 1859
Schwab, Eugen, 22; Hermann Theodor, 1850; Comal Co.
Schwab, J.—Neuland to Austin; Fortuna, 1860
Schwab, Val, 35, Elis. 27, Andreas 8, Alexius 4 — Hermann Theodor, 1850; Comal Co.
Schwaeckenwalte, W., 25 — Eichwerder to Yorktown; Weser, 1858

Schwanaeljack, Herm., 19; Brasilien or E. von Beaulieu, 1857
Schwanck, Aug. Wm.—Siestedt; Reform, 1849
Schwanke, J. with family — Weigersdorf to Bastrop; Fortuna, 1858
Schwante, Fr.; Ammerland, 1854
Schwarting, Anna—Minsen to Galveston; Fortuna, 1860
Schwarting, Fred, 19, Hanchin (F) 21—Franziska, 1847
Schwarz, Fr. and Louise—Wehdem to Brenham; Weser, 1860
Schwarz, J. H.—Burghassungen; Texas, 1853
Schwarzbach, G., wife Christine, son August—Lichtenau, Prussia; Franklin, 1853; Galveston
Schwarzbach, Gottlieb, 25; Colonist, 1850; Galveston
Schwarze, Heinrich—Treikenhorst (?); Magnet, 1851
Schwede, Christ. — Reckenthien, Prussia; Miles, 1852; Colorado Co.
Schween, F.—Hannover; Suwa, 1853
Schweigel (?), Joh., 29—Bavaria; Franziska, 1847
Schweimer, Emile, 32; Fortuna, 1858
Schweiss family—to Brenham; Weser, 1859
Schweizer, Carl 25, Hein. 21—Kahla; Hamburg, 1849; De Witt Co.
Schwenke, Diedrich, 22—Oldenburg; Franziska, 1847
Schwerberger, Wendelin, Mary, Marg. — Hornau to New Ulm; Fortuna, 1860
Schwerdfeger, H. J. A.—Oldenburg; Neptune, 1848
Schwertfeger, Hein., 22—Cöslin; Brasilian, 1850
Schwerdfleger, Ant., 42—Saxony; Joh. Dethardt, 1848
Schwaboda, Joh. and wife—Mähren; Weser, 1854
Schwinn, Maria—Yullau (Tullau) to Houston; Iris, 1858
Seber, Fr.—Friedrichsrode; Gessner, 1855
Sechling (Sechting?), August — Hannover; Franziska, 1854; Fayette Co. or Austin Co.
Sedtmeyer, Lorenz—Wolfgang; Lucie, 1854
See, Joachim and wife—Schwerin, Mecklenburg; Sophie, 1852
Seege, Hein.—Bielefeld; Weser, 1854

Seeger, C.—Buchs to New Ulm;
Fortuna, 1860
Seehagel, Ferd., Charl—Tarkawo
(Tankow?) to Cypress, Harris
Co.; Fortuna, 1860
Seehagel, Marie, Wilhme, Floren-
tine, Ernestine—Tarkawo ('Tan-
kow?) to Cypress; Fortuna,
1860
Seekamp, R.—to Galveston; Wes-
er, 1859
Seel, ...—Grafenberge to Gal-
veston; Iris, 1858
Seelhorst, Marg.—Versmold; 2
persons; Texas, 1853
Seeliger, E. G.—Heidersdorf; 5
persons; Reform, 1851
Seeman, Maria, 18—Grevsdorff,
Mecklenburg; Washington, 1852
Seeman, Meta—Braunschweig;
Gessner, 1854
Seemann, Marg. — Schoenkirchen,
Holstein; Hampden, 1854
Seffel, Wenzel, wife and 5 ch.—
Reichenberg to San Antonio;
Weser, 1857; Bexar Co.
Segger, Fried.—Hannover; Suwa,
1853
Segbelig, Louis—Breslau, Prussia;
Miles, 1852
Sehlmer (or Schlmer), W.—Goertz,
cf Schlemmer; wife and 2 sons,
¾ and 3½ yrs.; Hampden, 1854
Seidel, A. — Prussia; Friedrich
Grosse, 1853; Goliad Co.
Seidel, Bernhard; Seidel, Franz.—
Cassborn (Kassebohm?); Nep-
tune, 1854
Seidler, D.—Paulwitz to Austin
Co.; Juno, 1860
Seidler, Joh. and family; Ammer-
land, 1854
Seidelmann, Dor. — Seehausen to
Industry; Iris, 1860.
Seiler family, 5 persons—Gräfen-
bain to Galveston; Iris, 1859
Sellmer, Anna—Posen to Galves-
ton; Iris, 1857
Selm. Marie—to Galveston; Weser,
1859
Selszack, Joh., Anna—Vienna;
Suwa, 1853
Seltrecht, A. T. F.—Mollenstorf;
Leibniz, 1850
Sembala, Maria, Louisa — Sobie-
schen (Sobieszyn) to Indianola;
Juno, 1860
Semmel, Bertha—Posen; Adol-
phine, 1859
Semmler. M. Ferd., 35—Limbadr
(?); Canapus, 1848; Comal Co.
Sendler, Alex.—Württ.; Texas,
1853

Senf (Seuf?), W.—Prussia to San
Antonio; Gessner, 1860
Senger, Elis., 58, William 17;
Sophie, 1852
Senne, H.—Hannover to Bastrop;
Iris, 1857
Senne, Henry—Steinhude to Johns-
ville (Erath Co.); Gaston, 1860
Sensel, Marg.—Reffenroth?;
Texas, 1853
Sensel, Veronica—Kassel; Texas,
1853
Settegast, M. W., 7 persons—Bieb-
rick, arr. Gal. ship? date?
Settegast, Herm.—Düsseldorf; Re-
form, 1849; Bexar Co.
Settgast, Chr.—Rependorf, Meck-
lenburg to Galveston; Basser-
mann, 1851
Seubert family—to Galveston;
Weser, 1859
Seuf, W. See Senf, W.
Severin, Stine, 22 — Brockhusen,
Mecklenburg; Herschel, 1855;
Austin Co.
Seyffarth, Aug.—Altenburg; Re-
form, 1851; Fayette Co.
Seydler, Babette—Bischoffsgrün;
Weser, 1854
Seydler, Ernestine—Bautzen,
Prussia; Franklin, 1853
Seydler, Fr. Aug. 26, J. Gustav
28, Wilh. 24 — Bautzen; Ham-
burg, 1849; Fayette Co.
Seyer, Joh. Christ. 56, Louise 69—
West Prignitz to Houston; Iris,
1859
Sich, Christian, 38, Caro. 30, Jo-
hanna ¾ — Prussia; Chas. N.
Cooper, 1847
Sichart, Fred., 27—Hannover;
Franziska, 1847
Sichel, Joachim—Bluethen, Meck.;
Copernicus, 1852; Bexar Co.
Sickenius, Caro.—Darmstadt to
Kerr Co.; Gaston, 1860
Sickert, W., Henriette, William—
Berlin to Galveston; Fortuna,
1860
Sickor, Georg—Dresden; 4 per-
sons; Reform, 1851
Sidow, Aug. and Rosina—Posen to
Houston; Juno, 1860. See Sydow
Siebel, C.—Bremen; Gessner, 1855
Sieber, Christoph, 28, Hanna Chris-
tine 60, Carl Hein. 25, Moritz
18—Saxony; Chas. N. Cooper,
1847; Comal Co.
Sieber, Joh. Dana, 31, Hana Chris-
tiane 29, Hanna 4, Louis ¾—
Saxony; Chas. N. Cooper, 1847
Siebert, Sophia—Rohden; Texas,
1853

Siedenstopp, Joh., 48, Wilhme 29; Herschel, 1850
Siegfried, Veronica, Marie—Durgau, Switz.; Lucie, 1854
Sieghorst, Carl L.—Berlin; Suwa, 1853
Siegle, L.—Heilbronn; Juno, 1860
Siegmann, P.—Prussia; Friedrich Grosse, 1853
Sieling, Antoinette—Galveston to Galveston; Weser, 1860
Sieling, Madame H. and daughter —Galveston; Gaston, 1857
Siemring (Siemering), August — Dahlhausen, Prussia; Republic, 1851; teacher at Fredericksburg and editor San Antonio Zeitung
Sieper, Marg., 26; Creole, 1852
Sievers, Anton, 24; Canapus, 1848
Sievers, Fritz and Elise—to Galveston; Weser, 1859
Sievers, Hein., 27, Sophie 35; Hamburg, 1849; Austin Co.
Sievert, Doris — Pritzwalk, Prussia; 4 ch., ¼-6 years; Hampden, 1854; Austin Co.
Siffel, Steph(an)—Friedland; Canapus, 1849
Simm, Georg, Joh., Agnes, Mary, Magda.—Rakel to Cunningham, Lamar Co.; Fortuna, 1860
Simmauk, Andreas, 50, Maria 40, Samuel 11, Anna 10, Magda. 5, Christian 2, Mary 1—Golbitz to Resperek?; Iris, 1859
Simme, J. and wife—Rackel; Anton Gunther, 1860
Simon, Chr., 48, Joh. 50, Fried. 23, Aug. 17; Neptune, 1850; Victoria Co.
Simon, Martha—Pfiffe to San Antonio; Weser, 1860
Simonis, Christiane; Hamburg, 1849
Sindstaebter, Chr. — Reitzengeschwenda; Reform, 1851
Singvogel, Sebastian—Geislingen; Weser, 1854
Sinn, Christine—Mückenberg to Neighbor's Creek; Iris, 1859
Sinram, Fried. — (St.?) Petersburg, Russia; wife and 2 ch., 10 and 13 years; Washington, 1852
Sittig, Wilh.—Schmalkalden; Henriette, 1843 (1853)
Sklouzal, Theresia; Jeverland, 1860
Skwortz, Joseph and family—Himlowitz (Himmelwitz?); Weser, 1854

Stadeck, John, Maria, John, Franziska, Ignaz, Conrad, Theresa, Juliane—Austria; Jeverland, 1860
Slege, Hein.—Hannover; Suwa, 1853
Slievensky, Jos.—Königgratz; Herschel, 1851
Slivensky, Caro.—Prag(ue) to Bastrop; Iris, 1861
Slowatschek, Paul and M. with wife and 2 ch.—Gacenka (Jasenka); Juno, 1860
Smirack, Johanna—Austria; Jeverland, 1860
Smolik, Ignaz, Katherine—Misliboritz to Austin; Gaston, 1860
Soder, F.—Madgeburg; Gessner, 1855; Austin Co.
Soefge, Heinrich, wife Anna, nee Willmann; Friedrich Grosse, 1853; Comal Co. 1860
Soellner, Dor.—Berlin; Suwa, 1853
Soelner, C.—Halle to Brenham; Weser, 1860
Sohns, C.—Wüngsowitz (Wenglowitz) to Galveston; Weser, 1858
Solbrig, Herm. Theod.—Leipzig; Herschel, 1851
Somer, Joh., 47, Ann. Marg. 45, Gesha 16, Anne 11; Franziska, 1849
Sommer, August 31, Alwine 29, Ludwig 7, Wilhilme 2 — Neu-Strelitz, Meck.; Miles, 1855; Guadalupe Co.
Sommer, F., wife and 4 ch.—Bullendorf; Minna, 1854; Washington Co.
Sommer, Marie—Riggersdorf, Bohemia; Mississippi, 1855
Sommer, Pauline, 24—Jauer; John Frederick, 1850
Sommerfeld, Anna — Springberge to Houston; Iris, 1860
Sommerfeld, W.—Prussia to Houston; Juno, 1860; Washington Co., 1870
Sommerlate, A., 30, Caro. 23, Fried. 5, Aug. 2, Leopoldine 50, Friedke 20; Fortuna, 1858; Lavaca Co.
Sommeletter, C.—Wörlitz to Frelsburg; Iris, 1857
Sommers, Franz, Anna — Bullendorf; Minna, 1854
Sondershausen, Ta (Theodora?)— Stadtilm Thuringia; Hampden, 1854
Sosatzky, L.—Burg; Texas, 1853
Sparmann, Aug.—Berthelsdorf; Neptune, 1853

Specht, Juliane—Württemburg; Franziska, 1854
Speier, Mathilda, 20—Kassel; Weser, 1858
Speisser, Maria, Barbara—Essingen to New Braunfels; Gaston, 1857
Spengler, Fr. Carl, 29—Berlin; Hamburg, 1849
Spickels, Eilert, 65, Anna Cath. 54, Eilert 35, Gehr. 17, Gerd. 12, Cath. 14 — Jaderbollenhagen; Helen & Elise, 1847
Spickels, Jan. 29, Geshe Marg. 24, Gehr. 4, Marg. Cath. 3, Joh. Chr. 8 days (born on board); Helen & Elise, 1847
Spies, H.—Schameder to Shelby; Fortuna, 1860
Spiess, Christian and family; Galliott Concordia, 1854; Washington Co.
Spiess, Joh. and family (4)—Oermelingen; Solon, 1852; Colorado Co.
Spiess, Martin—Oermelingen; Solon, 1852
Spikermann family—to Petersburg; Weser, 1859
Spiller, Louis—Bernstadt, Prussia; Sophie, 1852
Spillmann, F. H., 28, Anna 22; Hermann Theodor, 1850
Spillman, H.—Prussia to Austin; Gessner, 1860
Spinas, A.—Zürich to Galveston; Iris, 1859
Spindler, Jos.—Dahlhausen; Herschel, 1851
Spitzschack, Carl—Berlin; Washington, 1852
Sponholz, Carl—Ruelow, Mecklenburg-Strelitz; Sophie, 1852
Spreen, Franz, 35, Charlotte 35, Wilhme 10, Henriette 9, Wilh. 4, Franz 6, Christine 24; Hermann Theodor, 1850; Austin Co.
Spreer, Henriette—Wehdem to Brenham; Weser, 1860
Spremberg, Dor., 4 persons—Garkau; Texas, 1853
Sprems, W.—Wehdem to Houston; Weser, 1858
Sprenger, Christian, 34; Creole, 1852
Springer, Carl, 43, Marie 28, Albert 7, Marie 3, Paul 16—Saxony; Reform, 1850; Fayette Co.
Springer, J. G. B., Meta—Varel; Solon, 1852
Springfield. Carl, 30—Mecklenburg; Colonist, 1848

Springmann, Max—Hannover; Friedrich Grosse, 1853
Spütz, Wilh.—Breslau; Neptune, 1854
Staake, Aug., 23—Free Town; Antoinette, 1848; Bexar Co.
Staats, ..., 2 daughters—Hoheneggelsen to Zaria(?); Fortuna, 1858
Staats, Bertha, 28—Schermcke to Galveston; Weser, 1859
Staats, Heinrich—Wenden; J. W. Buddecke, 1853
Stach, A.—Prussia; Friedrich Grosse, 1853
Stache, August — Niederwaltersdorf, Meck.; Franklin, 1853
Stacho, Cath.—Weglewo to New Braunfels; Gaston, 1860
Stadtzirk, T.—Gleiwitz to Austin; Iris, 1858
Staedtler, Mrs. Johanne, son Carl, 0 years lod—Rudolstadt, Thuringia; Therese Henriette, 1853
Staffehl, Carl and wife—New Orleans; Copernicus, 1852
Stahl, Carl, 20, Leonhard 12; John Holland, 1848; Comal Co.
Stahl, Carl, 27, Lina 24—Elberfeld; Franziska, 1849
Stahl, Fried.—Kuwinkel, Meck.; Washington, 1852; Guadalupe Co.
Stahl, J. — Württ. to Galveston; Jeverland, 1860; Comal Co. 1865
Stahlberg, F.—Friesack to Galveston; Iris, 1860
Stahmer, Anna, with 3 ch.—Bergedorf to Galveston; Republic, 1851
Stakh, Joh., 32, Joh. 24, Veronika 24, Thomas 1; Brasilian or E. von Beaulieu, 1857
Stalle, Carl; Ammerland, 1854
Stammer, E. H., 18, and Franz H., 49—Bergedorf; Alexander, 1850
Stanic, Franz and Johann—Böhmen; Weser, 1854
Stanke, Carl—Leibnitz; Neptune, 1854
Stansfield, Edw., 14, Joh. W. 24—Leeds (England); Hamburg, 1849
Stapf, Otto, 33, Mary 26, Ernst 2, Georg ¾; Herschel, 1850; Austin Co.
Staphel, Carl. 28, Johanna 19; Natchez, 1847
Starke, Christine, Auguste—Berlin; Texas, 1853
Starke, Hrn.—Eisenach; 3 persons; Neptune, 1853; Comal Co.

Starke, Otto, Max—Berlin; Solon, 1852; Comal Co.
Starts, H.—Wenden to Houston; Gessner, 1860
Starzensky, S., wife and son—Gnesen; Neptune, 1854
Staudt, Jac, 8 persons — Rauenthal; arr. Gal. ship? date?
Stauke, Franz, 28—Prussia; Reform, 1850
Stausenberger (Stautzenberger), Frz, 3 persons—Doersdorf; arr. Gal. ship? date?; Guadalupe Co.
Stausenberger (Stautzenberger), G. P. and Fr., 9 persons—Doersdorf; arr. Gal. ship? date?; Guadalupe Co.
Stavenhagen, E. — Charlottenburg to Galveston; Fortuna, 1860
Stawinoha, A n d r e a s, Marianne, Theresia, Marianne, Ignaz—Austria (had coffee house in Vienna); Jeverland, 1860; Lavaca Co.
Stawinoha, Joseph, Johanna, Agnes, Franz, Ignaz — Austria; Jeverland, 1860
Stechlich, Ed and Franz — Tolau, Prussia to Galveston; Bassermann, 1851
Steck, Gottlieb and family; Ammerland, 1854
Steer, Wilh. Fr.—Behrendorf, Holstein; Copernicus, 1852
Steffansen, Caroline, 16, with Joh. H. Jessen — Svendborg, Denmark; Gutenberg, 1855
Steffen, Maria, 12; Magnet, 1852
Steffen, Michel, 29, Hanne 6 (f), Henriette 4, Mina 26; Hermann Theodor, 1850
Steffens, F.—Hildesheim to Galveston; Juno, 1860
Stehl, Carl, 27; Herschel, 1849
Steiber, Anna—Dettingen; Solon, 1852
Stein, Christian, 34, Doris 35, Hein. 8, Christian 5, Hans 3—Neumünster, Holstein; Gutenberg, 1855
Stein, Diedrich—Marktsuhl; Henriette, 1843 (1853); Austin Co.
Stein, H.—Hannover to Houston; Gessner, 1860
Steinbrinker, Joh., 44, Elis. 44, Cath. 17, Hein. 14, Fried. 2; Solon, 1850
Steinbrucker, Carl—Warmbrunnen to Latium, Washington Co.; Juno, 1860
Steinbusch, Ludwig, 40—Württ.; Joh. Dethardt, 1848

Steindel, E.—Herschel, 1849
Steindorf, Ferd.—Polensko; Gessner, 1854
Steiner, Fried.—Oberhausen; Solon, 1852
Steines, A. L. L., 35—Hamburg; Hamburg, 1849
Steiness, Wilhelm, wife and 3 ch. —Torgau, Prussia to Galveston; Bassermann, 1851
Steines, Doretha, 21, Joh. 2—Berlin; Neptune, 1850
Steingraber, F,. 28; Alexander, 1850
Steinhagen, ... and wife—Kroeplin, Meck.; Basserman, 1851
Steinhagen, C. F., 33; Galliott Flora, 1849; Grimes Co.
Steinhagen, Georg—arr. Galveston Oct. 1851; Austin Co.
Steinhauser, Fidel, 37; Galliott Flora, 1849; Austin Co.
Steinhauser, L.—Weimar to San Antonio; Gessner, 1860
Steinhoff, Mrs., 28, John ½, Johanne 14; Wilhelm, 1858
Steinland, W.—Braunschweig; Hermann Theodor, 1853
Steller, J.—Prussia; Friedrich Grosse, 1853
Stelter, A.—Callies to Galveston; Weser, 1857
Stelter, Elis. and Henriette—Peppner to Galveston; Weser, 1860
Stennis, Eduard, 32; Colonist, 1848
Stepheck (Stefek), Theresia—Austria; Jeverland, 1860
Sternberg, ..., wife and 1 child—Ruehn; Leibniz, 1850
Sternberg, Jacob, wife and 9 ch.—Neutschlemmin, Meck. to Galveston; Sarah, 1851
Stettner, Hein, — Triest, Austria (since 1947 called Free Territory); J. W. Buddecke, 1853
Steuberg (Steubing), Joh. Hein., 56, Wilhme 50, Joh. Geo. 21, Hein. Chs. 19, Hein. 16, Wilhme 13, Wilh. 10—Bicken, Nass; Antoinette, 1848; Comal Co.
Steucke, Paul, 29; Brasilian, 1857
Steves, Edward, Robert, Heinrich and Laura — Prussia; Neptune, 1849; Bexar Co.
Stichler, F.—Serno; Adolphine, 1859
Stiebel, Chrissina, 26, male, farmer; Herschel, 1850
Stieber, G. and family—Oranienbaum; Gessner, 1854
Stieble, Friedr.—Zerbst to New Ulm; Weser, 1860

Stieghan, Hein., 27—Allerbüttel;
Joh. Dethardt, 1848
Stiegler, Marie, 18; Franziska,
1849
Stiel, F. H., 28—Galveston;
Herschel, 1849
Stock, Aug. and Joh.—Cassel;
Weser, 1854; Colorado Co.
Stock, Hein.—Reffenroth; Texas,
1853
Stock, Louise and Marg.—Cassel;
Henriette, 1843 (1853)
Stoeber, N.—Kyritz; Lucie, 1854
Stoeckel, D. and family—Rehburg
to Brenham; Weser, 1857
Stoeckhardt, H. A.—Dresden to
Galveston; Weser, 1857
Stoehr, Marie—Aldstadt; Texas,
1853
Stoertjer, Anna—Garz, Holstein;
Hampden, 1854
Stoetzner, Zacharias—Altenburg;
Lucie, 1854
Stoeves, Franz—Creweld; Texas,
1853
Stoffel, Hein., 83, Lena 23, Aug.
14, Eugen ½; Magnet, 1852
Stoffelmann, Gerh., 46, Marg. 40,
Anna 6—Beckhausen; Neptune,
1850
Stoffers, H.—Marton (Marten?)
to Houston; Weser, 1858
Stoffers, Helene—Rastede; 2 per-
sons; Texas, 1853
Stoffers, Joh., 30; Solon, 1850
Stoll family—to Independence;
Weser, 1859
Stolle, Joh. Fr., 28 — Sufeld;
Canapus, 1848; Colorado Co.
Stolte, Christian, 31, Friedke 23;
Sophie, 1852; Comal Co.
Stolz, Caro.—Driesen to York-
town; Iris, 1860
Stolze, Maria, Rosina—to Galves-
ton; Weser, 1859
Stolze, R.—Werningerode to Gal-
veston; Iris, 1860
Stolze, Johanne—Dresden to Gal-
veston; Fortuna, 1860
Stolzenbach, J.—Hamburg; Lucie,
1854
Stophel, Carl — See Staphel, Carl
Stork, G.—Baruchheim (Baruth-
heim?); Gessner, 1854
Strach, Fried. and family; Galliott
Concordia, 1854
Strachbein, Fr., 6 persons—Frohn-
hausen; Reform, 1851; Gillespie
Co.
Strachezcki, Fr.—Kuduwitz(?);
Mississippi, 1855
Strack, Hein.; Joh. Ed. Grosse,
1853

Strade, Franz and family—Hump-
oletz, Bohemia; Weser, 1854
Strak, Joh.; Joh. Ed. Grosse, 1853
Strate, Wilhme—Sternberg to Gal-
veston; Weser, 1858
Straube, ... —Mittelwalde;
Magnet, 1851
Strauss, Franz—Fleingen? Gess-
ner, 1854
Strauss, Heinrich, wife and 4 ch.
½-8 years old — Wandsbeck,
Holstein; Sophie, 1852; Austin
Co.
Strauss, Madame and child—Hil-
desheim to Galveston; Weser,
1857
Strecker, Chr., wife and 2 ch. ½
and 3 years old—Bellin, Hol-
stein; Washington, 1852
Stredde, Joh. A.—Prussia; Nep-
tune, 1848
Streithorst, Aug. 32, Fried. 6;
Neptune, 1850
Stremme, Conrad, 45; Magnet,
1852; Travis Co.
Stressner, Wilhme; Neptune 1848
Streubel, Theresa, 22; Galliott
Flora, 1849
Streuer, H. with wife — Briggen
(Brüggen?) to New Braunfels;
Iris, 1858
Stricker, C.—Riste (Rüste);
Gessner, 1855
Striegler, J. F. G., 41, Christine
41, Ernestine 18, Alphorstine
(Albertine?) 16, Arthur 15,
Wilhelm 13, Nicolaus 12, Ida 11,
Friedr. 7, Olga 4, Jens ¼—
Svendborg. Denmark; Gillespie
Co. 1860; Gutenberg, 1855
Striepe (Striesse?). Christ., 40—
Gs. Sch.?; Joh. Dethardt, 1848
Stroebel, Barbara—Plieningen;
Solon, 1852
Stroehmer, F.—Herzberg to San
Marcos; Iris, 1858
Stroeker, Marie—Bocholzhausen?
to Galveston; Iris, 1860
Strohboecker, David and family
(5) — Plieningen; Solon, 1852;
Kendall Co.
Strohmeier, Catharina — Udenhau-
sen to Round Top; Iris, 1857
Strohmeier, John and wife—Uden-
hausen to Colorado Co.; Gaston,
1860
Strohmeyer, Emil, 23; Louis, 1848
Strube, Adolph and wife—Galves-
ton to Galveston; Gaston, 1860
Strube, Auguste, 23—Leipzig;
Franziska, 1849; Lavaca Co.
Strube, Fried., 26; Natchez, 1847

Strube, J., 54, Dor. 50, Dor. 24,
Maria 16, Wilh. 14 — Prussia;
Alexander, 1850
Struck, Theresa—Lippstadt to Galveston; Weser, 1860
Struebing, G.—Geber; Gessner, 1855
Strumann, P.—Prussia; Friedrich Grosse, 1853
Strunke, Hein. and Johanna—Berlin; Suwa, 1853
Struve, Charles, 18, and Ernst, 59 —Holstein; Alexander, 1850
Struwe, Joh. Fried., 52, Eva 44, Dor. 8, Maria 36—Moellenbeck, Meckl.; John Frederick, 1850
Stubbelmann, Lother; Herschel, 1849
Stubenhofer, Jacob; Galliott Concordia, 1854
Stubenmuch(?), Ferd., 32, Johanna 33; Sophie, 1852
Stuckenbrock, W.—Arolsen; Weser, 1854
Stuckert, Albert and August—Loitz, Mecklenburg-Strelitz; Sophie, 1852
Stuckler, Jos. and Pauline—Neuchatel; Mississippi, 1855
Stuecker, Henriette—Erlinghausen to Galveston; Iris, 1857
Stuermer, G.—Obersdorf; Lucie, 1854
Stueve, Lena, 25—Vechta; Antoinette, 1848
Stukas, Wilh.—Schlieben, Prussia; Mississippi, 1855
Stultemann, Antonie; Joh. Ed. Grosse, 1853
Stumke, Joh., 66; Hermann Theodor, 1850
Sture, Henri, 26—Prussia; Joh. Dethardt, 1848
Sturm, C.—Bernburg; Neptune, 1854
Sturm, Ernestine—Bernstein; Minna, 1854
Sturm, Nicolaus Georg, wife and 4 ch. — Roda, Sachsen-Weimar; Republic, 1851
Sturmm, Lud., 36; Reform, 1850
Stussee, Cath.; Joh. Ed. Grosse, 1853
Suders, Fr.; Herschel, 1849
Sueltenfuss, H. and W.—Düsseldorf; Iris, 1859
Sueltenfuss, Marie—Düsseldorf to San Antonio; Iris, 1859
Suenemann(?), Ferd., 14; Solon, 1850
Suess, ... —Marburg to Mill Creek; Iris, 1858

Suhr, Elis., 29—Braunschweig; Franziska, 1847
Suhrland, Fried., 45, Marg. 40— Hamburg; Natchez, 1847
Sulemmer — See also Schlemmer
Sutor, Fried.—Schneidemühl; Henriette, 1843 (1853)
Suttenfuest, A., 30, and lady, 27; Herschel, 1849
Sutter, Georg—Rünenberg; Solon, 1852
Swiatowsiak, Jos.—Poland; Lucie, 1854
Sydow, J. with family—Callies to Austin; Weser, 1857
Sydow, J. Friedr., with wife and child—Callies to Galveston; Weser, 1851
Syrzinek, Georg, Barbara, Georg; Austria; Jeverland, 1860

— T —

Taiber, Jos. and Cath.—Vienna; Suwa, 1853
Tamke, August and Julta—Braunschwig; Antoinette, 1854
Tampke, Andreas, 20, Allient (Albert?) 21; Herschel, 1849; Medina Co.
Tanisch, Carl, 52, Friedke 46, Adelheid 18, Ludwig 14, Herm. 7, Albert 5; Creole, 1852
Tanish, Jacob, 40; Creole, 1852
Tannhaeuser, A., 5 persons—Prussia; Friedrich Grosse, 1853
Tapken, A., 23, Cath. 11, Gesina 43; Herschel, 1850
Taubert, H.—Kaltenburgsfeld (Kaltenlengsfeld); Magnet, 1851
Tausch, Leop(old), 26—Prussia; Joh. Dethardt, 1848
Tauterbach, Hein., 25; Creole, 1852
Taylor, Charles, 23—Hamburg; Chas. N. Cooper, 1847
Tchecke, Franz, 7 persons—Allendorf; Neptune, 1854
Teber, E.—Salzbrunn; Gessner, 1854
Tegenhard, Joh., 2 persons—Burghasungen; Texas, 1853
Tegge, Joach(im), 24 — Steimke; Helen & Elise, 1847; Colorado Co.
Telge, W.—Hannover to Houston; Gessner, 1860
Telgmann, H. — Braunschweig; Neptune, 1853; Kendall Co.
Tell. Catharine, 11; Herschel, 1850
Tellinger, Wm.—Hannover; Neptune, 1848
Tellmann, W.—Oppendorf; Adolphine, 1859

Telschow, C.—Pritzwalk; Hamburg, 1849
Teltz, Andr. Fr.—Friedland; Leibniz, 1850
Temperli, J.—Durgau, Switz.; Lucie, 1854
Tendler, Wilh., 5 persons—Heilegendorf, Han.; Neptune, 1853
Tesch, Joh. Ludw., 35, Anna 32, Minna 8, Louis 6, Carl 3, Dor. ½ — Nebelin; Brasilian, 1850; Austin Co.
Teschner, Al.—Magdeburg; Hermann Theodor, 1853
Tesen, Bertha, 23—Holstein to Mobile; Chas. N. Cooper, 1847
Tess, H.—Posen to Houston; Juno, 1860
Tessner, Wm.—Prussia; Neptune, 1848
Teulmeyer, Wilh., 58, Louise 54, Fritz 19, Elise 21, Louise 12, Wilhme 10—Salzoffen (Salzkotten?); Neptune, 1857
Thalmann, Lebrecht, wife and 3 ch. 1½-7 years—Poesneck, Meiningen; Copernicus, 1852
Thanert, Dr. H.—Dresden to Galveston; Weser, 1858
Theiss, P. J., 8 persons—Offenbach, Nassau; Mississippi, 1855
Theiwes, Marie, 18 — Einbeck to Indianola; Weser, 1859
Thel, Amalie, 30; Franziska, 1849
Theuss, Georg, wife and ch.—Hollenhahn; Henriette, 1843 (1853)
They, F(riedri)ch, wife Maria—Celle; Leibniz, 1850
Thie, Abraham, 18—Posen to Galveston; Weser, 1859
Thel, A.—Prussia; Friedrich Grosse, 1853
Thiele, Aug.—Bernburg; Neptune, 1854
Thiele, Claus, and family, 3 persons—Kimmernitz, Prussia; Washington, 1852
Thiele, Daniel, Ernestine—Meloslawice (Melovice?) to Washington-(on-the-Brazos); Weser, 1860
Thiele, Ferd., 23, Caro. 25; Herschel, 1849
Thiele, Gustav—Senst to New Ulm; Fortuna, 1860
Thiele, Heinrich — Bärenburg to Houston; Fortuna, 1860; Austin Co.
Thielemann, W.—Oppendorf to Houston; Weser, 1858
Thielen, Adolph—Celle, Han.; Washington, 1852

Thieman, Carl, 15—Westrup, Prussia; Fortuna, 1858
Thieme, ... —Bavaria to Galveston; Anton Gunther, 1860
Thiemen, C. H.—Hille; Weser, 1854
Thien, Helene, 23; Solon, 1850
Thies, Joh., Betty—Bremen to Galveston; Weser, 1860
Thiesen, Robert, 29; Herschel, 1849
Thoischen, E.—Christiansand, Denmark; Copernicus, 1852
Thomas, Chr.—Hoheneiche; Weser, 1854
Thomas, Nic., 4 persons—Neufelden, Austria; Estafette, 1850; Washington Co.
Thomsen, Cath., 13 (fem)—Holstein; Alexander, 1850
Thon (Than?), Carol, 24—Stadthagen; Canapus, 1848
Thonig, A.—Rackel; Anton Günther, 1860
Thorade, John Fr.; Joh. Ed. Grosse, 1853
Thorngrel, J.—Copenhagen, Den.; Leibniz, 1850
Thorstraten, C.—Föhr to Galveston; Juno, 1860
Thuem, Fried.—Boitzenburg; Therese Henriette, 1853
Thuemler, Rieke—Reudnitz, Saxony; Miles, 1854
Thuerge, J. S., 3 persons—Saxony; Friedrich Grosse, 1853
Thuermann, Alexander—Sergan; Texas, 1853
Thuessing, ... —Münster to Galveston; Iris, 1858
Thunmann, Wm., 29—Cable (Kahla?); Canapus, 1848
Thuns, Carl—Eilau, Prussia; Miles, 1854
Thurman, H.—Hagenburg; Reform, 1849
Thusen, Robert, 29; Herschel, 1849
Tiede, Matthias—Laasche; Franklin, 1853
Tiekoetter family, 4 persons—Berlin; Suwa, 1853
Tieman, Henriette—Oppenwehe to Galveston; Weser, 1857
Tietze, Joh. Hein., 32 — Bremen; Joh. Dethardt, 1848; Galveston
Tillmann, E., 23; Herschel, 1849
Tillman, H.—Oppendorf to Houston; Weser, 1858
Tillner, Ernst W.; Neptune, 1849
Timäus family—Bärnsdorf; Adolphine, 1859
Tippe, Ernst, 21; Solon, 1850
Tippert, Michael, 37; Creole, 1852

Tips, Conrad, Anna Carol—Prussia; Neptune, 1849; Guadalupe Co.

Tischendorf, Carl—Hamburg; Hampden, 1854

Tischler, Heinrich with wife—Rehburg to Brenham; Weser, 1857

Tobolla, John, Veronica, Marianne, Franz, Joseph, Thomas — Austria; Jeverland, 1860

Todtmann, Anna—Ottensen, Holstein; Therese Henriette, 1853

Toekel, E.—Rehburg to Galveston; Weser, 1858

Toepperwein, Ferdinand, wife and 6 ch. ages 4-15; Neu-Ruppin; John Frederick, 1850; Gillespie Co. 1860

Toerner, C., 2 persons—Eltville; arr. Galveston, ship? date?

Tomson, H.—Foehr to Galveston; Juno, 1860

Tonne, Diedrich, 27; Sophie, 1852; Comal Co.

Trambowsky, Carl, Gustav—Reichenbach; Weser, 1854

Trapp, Josephine—Hilders to San Antonio; Fortuna, 1860

Trappe, Hein. and Marie—Fuhrenberg; Henriette, 1843 (1853)

Traudgen, Carl, 33—Svendborg, Denmark; Gutenberg, 1855

Trautwein, Hermann — Bernstadt, Prussia to Galveston; Republic, 1851; De Witt Co.

Treder, A. and Pauline—Belgard to Galveston; Iris, 1857

Trefflich, Hein. and family, 6 persons—Hassleben, Prussia; Washington, 1852

Trente, Joh.; Joh. Ed. Grosse, 1853

Trenzler, Marie—Tretzdorf (Fretzdorf?), Prussia to Galveston or Indianola; Franklin, 1852

Tresimer, Carl—Berlin; Suwa, 1853

Treuholz (Trenholz?), C., 2 persons—Danzig; Hamburg, 1849; Victoria Co.

Treute, Cath.; Joh. Ed. Grosse, 1853

Tricke, Henry, Henriette, Henriette, Henry, Henriette, Louisa—Hannover to New Braunfels; Weser, 1860

Triebe, Georg, 53, Hry. 15, Joh. 13, Fried. 10; Alexander, 1850

Triebel, Joh., 38, Johanna 40. Amalie 9, Auguste 5, Friedke 4; Creole, 1852; Victoria Co.

Trolle, Auguste—to Victoria; Weser, 1859

Trollmann, F., wife and 3 ch. and Trollmann, F. and wife—Stetterling; Weser, 1854

Truetschel, Hein., 24; Creole, 1852

Tschiedel, A.; Ammerland, 1854

Tschirschnutz, Hein., 27—Prussia; Joh. Dethardt, 1848

Tschudi, Mad.—Galveston to Galveston; Iris, 1861

Tuebel, Michael, 34, Anna Cath. 34, Fried. 10; Creole, 1852

Tuemmler, ... —Esensham to Frelsburg; Iris, 1858

Tuemmler, Joh., 35, Friedke 31, Friedke Pauline 4, Ernestine Louise 2, Theodor 9/12; Creole, 1852

Tuhrs, J.—Altingen; Neptune, 1855

Turmell(?), Ernestine, 24; Reform, 1850

Tzirnoch (Czirnoch), Marianne—Austria; Jeverland, 1860

— U —

Ueckert, C. with family—Tunton (Tuntel?) to Houston; Weser, 1858; Austin Co.

Uhe, Jacob—Wittenberg; Juno, 1853

Uhlich, F.—Annaberg to New Ulm; Weser, 1858

Uhlig, D., wife and 4 ch.—Lengefeld; Lucie, 1854

Ulbricht, Carl W. — Friedeberg; 2 persons; Neptune, 1853; Fayette Co.

Ullmann, G.—Lengefeld; Lucie, 1854

Ulrich (Ullrich), Aug. and wife—Eubis (Euben?); Lucie, 1854; Fayette Co.

Ullrich, Johann—Uttrichshausen; Weser, 1854

Ullrich, Sebastian, with family, 4 persons — Wustensachsen; Henriette, 1843 (1853)

Ulrich, Johann—Hamburg; Hampden, 1854

Ulrich, Wilh.—Luetjewisch, Schleswig to Galveston; Franklin, 1852

Umla, A. and wife—Bratz to Bastrop; Iris, 1857

Umland, Hein., 42, Elise 35, Auguste 10, Emma 7, Johanna 5, Wilh. 5, Julius 11/12—Hamburg; Hamburg, 1849; Austin Co.

Umland, Jacob—Freiburg, Hannover; Sophie, 1852

Urbahn, Albert, 28—Bremen; Antoinette, 1848; Bexar Co.

Urbanach, Agnes—Albrechtsdorf; Minna, 1854

Urbantke, Fried., Julius, Auguste —Bielitz to Millheim; Gessner, 1860
Urbantzck, Jakob and family—Rajemisch?; Weser, 1854
Urbecke, C.—Prussia; Friedrich Grosse, 1853
Urner, A.—Prussia; Friedrich Grosse, 1853

— V —

Vahl, Alexander, 32, Elise 25— Wolgast, Prussia; Brasilian, 1850
Vass, H.—Braunschweig; Franziska, 1854
Veinhorn family, 6 persons—Hannover; Suwa, 1853
Velsch, Carl—Graepelin; Leibniz, 1850
Velten, H. and Jac., 4 persons; Estafette, 1850; Gillespie Co.
Verlocher, Madame A., 2 children —Switzerland to Galveston; Weser, 1857
Verwib, Minna—Danzig; Texas, 1853
Vetter, Andr.—Weschnitz; Magnet, 1851
Vetter, C. F. A., 48, J. S. (female) 43, A. H. 20, J. R. 19; Galliott Flora, 1849; Guadalupe Co.
Vetter, Th. and family; Ammerland, 1854
Vetterlein, F.—Saulwitz to Sisterdale, Kendall Co.; Gaston, 1857
Vetters, Caroline—Friedland; Franklin, 1853
Vettner, Fr. and famly; Ammerland, 1854
Vibruck, Christine, Caro.—Brake to Galveston; Weser, 1860
Vibruck, Friederike—Dresden to Indianola; Weser, 1860
Vieck, H.—Popendorf, Holstein; Hampden, 1854; Austin Co .
Viereck, Hein. and wife—Nebbelin, Meckl.; Washington, 1852; Fayette Co.
Viereck, Joachim, wife and 2 ch.— Webelin, Prussia; Bassermann, 1851; Fayette Co.
Viereck, Johanna, 20 yrs.—Schwerin, Meckl.; Franklin, 1852; Fayette Co.
Viereck, Louise, 25 yrs.—Weitendorf, Meckl.; Franklin, 1852; Fayette Co.
Vieweger, S. J.—Saxony; Neptune, 1848
Vock, Georg—Benz, Denmark; Copernicus, 1852

Voelker, Eugen, 2 persons—New Braunfels, Tex.; Magnet, 1851
Voelkerath, Fried. Arnold — Bilk, Dusseldorf, Prussia; arr. Gal. 1848; Comal Co.
Voessek, Aug.—Berlin; Suwa, 1853
Vogel, C. and P.—AltenBuseck to Richmond; Weser, 1858
Vogel family—to Colorado (Co.?): Weser, 1859
Vogel, G. — Montivie (Montivilliers? (France) to New Braunfels; Iris, 1859
Vagelsag (Vogelsang), Ernst and Wilhme; Joh Ed. Grosse, 1853: Fayette Co.
Vogelsang, G.; Herschel, 1849; Fayette Co.
Vogelsang, Herm.—Elberfeld; Lucie, 1854
Vogelsang, Jacob—Hannover; Neptune, 1848
Vogelsang, Jacob, 46, Hetta 27. Doris 21, Theo. 18, Ernst 12, Fried. 8—Uplethe (Upsede?): Neptune, 1850; Austin Co.
Vogelsang, Otto, 43 — Lauenburg; Fortuna, 1858; Austin Co.
Vogelsang, Peter, 18; Solon, 1850
Vogelsang, Peter—Elberfeld; Lucie, 1854
Vogelsang, W. and family; Ammerland, 1854
Voges, Diedrich, 28—Bissendorf, Han.; Colonist, 1850; Comal Co.
Vogg, C. Frederick, 21—Württ.; Chas. N. Cooper, 1847
Vogle, Aug., 25—Zedenick; Wilhelm, 1858
Vogt, Christ. Ludwig and family (7)—Langenwiesen; Solon, 1852
Vogt, Carl. 19—Hesse; Chas. N. Cooper, 1847
Vogt, E.—Hesse; Friedrich Grosse, 1853; Guadalupe Co.
Vogt, J. and wife—Breslau; Gessner, 1855; Fayette Co.
Vogt, M.—Hesse; Friedrich Grosse, 1853
Vogt, Maria—Hirschberg to Bellville; Fortuna, 1858
Vogt, Wilg (Wilh.?), Henriette— Berlin; Suwa, 1853; Guadalupe Co.
Voight, Adam, 28; Hermann Theodor, 1850
Voigt, Andreas, 59, Friedke 36; Hermann Theodore, 1850; Comal Co.
Voigt, Auguste, 3 persons; Joh. Ed. Grosse, 1853

Voigt, Ignaz—Buchhofen; Lucie,
1854; Victoria Co.
Voight, Joh., 18; Alexander, 1850;
Fayette Co.
Voigt, Michael and wife, 2 ch. 16
and 18 years—Rohrbach, Saxony
to Galveston or Indianola;
Franklin, 1852
Voigt, Michael, 43, Marie 37,
Herm. 15, Wilh. 13, Franz 11,
Albrecht 9, Carl 7, Thelka 5,
Otto 2, Gustav 1—Sachsen-Mein-
ingen; Franziska, 1847; Victoria
Co.
Voight, Samuel, 47 (died), Augus-
ta 47, Ferd. 27, Ed 19, Caro.
(died), Hein 16, Adolph 9—
Sachsen - Meiningen; Chas. N.
Cooper, 1847
Volbert, Marcellus—Anzefahr;
J. W. Buddecke, 1853
Volckhard, F. — Markelitz(?) to
Lockhart; Gaston, 1857
Volk, Christoph, 19 — Erlingheim,
Württ.; Wilhelm, 1858
Volkens, Johann—Schleswig, Hol-
stein; Washington, 1852
Volland, Christian, 3 persons—Nie-
derVellmer; Hermann Theodor,
1853
Volling, H.—Lesse; Lucie, 1854
Vollmer, Anna, Friedke—Oberkau-
fungen to Washington-(on-the-
Brazos); Fortuna, 1860
Vollmar, S. G.—Prussia; Neptune,
1849; Colorado Co.
Vollrath, F. W.—Gaschwitz, Prus-
sia; Franklin, 1853
Vollrath, J. E. T. and wife—Ilme-
nau to Galveston; Republic, 1851
Volrath, L., 28; Herschel, 1849;
Wilson Co.
Volst, Gustav, Henriette—Gurkow
to Yorktown; Fortuna, 1860
Voltz, Fred., 22; Louis, 1848
Voltz, Ferdinand, 23—Darmstadt,
arr. Gal. 1847; Comal Co. 1849
Vomweg, Wilh.—Fachbach; Texas,
1853
von Buren, Theresa — Hildesheim
to Galveston; Weser, 1857
von Bueren, G. and family—Brem-
en to Galveston; Iris, 1860
Von der Cammer, Hein.—Hamburg
to New Orleans; Washington,
1852
von Cloudt. Fried.. 32—Hannover;
Joh. Dethardt, 1848; Blanco Co.
Coreth, Count Ernst, Agnes 35,
Agnes 14, Carl 13, Rud. 11, Amalie 8. Joh. 5. Franz 3, Maria 1
—Texas; Colonist, 1850; Comal Co.

Coreth, Count Ernst, from New
Braunfels; Maryland, 1859
von Donop, Otto; Magnet, 1852;
Kendall Co.
von Duelmen, Wuessig — Emmerich; Juno, 1853
von Els, Bertha—Düsseldorf;
Neptune, 1853
von Gelgenheiml, Ferd., 27—Breslau; Colonist, 1850
von Hademann, Aug., 22—Poppe-
lau; Colonist, 1850
von Hippel, Moritz, 31; Colonist,
1850
von Knobelsdorf, Julia—Danzig;
Mississippi, 1855
von Lausel, Otto—Elberfeld;
Reform, 1849
von Lichtenberg, Ernst, 28 (died
1849), Ludwig 25—Mainz; Louis,
1848; Comal Co.
von Loehr, Anton, 15—Koblenz;
Franziska, 1849
von Marschall, Guillamme, 26, Louise Caroline 22, Charles 10/12,
Mathilda 23—Nassau; John Holland, 1848
von Maudeville, Adelbert—Cöslin;
Juno, 1853
von May, Leopold — Hausberge,
Prussia; Mississippi, 1855
von Plonnies, Carl, 21; Brasilian
or E. von Beaulieu, 1857
von Quitzow, Wilhelm—Rostock,
Meckl.; Copernicus, 1852
von Rastmann, G.—Darmstadt;
Neptune, 1853
von Ratzmann, ..., 21; Louis,
1848
von Roggenbuche, Oscar — Sahl
(Suhl?); Gessner, 1854; Kendall
Co.
von Rosenberg, Alex., 14—Menel,
East Prussia; Franziska, 1849;
Fayette Co.
von Rosenberg, Carl, 54, Amanda
41, Wilhelm 28, Augusta 23, Johanna 25, Joh. 23, Eugen 19,
Lena 15, Alex 14, Walter 9—
Menel; Franziska, 1849; Fayette
Co.
von Rosenberg, Eugin—Menel;
Franziska, 1849; Fayette Co.
von Rosenberg, J., 23—Menel;
Franziska, 1849; Fayette Co.
von Rosenberg, Wilh., 28—Menel;
Franziska, 1849; Travis Co. 1858
von Spiegel, Lieut.—Wetzlar;
Ship? Date?
von Stein, Carl, 58. Elisa 68, Al-
vine 32—Köln; Franziska, 1848

von Stein, Eduard, 21—Köln; Louis, 1848; Comal Co.
von Stein, Emil, 30, Charl. 25, Alfred 2; Louis, 1848; Comal Co.
von Strube, Hein., 45, Minna 26, Amandus 10, Louis 8, Stephanie 1; Colonist, 1848; Bexar Co.
von Thiele, Ida—Dresden to Houston; Gaston, 1857
von Thies, Arnold—Behrenburg to New Ulm; Weser, 1860
von Well, Hendrine—Cöln; Juno, 1853
von Westphalen, Edgar, 27—Prussia; Chas. N. Cooper, 1847
von Westphalen, Edgar — Bremen to Galveston; Reform, 1851
von Zeuner, Carl—Berlin; Neptune, 1853
Vonsetter, Eugene, 27; Louis, 1848
Vorbendaumen, H. and family — Borgholzhausen to Galveston; Fortuna, 1858; Mason Co.
Vosage, Christian, 27—Braunschweig; Franziska, 1847
Voskamp, Joh. Hein., 32—Engter; Antoinette, 1848; Austin Co.
Voss, Adolph—Prussia; Antonette, 1854
Voss, August, 24, Konradine 22; Creole, 1854
Voss, Carl, 23, Marie 24, Carl 2, Lene 55—Willarshagen. Meckl.; Herschel, 1855; Guadalupe Co.
Voss, Dorothea, 17—Kuwinkel, Mecklenburg; Washington, 1852
Voss, Ludwig, 28, Auguste 25, Wilh. 6/12, Wilhelmine 2; Creole, 1852

— W —

Wacke, Sophie, 24 — Jessnitz, Meckl.; Copernicus, 1852; Austin Co.
Wachsmuth, Fried.—Dessau; 6 persons; Neptune, 1853
Waertzner, L.—Wolkenstein; Gessner, 1855
Wagen, Anton—Benhausen; Weser, 1854
Wagenbret, F.—Ellerich (Ellerüh) to Galveston; Weser, 1860
Wagener, Adolph—Landsberg, Prussia; Miles, 1854
Wagener, Fried., 36—Wittstock; Hamburg, 1849
Wagener, J.—Prussia; Friedrich Grosse, 1853
Wagener, Joachim—Posen, Prussia; Franklin, 1853

Wagener, Julius — Hamburg; Washington, 1852; Guadalupe Co.
Wagenfuehr, Andreas, 20; Solon, 1850; Blanco Co.
Wagenfuehr, Aug., 38, Christine 38, Joh. 9, Fried. 4, Hein. ¾; Solon, 1850; Comal Co.
Wagenfuehr, Friedr. anl family—Rhoden; Weser, 1854; Comal Co.
Wagner, ... —Cassel to Galveston; Iris, 1858
Wagner, A.—Potsdam to Galveston; Iris, 1860
Wagner, A.—Poland; Franziska, 1854
Wagner, Carl—Saxony; Friedrich Grosse, 1853; Guadalupe Co.
Wagner, Eduard, 25—Amorbach; Neptune, 1853
Wagner, Friedr.—Rohrbach, Saxony to Galveston or Indianola; Franklin, 1852
Wagner, J. and E.—Maffersdorf; Gessner, 1855
Wagner, J. S., Marie—Enkirch; Anna Louisa, 1857
Wagner, Joh. Ph., 40, Samuel 35, Anne Marie 26; Anna Louisa, 1857
Wagner, Julius, 32, Emilie 29— Texas; Franziska, 1849; De Witt Co.
Wagner, Konrad, Cath., Christine —Hesse to Castroville, Medina Co.; Weser, 1860
Wagner, Paul—Oldenburg; Reform, 1851; Bexar Co.
Wagner, Philipp and family — Prussia; Antoinette, 1854; Comal Co.
Wagners, Carl, Magda.—Weigersdorf to Bastrop; Fortuna, 1858
Wahl, Theodor—Quedlinburg; Reform, 1849
Wahl, Vincenz—Buchholz; Henriette, 1843 (1853)
Wahls, Johann, wife and 2 ch. 2 and 6 years—Viettluebe, Meckl.; Washington, 1852
Wahrmann, August—Tempelburg, Prussia; Therese Henriette, 1853
Waker, Mathias and family (6)— Schauenhausen; Solon, 1852
Wakerburg, Marie—Kassel; Solon, 1852
Wald, T. and Joh.; Ammerland, 1854
Waldschmidt, W.—Hesse; Friedrich Grosse, 1853

Waliczeck, Peter, Eveline, Anna, Franz, Marianne, Eveline—Austria; Jeverland, 1860; Austin Co.

Walley, Fried., 32; Herschel, 1849

Walter, Adam—Bruledorf?; 3 persons; Texas, 1953

Walter (Waller?), Carl, 36, Pauline 26, Auguste 4, Pauline 1—Baden; Reform, 1850; Grimes Co.

Walter, H.—Hizdorf (Hitzendorf?); Neptune, 1854

Walter, Hein., 27, Caro. 24—Wol gast, Prussia; Brasilian, 1850

Walter, Julius and family—Saxony; Neptune, 1848

Walther, Guenther — Offenbach; wife and daughter ½ year old; Miles, 1854

Walther, Lina—Vilbel to Victoria; Weser, 1860

Walther, W.—Gössitz; Reform, 1851

Walther, Wilh., 50, Caro. 25; Natchez, 1847

Walz, Ottilia—Liegnitz; 4 persons; Hermann Theodor, 1853

Wanasch, A. and wife—Maltitz; Anton Günther, 1860

Wanieck, Franz, Johanna, Franz, Marianne—Austria; Jeverland, 1860

Wanieck, Veronica, John, Veronica—Austria; Jeverland, 1860

Warnecke, A.—to Houston; Weser, 1859

Warnke, Fried.—Königslutter; J. W. Buddecke, 1853

Warnken, Meinert, 25; Solon, 1850

Warring, Fried., 27; Sophie, 1852

Wasselberg, Fried., 24; Magnet, 1852

Wassermann, Georg and Cath. age 15 — Kaltenlengsfeld, Sachsen-Meiningen; John Frederick, 1850; Austin Co.

Wassermann, George—Marktsuhl; Henriette, 1843 (1853)

Wassmund, J.—Gewitzin; Leibniz, 1850

Wattke, Ch. Joh.—Lukau; Texas, 1853

Watts, M. E. and Cath.—Kassel; Weser, 1854

Watz, Heinrich—Kassel; Texas, 1853

Waumann, Auguste, 27—Dresden; Antoinette, 1848

Waumann, F. Aug., 27—Chemnitz; Antoinette, 1848

Waur, Mrs. Ida, 34, Adele 8, Elise 6, Henrich 3, Joh. ½—Strelitz, Meckl.; Weser, 1858

Webbe, H.—Prussia; Adolphine, 1859

Weber, A.—Dresden to Galveston; Weser, 1860

Weber, Carl Anton—Falkenbach; 11 persons; Neptune, 1853

Weber, Carl Fr., 28—Weimar; Canapus, 1848

Weber, Friedrich—Buchholz, Prussia to Galveston or Indianola; Franklin, 1852

Weber, Gottfried, wife and 3 ch.—Ebersbach; Minna, 1854; Victoria Co.

Weber, H. D.—Feldhein, Switzerland; Mississippi, 1855

Weber, Joh.—Honsbach; Reform, 1849

Weber, Mathias, 22—Köln; Franziska, 1849; Galveston

Weber, O.—Altendorf to San Antonio; Weser, 1860

Weber, Quivatius, 28—Hilderg; Neptune, 1850

Weber, S.—Lippe Detmold to Indianola; Juno, 1860

Weber, Wilh., 19—Köln; Franziska, 1849; Galveston

Weberling, T.; Ammerland, 1854

Wechsler, Jos.—Eltville; Ship? Date?

Wedekind, Gustav—Weimar, Sachsen Weimar; Franklin, 1852; Blanco Co.

Wedemeier, H. and Johanne—Hannover to Galveston; Weser, 1860

Wegand, Hein.; Joh. Ed. Grosse, 1853

Wegeheft, J. — Oppenwehe to Washington- (on-the-Brazos); Weser, 1857

Wegemann, L.; Herschel, 1849

Wegener, Andreas, 22; Solon, 1850

Wegener, Carl, wife and 3 ch. ¾ to 7½ years — Gartz, Prussia; Washington, 1852

Wegener, Fr.. 36—Wittstock; Hamburg, 1849

Wegener, J., 6 persons — Prussia; Friedrich Grosse, 1853; Austin Co.

Wegener, Marg.—Wustensachsen; Henriette, 1843 (1853)

Wegener, Johann — Lalendorf, Meckl. to Galveston; Sarah, 1851

Wegener, Martin and wife, 6 persons — Dullrufka, Prussia; Mississippi, 1855

Wegener, Sophie — Falkenhagen, Prussia to Galveston or Indianola; **Franklin,** 1852
Wegner, Carl—Berlin to Galveston; **Republic,** 1851
Wegner, Friedrich, wife Friedrike, son Friedrich 0 year old—Barentin, Prussia; **Franklin,** 1853
Wegner, Cath. and Julia and 2 ch., 2½ and 4½ years old—Altona; **Leibniz,** 1850
Wegner, Hein., 26—Gramingen (Groningen); **Joh. Dethardt,** 1848
Wehe, H. and Carl—Anhalt, Dessau; **Antoinette,** 1854; Comal Co.
Wehecke, Carl—Netze, Han.; **Hermann Theodor,** 1853
Wehl, Franz, wife and ch.—Rückersdorf; **Minna,** 1854
Wehling, Friederike—to Galveston; **Weser,** 1859
Wehmann, W.—Wehdem to Brenham; **Weser,** 1860
Wehmeier, Doris, 30, Elis. 2; **Fortuna,** 1858
Wehmeier, H., 28—Wehdem to Brenham; **Iris,** 1859
Wehmeier, Karl, Caro.—Wehdem to Brenham; **Weser,** 1860
Wehmeyer, Franz — Hildesheim; 3 persons; **Texas,** 1853; Gillespie Co.
Wehmeyer, Hein., 16; **Hermann Theodor,** 1850
Wehn, Fried., Louis and 2 ch.—Kerpernitz; **Minna,** 1854
Wehn, Wilhelmine—Schweidnitz, Silesia; **Minna,** 1854
Wehner, George and Anna—Kleinensiehl; **J. W. Buddecke,** 1853
Wehring, C.—Oppendorf to Houston; **Weser** 1858
Wehring, Hermann—Oppendorf to Washington- (on-the-Brazos); **Weser,** 1857
Wehring, Louise—Prussia to Brenham; **Weser,** 1860
Wehrmann, Caro.—Gross Elbe; **Texas,** 1853
Weichhahn, Wilh., wife and 2 ch.—Poland; **Franziska,** 1854
Weide, Christ.—Watolow, Meckl.; **Washington,** 1852
Weide, Fr. Wilhelm—Flensburg, Denmark; **Copernicus,** 1852
Weidermann, W.—Gössitz; **Reform,** 1851
Weidner, Fried. Lebrecht and family—Oberlichtenau, near Polnitz, S a x o n y; **Galliott Concordia,** 1854; Comal Co.

Weigand, Anton, 27—Hesse; **Joh. Dethardt,** 1848
Weige, Carl and Minna; **Ammerland,** 1854; Austin Co.
Weigel, Aug., 25—Saxony; **Colonist,** 1848
Weighardt, Eliz., 24—Prussia; **Joh. Dethardt,** 1848
Weilbacher, Peter, 23; **Magnet,** 1852
Weilmann, Juliane—Falkenburg to New Braunfels; **Iris,** 1860
Weilshauser, Emil, 22—Oppeln; **Colonist,** 1850
Weims, Elis.—Schlürbach; **Weser,** 1854
Weinberg, C.—Levern to Galveston; **Iris,** 1858
Weindorff, Carl, wife and 2 ch., 0-7 years — Bagenitz, Prussia; **Therese Henriette,** 1853
Weinert, A. and family—Mittweida to La Grange; **Iris,** 1857
Weingarten, Ph. and family, 3 persons, 14-50 years — Okenheim, Westphalia; **Hampden,** 1854
Weinhold, Jos., 29, Joh. 11, Christ. 6—Silesia
Weinknecht, J. and wife—Rendowitz; **Gessner,** 1855
Winström (Weinstrom), Ida, 4 persons — Prussia; **Friderich Grosse,** 1853; Comal Co.
Weise(?), Gottlieb, 50; **Magnet,** 1852
Weisenberg family—to Galveston; **Weser,** 1859
Weiss, Adolph, 27; **John Holland,** 1848; Bexar Co.
Weiss, Anton—Mühlhausen; **Weser,** 1854
Weiss, Franz, Bertha—Sahl (Suhl?); **Gessner,** 1854
Weiss, Fried., 48; **Sophie,** 1852; Washington Co.
Weiss, Jos.—Friedland; **Canapus,** 1849
Weissensee, Barbara, 24—Fulda to Coleto; **Iris,** 1859
Weiter, Joh., 39, Elis. 36, Hein. 14, Maria 12. Henriette 9, Fried. 6, Val. 3, Marg.(?) — Germany; **Natchez,** 1847
Welke, W. Rob.—to New Ulm; **Solon,** 1852
Wellers, Cath., 21; **Neptune,** 1850
Wellmann, Gesine—Oldenburg to Harrisburg; **Gessner,** 1860
Wende, Carl—Scheldberg; **Solon,** 1852
Wendel, F., wife and 3 ch.—Hesse; **Franziska,** 1854; Colorado Co.

Wendell family, 7 persons — Alt-Marschen to Coleto; Iris, 1859
Wendel, Gottfried, 24—Schweksznen, Poland; Brasilian, 1850
Wendel, Hein. 42, Anna Elise 39, Adam 16, Marie 10, Fried. 7, Martha 5, Joh. 1—Alt-Morschen to Coleto; Iris, 1859
Wendler, ... —Alt-Burkow to Muelheim (Millheim, A u s t i n Co.); Anton Gunther, 1860
Wendling, Hein., 44, Friedke 37, Friedke 8, Wilhme 7, Ludw. 6, Ernestine 3, Auguste ½—Wittstock; Brasilian, 1850
Wendt, Christian, wife and 5 ch., 2-17 years—Pragsdorf, Meckl.-Strelitz; Sophie, 1852; Austin Co.
Wendt, Friedrich, wife and 4 ch., 23-36 years old—Ruelow, Mecklenburg-Strelitz; Sophie, 1852; Austin Co.
Wenhard, Gottfried, 4 persons; Joh. Ed. Grosse, 1853
Wennmohs, A.—Porchim; Hamburg, 1849
Wennhoser, H.—Prussia; Friedrich Grosse, 1853
Went, Anna — Barkzin (Barksen) to Rose Hill (Harris Co.); Iris, 1859
Wentz, Isaac and family—Oggersheim; Weser, 1854
Wenzel, ..., wife and son—Rückersdorf; Minna, 1854
Wenzel, F. A. and family, 10 persons, 8-56 years old—Lichtenhagen, Prussia; Hampden, 1854
Werbach, Aug., 35, wife Wilhme 38, Sophie 3 years old—Pansin; Brasilian, 1850
Wernau, Chr.; Ammerland, 1854
Werner, Anna—to San Antonio; Weser, 1859
Werner, Anton and f a m i l y — Schemisof (Schemisal?); Weser, 1854; Comal Co.
Werner, Aug.; Ammerland, 1854
Werner, Caro. and Wilhme—Scheidenberg to Round Top; Fortuna, 1860
Werner, Fr., 24—Meschede; Canapus, 1848; Kendall Co.
Werner, H., wife and child—Westerfeld; Lucie, 1854
Werner, Hein., Elis., Christine, Marie—Upen to Schönau; Gaston, 1857
Werner, Hermann—Beeskow, Prussia; Washington, 1852; Houston

Werner, J—Cappeln to Boerne; Iris, 1858
Werth, Aug.—Lübbecke; Gessner, 1854
Wesemann, F.—Oldenburg; Weser, 1854
Wesenburg, Carl—Neu-Ruppin; John Frederick, 1850
Wessels, Gesine, with 3 ch.—to Frelsburg; Iris, 1858
Wessels, Henriette, Ludewike, Amalie — Vegesak to Galveston; Weser, 1860
Wessels, J. and Antoinette—Bremen to Galveston; Weser, 1860
Wessely, Franz; Galliott Concordia, 1854
Wessendorff, Bernhard, 2 persons; Galliott Concordia, 1854
Wesser, Friedr.—Saxony; Friedrich Grosse, 1853
Westen, P.—Rügeberg to La Grange; Fortuna, 1858
Westerfeld, Joh. G.—Holzhausen; 4 persons; Neptune, 1853; Comal Co.
Westerlage, Phil., 30, Angela — Prussia; Joh. Dethardt, 1848; Galveston
Westerwald, C.—Hannover to Houston; Gessner, 1860
Westphal, Maria—Krabow; Leibniz, 1850
Westphal, Caro., 16; Solon, 1850
Westphal, Jochen, 59, Stine 58, S o p h i a 27 — Behnkenhagen, Mecklenburg; Herschel, 1855
Wetterlahn, Gottlieb—Naulitz; Neptune, 1854
Wettermann, Aug. — L u m b a c h (Lumbeck? Rumbach?); Reform, 1849
Wichmann, J. E., 35; Herschel, 1850
Wicke, Franz, John and Anna; Jeverland, 1860; Fayette Co.
Wicke, H.—Altenhausen; Texas, 1853
Wicke, Hein., 20; Sophie, 1852
Wickeland, Fritz, 18—Bremen; Anna Louise, 1857
Wickmann, F. W.—Reiskersdorf? to Brenham; Fortuna, 1860
Wiebusch, Joh. H. and wife, 5 persons—Hausberge, Han.; Mississippi, 1855
Wiebusch, Ludwig, 26—Osnabrück; Joh. Dethardt, 1848
Wied, Georg Wilh. and family; Galliott Concordia, 1854
Wied, Jacob, 4 persons; Galliott Concordia, 1854

Wied, Marie; Joh. Ed. Grosse, 1853
Wiede, W.—Waterloo, Belgium to Brenham; Juno, 1860
Wiedemann, Michael, 43, Caro. 36, Caro. 12, Eduard 7, Leopold 3, August—Prussia; Natchez, 1847
Wiedemar, M. R.—Obereinsberg; Miles, 1854
Wiederhold, Samuel—Udenhausen; 3 persons; Neptune, 1853
Wiedmann, G. and wife—Gebron; Weser, 1854
Wiedner, Hein., 4 persons—Stetterling (Stetternich?); Texas, 1853
Weifer ('Weiser?), Kate—Wengerohr to Washington-(on-the-Brazos); Fortuna, 1860
Wieg, Friedrich—Velkböken, Mecklenburg; Copernicus, 1852
Wiegand, Hein., 20; Brasilian or E. von Beaulieu, 1857
Wiegand, J. and Appolonia—Loitsch; Weser, 1854
Wiegand, Wilhelmine and Susanne —Darmstadt; Gessner, 1854
Wiegel, Christian—Braunschweig; Suwa, 1853
Wieglow, Ch., wife Maria—Pritzwalk, Prussia; Hampden, 1854
Wiegmann, Ernst, 20—Isenbüttel, Han.; Joh. Dethardt, 1848
Wiegmann, J. and wife—Hannover; Franziska, 1854
Wiegmann, Joh. Hein., 30—Hoya; Joh. Dethardt, 1848
Wieland, J., wife and child—Unterwatsdorf; Lucie, 1854
Wieland, Joseph—Unterwatsdorf; Lucie, 1854
Wiemanm, Henry F., 24—Engter; Antoinette, 1848
Wiener, Luise—Dargun, Meckl.; Hampden, 1854
Wiener, Johann and Anton—Gross-Neder to Galveston; Juno, 1860
Wienstruck, Wilh., 36, Marie 20; Hamburg, 1849; Austin Co.
Wiese, F., 16—Wehdem to Brenham; Iris, 1859
Wiese, Henry and Wilh.—Wehdem to Brenham; Weser, 1860
Wiese, Heinrich and Eggert — Rathjendorf, Schleswig to Galveston or Indianola; Franklin, 1852
Wiesemann, Chr. and child; Ammerland, 1854
Wieser, Franz. wife and 4 ch.—Hannover; Franziska, 1854
Wiester, H.—Prussia; Franziska, 1854

Wiezold, Franz Wilh., 19 — Frieberg, Sachsen (Saxony); Gutenberg, 1855
Wigand, Fried.; Galliott Concordia, 1854
Wilberg, Jos.—Entrup; Canapus, 1849
Wilde, Carl Eugen — Frankfurt, Prussia to Galveston; Bassermann, 1851
Wildesheim, Franz—Coswig to New Ulm; Weser, 1860
Wilgeroth, Aug. Chr., 26, Christian, 23; Solon, 1850
Wilharm, Caro.—Sulbeck; Lucie, 1854
Wilhelm, F., 14; Fortuna, 1858
Wilhelm, Johann and wife—Neu-Köbelich, Meckl.-Strelitz; Sophie, 1852
Wilke, A. with family—Burg to Fredericksburg; Weser, 1858
Wilke, Christian—Bernburg; Neptune, 1854
Wilke, Heinrich—Burg, Prussia to Galveston; Republic, 1851; De Witt Co. 1860
Wilke, Herm.; Ammerland, 1854
Wilke, L.—Altenhausen to Houston; Iris, 1860
Wilken, H., 32—Etzel; Fortuna, 1858; Calhoun Co.
Wilkening, H. with family—Rohberg to Galveston; Weser, 1858
Will, Joh., 45, Christine 30, Louise 13, Maria 8; Hermann Theodor, 1850
Wille, Richard, 6, Robert 4 (with Heyer, Fritz?) — Torgau, Prussia; Herschel, 1855
Willinger, Hanna—to Houston; Weser, 1859
Willenberg, Aug.—Berndorf; Canapus, 1849; Bastrop Co.
Willmann, Anton—Rauschwitz, Silesia; Friedrick Grosse, 1853; Comal Co.
Willmann, Joh., 8 persons—Prussia; Friedrich Grosse, 1853
Willmann, Joseph, and 5 ch.; Friedrich Grosse; Comal Co.
Willms family, 5 persons—Gerstemünde to Galveston; Iris, 1859
Wilms, Joachim, 40—Perleberg; Brasilian, 1850
Willms, Peter—Düsseldorf; Weser, 1854
Wilms, Silbert—Wrisse to Meyersville; Weser, 1857
Wilms, Therese, 6 persons—Perleberg; Texas, 1853

Wilms, Wilhelm—Wrisse to Meyersville; **Weser,** 1857
Willner, Johann, wife and sister—Vietluebbe, Mecklenburg; **Washington,** 1852
Wimmer, O.—Schneeberg to Houston; **Iris,** 1860
Winckler, Carl, 43; **Magnet,** 1852
Windel, Ernst—Hannover; **Juno,** 1853
Windel, F.—Prussia to Independence; **Weser,** 1860
Windel, Joh. and family—Centaver (Contawa?); **Weser,** 1854
Wink, Georg Paul, 47, Anna Marie 41, Francisca 11, Josef 9, Magda. 7, Jean 5, Anna 2; **John Holland,** 1848; Colorado Co.
Wink, Jean, 41; Antonie 35, Anna Marie 10, Rosina 6, Peter ½; **John Holland,** 1848; Colorado Co.
Wink, Louis, 21, Cath. 20; **John Holland,** 1848
Winkel, Carl—Meichow; **Gessner,** 1854
Winkelmann, F.—Oppendorf to Houston; **Weser,** 1858
Winkelmann, Wilh., 27; **Solon,** 1850; Washington Co.
Winkelmann, W. with family—Oppenwehe to Houston; **Weser,** 1858
Winkler, A.—Weigersdorf to New Ulm; **Fortuna,** 1858
Winkler family—Weigersdorf; **Adolphine,** 1859
Winkler, J. — Ottmanshausen to New Braunfels; **Iris,** 1857; died spring of 1859
Winkler, Joh., 24, Marg. 22—Fichlbach?; **Wilhelm,** 1858
Winninger, Jul., 28—Arolsen; **Canapus,** 1848
Winter, F.—Lemförde to Galveston; **Juno,** 1860
Winter, Wilh., 50, Johanne 20, Wilh. 18—Quedlinburg; **Franziska,** 1849; Fayette Co.
Winterfeldt, Friedrich, wife and 5 ch. up to 14 years—Perleberg, Prussia to Galveston; **Bassermann,** 1851
Winterhand, Paul—Baden; **Weser,** 1854
Wipprecht. Rud., 24—Nebra, Thuringia; **Herschel,** 1849; Guadalupe Co.
Wirsich, Joh. Gotth.—Breslau; **Solon,** 1852
Wirth, Philippine—Stolpe; **Magnet,** 1851

Wisner, W.—Prussia; **Friedrich Grosse,** 1853
Wissroth, A., wife and dau.—Galveston to Galveston; **Weser,** 1857
Wisserothe, Aug.—Sehlde; **Neptune,** 1854
Wisserothe, Hein.—Galveston; **Neptune,** 1854
Witt, Anna—Schleswig, Schleswig; **Hampden,** 1854
Witt, Hein., Caro., Ida Friedr., Aug. — Neudorf to Richmond; **Fortuna,** 1860
Wittbecker, Wilh.—Berlin; **Suwa,** 1853
Witte, J. L. R., 25, Marg. 25—Alt-Belitz, Prussia; **Herschel,** 1855
Witte, Victor (Pastor), 29, Anna 21, Marie 2, Helene ¾—Hannover; **Neptune,** 1850; Austin Co. 1850
Witte, W.—Bocholzhausen to Galveston; **Iris,** 1860
Witte, Wilhelm—Perleberg, Prussia to Galveston or Indianola; **Franklin,** 1852
Witthoeft, Sophia, 18—Wittenberg, Holstein; **Gutenberg,** 1855
Witthoeft, Carl H. A., 33, Louise 34, Carl 8, Fritz 3—Wittenberg, Holstein; **Gutenberg,** 1855
Witthoef, Doris, 5, Dietrich 1—Wittenberg, Holstein; **Gutenberg,** 1855
Witting, Fried., 21 — (Alt)-Morschen; **Solon,** 1850; De Witt Co. 1860
Witting, Georg, 24; **Creole,** 1852; Lavaca Co.
Wobst, J o h a n n — Baumgarten, Mecklenburg to Galveston; **Sarah,** 1851
Woeffler, Louis, 5 persons; Oppeln; **Reform,** 1851
Woerm, Friedke—Württ.; **Franziska,** 1854
Woehler, ... and wife—Teterow, Meckl. to Galveston; **Republic,** 1851
Wohlk, Asmus and wife Caro.—Hamburg; **Hampden,** 1854
Woiteck, Johann, wife and 4 ch.—Gacenka (Jasenka) to Industry; **Juno,** 1860
Woityna. Stanislaus and family—Tost; **Weser,** 1854
Wolf, brothers and sisters—Wörlitz to Lexington; **Iris,** 1857
Wolf, Ferd., 29—Prussia; **Joh. Dethardt,** 1848
Wolf, G.—Lützow to New Ulm; **Weser,** 1860

Wolf, H.—Fallersleben to Springfield; Gaston, 1857
Wolf, J. C. L., 77, died; Cath. 73; Hamburg, 1849
Wolf, Jos. 28, Leonhard, 27—Bavaria; Franziska, 1849
Wolfer, Christian — Plieningen, Württ.; Texas, 1853; Galveston
Wolfer, Ferd. (Fred.), wife Dorothea nee Koch — Plieningen, Württ.; Texas, 1853; Galveston
Wolfermann, Anton — Reichenwalde; Mississippi, 1855
Wolff, C. C.—Württemberg to San Felipe; Gessner, 1860
Wolff, Eugen—Prussia; Antoinette, 1854; Galveston
Wolff, Ferd., 30—Prussia; Natchez, 1847
Wolff, Johann, wife and 1 child ½ year old—Stettin, Prussia; Copernicus, 1852
Wolff, Julius—Schlage, Prussia to Galveston; Bassermann, 1851
Woling, Rud. — Krotoschin, Prussia; Washington, 1852
Wolken, Stephan, 7 persons—Forst; Texas, 1853
Wolle, Carl Wm. and family—Prussia; Neptune, 1848
Woller, R., wife and child—Unterheide; Lucie, 1854
Wolter family—to Galveston; Weser, 1859
Wolter, Friederike, 22—Penwick, Meckl.; Copernicus, 1852
Woltersdorf, Carl, 30—Perleberg; Colonist, 1850; Fayette Co.
Woltersdorf, Jost. H., 33—Prussia; Joh. Dethardt, 1848
Woltz, Kath. — Belsenberg to Neighbor's Creek (Comal Co.); Iris, 1859
Wolzenn, John, 34, Gertrude 34, John 8, Gertrude 4, Anna 2; Magnet, 1852
Wolzenn, Math., 30; Magnet, 1852
Wonach, Cath.—Sommerfeld to Goliad; Iris, 1859
Worlofsky, Joh.; Galliott Concordia, 1854
Worner, G.—Württ.; Franziska, 1854
Wotipka, Johann and wife—Mähren; Weser, 1854; Austin Co.
Wotipka, Johann, wife and child—Mähren; Weser, 1854; Austin Co.
Wrage, J., 24—Prussia; Colonist, 1848

Wrana, Jacob, Veronica, Veronica, Barbara, Franz—Austria; Jeverland, 1860
Wrase, Friedrich, wife and 3 ch.—Althuetten, Prussia to Galveston; Republic, 1851
Wrehner, Widow—Oppendorf; Adolphine, 1859
Wreziona, A.—Tarnau; Gessner, 1855
Wuensch, A.—Schleusingen to Columbus; Fortuna, 1860
Wuenscher, Chr. Fried., 50, Rosine 40, Fried. Wilh. 24, Carl Wilh. 16, Rosine Theresa 8, Richard 2—Prussia; Joh. Dethardt, 1848
Wuermueller, Joseph—Schönau; Lucie, 1854
Wuerth, Heinrich, Friedricke—Essingen to New Braunfels; Gaston, 1857
Wueste, Louise—to Indianola; Weser, 1859
Wuesthoff, Robert, 21—Perleberg; Colonist, 1850; Bexar Co.
Wulf, Wilhelm—Grube, Holstein; Hampden, 1854
Wulff, Sosshia—Krabow (Krachow?); Leibniz, 1850
Wulff, H., 29—Gehlsdorf, Meckl.; Herschel, 1855
Wulfring, E. R., 27; Herschel, 1849
Wunder, L. and wife—Böhm; Weser, 1854
Wunderlich, F. with family — Greifswalde to New Braunfels; Weser, 1858; Comal Co.
Wunderlich, Jost, 37, Mary Elisa, Geb. Wied. 37, Elisa 11, Frederic 10, Henry 3 — Feudingen; Antoinette, 1848; Austin Co.
Wunsch, Carl Gott., 39, Christiane 38, Carl Gottl. 17, August G. 10, Ernst G. 8, Wilh. G. 7, Gottlieb 5—Saxony; Joh. Dethardt, 1848
Wurst, Caro. — Bleidelsheim? to New Braunfels; Iris, 1859
Wustenbarsch, Augustus — Lülfitz to Colorado Co.; Gaston, 1860
Wusterich, Otto, 41; Reform, 1850
Wuth, C.—Hesse; Friedrich Grosse, 1853
Wywial (Wywral), Joseph, Barbara—Austria; Jeverland, 1860

— Z —

Zabe, W.—Burg to Galveston; Iris, 1860
Zabel, L.—Dembowo (Dembno?) to Brenham; Iris, 1860

Zach, Joseph and family—Sceycera (Scheyern); Gessner, 1854
Zahn, Gottlieb, 48, Maria 38, Maria 14, Wilhme 12, Emelia 5/6, Carl 23 — Prussia; Hamburg, 1849
Yahren (Zahren?), J.—Millich to San Antonio; Iris, 1857
Zahren (Yahren?), W.—Millich to San Antonio; Iris, 1857
Zander, A. H. B., 47, Marg. 47, Adolphine 11; Hamburg, 1849; Fayette Co.
Zander, Fried., 47, Friedka 35, Wilh. 3, Auguste 2, Fried. ¼ (died) — Eimsbüttel; Hamburg, 1849; Austin Co.
Zauder? (Zander), Max, Minna, Sabra — Nackel to La Grange; Gessner, 1860
Zanje, Peter, 50, Caro. 30, Louise 24, Anna 22, Carl 18, Auguste 16, Albertine 12, Johanne 6—Prussia; Chas. N. Cooper, 1847
Zapp, Eleanore, 22, Carl 3—Nunderath; Anna Louise, 1857
Zarsky, Franz, Theresia—Austria; Jeverland, 1860
Zaschke, M.—Prussia; Friedrich Grosse, 1853
Zauder (Zander?), H.—Bromberg; Adolphine, 1859
Zech, Michel; Joh. Ed. Grosse, 1853
Zeh, Chs. Wm., 22; Galliott Flora, 1849
Zehnder, And.—Schöftland, Switzerland; Lucie, 1854
Zeidler, Barbara, 20—Adorf; Hamburg, 1849
Zeiss, L. and R.—to Brenham; Weser, 1859
Zeller, G., Eltville; 3 persons; ship? date?
Zenke, Therese—Glogau; 3 persons; Herschel, 1851
Zenner, Peter, 35; Sophie, 1852; Gillespie Co.
Zensch, Fried., 29; Brasilian, 1857
Zentner, Franz; St. Pauli, 1847
Zentz, Wilh., 29; Galliott Flora, 1849
Zerbach, Joh., 60, Elis. 66; Solon, 1850
Zerbel, Carl Wlh.—Callies to Galveston; Weser, 1859
Zerbst, Carl Wilh.—Buetzow; wife and 2 ch. 9 and 16 years (Hamburg Archives); Brasilian, 1850
Zerbst. Carl Wilh., 49. Henriette 42, Carl Wilh. 16, Auguste 9; (U. S. Microfilm); Brasilian, 1850

Zesch, Rob.; Ammerland, 1854; Mason Co.
Zethern, F. — Niederwaltersdorf, Mecklenburg; Franklin, 1853
Zetzmann, Friederike — Ahnebeck to Frelsburg; Fortuna, 1860
Zickala, Joseph, Anna, John—Austria; Jeverland, 1860
Ziedler, Elis.—Kaiserhammer to Indianola; Weser, 1858
Ziegelbauer, W. and wife—Böhmen; Weser, 1854
Ziegenhagen, Friedr.—Prussia; Antoinette, 1854
Ziegler, August—Borgholzhausen; J. W. Buddecke, 1853; Lavaca Co.
Ziegler, Franz, Agatha; Galliott Concordia, 1854
Ziegler, Joh.—Schwaben; Weser, 1854
Zielke, Johann and wife Anne; Posen; Miles, 1853
Ziems, L., 58, Sophia 54, Jochen 14; Nienhusen, Mecklenburg; Herschel, 1855
Zientz, Albert—Kotulien(?); Weser, 1854
Zieriaks, Ludwig—Buetzow; Leibniz, 1850
Ziesang, Carl—Schwerin, Mecklenburg; Washington, 1852
Zimmermann, Christian, 41, Wilhme 33, Hanna 8, Friedke 4, Aug. 2; Brasilian or E. von Beaulieu, 1857; Fayette Co.
Zimmermann, Daniel, 16; Sophie, 1852; Calhoun Co. 1860
Zimmermann, Marg.—Riechenberg to Indianola; Iris, 1859
Zimmermann, Reiner Jannes; Galliott Concordia, 1854; Fayette Co.
Zindahl, Christ., wife and 1 ch. 19 years old — Wangerin, Prussia; Washington, 1852
Zindeler, Julie—Schmuessen, Prussia; Hampden, 1854
Zinram, A. and family — Walkenried; Gessner, 1854
Zirjacks, C. — Moltnow, Mecklenburg; Hampden, 1854
Zobel, Christine, 29—Butterstieg, Holstein; Brasilian, 1850; Fayette Co.
Zoche. Franz; Galliott Concordia, 1854
Zoeller, Adolph—Darmstadt; Neptune, 1853
Zoeller. Philipp; St. Pauli, 1847; Kendall Co.
Zollinger, Hein.—Uster, Switz.; Lucie, 1854

Zowurka, Martin, 31, Cath. 34, Euphenia 7, Eva 5, Johanna ¾—Tarnau, Prussia; Miles, 1855

Zuch, Ludwig, Wilhme, Robert—Gurkow to Yorktown; Fortuna, 1860

Zucke, Johann—Schwarzee, Prussia to Galveston; Sophie, 1850

Zulaus, Verena—"Aus der Schweiz" to Cat Spring; Gessner, 1860

Zurawski, J. and M.—Lamenstein to Fredericksburg; Iris, 1859

Zuruda, Martin, 31—Tarnau, Prussia; Miles, 1855

Zwernemann, Ludwig — Udenhausen; Neptune, 1853; Fayette Co.

Zwesch, Franz—Neu-Ruppin; John Frederick, 1850

Zwieb, Marie—to Galveston; Weser, 1859

Zwollaneck, Joh. and family—Humpoletz, Bohemia; Weser, 1854

Zzarzay, F. and wife—Olmütz, Moravia; Gessner, 1855

Bibliography

BIBLIOGRAPHY

BOOKS

Barkley, Mary Starr. *History of Travis County and Austin, 1839-1899*. Waco, Texas: Texian Press, 1963

Batte, Lelia M. *History of Milam County, Texas*. San Antonio: The Naylor Co., 1956

Benjamin, Gilbert G. *The Germans in Texas, A Study in Immigration*. Philadelphia, 1909

Biesele, Dr. R. L. *History of the Early German Settlements in Texas, 1830-1860*. Austin, Texas: Von Boeckmann-Jones Co., 1930

Biggers, Don, *German Pioneers in Texas*. Fredericksburg, Texas: Fredericksburg Publishing Co., 1925

Boethel, Paul C. *A History of Lavaca County*. Austin, Texas: Von Boeckmann-Jones, 1959

Bracht, Victor. *Texas in 1848*. Elberfield, Germany, 1849

Caldwell, Lillian Moerbe. *Texas Wends, Their First Half Century*. Salado, Texas: The Anson Jones Press, MCMLXI

Cat Spring Agricultural Society. *The Cat Spring Story*. San Antonio: The Lone Star Printing Company, 1956

Day, James M. *Maps of Texas, 1527-1900. The Map Collection of the Texas State Archives*. Austin, Texas: Pemberton Press, 1964

Ehrenberg, Hermann. *With Milam and Fannin, The Adventures of a German Boy in Texas' Revolution*. Translation by Charlotte Churchill. Austin, Texas: The Pemberton Press, 1968

Fehrenbach, T. R. *A History of Texas and Texans*. New York: The MacMillan Co., 1968

Geiser, Samuel Wood. *Naturalists of the Frontier*. Dallas, Texas: Southern Methodist University Press, 1948

Geue, Chester W. and Ethel Hander. *A New Land Beckoned, German Immigration to Texas, 1844-1847*. Waco, Texas: The Texian Press, 1966

Gillespie County Historical Society. Compilers: *Pioneers in God's Hills, A History of Fredericksburg and Gillespie County People and Events*. Austin, Texas: Von Boeckmann-Jones, 1960

Gracy, Alice Duggan, Jane Summer, and Emma Gene Sealy Gentry. *Early Texas Birth Records, 1838-1878*. Austin, Texas: Privately published, March, 1969

Haas, Oscar. *History of New Braunfels and Comal County, 1844-1946*. Austin, Texas: The Steck Company, 1968

Jackson, W. H. and S. A. Long. *The Texas Stock Directory or Book of Marks and Brands, 1865*. San Antonio: The Herald Office, 1865; Reprint, The Book Farm, New Braunfels, Texas; Heartman's Historical Series No. 77

Jordan, Dr. Terry G. *German Seed in Texas Soil, Immigrant Farmers in Nineteenth-Century Texas*. Austin, Texas-London: University of Texas Press, 1966

Lotto, F. *Fayette County, Her History and Her People*. Schulenburg, Texas: Sticker Steam Press, 1902

Meusebach, John O. *Answer to Interrogatories*. Austin, Texas: Pemberton Press, 1964

Olmstead, Frederick Law. *A Journey Through Texas or Saddle Trip on the Southwestern Frontier*. New York: Dix, Edwards & Co., 1857

Our God Is Marching On, A Centennial History of the Bethlehem Lutheran Church, Round Top, Texas. Austin, Texas: Von Boeckmann-Jones, 1966

Ousley, Clarence. *Galveston in 1900*. Atlanta, Ga.: William B. Chase, 1900

Ransleben, Guido E. *A Hundred Years of Comfort in Texas*. San Antonio: The Naylor Company, 1954

Roemer, Ferdinand. *Texas, with Particular Reference to German Immigration*. Translation by Oswald Mueller. San Antonio: Standard Printing Co., 1935

Rose, Victor. *History of Victoria County*. A republishing, Edited by J. W. Petty, Jr. San Antonio: Lone Star Printing Company, 1961

Sadler, Jerry. *History of Texas Land*. Austin, Texas, 1964

Santleben, August. *A Texas Pioneer*. Edited by I. D. Afflick. New York and Washington: The Neale Publishing Company, 1910. Facsimile edition from the Press of W. M. Morrison, Waco, Texas, 1967

Schmidt, Charles F. *History of Washington County*. San Antonio: The Naylor Company, 1949

Soergel, Alwin H. *Für Auswanderungslustige! Briefe eines unter den Schutze des Mainzer Verein nach Texas ausgewanderten*. Office of the *Herald*, Published and distributed in Leipzig, 1847

Tiling, Moritz. *German Element in Texas from 1820-1850*. Houston, Texas: Moritz Tiling, 1913

Trenckmann, W. A. *Austin County*. Bellville, Texas, 1899

Webb, Walter P. and H. Bailey Carroll, Editors. *Handbook of Texas*, 2 vols. Austin, Texas: The Texas State Historical Society, 1952

Williams, Annie Lee. *History of Wharton County, 1846-1961*. Austin, Texas: Von Boeckmann-Jones, 1964

MAGAZINES

Texana, Vol. V, No. 2, Summer 1967. "Die Lateinische Ansiedlung in Texas," translation by C. W. Geue; Texian Press, Waco, Texas

Texana, Vol. VI, No. 3, Fall 1968. "The Patterns of Origins of the Adelsverein German Colonists," by Dr. Terry G. Jordan; Texian Press, Waco, Texas

Deutsche-Texanische Monats-Hefte, Year 11, No. 2, August 1906, pp. 48-54, San Antonio: Editor—L. F. Lafrentz. "The Germans in Texas before the Mass Immigration in the Year 1844."

Ibid. Year 11, No. 3, September, 1906, pp. 88-92

Ibid. Year 11, No. 4, November, 1906, pp. 128-129

Ibid. Year 12, No. 2, March-April, 1908, pp. 45-51

Neu-Braunfelser Zeitung Jahrbuch fuer 1940. "Arrival of Bremer Bark *Weser*"

Southwestern Historical Quarterly, Vol. XXXII, No. 4; April, 1934. "A Critical Study of the Siege of the Alamo and of the Personnel of Its Defenders: V. Historical Problems Relating to the Alamo," by Amelia Williams

Ibid., Vol. XLIII, Vol. 1; July, 1939. "The Men of Goliad" by Herbert Davenport

NEWSPAPERS

Allegemeine Auswanderungs-Zeitung, July 8, 1852; Rudolstadt, Germany

New Braunfels Zeitung-Chronicle, series of articles by Oscar Haas on "Early New Braunfels," 1965; *New Braunfels* [Tex.] *Herald*

Neu-Braunfelser Zeitung, 1852-1861

Neu-Braunfelser-Zeitung, 100th Anniversary Edition. Neu-Braunfelser Zeitung Publishing Co., New Braunfels, Texas, 1952

Die Union, Galveston, Texas, 1858-1860

Galveston Zeitung, 1851, Galveston, Texas

CHURCH BOOKLETS

Centennial Anniversary Zion Lutheran Church, Fredericksburg, Texas, 1852-1951

History of the First Evangelical Lutheran Church, 1850-1950, Galveston, Texas

History of the Hilda Methodist Church, Mason County, 1862-1962

History of the First Protestant Church, 1847-1947, New Braunfels, Texas, by Oscar Haas

Hundredth Anniversary of St. John's Lutheran Church, New Ulm, Texas, 1867-1967

One Hundred Years Trinity Lutheran Church, Frelsburg, Texas, 1855-1955

One Hundred Years of Methodism at Industry, Texas, 1848-1948

GAZETTEERS

In English—Hammond, C. S. & Co., *World Atlas*, Philadelphia, Pa., 1951
   Lippencott's Pronouncing Gazetteer and Geographical Dictionary of the World. 2 Volumes, Philadelphia, 1856: J. B. Lippencott and Co.
In German—*Müller's Grosses Deutches Ortsbuch*, Wuppertal-Nachstebreck, October, 1953: Post Meister A. D. Müller
   Ortsverzeichnis I, Berlin—Tempelhof, May, 1944

MICROFILMS

Microcopy 575, Roll 3: Copies of Lists of Passengers Arriving at the Port of Galveston, Texas, 1846-1871. The National Archives and Record Service, General Services Administration Service, Washington, D. C.
Microfilm Records of United States Census Reports for 1850, 1860, and 1870.

OTHER SOURCES

Verein Collection and Wied Collection in University of Texas Archives, Austin, **Texas**

Index

INDEX

Cornitus, H. O.: 20
Counties, new: 25, 37
Courtmann, George—see
Kurtmann
Courtmann, Henry: 8, 9
Crimean War: 31
Crueger, David: 4

— D —

Dangers, B.: 27
Darmstadt, Germany: 20, 21
Darmstaedter Farm: 20
Dedrick, Georg: 4
De Leon, Martin: 11
Degener, Eduard: 21
Denmark: 8, 13, 31, 35
Deutsche-Texanische Monats-
Hefte: 3, 4
DeWitt's Colony: 10
DeWitt County: 36
De Zavala, Lorenzo: 11
Dietrich, Franz: 3, 7
Dillenburg, Nassau: 16
Dirksen, Joseph: 2
Dombrinski, M.: 7
Dorsheimer, Andreas: 4
Dosch, Ernst: 20
Douai, Dr. Adolf: 21, 27, 28
Dresel, Emil: 21
Dresel, Gustav: 13
Dresel, Julius: 21
Dresel, Rudolph: 21

— E —

Ealender, Joseph: 4
Earnest (Ernst), F. B.: 2, 3, 4, 9
East Central Texas counties: 36
Eberly, Jacob: 4
Ebinger, J. G.: 27
Ehrenberg, Hermann: 3, 6, 7
Eigenaur, Conrad: 4, 7
Eilers, Bernhard: 4, 9
Eisenlohr, G. W.: 27
Eisterwald, C.: 4
Elberfeld, Germany: 13
Ellinger (Ehlinger?), Jos.: 9
Elm, Fr.: 4
El Paso, Texas: 19
El Sol Colorado: 19
Emanuel, Albert: 9
Emigration, reasons for: 13, 31, 32
Empresarios: 10
England: 8, 35
Epidemic of 1846: 17, 18
Erath, Georg P.: 3, 9
Ernst, Caroline: 2
Ernst, Fr.: 2, 3, 9
Ernst, Mrs. Fr.: 2
Ervendberg, Pastor: 26, 27
Europe, immigrants from: 35

Eversburg, Albert: 20
Eyler, Jacob: 4

— F —

Fachwerk houses: 25
Falk, John: 3
Fannin, Col. James: 6, 7
Fayette County: 11, 36
Felder, Carl: 9
Ferdinand (ship): 15
Findelmann, E. C.: 4
Finner (Fenner), Robert: 7
Fischer, Dr. Joh.: 28
Fisher, Henry: 3, 14
Fisher, J. H.: 7
Fisher-Miller contract: 14
Fisher-Miller grant: 3, 18-21, 23;
disadvantages of, 14; opened to
settlers, 19
Fisher-Miller grant: counties of,
25; size of, 25
Flach, Christian: 20
Flake, Ferdinand: 27
Fleming, Peter and Robert: 4
Fordtran, Charles: 2, 9
Formann, Abraham: 9
Forts in Texas: 19-20
France: 35
Franks, S. H.: 28
Frederick, John: 4
Fredericksburg: 11, 16, 17, 18, 20,
25, 26, 27
Frels, William: 3, 9
Frelsburg, Texas: 3, 11
French settlers: 11
Friedlander, Wm.: 4, 9
Friederich, Wm.: 21
Frontier of Texas, advance of: 37
Fullenweider, Peter: 9

— G —

Galveston: 11, 13, 15, 33, 34
Galveston County: 36
Galveston Der Union: 33
Galveston News: 21
Galveston Zeitung: 33
Garza, Raphael: 15
Geiger, Jacob: 9
General Land Office: 2, 3, 4
German emigration, reasons for:
13
German Emigration Co.: 23
German immigrants: 13, 14, 21, 23,
33, 34, 36
German newspapers in Texas: 27
Germans: at Goliad, 7, 8; in Texas
before 1836, 4, 5; in Texas Rev-
olution, 8, 9; in Republic of
Texas, 4, 5; killed in Alamo, 8;
killed at Goliad, 7, 8
Germany: 8, 15
Geubner, G.: 27

Varrelmann, Dr. John D.: 3
Vehlein's Colony: 11
Veramendi family: 15
Verein: 11, 12, 15, 21, 22, 23, 31
Verein immigrants: 17, 37
Victoria County: 36
Victoria, Texas: 6
Vienna: 32
Vogt, Adam: 20
Volkmar, J.: 8
Voss, Georg: 8
von Bieberstein, Herm.: 20
von Breitenbach, Louis: 21
von Claren, Lieut.: 19
von Lichtenberg, Ernst and Lud.: 20
von Roeder family: 3
von Roeder, Joachim, Louis, Otto, Rud. and Wm.: 9
von Rosenberg, Ernst: 2
von Rotsmann, Baron: 20
von Wrede, Fr. W.: 3, 5, 13, 19, 27
v. Zacharias, L.: 9

— Z —

Zekainski, J.: 9
Zink, Nicholas: 21
Zizelmann, Ph. Fr.: 27
Zoeller, Father: 27
Zoeller, Philip: 20
Zuber, Abraham: 5
Zuber, Wm.: 9
Zumwalt, Andrew: 9

— W —

Wagner, William: 9
Waisenfarm: 28
Washington County: 3, 11, 20, 36
Washington-on-the-Brazos: 10
War with Mexico: 17
War in U. S. Between North and South: 37
Weisgerber, F.: 27
Wends of Texas: 34
Wendt, H.: 27
Weppler, Phil.: 9
Wertzner, Chr. G.: 9
West Texas counties: 36, 37
Westphal, Baron: 21
Wharton County: 36
Wickmann, Edward: 5
Wiesbaden, Germany: 16
Wilhelm, A. and R.: 9
Wilhelm, Sarah: 3
Wilke, Henry: 9
Willmuth, Louis and Wm.: 5
Winter, A: 8
Witte, Bernhard: 20
Wolfenberger, Sam: 5, 9
Wolters, Jacob: 3
World Atlas, Hammond's: 34
World War II: 33
Wutherich, Ulrich: 8

— Y —

Yeager, S. W.: 5
Yordt, D. F. F.: 3
York's Creek: 25

www.ingramcontent.com/pod-product-compliance
Lightning Source LLC
Chambersburg PA
CBHW070427270326
41926CB00014B/2977